The White Scourge

American Crossroads
Edited by Earl Lewis, George Lipsitz, Peggy Pascoe,
George Sánchez, and Dana Takagi

The White Scourge

Mexicans, Blacks, and Poor Whites in Texas Cotton Culture

Neil Foley

UNIVERSITY OF CALIFORNIA PRESS

Berkeley / Los Angeles / London

University of California Press
Berkeley and Los Angeles, California

University of California Press, Ltd.
London, England

First Paperback Printing 1999

Library of Congress Cataloging-in-Publication Data

Foley, Neil.
     The white scourge: Mexicans, Blacks, and poor whites in Texas
cotton culture / by Neil Foley.
         p.   cm.—(American crossroads; 2)
     Includes bibliographic references (p.   ) and index.
     ISBN 0–520–20723–8 (cloth: alk. paper). — ISBN
0–520–20724–6 (pbk.: alk. paper)
         1. Texas—Race relations.   2. Cotton picking—Social aspects—
Texas—History—20th century.   3. Cotton growing—Social
aspects—Texas—History—20th century.   4. Afro-Americans—
Texas—History—20th century.   5. Mexican Americans—Texas—
History—20th century.   6. Whites—Texas—History—20th
century.   7. Texas—Social conditions.   I. Title.   II. Series.
F395.A1F65   1997
305.8′009764—dc21   97–10222

Printed in the United States of America
08   07   06   05   04   03   02   01   00   99
9   8   7   6   5   4   3   2   1

It was the whiteness of the whale that above all things appalled me. . . . Though in many natural objects, whiteness refiningly enhances beauty, as if imparting some special virtue of its own, . . . and though this pre-eminence in it applies to the human race itself, giving the white man ideal mastership over every dusky tribe; and though in other mortal sympathies and symbolizings, this same hue is made the emblem of many touching, noble things—the innocence of brides, the benignity of age . . . yet for all these accumulated associations, with whatever is sweet and honorable and sublime, there yet lurks an elusive something in the innermost idea of this hue, which strikes more of panic to the soul than that redness which affrights in blood.

Herman Melville, *Moby Dick*

To Angela, Sabina, Bianca, and Sophia;
To Raymond P. Foley; and
In memory of my mother,
Maria Lilia Trejo Foley, 1919–1990

Contents

Illustrations

Photographs follow pp. 96 and 192

Tables

Maps

Preface and Acknowledgments

Growing up in Alexandria, Virginia, in the suburbs of Washington, D.C., during the 1950s and 1960s, I realized that however one might characterize the federal city, it was not then a multiracial city. Like the rest of the South, its culture was black and white. I first met our Mexican and Mexican American relatives on a visit to my mother's family in Deming, New Mexico, when I was five years old. In the deserts of southern New Mexico, less than an hour's drive from the border with Chihuahua, Mexico, everyone spoke Spanish—cousins, aunts, uncles, neighborhood children—and many, like my grandparents, spoke no English at all. We Foleys were *agringados* ("whitened" Mexicans) from the East, whose Anglo father was a Spanish-speaking second-generation Irishman. His parents emigrated from County Kerry, Ireland, about the same time my mother's parents immigrated to the United States after the outbreak of the Mexican Revolution in 1910. The East was a long way from the Southwest, where my mother had grown up, and from the West I had seen on television, with its broad, dry landscapes, big sky, and treeless plateaus. Although the Washington area was the East to my relatives in New Mexico, to me its cultural rhythms and racial barriers against the large black population made it seem more like the South than anything else. Like most southern places, the District of Columbia and Alexandria had little experience with those who were neither unambiguously white nor black. As hybrid Irish-Mexicans, we were simply "The Foleys," a family of eight children located somewhere on the fringe of whiteness.

My mother, Maria Trejo, in seeking to avoid the harsh discrimination that she witnessed against blacks in the District of Columbia and Vir-

ginia in the 1940s and 1950s and that sometimes she herself experienced
when she was denied service at downtown lunch counters and department stores, sought to convince neighbors, strangers, and lunch-
counter personnel that she was white—not exactly Anglo, of course, but
white nonetheless. For the first time in her life, she could not be what
she had always been in the Southwest—a *mexicana*. Discrimination
against African Americans and strict segregation in the capital city made
my mother self-conscious about her Mexicanness, since there was no
Mexican community to which she could turn to affirm her ethnocultural
heritage. There simply was no room for being brown in a black-and-
white city.

Writing this book has reminded me of how the rigid boundaries of
black-white race relations fail to account for groups, like Mexicans, located somewhere in the ethnoracial borderlands between whiteness and
blackness. In choosing central Texas as my laboratory for examining race
relations, I explore how Mexicans, blacks, and poor whites negotiated
and manipulated the racial space in this borderlands province between
the South, the West, and Mexico.

For guidance along the way I have had the counsel and support of
many friends and mentors, beginning with Rebecca Scott and Tom
Holt, who first encouraged me to pursue my interest in cross-cultural,
transnational, and interracial history. At the University of Michigan Rebecca Scott helped me make the transition from English literature to the
social history of the United States and Mexico. Her scholarly standards
inspired me to do my best work, and her friendship sustained me
throughout my graduate-school career. Angela Hinz, Hal Woodman,
John Chávez, Ramón Gutiérrez, Terry McDonald, Leslie Rowland, Ricardo Romo, Thad Sitton, Myron Gutmann, Zaragosa Vargas, Patricia
Nelson Limerick, Julie Saville, Sylvia Pedraza, Jerry and Maria Huntley,
Jim McIntosh, Tom Holt, Fred Cooper, and Steven Hahn all offered
valuable advice and encouragement early on.

I was also fortunate to receive generous financial support while a
graduate student at the University of Michigan. The Andrew Mellon
Foundation and the Rackham Graduate School awarded me the CIC
Predoctoral Fellowship. The Project for the Comparative Studies of
Postemancipation Societies (funded by the Kellogg Foundation and
codirected by Rebecca Scott, Thomas Holt, and Frederick Cooper) pro-
vided me with a research assistantship for three years, as well as a travel
grant to conduct research in Texas. I also owe a debt of gratitude to the
Rackham Graduate School for awarding me the César Chávez / Rosa
Parks / Martin Luther King, Jr. Postdoctoral Fellowship at the University

of Michigan; and to the University of Michigan's Center for Afroamerican and African Studies for providing a home and staff support.

The Ford Foundation, through the National Research Council, awarded me a postdoctoral fellowship for minority scholars, which enabled me to complete the research for this book. The Center for American History at the University of Texas provided an office and staff support while I was a Ford Fellow. The University Research Institute and the Center for Mexican American Studies at the University of Texas at Austin provided generous research grants for research and writing during the summers. The University of Texas also awarded me a subvention grant from the University Cooperative Society.

The staffs at libraries and archives in which I conducted research deserve mention for their support and professionalism. I thank the staffs at the Center for American History, the Benson Latin American Collection, the Harry Ransom Humanities Research Center, Texas State Archives, the Bancroft Library, the Texas Institute of Culture, and the National Archives.

A number of scholars took time to read all or parts of the manuscript and offered me solid advice. For their efforts I am grateful to Angela Hinz, David Gutiérrez, Ramón Gutiérrez, George Lipsitz, Robin D. G. Kelley, David Roediger, Virginia Scharff, David Montejano, Gunther Peck, Pete Daniel, Joan Jensen, Michael Stoff, Kevin Kenny, Elliott Young, Jerry Huntley, John Chávez, Sarah Deutsch, George Sánchez, Robert Crunden, Rebecca Scott, Earl Lewis, and Michael Rogin. I would also like to express my special thanks and appreciation to Teresa Palomo Acosta, who shared with me her family's photographs and invited me into her home. I also owe a debt of gratitude to Adriana Ayala and Patricia Martínez, young scholars who served as research assistants at various stages of this project. Finally, I would like to thank editors Monica McCormick and Scott Norton of the University of California Press and copyeditor Sarah Myers for their patience and professionalism in guiding this book to completion.

Over the years I have enjoyed the company and support of my parents and my brothers and sisters and their families, who have put me up on many occasions and put up with me on the rest. To my own family I owe the biggest debt of gratitude. Angela Hinz convinced me to return to graduate school and pursue my interest in the history of race in America and in the history of Mexicans in the United States. She has been my best critic and best friend. To our young daughters, Sabina, Bianca, and Sophia, thank you for sending me off each day with a smile and a kiss. Your love sustains me.

Introduction

When one thinks of sharecroppers, images of the plantation South come to mind—poor folks, blacks and whites, dressed in overalls, their wives cooking, washing, and raising children in one-room shacks with no running water and very little furniture, while partially clothed children play at their feet. One perhaps thinks of the plantation world of the Mississippi Delta, the "most southern place on earth," according to the historian James Cobb, where thousands of mostly black sharecroppers tilled the land with mules and plows not much changed from Reconstruction days. One conjures images of riding bosses, planters, credit merchants, fatback and molasses, boll weevils, and unending poverty for the men, women, and children, many suffering from pellagra and rickets, who worked from "sun to sun" dragging long cotton sacks on farms they did not own. This was the New South of the first four decades of the twentieth century, a region tenaciously rural and constant in its loyalty to the culture of cotton.[1]

Whatever image of the South one summons, it largely excludes Texas cotton farmers, even though Texas, as a slave state of the Confederacy, experienced defeat and Reconstruction and became the nation's leading cotton-producing state by 1890. The postbellum image of the South also overlooks twentieth-century Texas and its large population of Mexicans, both native-born and immigrant, who came increasingly to displace Anglos and blacks on cotton farms in central Texas after 1910. As part of the Spanish borderlands before 1821 and as a Mexican state until 1836, Texas has had a long history of interaction between Mexicans and Anglos, as well as between masters and slaves on plantations in east Texas.[2] East

Texas, for example, fits comfortably within the cultural and historio-graphical boundaries of the South, with its history of slavery, cotton, and postemancipation society. South Texas, however, shares more com-monalties with the history of the "trans–Rio Grande North" and Mex-ico than with the U.S. South. These discrete cultural regions of east and south Texas overlap in south-central Texas from Waco to Corpus Christi, where cultural elements of the South, the West, and Mexico have come to form a unique borderlands culture. Spanish, French, Ger-man, African, Mexican, English, Polish, Czech, and other groups have left their cultural mark in a society of such great social heterogeneity and hybridity that one geographer has called it the "shatter belt." Texas is thus culturally and historiographically at some distance from the "most southern place on earth," but its cotton culture nevertheless makes it rec-ognizably southern, even if the state's large Mexican population contin-ues to link it with other western states and Mexico (see Maps 1 and 2).[3]

As the cotton culture of the South advanced westward, Texas retained the image of a state more western than southern, in part because, as one Texas historian has noted, cotton makes Texas seem "too southern, hence Confederate, defeated, poor, and prosaic."[4] In Texas, "unlike the Deep South," wrote the anthropologist Oscar Lewis, "there was no leisure class to romanticize cotton farming, and it could at no time com-pete with ranching in capturing the imagination of the people as an ideal way of life."[5] Tourists flock to San Antonio more than any other Texas city because it alone captures the image that Texans most like to project of themselves—defenders of the Alamo, victors in the war against Mex-ico, pioneers in the western wilderness, manly cowboys and rich cattle barons. But while longhorns, Stetson hats, and the romance of ranching have replaced cotton, mules, and overalls in the historical imagination of Anglo Texans today, the fact remains that most Anglo Texans were de-scended from transplanted Southerners who had fought hard to main-tain the "color line" in Texas and to extend its barriers to Mexicans. Many Anglo Texans thus often wore two hats: the ten-gallon variety as well as the white hood of the Invisible Empire.[6]

The large presence of Mexicans in Texas is one obvious feature that has distinguished Texas from the rest of the South and unites it with other states of the Southwest and West with large Mexican populations. Indeed, if we count Texas as a southern state, following the lead of the census, until 1930 the South—not the West—was home to more Mexi-cans than was any other region of the country.[7] One central Texas landowner referred to the region as "the West" because, he explained,

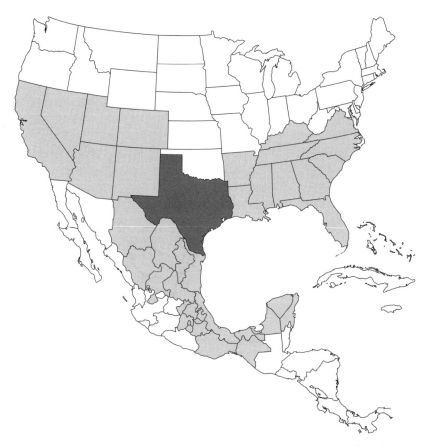

Map 1. Texas as a Border Province between the South, the West, and Mexico.

central Texas was the western part of the cotton belt—it was, in other words, "the West" of "the South."[8] In shifting their self-image from South to West, Anglos may have been influenced by the growing presence of Mexicans in Texas after 1900 and the proportional decrease in the percentage of blacks in the population.[9] The fusing of the cultural practice of the South and the West for more than a century in Texas led one Work Projects Administration (WPA) author to observe in 1940: "More Southern than Western is the State's approach to most political and social questions; more Western than Southern are the manners of most of its people."[10] Central Texas at least remained southern in its maintenance of Jim Crow segregation of Anglos, blacks, and Mexicans, but as the development of large-scale industrial "cotton ranches" shifted cotton production from the South to the West after 1920, the growing

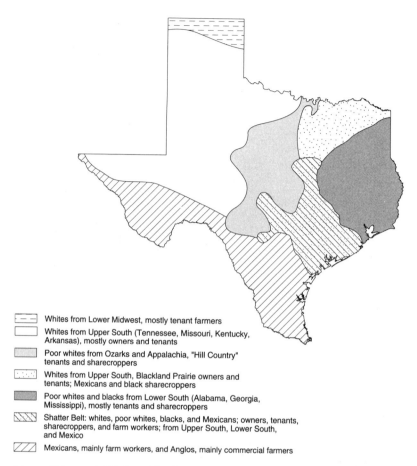

Whites from Lower Midwest, mostly tenant farmers

Whites from Upper South (Tennessee, Missouri, Kentucky, Arkansas), mostly owners and tenants

Poor whites from Ozarks and Appalachia, "Hill Country" tenants and sharecroppers

Whites from Upper South, Blackland Prairie owners and tenants; Mexicans and black sharecroppers

Poor whites and blacks from Lower South (Alabama, Georgia, Mississippi), mostly tenants and sharecroppers

Shatter Belt: whites, poor whites, blacks, and Mexicans; owners, tenants, sharecroppers, and farm workers; from Upper South, Lower South, and Mexico

Mexicans, mainly farm workers, and Anglos, mainly commercial farmers

Map 2. Ethnoracial/Cultural Regions of Texas. Adapted from Terry G. Jordan, John L. Bean Jr., and William M. Holmes, *Texas: A Geography*, Geographies of the United States Series (Boulder, Colo.: Westview Press, 1984), 91.

reliance on Mexican farm workers made parts of south-central Texas seem less like the Mississippi Delta and more like the San Joaquin Valley of California.[11]

The cotton culture of central Texas represents a special case for the study of class formation and white racial ideology precisely because it brings together two sets of race and class relations—blacks and whites in the South, and Mexicans and Anglos in the Southwest. The fusion of cotton and cattle culture, of plantation and ranch, created a hybrid economy that mixed mostly small farmers (whether as tenants or sharecroppers on plantations or owner-operated family farms) with large-scale, industrialized cotton ranches that employed hundreds of farm workers. In south-central Texas many blacks and poor whites were displaced as tenants and sharecroppers and were reduced to farm workers, along with Mexicans, on corporate cotton ranches. At the same time, white farm owners in central Texas replaced white and black tenants with Mexican sharecroppers because owners believed they could better control and exploit Mexican immigrants. The quintessentially southern image of blacks and poor whites on sharecropper farms was yielding to a hybrid southwestern culture in which Mexicans transgressed the racialized boundaries between farm worker, sharecropper, and share tenant and forged new identities in the racially charged borderlands between whiteness and blackness.

In rupturing the black-white polarity of southern race relations, the presence of Mexicans in central Texas raises some interesting questions about the way in which "whiteness" itself fissured along race and class lines. White Texans had a long history of invoking the color line in their social, economic, and political interactions with African Americans, but they had little experience in plantation society with what one contemporary sociologist called "partly colored races."[12] Were partly colored Mexicans, in other words, white or nonwhite? As a racially mixed group, Mexicans, like Indians and Asians, lived in a black-and-white nation that regarded them neither as black nor as white. Although small numbers of Mexicans—usually light-skinned, middle-class Mexican Americans—claimed to be Spanish and therefore white, the overwhelming majority of Texas whites regarded Mexicans as a "mongrelized" race of Indian, African, and Spanish ancestry. In Texas, unlike other parts of the South, whiteness meant not only not black but also not Mexican.[13]

Whiteness also came increasingly to mean a particular kind of white person. Not all whites, in other words, were equally white. In the first two decades of the twentieth century, the eugenics movement, which advanced the theory that behavior and racial traits were genetically determined and therefore inherited, influenced popular thinking on issues ranging from immigration restriction to prohibition of interracial marriage, sterilization, and the decline of the white civilization by barbarians from within as well as without.[14] Eugenicists had lost confidence in the social Darwinist notion of "survival of the fittest"—what worried them most was survival of the unfit. "Race scientists" influenced by eugenics, like Madison Grant and Lothrop Stoddard, popularized the idea that the "Nordic" race was in danger of being overwhelmed not only by the "rising tide" of dark people in the world but also by the biological reproduction of "defective" whites. In 1922 Vice President Calvin Coolidge echoed the theories of Stoddard and Grant when he claimed that

Nordics became biologically inferior whites when mixed with other races. At its extreme, eugenics called for the sterilization of "moronic," criminal, insane, drunken, sexually perverse, and other "cacogenic" (bad-gened) whites.[15] While immigrant Jews, Slavs, Italians, and Irish were "becoming white" in the urban areas of the East, poor whites in Texas and elsewhere in the South were heading in the opposite direction—losing whiteness and the status and privileges that whiteness bestowed. Poor whites in the cotton South came not only to be seen as a social problem but also to be located in the racial hierarchy as the "trash" of whiteness.[16]

Successful whites—cotton growers, merchants, bankers, and those whom eugenicists often called Nordic whites—began to racialize poor whites as the "scrubs and runts" of white civilization, both as an excuse to displace them and as a justification for the impoverished condition of those who remained.[17] Edward Everett Davis, a researcher who wrote numerous articles on cotton culture in Texas during the 1920s and 1930s, wrote an inferior novel published in 1940, titled *The White Scourge*, in which he portrayed cotton as the scourge of southern society because it attracted "white trash" like "iron filings to a magnet." The cotton culture of the South provided an elemental means of subsistence for "lowly blacks, peonized Mexicans, and moronic whites," Davis mused, which enabled them to reproduce their "hideous kind" and populate the cotton belt with "America's worthless human silt."[18] But the novel also suggests that "trashy" whites, not cotton, were the real "white scourge"— the "human debris" of whiteness—that posed a serious menace to the rest of white civilization. Davis encouraged east Texas Congressman John Box, one of the leading immigration restrictionists of his day, to read Stoddard's popular *The Rising Tide of Color against White World-Supremacy*, published in 1920, to understand the urgency of restricting the "lower races" from admittance to the United States because they frequently intermarried with "marginal" whites who had "just enough intelligence to beget children, hew wood, draw water, and pick cotton."[19]

Although more than twenty-five states had enacted sterilization laws by 1925, sterilization as a eugenic solution to eradicating inferior "germ plasm" had been largely ineffective. Davis argued that the only way to preserve the "racial hygiene" of the white race in the South was to abolish cotton agriculture, because it provided a means of subsistence for "feeble-minded" poor whites, as well as for racially inferior Mexicans and blacks. Taxing the land to force landowners to sell to small farmers, Davis believed, would enable white farmers to restore the racial virility and manhood of the South. In using the title of Davis's novel for this book, I suggest that the scourge of the South and the nation was not cotton or poor whites but whiteness itself—whiteness not simply as the pinnacle of ethnoracial status but as the complex social and economic matrix wherein racial power and privilege were shared, not always equally, by those who were able to construct identities as Anglo-Saxons, Nordics, Caucasians, or simply whites. Poor whites, always low-ranking members of the whiteness club, were banished in the early twentieth century on the grounds that they were culturally and biologically inferior. The "wages of whiteness" conferred privilege on those who were able to claim whiteness, as historian David Roediger has ably shown, but they also invoke the biblical injunction that the "wages of sin" is death—death to the notion of racial, and therefore social and economic, equality.[20]

The heterogeneity and hybridity of whiteness became more transparent in this region, where whites were both the most successful landowners and among the most impoverished sharecroppers. White tenants blamed the system for their inability to escape tenancy, while bankers, landlords, and credit merchants became ever more critical of the tenant class, implying that failure to ascend the ladder to ownership reflected the incompetence or laziness of Mexican, black, and "sorry white" tenants rather than any deficiency in the system itself. Many Mexicans, on the other hand, moved from migrant work to sharecropping and share tenancy over time and often had as much claim to whiteness as did some of the poor whites with whom they competed.[21] The emergence of a rural class of "white trash" made whites conscious of themselves as a racial group and fearful that if they fell to the bottom, they would lose the racial privileges that came with being accepted for what they were not—black, Mexican, or foreign born.[22]

Behind this geography of region thus lie complex and often overlapping geographies of racial power and difference. The cotton culture of this fertile region of central Texas was not racially static or bipartite but a site of multiple and heterogeneous borders where different languages, experiences, histories, and voices intermingled amid diverse relations of power and privilege. Partly for these reasons, the categories of Anglo, black, and Mexican are wholly inadequate—and even misleading—in describing the highly miscegenated culture of central Texas. Anglo, for example, exists as a label principally in opposition to Mexican and denotes, rather crudely, all non-Mexican whites, thereby conflating widely diverse cultural groups in Texas, such as Germans, Czechs, Wends, Irish,

English, Polish, and French—to say nothing of Protestants, Catholics, and Jews. In reducing all whites of European descent into one category, the term *Anglo* thus fails completely to identify any single ethnic group—too often they all tend to look alike. The Irish, for example, remained outside the circle of whiteness until they learned the meaning of whiteness and adopted its racial ideology. Texas Germans who belonged to the Republican Party did not share the racial animosity of other whites toward Mexicans and blacks and were frequently suspected of being traitors to their race. Some German landowners not only rented to Mexicans and blacks, as did other whites, but socialized with them and, in some cases, formed political alliances with them.[23] Since not all European groups became white at the same time or came to enjoy the "property right" in whiteness equally, the fissuring of whiteness in the region into Nordic white businessmen farmers and poor white tenants is a central concern of this study, for "white trash" ruptured the convention that maintained whiteness as an unmarked and normative racial identity. Most whites nevertheless occupied a position in the social structure and in the agricultural economy more like one another than like Mexicans, Mexican Americans, and African Americans. Consequently, I sometimes use the term *Anglo* when discussing relations between whites and Mexicans, because some Mexicans claimed to be white.

Anglo Texans, for their part, often failed to differentiate between Mexican Americans and Mexican immigrants, referring to both simply as Mexicans, a word that conflated race with nationality. This fact became painfully clear to American citizens of Mexican descent during the repatriation drives of the 1930s, when immigration officers routinely deported Mexican Americans along with resident Mexican nationals.[24] For many white Texans, a Mexican American was simply a contradiction in terms, a hybridization of mutually exclusive races, nationalities, and cultures.[25]

The use of the term *Mexican* also glosses over intra-ethnic conflict that characterized relations between Mexican immigrants and Mexican Americans during the first decades of the century. Mexican nationals frequently referred to Mexican Americans as *pochos* (gringoized Mexicans) or agringados, while many Mexican Americans favored immigration restriction, claiming that Mexican immigrants took away jobs and lowered wages. Some Mexican Americans also began to embrace whiteness by representing themselves as Latin Americans and Spanish Americans who feared that the constant influx of poor and largely illiterate agricultural workers reinforced the Anglo stereotype of Mexicans as nonwhite peons and "birds of passage."[26]

Although most scholars recognize the inadequacy of terms like *Anglo* and *Mexican*, many still regard the category of black or African American as unproblematic, readily identifiable, and easily, if mistakenly, defined. After centuries of thinking of blacks as a separate racial group, we often overlook the fact that Black Americans, like Mexicans and Anglos, are also ethnically diverse and represent generations of intermarriage with Anglos, Mexicans, Asians, Indians, and other groups. Our stubborn refusal to recognize black ethnicity stems from what the African American novelist Ishmael Reed has termed America's "secret of miscegenation," which underlies our insistence on the separateness of whiteness and blackness. To illustrate the power of miscegenation's secret in the social construction of whiteness, Reed explained that when he mentioned his Irish-American heritage to a professor of Celtic studies, the professor's only response was to laugh.[27] Some people still wonder how a black person could also be part white if, as many have been acculturated to believe, it is impossible for a white person to also be part black.[28] Although Anglos and Mexicans relied on some monolithic, reified notion of blackness for their own race-making purposes, the so-called one-drop rule of southern racial ideology placed constraints on the ability of African Americans to exploit the ethnoracial fissures forming in central Texas during the first half of the century.

Despite the contradictions inherent in the nomenclature, I use the terms *Anglo/white, black*, and *Mexican* because they conform to the ways in which these diverse groups constructed their own identities as distinct from members of the other groups. However imaginary the homogeneity of these communities might be, the boundaries separating the groups were real enough: For example, central Texas Czechs and Germans, who spoke different languages and often attended different churches and schools, still thought of themselves as whites when they were in the company of Mexicans and blacks.

In culturally crisscrossed central Texas, overlapping economic systems and racial hierarchies enable us to examine how systems of domination and subordination were structured through processes of racialization and white racial construction. Over time, the region's poor whites and Mexicans, more so than African Americans, underwent significant transformation in their ethnoracial status and identity. However, in order to understand some of these changes, we need first to have a basic understanding of the complex system of land tenure in the cotton South, which contemporaries sometimes called the "agricultural ladder."

The notion of a ladder was a fundamental tenet of American agriculture from the Civil War to the New Deal. It held that the young male farmhand could climb, rung by rung, through the stages of hired hand, sharecropper, and tenant farmer to farm owner. It guaranteed opportunities for all farmers, in theory at least, to move across social and economic boundaries toward farm ownership, which was both the symbol of and the passport to full citizenship in the democracy of rural America.[29]

In central Texas a sharp distinction separated sharecroppers and tenant farmers, in part because of the social and racial stigma attached to being a sharecropper. Sharecroppers were essentially wage hands hired to work on farms they did not own. Landowners hired them to produce cotton for the landowner. Instead of paying sharecroppers in wages, however, owners sold the cotton at the end of the harvest and paid them one-half of the proceeds of the sale, minus any debts the sharecroppers owed the owner for supplies. Sharecroppers were often called "halvers" because they worked for half of the cotton. They owned no tools or work animals, which the owner supplied. The owner also arranged credit for the sharecroppers and their families to purchase supplies at the town store, which sometimes the landowner owned himself.

Tenant farmers occupied a higher class position on the agricultural ladder than did sharecroppers, mainly because they owned their own plows, work animals, and tools. Since they owned their own capital, they were able to rent land from the owner for one-fourth of the cotton and one-third of the grain, usually corn they grew to feed their workstock. They kept three-fourths of the cotton and two-thirds of the corn as income. For this reason tenants, to use the vernacular of the time, rented "on thirds and fourths." As true renters, they owned the crop and therefore were legally entitled to sell it themselves. They established their own credit arrangements and worked without supervision by the landlord. Share tenants, in other words, thought of themselves as farmers, not as sharecroppers or farm workers. Sharecroppers, on the other hand, received cotton as wages for labor and legally were not accorded the status of renters or farmers. White sharecroppers nevertheless liked to think of themselves as farmers who only temporarily occupied the lower rungs of the agricultural ladder. As one might expect, therefore, the majority of share tenants in central Texas were white, whereas most Mexicans and blacks, who often owned little or no capital, were sharecroppers or migrant workers.[30]

The region I examine in this study differs from the usual southern patterns in important respects. First, central Texas did not have as extensive a history of plantation farming as did other southern states where plantations had operated before the Civil War and where blacks often constituted a majority of the workforce. Second, the majority of farmers in the central Texas cotton belt were white share tenants, not black sharecroppers; they farmed on the richest soil in Texas for cotton, the Blackland Prairie, and aspired to own their own farms, as had many of their white ancestors. Third, white owners and tenants came increasingly to rely on Mexican migrant labor to harvest the crop and gradually began to replace white and black sharecroppers with Mexican sharecroppers and wage laborers. These variations on the southern theme of cotton agriculture produced complex and odd configurations as Mexicans competed with blacks and as both groups competed with white tenants, sharecroppers, and wage workers. White tenants did not share the same economic interests with white sharecroppers; and among black, Mexican, and white sharecroppers and wage laborers, competition and racial prejudices frustrated efforts to organize effectively. Finally, white tenants worried over the introduction of yet another nonwhite group requiring its own schools, churches, and neighborhoods.[31]

Movement up or down the agricultural ladder raises a series of questions about economic competition and popular mobilization. Were there recognizable patterns of confrontation among the groups as each tried to effect certain economic and political outcomes? How did whites respond to the challenges to the racial order and defend their interests and privileges as whites? The legacy of antiblack racism in central Texas and of white Southerners' abhorrence of social equality with blacks led many white farmers to seek political alliances, however reluctantly at first, with Mexican sharecroppers and tenant farmers between 1910 and 1920. Together they formed numerous locals of the Socialist Renters' Union and Land League, founded in Texas in 1911, and organized against land monopoly, high rents, low wages, and inferior living conditions on cotton farms. The radicalism of Mexican workers in the Socialist Party, Renters' Union, and Industrial Workers of the World (IWW) complicated southern notions of whiteness that constructed white manhood, in part, in opposition to docile, peon Mexicans.

In examining the conflicts between owners and tenants, Anglos and Mexicans, blacks and whites, men and women, as well as the conflicts within different classes and races of farm men and women, this study assumes that whites are raced, men are gendered, and women are marked by class. Although the conflicts between landlords and tenants in the triracial borderlands of central Texas best exemplify the relationships among whiteness, race formation, and class, the story that follows links gendered notions of masculinity and agrarian whiteness to the various races and classes of farmers. The conjunction of race and gender, for example, is exemplified in the political discourse of the Socialist Party, in which manly courage was constitutive of whiteness. Socialist leaders accused white tenants of lacking the "white-hearted manliness" of Mexican tenants, who launched a revolution in Mexico and were among the most radical elements in the Texas Socialist Party.[32]

In analyzing the ways in which race and class interacted in the formation of an agricultural proletariat, we must also consider the meaning of each category within the context of gender relations. The interests of men and women were not necessarily identical in a society that subordinated women to men in the family and denied women any power in politics. Gerda Lerner makes the valuable point that the category of class is "genderic"—it is "expressed and institutionalized in terms that are *always different* for men and women."[33] For men and women of different races the "genderic" experience of class position is even more profound: A world of difference existed between the experience, for example, of an African American wife of a sharecropper and that of a white male sharecropper. Any race and class analysis of farming culture must therefore account for the labor of women (and children), because farming, by definition, was a collective endeavor that required their labor in the fields and in the household. Single men simply did not operate farms, and certainly the work provided by the hands of women and children was a prime consideration for owners in renting to share tenants or sharecroppers. In William Faulkner's novel *The Hamlet*, one of the first questions the landlord-merchant Jody Varner asks Ab Snopes, a sharecropper looking for a farm to rent, is, "How much family you got?" Varner rents the farm to Snopes when Snopes replies that he can put six hands into the field, four of whom are women.[34] The image of men plowing the fields behind their mules obscures the fact that men could not be tenants and sharecroppers in the first place were it not for the labor power of their wives and children.

For Mexicans, central Texas represented a vastly different culture from the ranch country of south Texas, where blacks were few and where Anglos, who began to settle the region before the Civil War, knew something of Mexican culture and customs. Central Texas was cotton country, and its people were primarily transplanted Southerners who had brought with them their particular history of interaction across the color line. Neither blacks nor whites had much experience or understanding of Mexicans, who frequently could not speak English and whose Catholicism made them suspect in the eyes of black Baptists or Anglo Methodists. But over time Mexicans became a part of the southern culture of the region, adapted to it, and at the same time transformed it into a unique cultural crossroads in the borderlands between the South and the West.

In the first chapter I explain how the Texas Revolution and the War with Mexico laid the foundation for racializing Mexicans as nonwhites. As cotton displaced cattle in the Blackland Prairie, a strip of fertile cotton counties stretching roughly from Dallas to San Antonio, white owners of cotton farms began to experiment with Mexican labor. Contemporaries began to allude to the "white man's problem" when they described the growing rate of white tenancy in central Texas and the increasing number of Mexican sharecroppers taking the places of white tenants on the farms. In chapter 2 I argue that immigration of Mexicans into Texas after 1910 constituted a "second color menace" in the western South and sundered the racial dyad of white and black. In the South the color line separated monolithic whiteness from debased blackness; in central Texas, however, Mexicans walked the color line. Heavily recruited by growers throughout the Southwest, Mexicans were represented variously as nonwhite "mongrels" who polluted the Anglo-Saxon racial stock and as almost white laborers who worked in unskilled occupations shunned by most whites. Eugenicists opposed the acceptance of Mexicans as whites because it sanctioned the mixing of Nordic whites with Indian Mexicans, while growing numbers of Mexican Americans sought acceptance within the ranks of the American working class by insisting on their status as whites.

How complex land-tenure arrangements among Mexicans, blacks, and poor whites shaped race, class, and gender identities of owners, renters, croppers, and wage hands is the subject of chapter 3, in which I argue that white sharecroppers increasingly came to be regarded as the scourge of the white race in Texas. Here I also look at the relationship of race and ethnicity to land tenure, landlord-tenant relations, credit practices, and notions of masculinity, with a focus on the social and economic processes by which Mexican, black, and white owners, renters, croppers, and laborers moved up and down separate and unequal agricultural ladders.

In chapter 4 I examine the efforts of the Socialist Party in Texas to organize Anglo and Mexican tenant farmers between 1911 and 1917. Under the leadership of the Irish immigrant Tom Hickey, a neophyte white Southerner and disciple of white supremacy, the Renters' Union and

Land League sought to build an interracial union like the Brotherhood of Timber Workers (BTW) in east Texas and Louisiana. Although the union officially opened its doors to black farmers in 1912, Hickey made no effort to recruit them, fearing a white backlash and charges of "social equality." He supported the Mexican Revolution and admired leaders like Emiliano Zapata and Pancho Villa, even as he called white tenants who would not join the union "coons" and peons for failing to live up to manly measures of whiteness. Hickey consistently failed to understand the transnational militancy of Mexicans who crossed the border into Texas imbued with the radical ideology of *magonismo*—a radical social movement led by the anarchist Ricardo Flores Magón—and later the Partido Liberal Mexicano (PLM).

The intersection of race and technology on large-scale cotton ranches is the subject of chapter 5. The growth of cotton ranches accompanied, and in many ways abetted, changes in the racial geography of the workforce. Large business farms like the Taft Ranch demonstrated the feasibility and efficiency of producing cotton profitably through mechanization and the "scientific management" of its Mexican, black, and white workers. Scientific management of a racialized workforce on corporate farms reflected—and in some ways implemented—the eugenicist notion that nonwhite Mexicans and blacks, as well as "sorry whites," were best handled under the close supervision of their Nordic superiors. In these industrial "factories in the field" white tenants of the New South encountered Mexican laborers of the Southwest and ultimately were displaced by them.

Chapter 6 is an analysis of the ways in which the ideology of yeoman manhood served as the linchpin of gendered whiteness. Mexican, black, and white farm women shared overlapping identities as women, mothers, wives, and daughters as well as owners, tenants, sharecroppers, and wage workers. Women of different classes and races contested gendered notions of farm life by transgressing the boundary between men's work and women's work and attacking the agrarian, patriarchal ideology that praised the role of the farmer's helpmate while ignoring her needs entirely. Mechanization, for example, was decidedly a masculine adaptation that put many men on tractors while women continued to haul water from not-so-nearby wells for cooking and cleaning. Agrarian whiteness excluded African American and Mexican women who spent more time doing "men's work" in the fields than did white farm women, regardless of tenure status, while more-privileged white farm women angrily denounced the work of extension agents for putting the needs of farm animals before those of farm children.

In the last two chapters I consider the impact of New Deal programs on the racialization of the rural workforce and the efforts of agricultural workers—Mexicans, blacks, and whites—to organize against the worst abuses of the new order. Landlords took advantage of loopholes in the federal cotton contract as well as the large reserve of Mexican laborers to evict poor whites from central Texas farms, while the Southern Tenant Farmers' Union (STFU) in Texas failed to acknowledge class distinctions between tenants and sharecroppers or between farmers and proletarianized farm workers. This "biracial" union was composed mostly of segregated locals of Mexican, black, and white sharecroppers and wage workers whose interests—wages, working conditions, job security—more closely resembled those of industrial workers than of central Texas share tenants who *hired* wage laborers, mostly Mexicans.

The story thus ends with the massive disruptions to the farm order of the South and Southwest caused by New Deal agricultural programs in the 1930s. At the national political level, the interstate migration of displaced white tenants—"Okies" and "Arkies"—brought to the nation's attention the growing social, political, and economic problems associated with the rapid development of agribusiness farming in the Southwest and West and its growing reliance on immigrant Mexican labor—a discovery that reified the racial boundaries of farmwork around "off-white" Okies and Mexicans.[35] John Steinbeck's 1939 novel *The Grapes of Wrath* chronicles not only the odyssey of displaced Dust Bowl tenant farmers from Oklahoma on the road to California but also their fall from agrarian whiteness and yeoman manhood, tropes intimately linked to the ownership of farmland.

A few words need to be said about the meaning of the term *central Texas*. Texas consists of four broadly defined cotton belts: east, west, south, and central.[36] For the purposes of this study, central Texas forms a diamond shape from Dallas in the north to Corpus Christi in the south, bounded by San Antonio in the west and Houston in the east. In the geographical morphology of Texas, this region is the site of the cultural core, not because it occupies the geographical center of the state but because, more than any other region, it displays, according to geographer Donald Meinig, the "full range of intercultural tensions" that exist between east Texas, west Texas, and south Texas.[37] In the ethnoracial borderlands of central Texas, the South, with its dyadic racial categories, first encountered the Southwest, where whiteness fractured along class lines and Mexicans moved in to fill the racial space between whiteness and blackness (see Map 3).

Finally, *The White Scourge* seeks to transcend the black-white and

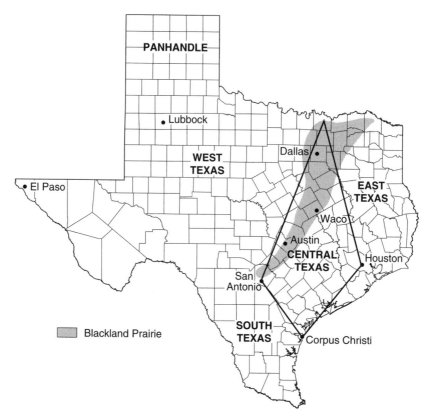

Map 3. Zone of Central Texas Cotton Culture.

Mexican-Anglo binaries of southern and western race relations that inform the history of Mexicans and African Americans in Texas. Historians of slavery and the plantation South focus on east Texas, that part of Texas that is most readily identifiable, culturally and historically, with the antebellum and postemancipation South. Historians of the West, on the other hand, incorporate Texas into the unfolding story of the Spanish borderlands and the U.S. Southwest, focusing on ranching, cattle, Indians, and Mexicans.[38] By situating these narratives within the larger context of agrarian transformation and white racial construction, *The White Scourge* bridges the chasm between African American and Southern history, on the one hand, and Mexican American and Southwestern history, on the other. In the borderlands of central Texas the westward advance of cotton culture produced profound changes in the lives of working men, women, and children in new, multiracial farming communities.

CHAPTER I

The Old South in the Southwest

Westward Expansion of Cotton Culture, 1820–1900

In December 1820 Moses Austin, father of Texas *empresario* Stephen F. Austin, was summoned to appear before Don Antonio Martínez, the Spanish governor of Texas in San Antonio de Bexar.[1] Moses Austin had come from Missouri to seek permission to obtain a Royal Commission to settle 300 families in Texas. Numerous questions were put to Moses, including what his reasons were for desiring to settle in Spanish Texas, to which he replied, through an interpreter, "to provide for his subsistence by raising sugar and cotton." Although the Spanish were deeply suspicious of American filibusters posing as settlers, Moses Austin was able to convince them that his colony, which included some slaveholders, had as its primary interest the growing of cotton and sugar and not revolutionary activity against the Spanish Crown.[2]

The Crown authorities reasoned that loyal farmer-colonists, with a high stake in the land, would provide a buffer against marauding Indians and prevent the intrusion of future filibusters from the United States. On January 17, 1821, the commandant of the eastern internal provinces, General Joaquín de Arredondo, notified Governor Martínez that the petition in the name of Moses Austin had been granted by the provincial council at Monterrey, located in Nuevo León, Mexico. In keeping with his father's agricultural objectives for the colony, Stephen F. Austin, in an address to the colonists in 1824, stated that they would be delivered from poverty through the cultivation of cotton, and on a later occasion he recommended to Governor Rafael Gonzales: "Nothing but foreign commerce, particularly the exportation of cotton to Europe, can enrich the inhabitants of this section of the State."[3] Thus the first cotton farmers and their slaves were introduced to the rich river-bottom lands of present-day east Texas in the first quarter of the nineteenth century.

Following the establishment of the Austin colony in Mexican Texas in 1821, the Mexican government, which won independence from Spain the same year, enacted a series of colonization laws in the 1820s that opened the door to white immigrants. Mostly from the upper and lower South, these white Americans crossed the Sabine River from Louisiana into Texas, where many quickly established cotton plantations in the eastern part of the province and along the rich coastal plains. The Mexican government offered each immigrant farmer one *labor* of land, or 177 acres.[4] Those who wished to graze livestock received a league (4,428 acres) or more, and empresarios like Moses Austin were entitled to five leagues for every hundred families settled.[5] At first these new immigrants had little contact with the Mexican population in Texas, the boundaries of which in the 1820s included San Antonio and La Bahía (Goliad) but not Laredo, which belonged to the Mexican state of Tamaulipas. The El Paso area, another center of mestizo population since the late seventeenth century, was located in the Mexican state of Chihuahua; and the present-day counties of the lower Rio Grande belonged to the Mexican state of Tamaulipas.[6] Less than a decade after 1821, however, owing to the liberal immigration laws, white immigrants from the United States outnumbered the Mexican population of Texas and increasingly began to foment rebellion against the Mexican government.

Numerous conflicts arose between the government of Mexico and Anglo and Mexican Texans (*tejanos*), particularly under the centralist rule of Antonio López de Santa Anna after 1834. Anglo Texans quarreled with the Mexican government over the enactment of antislavery laws, especially the Law of April 6, 1830, by which Mexico, in effect, closed the border between Texas and the United States to stop the flood of white "illegal aliens" from slaveholding states east of the Sabine River.[7] The Mexican government accurately reasoned that U.S. immigrants had felt little obligation to obey Mexican laws and were growing restless under a government that forbade slavery. Stephen Austin, once a loyal Mexican citizen who spoke Spanish and demonstrated his allegiance to the Mexican government on numerous occasions, succumbed to the demands of Texas slaveholders and nonslaveholders alike when he wrote in 1833: "I have been averse to the principle of slavery in Texas. I have now, and for the last six months, changed my views. . . . Texas *must be* a slave country."[8] A few years later, in 1836, the famous trio of southern-born whites,

Jim Bowie, Davy Crockett, and William Barrett Travis, gave their lives at the Alamo for the freedom of white men to own slaves.

After the bloody battles of the Alamo and San Jacinto, the Republic of Texas drafted its first constitution, in which it guaranteed the protection of slavery. Section 9 of the constitution reads, in part: "Congress shall pass no laws to prohibit emigrants from bringing their slaves into the republic with them . . . nor shall congress have the power to emancipate slaves; nor shall any slave holder be allowed to emancipate his or her slave or slaves without the consent of congress."[9] Texas whites had won in their revolt against Mexico what whites in the U.S. South would lose a few decades later with the outbreak of the Civil War, when slaves constituted approximately 30 percent of the population and when more than one-fourth of all Texas families owned slaves.[10]

From the beginning of the Republic of Texas, Indians and free blacks were denied the constitutional protections accorded to whites, while Mexicans occupied a nebulous, intermediate status between (nonwhite) Indian and (marginally white) Spanish. In many ways the Texas Republic represented the culmination of Anglo-Saxon beliefs in the racial inferiority of Mexicans as a result of centuries of racial mixing among Spaniards, Africans, and Indians.[11] Texas land policies, for example, sought to discourage the settlement of free blacks and Indians in the republic. The constitution of the Texas Republic retained the liberal land policies of Mexican Texas, but with the proviso that only white heads of family were entitled to purchase land. Texas whites and "Spanish" Mexicans who aided in the Texas revolt against Mexico were entitled to a first-class "headright" for one league and a labor of land, provided they could persuade the court that they were white and not of Indian or African descent. Shortly after statehood, for example, José María de la Garza, petitioning the commissioner's court of Refugio County (near Corpus Christi) for a league and a labor, stated that he was born in Texas "of Texas parents and is a free white person of Spanish and not of African blood."[12] Only by insisting on their Spanish blood and the absence of any African blood were some Mexicans, like José María de la Garza, able to claim whiteness in order to purchase land. Second-, third-, and fourth-class headrights, consisting of smaller land grants, were awarded primarily to encourage white people to settle in Texas. Whiteness was thus inscribed in Texas law as the quintessential property for both citizenship rights and landownership.[13]

Throughout the debates leading to annexation of Texas in 1845, politicians alluded frequently to the inferiority of Mexico and the Mexican race. In 1844 James Buchanan, who later served as secretary of state under President James K. Polk, argued that Mexico was incapable of re-taking the Republic of Texas because "Anglo-Saxon blood could never be subdued by anything that claimed Mexican origin." In the same year Levi Woodbury of New Hampshire argued that Texans were "men of the true Saxon race" who under Mexican rule were "humiliated, and en-slaved to Moors, Indians, and mongrels."[14] The slave Republic of Texas, in other words, had to be annexed to what the historian Alexander Sax-ton calls the White Republic in order to prevent white Texans from be-coming slaves to "mongrel Mexicans."[15]

The northern as well as southern belief in the inferiority of blacks also played a crucial role in uniting proannexation Northerners with proslav-ery Southerners. Most antislavery northern Democrats were appalled by the specter of millions of freed slaves migrating to the North. They hoped annexation would solve the agonizing racial problem of what to do with manumitted blacks in the white republic, the bête noire of America, according to the Irish visitor John Robert Godley in 1842.[16] An outspoken Negrophobe of the era, Mississippi Senator Robert J. Walker, warned that if slaves were freed and Texas were not annexed, millions of blacks would migrate to the North, where they would compete with whites for jobs. Texas, it was supposed, would become a safety valve for attracting both slaves and freed blacks to the doorstep of Latin America, where they could cross the border and become mingled with Mexicans. Annexation, then, would facilitate the relocation of blacks from the South to the "dumping ground" of the far-western frontier and hasten, according to a New York congressman, the "natural emigration" of blacks to "Mexico and the equator." The relocation of blacks to Texas and Mexico, expansionists also pointed out, would open land to poor white farmers in the South, as had the removal of unwanted Indians from Georgia in the 1830s. The annexation of Texas as a slave state thus became the great white hope of northern expansionists anxious to emancipate the nation from blacks, who, it was hoped, would find a home among the kindred population of "colored races" in Mexico.[17]

After the annexation of the Texas Republic, the United States went to war with Mexico. The immediate cause of the war was a boundary dis-pute between Texas and Mexico. The Republic of Texas had claimed that its western boundary was the Rio Grande; Mexico, which had never recognized the Republic of Texas or its annexation by the United States, claimed that the boundary between its twin states, Tejas and Coahuila, and the Gulf Coast state of Tamaulipas was at the Nueces River, which emptied into Corpus Christi Bay. The fact that the Rio Grande had never been the western or southern boundary of Texas was of little concern to the expansionist President Polk. As early as 1825, the United States, under President John Quincy Adams, had attempted to purchase the province from Mexico, but Mexico, torn by internal political divisions since winning independence from Spain in 1821, was not disposed to sell parcels of the homeland to the United States. Having failed to buy what it wanted, the United States sought a pretext to go to war in order to seize valuable ports on the Pacific from Puget Sound to the Gulf of California. A Whig congressman from Massachusetts, who was skeptical of President Polk's intentions, told his colleagues in the House of Representatives that Polk's objective in 1846 had not been "peace with Mexico, but a piece of Mexico."[18] When President Polk ordered General Zachary Taylor to cross the Nueces River, Mexican troops engaged him, and lives were lost on both sides. Polk immediately declared that "Mexico has invaded our territory and shed American blood on American soil." Although many Americans believed that the United States had provoked the war over land to which Mexico had at least a plausible claim, the voices of territorial expansion drowned out those of peace, and Polk asked Congress to declare war on Mexico.[19] The poet of the radical American experiment in democracy, Walt Whitman, added his voice to the chorus for war when he asked, in 1846: "What has miserable, inefficient Mexico . . . to do with the great mission of peopling the New World with a noble race?"[20]

Two years later the war was over. Fought by a southern president and a southern general, the struggle represented the territorial ambitions of the slave South and its white racial ideology as much as the North's pietistic notions of Manifest Destiny. Sam Houston was characteristically blunt—and honest—when he observed in 1848 that Americans had always cheated Indians, and since "Mexicans are no better than Indians . . . I see no reason why we should not go on the same course, now, and take their land."[21] The American General William Worth, a Northerner of southern sympathy and expansionist zeal, justified the seizure of Mexico's northern territory with the smug boast that "our Anglo-Saxon race [have] been land stealers from time immemorial, and why shouldn't they [be]?"[22] Though slavery would not be extended beyond Texas, mainly because it was thought that the cotton South had reached its geographical limits in Texas, the South and its southern senators had been among the war's most spirited defenders. The War with Mexico also made possible the extension of southern culture into the borderlands of what had been the northern states of Mexico. After the war, as white

Americans rushed to California to find gold and to Texas to buy cheap land, they brought with them the creed of white racial supremacy that had devastating consequences for the Mexicans, Indians, and Chinese whom they would encounter in the newly acquired American Southwest.[23]

The expansion of white Americans across the continent was completed in 1848, when Mexico ceded to the United States, by the Treaty of Guadalupe Hidalgo, all or part of the present states of California, Nevada, Arizona, New Mexico, Utah, and several others. In 1853 President Franklin Pierce added the Gadsden Purchase, a strip of land that now forms southern New Mexico and Arizona, to provide a southern route for a railroad to the Pacific. Those opposed to territorial expansion, particularly the Whigs, worried about the consequences of incorporating an inferior race into the union. Americans worried that these "colored mongrels," as citizens of the United States, might have the same rights as white people. Mexican Americans would then be entitled to hold seats in the Senate and House of Representatives. The southern senator John C. Calhoun, a fervent defender of slavery, opposed the incorporation of Mexico and its largely Indian population into the United States because, as he told the Senate, "We have never dreamt of incorporating into our Union any but the Caucasian race—the free white race."[24] Calhoun insisted that the color line be drawn at the Rio Grande and that the United States not extend its jurisdiction to the land and people south of it. "Ours is the government of the white man," Calhoun added, urging Congress to avoid "the fatal error of placing the colored race on an equality with the white." The nephew of Andrew Jackson, Andrew Donelson, also opposed acquiring all of Mexico and warned President Polk in 1848: "We can no more amalgamate with her people than with negroes."[25] Even those who wished to take all of Mexico's land as the spoils of war shared Calhoun and Donelson's concern over absorbing nonwhite people into the white republic, some even suggesting that Mexico's nonwhite population be removed to isolated reservations like their Indian kin in the United States. It is not surprising, then, that the new border between Mexico and the United States was drawn in such a way as to take as much land and as few Mexicans as possible.[26]

While the War with Mexico resulted in the confluence of the South with the Mexican borderlands, Mexicans began to bridge the cultural divide in the years between that conflict and the Civil War, accentuating some interesting differences between the two regions in the construction of whiteness. In 1848 Santiago Tafolla ran away from home in Santa Fe, New Mexico, and hitched a ride on the Santa Fe Trail to St. Louis. On the journey to St. Louis, Tafolla met Robert Matthews, a plantation owner in Georgia who offered to help him improve his English and find him work as an overseer on a plantation in Charleston, South Carolina. Until Tafolla arrived in South Carolina he had no experience of slave society or African Americans in general. But he remembered hearing his first lesson in southern race relations from a Mexican woman in St. Louis who warned him that once in the deep South he must never associate with Negroes. Later Robert Matthews's brother hired Tafolla as the superintendent of his plantation near Talbaton, Georgia, where an "old negro" supervised the day-to-day work of the slaves while Tafolla's duty was to maintain order among them. "It was necessary to have a white person stay on the place," Tafolla later wrote in his autobiography, "so that he could know everything that happened."[27] In Santa Fe Tafolla was perhaps Hispano or Spanish American, as distinct from *indio* or Indian, but in the plantation South, as he learned in St. Louis, one was either Negro or white. Southern necessity required that Tafolla become a white person.

On a visit to Robert Matthews's plantation in Talbaton, Georgia, some of the townsfolk came out to see the "Mexican boy." Some, according to Tafolla, "expressed surprise and would say, 'He is nearly white,' while others would say, 'He is as white as anybody.'" Tafolla recalled how Mrs. Matthews's daughter asked her: "Mama, is Mexican Jim sure enough white?" The young girl most likely had never seen a Mexican before. Her mother replied: "Daughter, James' [Santiago's] blood is as free from negro blood as yours or mine." Mrs. Matthews's response that Tafolla was a white man must have come as a relief to Tafolla, for in Santa Fe the occupation army of the United States in 1848 did not regard the newly conquered Hispanos as white, and in Texas, where Tafolla eventually settled, Anglos were more likely to call Tafolla a "greaser" than a white man. Nevertheless, it must have been plain to the planter's daughter that although Tafolla was not an African American, neither did he look quite like other white people in Georgia. Mrs. Matthews's daughter no doubt was used to seeing mulattos, which is perhaps why she did not ask whether Tafolla was "sure enough black." In the South, at least, the absence of "negro blood" conferred whiteness on Mexican Jim, perhaps history's only Mexican overseer on a slave plantation in the antebellum South.

Tafolla's whiteness proved ephemeral the moment he left the deep South, illustrating the ever-problematical process of identity formation for those, mainly Mexicans, whose ethnoracial identities were shaped as much by region as by class, skin color, language, religion, and culture. In Baltimore, Maryland, where he joined the U.S. army in 1855, he lost his status as a white man. There his commanding officer required him to perform menial tasks because of his "Mexican extraction." Dissatisfied with northern whites' unwillingness to recognize him as a white person, he left the army after five years and returned to the Southwest, where he married a tejana and settled in San Antonio. In 1862 he joined the Confederate army, but he deserted two years later because his Texas superiors refused to recognize and treat him as a white person and, more urgently, because his fellow white companions in the army had planned to lynch him.[28]

With few exceptions Anglo-Texan constructions of whiteness rarely included people of Mexican descent, and then only when they occupied important social and economic positions. When Anglo Texans married Mexicans, they often juggled the nomenclature to whiten their spouses by calling them Spanish Americans or simply Spanish. Mexican men, however, were only rarely accorded status as white persons, such as when they were owners of large ranches with marriageable daughters. Once back in Texas, "Mexican Jim" thus reverted to being the Mexican Santiago Tafolla, for in Texas, unlike antebellum Georgia, Mexicans were still "Mexicans."

On the eve of the Civil War, white Texans had grown increasingly suspicious of Mexicans, who were frequently accused of complicity with the slaves in insurrectionary plots and of aiding fugitive slaves to escape to freedom in Mexico. White Texans had long resented the Mexican government's refusal to return fugitive slaves after the Texas revolt in 1836, a fact which contributed to the general suspicion of Mexicans in what was once Mexican territory. Mexicans, according to one newspaper account, instilled in the slaves "false notions of freedom" and made them "discontented and insubordinate."[29] In 1856 the *Galveston News* published a letter describing the complicity of Mexicans in a purported slave uprising in Colorado County in which all white males were to be murdered and the "young ladies . . . made the brides of the diabolical murderers of their parents and friends." A committee was formed to investigate the rumors of insurrection. Shortly afterward, 200 slaves were found to have violated the law against possessing weapons. The evidence consisted of having found in the slaves' possession some bowie knives and a number of pistols. Every Mexican without exception was implicated in the plot, arrested, and ordered to leave the county within five days under penalty of death, and a resolution was passed "forever forbidding any Mexican from coming within the limits of the county."[30] One of the prime movers of the plot was identified as a Mexican named Frank, though he was not one of the ringleaders who were hanged. Many whites hoped that he might be arrested and "have meted out to him such reward as his black deed demands."[31] Frederick Law Olmsted, a critic of the Old South "slavocracy," observed that to "the vulgar mind of the South," Mexicans were "considered to be heathen; not acknowledged as 'white folks.' "[32]

White Texans also objected to the tendency of Mexicans to intermarry with slaves because Mexican and black men and women often ran away together. Mexicans "hate the ascendant race," observed Olmsted, and "involuntarily associate and sympathize with the negroes."[33] In Matagorda County, west of Galveston along the Gulf Coast, all Mexicans were ordered to leave the county because they "hang around the plantations," take the "likeliest negro girls for wives," and "run them to Mexico."[34] As a result, planters in some east Texas counties banished whole populations of Mexicans from their homes and forbade them on pain of death to return to the plantations. Wherever Mexicans came into contact with slaves in antebellum Texas, wrote Olmsted in 1857, "it has been found necessary to treat them as outlaws."[35] For many east Texas cotton farmers, Mexicans were thus not "white folks" because they performed "black deeds": They crossed the color line as well as the border in aiding slaves to freedom in Mexico.[36]

After emancipation, Mexicans no longer represented a threat to former slaveholders. In one of the ironies of Texas history, Mexicans had been driven out of east and central Texas counties before the Civil War only to be vigorously recruited to return in the decades afterward, especially to the newer cotton region of central Texas, to help family farmers chop (weed) and pick their cotton. Some Anglos began to experiment with Mexican labor as an alternative or supplement to freedmen labor, which they worried had become too unreliable. Judge Cowan of Caldwell County, near Austin, observed in 1867 that planters were generally dissatisfied with the experience of freedmen's labor and were determined to attract Anglo immigrants, mostly from other southern states, to settle in the county. Some had already begun to use Mexican labor on central Texas farms. In 1867 a Freedmen Bureau officer in Bastrop County, near Austin, reported that a planter had shot a freedman and his Mexican friend for leaving the plantation to seek higher wages and better working conditions on a nearby plantation. Another central Texas planter who had experimented with Mexican labor in 1874 found Mexicans to be more reliable workers than "Fifteenth Amendments," the metonymic equivalences for former slaves.[37]

To attract white settlers to central Texas, ranch owners in the 1880s offered to sell tracts of land for almost nothing, because few roads extended into the region and railroads had still not penetrated beyond the more populous counties of east Texas.[38] The prospect of obtaining large tracts of cheap land attracted land-hungry settlers from other states and from Europe and made Texas second only to California in the average size of its farms. Even farmers with little or no land were able to claim range rights to pasture large herds of cattle on the public domain.[39] Central Texas was particularly suited for cattle raising because of its climate and rich grasslands, as well as the state's liberal land policies.

Early settlers in central Texas raised more cattle and corn than cotton. During the 1870s and 1880s cattle drives from south Texas to railway links in the North reinforced the image of Texas as western even though east Texas remained culturally and economically southern. Trail drives were at first small-scale operations owing to the expense of the drive, the difficulties of overland herding, and the distance to markets. Most cattle were left to roam the vast, open spaces of south and central Texas, where they continued to multiply. In 1870 more than 5 million longhorns roamed the Texas prairies, most of them mavericks that could be claimed by anyone who cared to affix a brand. Good steers, which could be purchased in Texas for $4.00 a head, could be sold in the North for up to $40.00 a head. A few astute Texans realized huge profits from driving large herds to railroad connections in Missouri and, later, Kansas. The era of the Long Drive, with its powerful images of cowboys and roundups, was to endure for two decades following the Civil War. But during that twenty-year span the population of Texas was increasing rapidly, and new settlements pushed the cattle industry steadily westward beyond the central prairies and onto the rolling plains of west Texas. The days of the Long Drive were also numbered by the introduction of barbed wire and the enactment of quarantine legislation during the 1880s in Kansas, Colorado, Nebraska, and the territories of New Mexico and Wyoming. The quarantine constituted an absolute embargo against the transportation of Texas cattle into or across those states in order to prevent the spread of Texas cattle fever to cattle in other areas.[40]

As a western adaptation, barbed wire played a decisive role in transforming central Texas from cattle to cotton. The introduction of barbed wire in the 1870s sealed the fate of "free-grass" stockmen in central Texas who grazed their herds on the public domain and accelerated the pace of fencing in the range. Many cattle ranchers and some farmers began to see the advantages of barbed-wire fences. Once cattle outfits obtained title to lands or permanent claims to a portion of the range, they sought to fence in their land and their herds to protect against poachers and against overstocking the pasture with strays. But fences forced free-grass trail drovers either to cut fences and risk sometimes violent retaliation or to establish new trails around fenced property. Free-grass stockmen joined with some small farmers to oppose the fencing in of large tracts of public land, not only because it blocked access to trails and water holes but also because entire farming communities were sometimes fenced in. The result was an uneasy compromise: Laws were passed to make fence cutting a felony, but stockmen were required to place a gate in every three miles of fence and to refrain from fencing the public domain. One captain of a Texas cattle trail complained in 1884: "These fellows from Ohio, Indiana, and . . . other States—the 'bone and sinew of the country,' as politicians call them—have made farms, enclosed pastures, and fenced in water-holes until you can't rest; and I say, Damn such bone and sinew. . . . Fences, sir, are the curse of the country."[41] Barbed wire thus prepared the way for the development of large-scale ranching, land speculation, and absentee ownership of farmland.

The arrival of railroads onto the Great Plains widened the market for cattle considerably, but it also forced the cattle industry to seek less productive cropland farther west as growing numbers of settlers followed the railroads into the interior of Texas. Before the turn of the century the Panhandle came to typify the Texas cattle industry with its sprawling ranches and enormous herds. In 1877 Colonel Charles Goodnight established the first ranch in the Panhandle, called Palo Duro, which ultimately spread out over seven counties and contained a herd numbering 70,000, including 9,000 high-grade Herefords. As the population moved west, the trails also shifted west, so that by 1890 the prairies of central Texas had only 38.5 percent of the state's cattle in contrast with 47 percent in 1880 and nearly 70 percent in 1860. By 1880 the cattle drives had shifted farther to the west and vanished entirely with the construction of railroads throughout most of Texas in the 1880s. By then railroads had clearly demonstrated the economic advantages of moving range cattle to market by rail rather than by hoof.[42]

Railroads also provided the much-needed transportation to markets that made the production of cotton the most profitable enterprise in central Texas. Prior to the Civil War central Texas lay beyond the network of roads and rail lines that formed the all-important connection to commercial centers in the East. The rivers of central Texas were barely navigable, there were few bridges or ferries, and the roads were little more than paths for ox carts. Farmers had to pay high "wagoning" costs to have their products hauled hundreds of miles to market—usually to Galveston—a journey that required two or three months. Manufactured merchandise was also difficult to obtain and too expensive for most settlers. In 1875 Texas had only 1,650 miles of railroad track, virtually all of which was located east of Dallas and Austin and north of Corpus Christi. At the same time buffalo hunters successfully completed their bloody business on the Texas High Plains, making way for the expansion of livestock and rail lines west, while Comanches and Lipan-Apaches escaped farther west to avoid the fate of the buffalo. To encourage railroad construction, the state of Texas granted millions of acres from its public domain as railroad bonuses and made provisions for railroads to obtain land grants from the state. Between 1876 and 1882 Texas railroads received more than 32 million acres of land in return for 2,928 miles of track. By 1877 Texas led all states in railroad construction, and by 1904 it ranked first in railroad mileage.[43]

The ensuing transformations were rapid. A special report of the U.S. census on Texas in 1884 noted that the "building of new lines of railroad westward will probably be instrumental in extending the region of cotton production to the Llano Estacado [Panhandle] long before the census year of 1890."[44] Cotton production also spread to the Coastal Plains region around Corpus Christi, and elsewhere in the West railroads opened new regions to crop production and reconfigured others.[45] By 1890 Texas produced 20 percent of the nation's cotton and had become the nation's leading cotton-producing state, while the cattle kingdom continued to retreat into the Panhandle and south Texas (see Table 1). In 1908 a contemporary chronicler described the transformation of the region as a "contest for existence," in which stockmen and sheepmen gradually but inexorably lost ground to "the man with the hoe and the cotton planter."[46] The production of cotton was the engine not only of the Texas economy but of the entire South, whose cotton exports were increasing dramatically at a time when the nation was being integrated into the world economy at an unprecedented rate.

Throughout the last half of the nineteenth century, black/white east Texas and Mexican south Texas were converging on each other, as Mexicans gradually moved north and southern whites and blacks pushed

Table 1 *Cotton Production in Texas, 1860–1940*

	Number of Bales	Percentage Increase over the Preceding Decade	Percentage of U.S. Total
1860	431,463	—	8.0
1870	350,628	−23.0	11.6
1880	805,284	130.0	14.0
1890	1,471,242	83.0	19.7
1900	2,584,810	76.0	27.1
1910	2,455,174	−2.0	23.1
1920	2,971,757	21.0	26.1
1930	3,793,392	38.0	26.0
1940	2,724,442	−28.0	23.7

SOURCES: U.S. Bureau of the Census, *Eighth Census of the United States, 1860: Agriculture* (Washington, D.C.: Government Printing Office, 1864), 140–49; idem, *Ninth Census of the United States, 1870: Agriculture* (Washington, D.C.: Government Printing Office, 1872), 3: 250–60; idem, *Tenth Census of the United States, 1880: Agriculture* (Washington, D.C.: Government Printing Office, 1883), 3: 242–44; idem, *Eleventh Census of the United States, 1890: Agriculture* (Washington, D.C.: Government Printing Office, 1895), 5: 396–97; idem, *Twelfth Census of the United States, 1900: Agriculture*, part 1 (Washington, D.C.: Government Printing Office, 1902), 5: 434–35; idem, *Twelfth Census of the United States, 1900: Agriculture*, part 2 (Washington, D.C.: Government Printing Office, 1902), 6: 405; idem, *Fourteenth Census of the United States, 1920: Agriculture*, part 2 (Washington, D.C.: Government Printing Office, 1922), 6: 717–37; and idem, *Sixteenth Census of the United States, 1940: Agriculture* (Washington, D.C.: Government Printing Office, 1942), 3: 784–85 and 1: 477–95.

west onto the rich prairies of central Texas. The economic inducements drawing these two frontiers toward each other in central Texas were cattle and cotton. On the grassy prairie lands of central Texas the cattle and cowboys of Western culture—itself an amalgam of Mexican and Anglo ranching culture—were pushed farther west by the advancing frontier of southern cotton culture. The convergence of these cultures is best described by geographer Donald Meinig:

Cattle and cotton were the mainstays of much of Central Texas, but it was only here that the plantation and the hacienda, the two great patriarchal landed institutions richly idealized by the contending cultures, really met. But it was an unbalanced encounter of forces, and the military triumph of the one drove out the leadership of the other, so that both institutions were now ruled by the Anglo, the one worked by the Negro slave, the other still worked by the Mestizo vaquero.[47]

After the Civil War former slaves and vaqueros increasingly worked together on plantations and cotton ranches in central and south-central

Texas, while rapid immigration of southern whites into central Texas made it the "white belt" as well as the leading cotton belt of the state.[48]

After 1880, the Blackland Prairie was the most densely populated region of Texas until well into the twentieth century. This narrow region of approximately 24 counties contained, by 1900, almost 30 percent of the population in a state with more than 240 counties. Whites constituted an overwhelming majority of the population of central Texas; and African Americans continued to be concentrated in the older plantation counties of east Texas. Although the number of blacks in central Texas continued to increase between 1870 and 1900, their percentage of the total population declined from 23 percent in 1870 to 16 percent in 1900, as a result of the flood of Anglo immigrants into the region.[49] What came to distinguish central Texas from the rest of the cotton-growing South was its high percentage of white tenant farmers (see Table 2).

The Mexican-born population of the Blackland Prairie resided almost exclusively in San Antonio. At the southern tip of the prairie, San Antonio historically has been home to a large population of Mexicans. In 1870, for instance, 82 percent of the Mexican-born population in twenty-two Blackland Prairie counties resided in Bexar County (San Antonio). Only two other Blackland Prairie counties, Travis (Austin) and Hays (just northeast of Bexar), contained significant numbers of Mexicans in 1870.[50] Mexicans from San Antonio had traveled north to pick cotton in Blackland Prairie counties since the 1880s. The *San Antonio Express* reported in 1892 that Mexican cotton pickers from the south Texas county of Duval were traveling to Wharton County in the river-bottom plantation area of central Texas to pick cotton.[51] And according to one south Texas resident, Mexicans from both sides of the border in the lower Rio Grande Valley migrated in the 1890s into east Texas, following the cotton crop as far as the Sabine River (the border between Texas and Louisiana), where some crossed into Louisiana to work in the sugarcane fields.[52] In 1894 the *Beeville Bee* (Bee County, southeast of San Antonio) reported that approximately 5,000 Mexicans had passed through town on their way to the cotton fields to the north and that "For some months past there have been murmurs of discontent in certain quarters over the gradual but sure Latinizing of the laboring element of this county."[53] Droves of rural laborers from Mexico abandoned the fields and their debts on haciendas and migrated to Texas. After 1900, Mexicans settled north of San Antonio as sharecroppers, tenant farmers, or, in a few cases, farm owners.[54]

Table 2 *Whites and Blacks in the Blackland Prairie of Texas, 1860–1940**

	Whites	Percentage Increase over the Preceding Decade	Percentage of Total Population
1860	107,714	—	77
1870	172,661	60	78
1880	377,687	119	83
1890	570,903	51	83
1900	804,939	41	86
1910	914,695	14	82
1920	1,100,160	20	84
1930	1,309,930	19	84
1940	1,414,317	8	85
	Blacks		
1860	32,125	—	23
1870	49,848	55	23
1880	77,650	56	17
1890	116,766	50	17
1900	158,573	36	16
1910	196,525	24	18
1920	210,459	7	16
1930	241,218	15	16
1940	250,251	4	15

SOURCES: U.S. Bureau of the Census, *Eighth Census of the United States, 1860: Population* (Washington, D.C.: Government Printing Office, 1864), 472–91; idem, *A Compendium of the Ninth Census, 1870* (Washington, D.C.: Government Printing Office, 1872), 92–96; idem, *Twelfth Census of the United States, 1900: Population*, part 1 (Washington, D.C.: Government Printing Office, 1901), 557–60; idem, *Fifteenth Census of the United States, 1930*; Population Bulletin, First Series, *Texas* (Washington, D.C.: Government Printing Office, 1931), 1058–62; idem, *Sixteenth Census of the United States, 1940: Population* (Washington, D.C.: Government Printing Office, 1942), 1: 1041–44; and Mattie Bell, "The Growth and Distribution of the Texas Population" (Ph.D. diss., Baylor University, 1935), 64–71, 126–33, 166–73.

* "White" includes persons of Mexican descent. U.S.-born persons of Mexican descent were counted as white until the 1930 census established a separate category, in which "all persons born in Mexico, or having parents born in Mexico, who are not definitely white, negro, Indian, Chinese, or Japanese, should be returned as Mexican." The 1940 and subsequent censuses abandoned the category because of the confusion surrounding the distinction between white and nonwhite Mexicans. The Blackland Prairie counties are: Bell, Bexar, Caldwell, Collin, Comal, Dallas, Delta, Ellis, Falls, Fannin, Freestone, Grayson, Hays, Hill, Hunt, Kaufman, Lamar, Limestone, McLennan, Milam, Navarro, Rockwall, Travis, and Williamson.

Anglo cotton farmers also relied on Mexicans and African Americans to pick cotton during the harvest, sometimes using vagrancy laws to compel their labor. After the turn of the century many blacks in east Texas began to leave the countryside and take up residence in the towns and cities, where they hoped to find jobs in the growing industries.[55] At the northern end of the Blackland Prairie white farmers recruited black cotton pickers and sharecroppers from the Dallas area; at the southern end they recruited Mexicans from San Antonio. Mexicans had traveled up and down this San Antonio–Dallas corridor since the 1880s as migrants, but gradually they began to take up residence alongside Anglos and African Americans in this triracial regional community of Mexican, black, and white tenant farmers and farm workers.[56] Almost from its beginning the cotton economy of central Texas emerged as a hybrid culture situated between the South and the West and Mexico. At the center of these rapid cultural and demographic changes was the dramatic increase in the production of cotton in the Blackland Prairie (see Table 3).

On the Blackland Prairie a farmer could grow cotton year after year and never have to fertilize the soil. The folklorist William Owens recalled his mother's words when she moved to a farm on the Blackland Prairie: "You can make a better living by accident on the blackland than you can by trying on sandy land."[57] His mother knew what every other farmer of the blackland had learned since settling the region: The rich, thick, black soil made it ideal for the growth of cotton. The annual precipitation for the region of between thirty and forty inches was considered adequate for the cultivation of most crops, especially cotton. By 1900 the Blackland Prairie produced 43.5 percent of the cotton in Texas, and the state produced 27 percent of the nation's cotton, up from 8 percent in 1860. Between 1860 and 1900 the number of improved acres in Blackland Prairie farms increased an astonishing 963 percent.[58] By 1910 homeseekers were passing over the more populous sections of east Texas to locate in central Texas, where, according to a popular-magazine account, they succeeded in "making the transition at a single bound from range-farming to intensive small farming."[59] Just west of the Blackland Prairie the precipitation level dropped to below thirty inches, which effectively checked the westward expansion of cotton until methods of dry farming and irrigation were introduced during the 1920s. King Cotton had arrived in the West, and by 1923 more cotton was produced west of the Mississippi River than east of it.[60]

Whither went King Cotton there also went his retainers, which included a vast army of sharecroppers and tenant farmers, credit mer-

Table 3 *Cotton Production in the Blackland Prairie of Texas, 1860–1940**

	Number of Bales	Percentage Increase over the Preceding Decade	Percentage of State Total
1860	33,334	—	7.7
1870	103,276	210.0	29.5
1880	269,821	161.0	33.5
1890	574,544	115.0	39.4
1900	1,124,417	94.0	43.5
1910	1,047,537	−6.8	42.7
1920	988,248	−5.7	33.3
1930	1,129,505	14.3	29.8
1940	741,749	−34.3	27.2

SOURCES: U.S. Bureau of the Census, *Eighth Census of the United States, 1860: Agriculture* (Washington, D.C.: Government Printing Office, 1864), 140–49; idem, *Ninth Census of the United States, 1870: Agriculture* (Washington, D.C.: Government Printing Office, 1872), 3: 250–60; idem, *Tenth Census of the United States, 1880: Agriculture* (Washington, D.C.: Government Printing Office, 1883), 3: 242–44; idem, *Eleventh Census of the United States, 1890: Agriculture* (Washington, D.C.: Government Printing Office, 1895), 5: 396–97; idem, *Twelfth Census of the United States, 1900: Agriculture*, part 1, *Farm Live Stock, and Animal Products* (Washington, D.C.: Government Printing Office, 1902), 5: 434–35; idem, *Twelfth Census of the United States, 1900: Agriculture*, part 2, *Crops and Irrigation* (Washington, D.C.: Government Printing Office, 1902), 6: 405; idem, *Fourteenth Census of the United States, 1920: Agriculture*, part 2 (Washington, D.C.: Government Printing Office, 1922), 6: 717–37; and idem, *Sixteenth Census of the United States, 1940: Agriculture* (Washington, D.C.: Government Printing Office, 1942), 3: 784–85 and 1: 477–95.

* The Blackland Prairie counties are: Bell, Bexar, Caldwell, Collin, Comal, Dallas, Delta, Ellis, Falls, Fannin, Freestone, Grayson, Hays, Hill, Hunt, Kaufman, Lamar, Limestone, McLennan, Milam, Navarro, Rockwall, Travis, and Williamson.

chants, ginners, and cotton pickers. The transformation of a nearly all-white landowning class to a predominantly white tenant class took place gradually during the fifty years between 1880 and 1930. A writer for *Scribner's Magazine* reported in 1874 that "the farmers of the northern tier of Texas counties were independent, self-reliant, prosperous men, who took pride in their occupation and had no desire to live in town. Even then tenant farming had developed in Texas from the half-and-half to a third-and-fourth; though tenants were exceedingly scarce."[61] By 1900, however, the proportion of tenant-operated farms had climbed to 49.7 percent of all farms, and in the Blackland Prairie the percentage had risen to 60.3 percent (see Table 4).

After 1900, moreover, share tenants on "thirds and fourths" were gradually being reduced to "half tenants" (who paid half instead of one-fourth of the cotton as rent) and sharecroppers. Rising land values, the high cost of credit, and the low price of cotton all contributed to the

Table 4 *Tenant-Operated Farms in the Blackland Prairie and in the State of Texas, 1880–1940**

	Blackland Prairie		
Year	Total Number of Farms	Number of Tenant Farms	Percentage of Farms Operated by Tenants
1880	51,836	21,507	41.5
1890	68,406	34,991	51.2
1900	103,682	62,539	60.3
1910	106,488	66,042	62.0
1920	109,943	69,249	64.8
1930	111,119	79,169	72.2
1940	80,067	46,051	57.5

	Texas		
Year	Total Number of Farms	Number of Tenant Farms	Percentage of Farms Operated by Tenants
1880	174,184	65,468	37.6
1890	228,126	95,510	41.9
1900	352,190	174,991	49.7
1910	417,770	219,575	52.6
1920	436,033	232,309	53.3
1930	495,489	301,660	60.9
1940	418,002	204,462	48.9

SOURCES: Calculated from U.S. Bureau of the Census, *Report on the Productions of Agriculture as Returned at the Tenth Census, 1880* (Washington, D.C.: Government Printing Office, 1883), 89–93; idem, *Report on the Statistics of Agriculture in the United States at the Eleventh Census, 1890* (Washington, D.C.: Government Printing Office, 1895), 182–89; idem, *Twelfth Census of the United States, 1900: Agriculture*, part 1, *Farm Live Stock, and Animal Products* (Washington, D.C.: Government Printing Office, 1902), 5: 124–31; idem, *Thirteenth Census of the United States, 1910: Agriculture* (Washington, D.C.: Government Printing Office, 1913), 7: 632–77; idem, *Fourteenth Census of the United States, 1920, Agriculture*, part 2 (Washington, D.C.: Government Printing Office, 1922), 6: 12–34; and idem, *Fifteenth Census of the United States, 1930: Agriculture*, part 2 (Washington, D.C.: Government Printing Office, 1932), 2: 1360–1401.

* The Blackland Prairie counties are: Bell, Bexar, Caldwell, Collin, Comal, Dallas, Delta, Ellis, Falls, Fannin, Freestone, Grayson, Hays, Hill, Hunt, Kaufman, Lamar, Limestone, McLennan, Milam, Navarro, Rockwall, Travis, and Williamson.

growth of tenancy in Texas. Although blacks outnumbered Anglos in some river-bottom counties near the coast and in some east Texas counties, in central Texas they constituted less than 16 percent of the population by 1900. According to a 1916 report on the "Land Question in the Southwest," tenancy was—in central Texas, at least—primarily a "white man's problem."[62]

Agricultural analysts at first regarded the tenancy problem in central Texas as a white man's problem because the vast majority of the tenants were whites, not blacks or Mexicans. However, over time some whites began to view white tenants, rather than the system of tenancy itself, as the problem. Poor whites who competed with blacks and Mexicans as sharecroppers came to be racially marked as inferior whites whose reproductive fecundity threatened the vigor of Nordic whiteness. The persistence of sharecropping among black farmers, on the other hand, was not regarded as a problem because most whites held the belief that African Americans were racially inferior to begin with and that sharecropping was their natural economic condition. Whites frequently alluded to the inability of African Americans to escape sharecropping as evidence of their inferiority rather than as representative of more pervasive systemic problems in land tenure and the proper functioning of the so-called agricultural ladder. Similarly, whites believed that because Mexicans were docile and nomadic by nature, they made ideal seasonal laborers to harvest the cotton during peak season and then, like "birds of passage," return to their enclaves in south Texas and Mexico. Whites who had slipped into sharecropping blamed their economic undoing on the growing number of Mexican sharecroppers to whom, they argued, landowners could charge higher rents and credit arrangements.[63]

Most Mexicans who worked on central Texas farms were generally hired as temporary laborers rather than as sharecroppers, but various studies in the first decades of the twentieth century noted the increasing numbers of farmers of Mexican descent, mostly sharecroppers, who had established themselves in central Texas.[64] Between 1910 and 1930 numerous farm owners in central Texas between San Antonio and Waco began to rent to Mexicans where they often replaced Anglo and African American sharecroppers and share tenants. Narciso Alderete, for example, left Mexico when he was fourteen and became a *mediero* (sharecropper) on the 500-acre Fall Family farm in McGregor, McLennan County, in the 1920s. His nephew, Andrés Acosta, left Uvalde County in south Texas with his family and settled in McGregor in 1933, where he too worked on the Fall Ranch before becoming a sharecropper on another Anglo owner's farm. Mr. Acosta and his wife, Sabina Palomo Acosta, who still live in McGregor, recalled how one Mexican family, the de Leóns, were able to purchase their own 150-acre farm in McGregor in 1943, after farming for more than ten years as a sharecropper and share tenant. Sabina Palomo Acosta and her family had picked cotton on the Taft Ranch for two years before settling near Waco in 1932.[65]

The presence of Mexicans and blacks in their midst as sharecroppers and day laborers became a visible reminder to white tenants that they were but one rung removed from the social, economic, and racial stigma of sharecropping. However, the changing rural economy was imposing hardships on all tenants. Rising land values and increased rents not only blocked Anglo renters from becoming owners but also effectively prevented blacks and Mexicans in central Texas from moving out of sharecropping arrangements to tenant farming on thirds and fourths. As sharecroppers, for example, Mexicans were subjected to the same hardships of high credit, chattel mortgage, bad crop years, and close supervision and control by landlords as were Anglo and black sharecroppers; indeed, Mexican immigrants were often more thoroughly exploited than were either Anglos or blacks. As Mexicans, however, they were blamed for the deteriorating economic conditions of rural life in central Texas.

As the cotton frontier moved west into the Blackland Prairie, the prospect of supplementing the resident labor force with Mexicans from the border counties and from Mexico itself became feasible and, for many farmers, desirable because, as many believed, the Mexican was "specially fitted for the burdensome task of bending his back to picking the cotton and the burdensome task of grubbing the fields."[66] E. E. Davis, a Texas specialist of rural research, characterized the "gradual but sure Latinizing" of central Texas as a silent invasion of voracious insects: "The Mexicans did not hit the interior cotton lands with the impact of a hurricane, but seeped in silently and undermined the rural social structures like termites eating out the sills of a wooden house."[67] But Davis was only partially correct: The wooden house had already been abandoned, its Anglo occupants evicted by owners who, like slum landlords, were seeking higher rents from a lower class of occupants.

Owners and absentee landlords also believed Mexicans were more tractable than Anglo or black renters. One owner in Nueces County said that he preferred Mexican sharecroppers to whites because the white, "being of the same race and breed," would feel that he has an "equal right with you, but the Mexican understands that he is to do what you tell him." A white sharecropper, he complained, "will say it's too wet or give some other excuse for not doing what you tell him." In addition to the perception that Mexicans were more "easily domineered" than whites, Anglo owners provided Mexicans with only the bare essentials in house furnishings: "The whites want screened houses, toilets, bed springs, a table and a stove. The Mexican asks only [for] wood and water." Mexicans made fewer demands that the roof be repaired and accepted inferior housing that the "proud white tenant would refuse to occupy." As for holding Mexicans "in subjection like the Negro," one owner boasted, "It is what we in the South thought and still think."[68]

Some owners preferred Mexican sharecroppers because immigrant Mexicans were more politically vulnerable than were other groups. Many of them had fled political and economic turmoil in Mexico and feared being deported or arrested under the provisions of Texas's vagrancy laws. Many also faced hostility from Anglo and black sharecroppers and cotton pickers who believed, not without reason, that Mexicans were taking jobs away from them and that Mexicans, who worked for lower wages, tended to lower the standard of living in their communities. As early as 1894, for example, a riot broke out between Mexicans and blacks in Beeville in Bee County, just north of Corpus Christi. Mexicans had been migrating to the county and competing for jobs held by predominantly unskilled black laborers. Anglo employers hired Mexicans at wages below those paid to blacks, thereby effectively displacing blacks with "cheap Mexican" labor. The friction culminated in a raid on the Mexican quarter by blacks and some "wild white boys" who "Ku-Kluxed" the Mexicans.[69] In the late 1890s the White Caps, a group of Anglo vigilantes, rose up in Hays County, south of Austin, to warn planters not to rent to Mexicans and blacks (and to rent to Anglos "at one-third and one-fourth only"). In three neighboring counties (Wilson, Gonzales, and DeWitt) white tenant farmers threatened violence against landowners who rented to Mexicans or hired them as laborers.[70] Rather than viewing all laborers and tenants as sharing a common identity, the majority of white tenants, according to the historian James R. Green, "pitted themselves against landlords and businessmen on the one hand, and against black sharecroppers and brown migrants on the other." They viewed their exploiters and their competitors as having formed "an unholy alliance dedicated to pushing poor whites off the land."[71]

The gradual displacement of white and black tenants by Mexicans was also symptomatic of the transformation that was taking place in Texas agriculture: Many small, family-sized farms were being consolidated into larger, plantation-style farms run by managers who exercised close supervision over tenants and sharecroppers. The economic and social position of tenants and some sharecroppers thus gradually changed from one in which they still made basic decisions about the crop to one in which they came more and more under the control and direction of the owner. Anglo and African American tenant farmers would be less likely to accept such a change in their status because they had become accustomed to a certain limited independence; Mexicans, on the other hand, may have viewed sharecropping and tenant farming as desirable alternatives to migrant labor or to unemployment in Mexico.

Faced with angry white tenants clamoring for lower rent, less supervision, and better living conditions, many landowners began to justify their preference for Mexican labor by ascribing to white tenants the indolence and improvidence they had previously associated with African Americans and Mexicans. Landowner disillusionment with post–Civil War black labor in the South is a thrice-told tale that does not bear repetition here, but one example from central Texas will illustrate how the racist assumptions of the farm-labor problem changed around the turn of the century.

In 1893 a congressional committee solicited letters from prominent cotton growers throughout the South to address a set of questions concerning the problems they faced in the production of cotton. I. A. Wimbish, of DeWitt County in south-central Texas, wrote that the new generation of former slaves had become "more lazy, thriftless, and unreliable" and would not work more than four hours a day or more than three days a week. His own, admittedly impractical solution was to have the government ship all freedmen to Liberia or the Sandwich Islands, so that in their place "active, energetic, honest, and industrious white men from the Middle, Northern, and Western States" could replace them on the farms. Scarcely twenty years later, owners in central Texas had changed their tune about "industrious white men" and "lazy, thriftless" Black Americans. Owners had discovered Mexican sharecroppers and preferred them to whites, who frequently complained of poor living conditions and who liked to think of themselves as partners in the operation of the owner's farm. A planter from the Brazos bottoms complained that "white tenants are the least desirable, they are ignorant and lazy and seem to try to do as little work as possible to get along." Another central Texas planter angrily denounced white tenants as a "worthless, lazy, lying, anarchist lot" and replaced all but one with black day laborers.[72] By 1915 landowners throughout central Texas complained about a new generation of thriftless and unreliable *white* tenants and sought to replace them with "active, energetic, honest, and industrious" Mexicans and African Americans. Whiteness thus fractured along racial as well as class lines as distinctions came to be drawn between white owners and landless poor whites, whom many owners believed were foreordained to remain tenants.

Mexicans had suddenly become, in the eyes of white landowners, the solution to the growing demand for a cheap and tractable labor force in the nation's leading cotton-producing state. A study of Ellis County near Dallas in 1915 revealed that "the negro, and the recent, but permanent, appearance of the Mexican is the cause of no small amount of resentment on the part of the tenant farmer." An unpublished report on the land question in Texas and Oklahoma in 1915 warned that "intra-class dislike has been heightened by the tendency of landlords to substitute Mexicans for negro and white tenants, and negroes for white tenants where the shares system is followed . . . [because] negroes are considered more amenable to supervision than whites, and Mexicans are more tractable than either negroes or whites."[73] As whites slipped from share tenants to the racially marked status of sharecroppers, they came perilously close to becoming racially marked themselves.

Whites worried that their race had become vulnerable to "pollution" by the growing population of poor whites on cotton farms and not-so-white Mexicans who had chopped and picked the cotton for decades. After the outbreak of the Mexican Revolution in 1910, thousands of Mexicans fled the tumult of civil war to take up residence across the border in Texas, creating in the minds of many whites a "second color menace." Poorer Mexicans were racially marked as alien others, unfit for citizenship and ineligible for whiteness. Their presence, however, transformed the racial geography of cotton culture in central Texas and restructured its class hierarchies.

CHAPTER 2

"The Little Brown Man in Gringo Land"

The "Second Color Menace" in the Western South

In 1908 Victor Clark, a federal investigator for the Bureau of Labor, wrote that Mexican farm laborers in the United States "do not occupy a position analogous to that of the Negro in the South. They are not permanent, do not acquire land or establish themselves in little cabin homesteads, but remain nomadic and outside of American civilization."[1] Mexicans remained "outside of American civilization" not simply because of their mobility, as Clark suggested—although mobility played an important role in distinguishing Mexicans from other classes and races of workers—but also because of their racial status as nonwhites, which Clark took for granted. When Mexican sharecroppers settled in central Texas farm communities, they were subject to segregation in schools, neighborhoods, churches, and public facilities, as were more permanently settled African Americans in the Jim Crow South, including Texas. "American civilization" for Clark, as for his contemporaries, meant white civilization, and being American was synonymous with being white.

The immigration of Mexicans into Texas after 1910, and especially during the 1920s, raised fears among Texas whites that Mexicans would destroy white civilization, while other whites who employed Mexicans on the farms and in industry argued that Mexicans were simply too inferior to represent a threat to white America. Poor whites and not-so-poor whites expressed the nativist conviction that Mexicans constituted an inferior race of "mixed breeds." "The question . . . now is not whether a few special interests, cotton, sugar beet, railways, etc., should be granted . . . free and unrestricted immigration from Mexico," wrote one Texas nativist opposed to Mexican immigration, "but whether or not White Civilization shall be preserved in the Southwest."[2] White tenant farmers directed their attention to Mexican immigration as a source of their economic distress and helped give the issue of race added importance in the ongoing debate on immigration restriction during the 1920s.[3] Regardless of whether one was for or against Mexican immigration, most Texas whites viewed practically all Mexicans as unambiguously nonwhite.

Mexican immigration to central Texas breached the centuries-old southern racial binary of white and black and represented a "second color menace" to many Texas whites, who feared the social, economic, and biological consequences of what one contemporary eugenicist called the "conflict of color."[4] After the outbreak of the Mexican Revolution in 1910 many Mexicans were drawn into the expanding cotton economy of the Southwest by comparatively high wages.[5] They established little cabin homesteads in central Texas, where for decades southern whites and blacks had depended on them to pick cotton. When owners began to replace African and Anglo American tenants and sharecroppers with Mexican sharecroppers, however, white tenants accused owners of betraying the whiteness of Texas and called on the state and federal governments to restrict the flow of Mexicans into the Southwest.[6] The presence of large numbers of Mexicans in central Texas thus exacerbated tensions between white tenants, who worried that Mexicans would be the ruin of white civilization, and white landowners and businessmen farmers who increasingly regarded poor whites with nearly racial contempt.

Over time Mexicans came to locate themselves in the ethnoracial middle ground between Anglo Americans and African Americans, not white enough to claim equality with Anglos and yet, in many cases, white enough to escape the worst features of the Jim Crow South.[7] Although Mexicans and Anglos lived in a segregated society that strongly discouraged social interaction, the line of separation was not as rigidly maintained between the two groups as it was between whites and blacks. In some towns, for example, Mexicans could attend Anglo schools if they were "clean," which often was a euphemism for "white" as well as an allusion to the eugenic maintenance of white "racial hygiene."[8] A farmer from Nueces County remarked: "I would not mind Jim Crowing the filthy Mexicans, but I would not Jim Crow a Mexican if he was educated and . . . nearer the white race."[9] E. E. Davis wrote that "The American children and the clean, high-minded Mexican children do not like to go to school with the dirty 'greaser' type of Mexican child. The better thing is to put the 'dirty' ones into separate schools till they learn to 'clean up' and become eligible to better society."[10] Albert Gregg, a Texas Mexican with an Anglo father, observed that only "clean Mexicans with Spanish blood and fair complexions" were allowed to sit next to "Americans."[11]

Clean and dirty thus often alluded less to physical hygiene than to class mobility ("clean up") and racial categories in separating nearly white Mexicans from mostly nonwhite ones.[12] During the 1920s, however, the decade of the heaviest immigration from Mexico, Mexican farmers and farm workers throughout Texas were regarded as nonwhite aliens who rarely passed the cleanliness test for whiteness. "If a Mexican bought a lot among the whites" in Caldwell County, explained a school superintendent in 1929, "they would burn him out." He then added: "We are just old, hard-boiled southerners in this county."[13]

In order to understand how Mexicans came to be racialized as nonwhites or hybrid "in-betweens," we need to examine the increasingly important role Mexican workers came to play in the Texas economy after 1900. In the twenty years from 1890 to 1910, the number of persons of Mexican descent in Texas more than doubled. In 1910 approximately 125,000 Mexican-born Mexicans resided in Texas, in addition to the 108,000 U.S.-born Mexicans who reported one or both parents as having been born in Mexico. The numbers of Texas Mexicans steadily increased after the outbreak of the Mexican Revolution in 1910.[14] Until 1930 the majority of all Mexicans living in the United States resided in Texas; after that date California overtook Texas as the home of the largest number of Mexicans in the country.[15]

The geographical pivot for the distribution of Mexican laborers to the cotton farms of central Texas was San Antonio, to which Anglos sometimes alluded as the "Mexican Capital of Texas" and the "mecca of Mexican life in Texas."[16] In 1911 a San Antonio newspaper reported that "a coach load of Mexican pickers passed through this city for the great cotton fields about San Marcos [near Austin] and tomorrow an entire train load will go over into the Brazos bottoms where there is a great demand for help." The pickers were accompanied by their wives and children, which was to the liking of the planters because "children as a rule will pick as much cotton as grown-ups."[17]

Women and their children began to accompany their husbands on the northern trek to Texas cotton fields because the large size of many Mexican families made Mexican labor especially attractive to Texas cotton farmers. In addition, cotton farmers and railroad companies believed that single males, or *solos*, were less likely to jump contracts if they were with their families. Before that time the majority of Mexicans entering Texas to work in the railroads and cotton fields were single males. A Mexican family often consisted of a husband and wife, their younger children, their married children with their families, cousins, grandparents, uncles, aunts, and other relatives, and sometimes family friends.[18] Although most Mexican women accompanied their husbands *al norte*, some women—single women, single parents, separated or divorced women, and widows—found work in Texas through the services of private labor contractors. The majority of these unaccompanied women, however, were *solas*, single females determined to earn enough on which to live and perhaps to send a portion of their earnings back to their families in Mexico or south Texas. Little is known about Mexican, Anglo, or African American women migrant farm workers and their children, although the Bureau of Labor estimated in 1920 that 50 percent of all immigrants from Mexico were women and children. As word of work spread back to Mexico, more women and children joined their husbands in the northward sally to the cotton fields and railroad yards. As one railroad official observed:

Ten years ago our Mexican immigrants were chiefly men. It was rare to see a woman among those who came through. . . . About 1900, men who had been in the United States and returned to Mexico began to bring back their families with them. . . . Most of the men who had families with them did not go back the following season, but some of the men without their families did, and some of them in turn came back the next year with their families to remain permanently. So the process goes on, with . . . a larger proportion of women and children among the immigrants each year, and a larger proportion remaining in this country.[19]

The economist Ruth Allen wrote that Mexican migration after World War I had become such a movement of families that the immigration of men, women, and children into Texas had become "effective and, shall we say, fear inspiring."[20]

Networks of railroads from Mexico to the border with Texas became the arteries for Mexican migration. Just as Anglo settlers followed the construction of railroads westward into central and south Texas in the late nineteenth century, Mexicans built and followed Mexican railroads into northern Mexico, where the railways connected at border towns with Texas railroads. To meet the heavy demand for Mexican track laborers, private employment agencies and independent labor contractors multiplied throughout Texas. One agency supplied 6,474 Mexican laborers to four railroad companies within a period of nine months in 1907. Six agencies operating in El Paso for eight months in 1907–1908 supplied 16,479 Mexican laborers to railroads, an average of 2,060 per month. By 1909 Mexicans had supplied most of the labor for track-maintenance crews in the Southwest. Asked in 1913 why so few white men remained in track work, an official for the Atchison, Topeka and Santa Fe Railroad replied that "the American" [that is, the white man] considered track labor "below his grade" and that, furthermore, "the Irishmen have all gone into politics and into the police departments."[21]

By 1913 many Irish immigrants, like other European ethnic groups, had become white Americans. However, before they completed their passage into whiteness, Democratic politics, and police departments, Anglo-Saxon nativists throughout the nineteenth century regarded the Catholic Irish as "apes" and " 'niggers' inside out." As nonwhite "Celtic beasts" they had performed track work along with Chinese "coolies," but by leading the anti-Chinese campaign in California and by playing a leading role in the violence against New York blacks during the 1863 Draft Riot, many Irish immigrants had, by the end of the century, demonstrated their willingness to embrace the values of white supremacy in return for access to white power and privilege.[22] Whites, however, rarely regarded Mexicans, including those who were born and raised in Texas and elsewhere in the United States, as American because American applied only to members of the white race, regardless of one's citizenship or nationality. Mexicans, including Mexican Americans, had become, like the Chinese, a culturally and biologically inferior alien race.

As railroad work drew Mexicans deeper into Texas and other southwestern states at the beginning of the century, farmers came to rely on the railroads to provide them with a steady stream of Mexican workers. Cotton farmers recruited Mexicans by offering higher wages than the railroads offered, thereby drawing workers from the railroads and saving for themselves railway fare and other expenses of recruiting. Many Mexicans who had been recruited by the railroads to work in central Texas "jumped train" before reaching their destinations in order to pick cotton for Texas farmers, thus forcing railroads continually to pump in fresh supplies of Mexican workers to offset the loss to agriculture. One official of the National Railroad in Mexico complained in 1907 that his company had recruited fifteen hundred laborers for work on the northern section of the railroad but that within a year nearly all of them had left to work in Texas. A railway official in Dallas reported that 50 percent of the Mexican track workers left to take jobs on cotton farms, and an independent labor contractor reported that whole gangs left the sections to pick cotton.[23]

In order to meet the growing demand for agricultural labor, an entire industry of private employment agencies and individual labor agents or contractors developed shortly after 1900. The passage of the 1917 Immigration Act, which required that each immigrant pay an $8.00 head tax and pass a literacy test, sharply reduced the number of legal immigrants but had practically no effect on the surreptitious entry of Mexicans into the United States. A Department of Labor report acknowledged that the law led to the creation of a new and thriving industry for transnational smugglers (called *coyotes*) and resulted in an increased demand for the services of employment agencies and labor contractors or *enganchistas* (one who "hooks").[24] Between 1918 and 1920 licensed private employment agencies in Texas reported that they had furnished positions for 156,223 men and women in agriculture, mostly cotton, and that more than 86 percent of the recruits were Mexicans[25] (see Table 5).

Shortly after the passage of the Immigration Act of 1917, planters and growers throughout the Southwest petitioned Secretary of Labor William B. Wilson to invoke a special provision of the act that allowed for the temporary admission and return of "otherwise inadmissible aliens" to offset the labor shortage created by America's involvement in World War I. In response to the lobbying efforts of agribusiness farmers, the secretary of labor waived the literacy test, the $8.00 head tax, and the 1885 prohibition of contract labor. The relaxation of immigration requirements eliminated the need for *coyotes* to smuggle Mexicans across the border; however, independent labor contractors, especially the rapidly proliferating employment agencies, seized the opportunity to direct the flow of Mexicans to the cotton fields of east, central, and west Texas. Although the need for labor contractors near the open border may have diminished somewhat, their services were in great demand elsewhere in the state.[26]

The temporary suspension of certain provisions of the Immigration Act of 1917 provoked a storm of protest from southwestern nativists, patriotic societies, the American labor movement, eugenicists, and congressmen, who challenged the secretary's authority to suspend restrictions enacted by Congress.[27] Wilson issued an order after the war that rescinded the program for temporary admission, with the predictable result that growers again claimed they could not continue to operate without Mexican labor. Progrower congressmen once more pressured the

Table 5 *Positions Furnished by Texas Private Employment Agencies,*
1918–1920

1918–1919	Males	Females	Total
Whites	4,429	416	4,845
Blacks	406	45	451
Mexicans	37,242	390	37,632
Subtotal	42,077	851	42,928
1919–1920			
Whites	12,333	452	12,785
Blacks	2,373	107	2,480
Mexicans	96,745	1,285	98,030
Subtotal	111,451	1,844	113,295
Total	153,528	2,695	156,223

SOURCE: Texas Bureau of Labor Statistics, *Sixth Biennial Report,*
1919–1920 (Austin, 1921), 18.

labor secretary to continue the program indefinitely, and Wilson reluctantly agreed to extend it until 1920. He appointed a special committee
of Department of Labor officials who, after conducting investigations in
twenty-five cities in ten western states to determine whether Mexicans
were competing with American workers, came to the conclusion that
they were not and that, furthermore, the agricultural industry of the
Southwest could not continue to expand without access to Mexican
labor. With the enactment of the Quota Acts of 1921 and 1924, further restricting European immigration, growers became ever more dependent
on Mexican laborers. The Texas labor commissioner reported that farmers were still "unable to meet competitive wage scales offered in the
urban labor markets," a problem the commissioner said could "only be
remedied and is being remedied by hiring Mexican labor."[28]

Not only did labor contractors recruit Mexicans who resided in south
Texas, many contractors, some of them Mexicans and Mexican Americans, traveled to Central Mexico to recruit laborers in violation of the
provision of the Contract Labor Law of 1885 forbidding the hiring of
foreign workers prior to their emigration. The standard pattern was for
a contractor to cross the border into Mexico and, with promises of high
wages, smuggle workers into Texas and onto trains headed for cotton
fields in central and north Texas.[29] Often they did not have to cross the
border to recruit laborers. The Alien Contract Labor Law only forbade
the hiring of Mexicans in Mexico; once they were in the United States,

contractors were free to hire them. Some contractors, not wishing to violate the letter of the law, would distribute business cards, flyers, and job advertisements on the U.S. side of the border, knowing that these materials would find their way into Mexico and thereby serve as an inducement to Mexicans to cross the border into their waiting arms.[30]

The American Federation of Labor (AFL), which represented mostly white workers, believed Mexicans would eventually compete with whites for jobs in industry and thus urged the Immigration Service in 1911 to halt this "torrent of peon poison."[31] Samuel Gompers, president of the AFL, complained that there were too many loopholes in the Contract Labor law that enabled Mexicans and labor contractors to exploit it. Mexican track laborers, for example, often returned to Mexico to recruit others, mostly family members, to return to the United States to work on the railroads. Newly arriving family members were "well drilled" as to the statements they should make to immigration officials in order to avoid acknowledging that a friend or family member had recruited them for a job in the United States, which would have been illegal. But in denying that a job awaited them, they ran the risk of being denied entry on the grounds that they would become charity cases or "public charges."[32] The obvious way around the red tape and contradictions of the law was to engage the services of labor contractors. The contractors often ignored the law altogether, for after 1910 it was enforced only casually in Texas.

As most immigration authorities were aware, and as Carey McWilliams correctly observed, the Contract Labor Law was "more often honored in the breach than in its observance."[33] American immigration officials were more concerned with the illegal smuggling into the United States of Asians, especially Chinese, and eastern Europeans who had entered the United States through Mexico than with stanching the flow of Mexican laborers from across the border.[34] Prior to the establishment of the Border Patrol in 1924, for example, immigration authorities relied on a force of sixty mounted men to patrol a 1,900-mile-long boundary. A member of the Border Patrol in Texas reported that during the harvest season his supervisor, under pressure from local growers, routinely issued verbal orders to "shut our eyes to the most flagrant immigration violations" by allowing Mexicans to cross the border illegally to pick cotton.[35]

Although cotton and fruit growers in Texas had become dependent on labor contractors to meet the increasing demand for Mexican labor, they resented having to pay middlemen contractors for ensuring an adequate labor supply at harvest time. The Fruit Growers' Association wired the secretary of labor in 1917, for example, that it needed 5,000 agricultural laborers but complained that it could not afford the financial outlay necessary to import Mexicans. Its solution was simple: "Cannot government handle the importation of Mexicans or others for us?"[36] Texas fruit growers, as well as cotton farmers, had seized on the idea that the state ought to take charge of supplying them with agricultural labor and thus, in effect, subsidize large-scale farmers. In this way, they argued, the government could control the flow of Mexican workers to agriculture and industry as well as provide the workforce for the expanding economy of the Southwest.

Until growers could persuade the state to become its own enganchista, the Texas Bureau of Labor Statistics came under increasing pressure from growers to regulate private employment agencies and independent labor contractors to protect them against fraudulent practices, such as agents "selling" Mexican laborers "by the head" to cotton farmers for a fixed period and then, a few days later, absconding with them to sell to another grower for a slightly higher price. Growers, of course, had no quarrel with enganchistas who violated the Contract Labor Law to supply them with Mexican laborers; but Texas growers increasingly believed there was little need for middlemen labor contractors in a state that bordered Mexico, and they especially resented the power that Mexican labor contractors wielded over the labor supply. In response to growers' complaints, particularly in view of the severe labor shortage created during World War I, the Texas Labor Bureau urged the governor to establish state-run "free" employment agencies to bring farmers and laborers together "protected against impositions" and to counter the "lax way in which the municipal governments protect the poor people against these unscrupulous agents."[37]

Mexican labor contractors became the villains of both growers, who relied on them, and the Texas Labor Bureau, which hoped to replace them with state-controlled white labor contractors. The bureau commissioner reported that Mexican *coyotes* smuggled Mexicans across the border for a fee of between $2.00 and $10.00 per person and then turned them over "to some man-catcher or employment agent, who proceeds to fleece them of any money they may have left." After Mexicans arrived at their destinations, they were told that a certain amount had been charged to each to cover the cost of transportation and employment fees, an amount which would be deducted from their earnings. "When they sometimes refused to comply," according to testimony before the Commission on Industrial Relations, "they are guarded until they work out what they owe. I have known of a number of Mexicans to be chained in Gonzales County and guarded by armed men with shotguns and made to work these moneys out."[38] A favorite practice of employers was to hide the clothes and shoes of Mexicans at night in order to "protect their investment" by forcing them to remain in their custody.[39] As one employer put it, "you can treat them in any manner and not be bothered with lawsuits, reformers and social uplifters."[40]

Mexican immigrants were among the most exploited workers in Texas, but they nevertheless resisted the worst forms of abuse "with their feet." Whenever work conditions became unendurable, they often simply walked away from the fields, or in the case of sharecroppers, "jumped" contract. As individuals, Mexicans had little bargaining power, but as a group they attempted to set limits on their exploitation. If one worker was mistreated, often an entire group of pickers would desert the farmer. "They are Bolsheviks and want to run every deal they are in on," complained a representative for the federal farm-loan program; "They will all sit down in the field and not work if they hear somebody is paying a couple of cents more. You . . . have to give it to them or fire them."[41] A Texas journalist was impressed by the solidarity of Mexican laborers when he wrote: "Let one man become disgruntled because he has been called down for picking dirty cotton . . . and the chances are that if he quits, the entire crew will shed their sacks and quit with him. The communists could take lessons in 'class consciousness' and 'solidarity' from the brown boys."[42]

Support for state-operated labor contractors or employment agencies did not, however, arise from a humanitarian concern for the well-being of Mexican migrant workers. The Texas Labor Bureau reported, incredibly, that white farmers—not Mexican laborers—were the chief sufferers because crooked agents supplied them with "low grade common labor" of the peon class.[43] By charging fees for each Mexican he delivered to cotton farmers, the labor contractor increased the cost of low-grade Mexican labor, which resulted in farmers having to pay "white-men's wages" for nonwhite workers.

Conceding that it was impossible to regulate private employment agencies and independent enganchistas, the state finally decided to take over the operation of recruiting labor from private agencies by directly competing with them. In 1923 cotton growers realized their long-sought goal when the Texas Labor Bureau opened state-operated employment offices in Waco, Fort Worth, Dallas, Amarillo, El Paso, and San Antonio. The San Antonio office furnished positions to Mexican cotton pickers in

south and central Texas and recruited laborers in the spring for clearing and "grubbing" land, chopping cotton, and other farm work.
Within a few years state-run free employment offices had reduced the
business of private agencies by more than 50 percent.[44] Texas growers
had succeeded in inducing the state to seize control of recruiting Mexican labor from Mexican labor contractors, and thus the Lone Star
State had become, in effect, the new enganchista of Mexican laborers.
Twenty years later the federal government would inaugurate the
Emergency Farm Labor Program, more commonly known as the Bracero Program, to provide agribusiness growers in the West and Southwest with more than 4.5 million temporary Mexican laborers from
1942 to 1963.[45]

Poor whites in central Texas blamed Mexican sharecroppers and wage
laborers who settled in their midst for the collapse of their cherished
dream of owning a farm. They focused on the perceived danger of race
mixing and the alleged inferiority of Mexicans rather than on the competitive business practices of commercial farmers. Although no one was
certain about how many Mexicans had become sharecroppers in central
Texas or whether these were recent immigrants or Mexican Americans
from south Texas, virtually all who testified before various congressional
hearings agreed with the contemporary sociologist Max Handman that
"a pretty definite replacement of the American tenant-farmer by the
Mexican" had been taking place between 1900 and 1930.[46] "Texas is becoming more and more a region of nonresident land owners," east Texas
Congressman Box testified, and "more and more the men of capital are
acquiring Texas land and foreclosing liens and otherwise putting Mexican tenants out on the farms, and the few remnants of white people . . .
are having to move away."[47] Occupational designations listed in the
1880, 1900, and 1910 manuscript censuses for Mexican-born and Texas-
born individuals residing in the town of Lockhart (the county seat of
Caldwell County, a few miles south of Austin), reveal that Texas-born
Mexicans were more likely to be listed as farmers (that is, tenants) than
were Mexican-born people, who were almost always listed as laborers.
Before 1920 the census did not distinguish between sharecroppers and
tenants, and it is likely that some Mexican laborers were actually sharecroppers. More research needs to be done concerning the options available to first- and second-generation Mexicans, but the little evidence
available on central Texas suggests that immigrant Mexicans first
worked as migrant farm laborers and later became sharecroppers, share
tenants on "thirds and fourths," and, in some cases, owners.[48]

Caldwell County was also one of the first counties of the "white belt" of central Texas—so called because white share tenants were once more numerous than blacks or Mexicans—to witness the passing of "Nordic-American tenants." Between 1870 and 1890 almost all of the tenants in this county community, called Keglar Hill, were "native whites," and the population was about equally landowners and tenants. A few black tenants resided in Keglar Hill before 1880, but apparently none after that date. "Then came the Mexicans," wrote Robert Montgomery, a professor of economics at the University of Texas in 1931. At first they came in the 1880s to pick cotton, and then in 1892 two or three families stayed and worked the land "on the halves." Within five years "every large landowner in the community was employing Mexican tenants," so that by 1900 there were no native white tenants in Keglar Hill. Of more than 300 whites who owned or rented land in Keglar Hill in 1885, not one remained in 1910. For the "receding Nordic," Montgomery gloomily concluded, "his world had vanished."[49] Keglar Hill was more than just a local example of the "rising tide of color" throughout the Southwest; it took on the symbolic resonance of an Imperial Texas in decline, of an empire of whiteness being destroyed by degenerate Mexicans.

Within a few years the people of Texas and other states of the Southwest awakened to the reality of an "invasion" of a large and—as many believed—largely unassimilable group thought to be racially inferior but nevertheless capable of competing with whites for jobs in agriculture and industry. Not only whites, as it turned out, but also many blacks found it impossible to compete with Mexicans on the farms. A black cotton picker in Texas complained that "Mexicans can live on next to nothing. A tortilla and a cup of coffee will stand them for a half-day. We eat meat and bread about the same as you-all [whites]. . . . More Negroes would come . . . if there were not so many Mexicans and they could get better wages."[50] E. E. Davis pointed out that it was a great mistake to believe that the majority of Mexicans continued to reside along the frontier of the Rio Grande: "In 1920 the greatest density of the rural Mexican population in Texas was in Caldwell County in sight of the dome of the state capitol."[51] "On every corner," wrote one resident, "the tamale and chile vendor is shouting his wares."[52] It would not be long before white and black Southerners would be eating chile with their fatback and tamales with their cornbread and molasses.[53]

As the nation turned its attention to the Mexican question after the passage of the Immigration Act of 1917, Texas industrial and agribusiness leaders descended in droves on Washington to lobby against any restrictions on Mexican immigration. Telegrams to the secretary of labor arrived daily from Texas cotton growers claiming to need thousands more Mexican pickers than were available. The biggest tribute that has been paid to the Mexican in the economic development of the Southwest, wrote the author and Mexican immigrant Ernesto Galarza, "was the panic which spread among his employers when restriction of immigration threatened." Employers suddenly jumped to the defense of the Mexican laborer and declared him, in the words of one employer, *"persona absolutamente grata"*—he is "a man," protested the employer, "rough diamond though he be."[54]

Texas growers had so thoroughly relied on Mexican labor to chop and harvest cotton that immigration restriction would mean nothing less than economic disaster for the state. They worried that in other cotton states in the South during World War I many black sharecroppers and farm laborers increasingly sought higher-paying work in cities and towns or left to join the army.[55] White agents of county defense councils attempted to persuade black farmers of their patriotic duty to remain on the farms and raise cotton, a "prime necessity of modern warfare," but quickly learned that "the common negro does not place much trust in the promises of white people." The Texas State Council of Defense therefore hired thirty African Americans to lecture to the "colored people" of Texas to discourage them from leaving the farms, but they left anyway.[56] One white resident of Dallas County reflected in 1920, "Wherever you will find a boll of cotton growing in Texas, you will find the negro pretty close around, or you did in olden times, but now since modern times . . . the negro has gone to the city and is seeking other employment."[57] While most Texas African Americans remained in the state, they were abandoning its farms in increasing numbers. Between 1900 and 1930 the number of black Texans living in towns and cities increased from 19 percent to 39 percent.[58] "Much depends on who reaches the Negro farmer first," wrote one field agent, "as to whether or not he remains on the farm—the Negro extension agent or the industrial labor agent."[59]

The debate over restricting the immigration of Mexicans aroused strong emotions on both sides. From the point of view of the eugenicists and other nativists, the immigration question was essentially a biological one: The Nordic race would be genetically compromised if it attempted to absorb so many inferior "seed stocks" from southern Europe and Latin America. Immigration restrictionists argued that most Mexicans did not return to Mexico, took jobs from white people, lowered the standard of living, and constituted a threat to the purity of the Anglo-Saxon racial stock.[60] One Nordicist wrote in the *Saturday Evening Post* that the deluge of inferior races flooding America would inevitably produce "a hybrid race of people as worthless and futile as the good-for-nothing mongrels of Central America and Southeastern Europe."[61] And a "hyberdized [*sic*] people," wrote the American eugenicist Charles Benedict Davenport, were "a badly put together people."[62] One outspoken nativist argued that if what was needed was the ideal laborer, then the Chinese and not the Mexicans ought to be permitted to immigrate, for the "Chinese coolie," he believed, was "the ideal human mule. He will turn less food into more work, with less trouble, than any other domestic animal. He does not even plague us with his progeny. His wife and children are in China, and he returns there himself when we no longer need him."[63] But Mexicans, he argued, could not be trusted to return to Mexico.

What was particularly distressing for those who believed in the absolute importance of maintaining the whiteness of America was that many whites opposed placing a quota on immigration from Mexico. Chambers of Commerce, the Farm Bureau, railroads, and virtually all of the agricultural growers of the Southwest insisted that any regulation of Mexican immigrants caused severe labor shortages and ruined many business enterprises.[64] Cotton growers and industry leaders in Texas were caught in a dilemma because, on one hand, they desired a large Mexican labor force that was available, tractable, and cheap; on the other hand, however, they were sensitive to charges that they were sacrificing the whiteness of America for higher profits. For many Anglo Texans, Mexicans were not whites and could not be assimilated into Texas society. Texas whites sometimes made a distinction between upper-class Latin Americans or white Mexicans and nonwhite Mexican peons who filled the ranks of the immigrant class. The nativist Chester Rowell claimed that "the Mexican peon is not a 'white' man. He is an Indian . . . [who] embodies no part of that fine Latin-American culture which charms visitors to Mexico City."[65] Growers who opposed restriction were sometimes more virulently anti-Mexican than were the openly racist restrictionists. F. E. Jackson, president of the Farm Bureau in Ysleta, Texas, shared with the anti-immigration nativists the belief that Mexicans were innately inferior. Mexicans, according to Jackson, were *chilis*, whom he described as "creatures somewhere in between a burro and a human being."[66] For people like Jackson, Mexicans almost had to be half animal to survive the poverty their low wages guaranteed them.

The point Jackson was trying to make was that you worked Mexicans like work animals; you did not debate whether they made good American citizens.

The most ardent opponent of Mexican immigration, Congressman John C. Box of east Texas, stated simply, "I am in favor of keeping Texas white."[67] Despite his racist assumptions, Box correctly observed that Mexicans were "basically Indian" and carried in their veins a "strain of Negro blood derived from black slaves carried to Mexico from Africa and the West Indies." By the "one-drop rule" of the South, Mexicans were blacks, and intermarriage between Mexicans and whites was thus leading to a "distressing process of mongrelization."[68] The idea that Mexicans were mongrels and therefore inferior to whites was not new, nor was it confined to narrow-thinking racists. The champion of freedmen rights in the South after the Civil War, Thaddeus Stevens, in describing the people of the territory of New Mexico, explained to his colleagues in Congress that Mexicans were "a hybrid race of Spanish and Indian origin, ignorant, degraded, demoralized and priest-ridden."[69] Some believed these racial hybrids were criminally inclined and carriers of diseases. A "full-blooded American" complained to Box that employers hired Mexicans because they were "cheap, nasty, diseased criminal labor."[70] "Herds of unwashed greasers," wrote one medical doctor from Fort Worth, entered Piggly-Wiggly and Helpy-Selfy stores and handled the fruit, vegetables, and fresh meat although they had not had a bath since they swam the Rio Grande and were "sizzling with disease."[71] Not to be outdone, Congressman Box read into the *Congressional Record* a magazine article characterizing Mexicans as "diseased of body, subnormal intellectually, and moral morons of the most hopeless type." The article concluded: "It is true that our civilization has swallowed and digested a good many nasty doses, but the gagging point has been about reached."[72] Gastronomical metaphors were often used to suggest that Mexicans were unfit for white consumption, prompting the historian David Montejano to write, "Uncle Sam simply had no stomach for Juan García."[73]

As nonwhites, Mexicans were accused of every conceivable social ill, of carrying diseases, lowering wages, accepting charity, displacing Anglo workers, molesting white women, and even stealing Irish-American melodies and claiming them as their own.[74] Without immediate action to block immigration, the "proud citizenship" of Texas would soon be forced to hear the "babble, quack and gobble of alien tongues."[75] Underlying the nativists' concern over Mexican immigration was the fear of losing control of their culture, of having it transformed by the presence of an alien and nonwhite "other." A doctor from Waco, in central Texas, wrote: "Waco is a white man's town, but how long, oh how long will their boasted white supremacy last in the face of a deluge of ignorant illiterates . . . who will choke the wheels of justice, overrun the public schools, pay little or no taxes . . . , and reduce the moral standing?"[76] And if Texas should meet its end in some undefined and unspecified way, "let it go down," another pleaded, "with . . . the people singing 'Hail Columbia,' the 'Star Spangled Banner,' and 'Nearer my God to Thee,' instead of a motley crowd howling 'Hoch der Kaiser,' 'Viva Italia,' and 'Vive Mexicano' [*sic*]."[77] The presence of Mexicans thus also served to heighten ethnic tensions among Texas whites, or more precisely, between native-born Southern whites and not-quite-white Germans and Italians.[78]

Mexicans had become the scapegoats for whites who worried that the growing population of Mexicans in Texas would create another "race problem" which threatened to establish a society segregated in three ways. Edgar Wallace, a representative of the AFL, believed that Texas already had one race problem with its black population for which "there is no answer."[79] Congressman Box reiterated his view that the presence of Mexicans in Texas created a race problem similar to that of the Old South when it imported slave labor from Africa "like beasts . . . howling like lost or homesick dogs . . . without a ray of hope in their poor darkened minds."[80] The superintendent of schools in Gregg County wrote Congressman Box in 1928: "If it isn't good for the North to let in white folks from across the Atlantic, how in the name of common sense can it be all right to let in hordes of another race across the Rio Grande?" F. J. Stuart of Dallas wrote Congressman Box that "Mexicans swarm across the Rio Grande like vermin escaping from a bonfire."[81] But landowners from central Texas complained that when they tried to recruit black laborers from east Texas to pick cotton, east Texas farmers raised "a mob violence howl" that central Texas growers were stealing their cotton pickers. When central Texas growers resorted to Mexican labor, the "east Texas bunch" raised a "congressional roar" that growers in central Texas were causing the wholesale displacement of white and black tenants and sharecroppers and were mongrelizing Texas with foreigners who were neither white nor black but a degraded mixture of Indian, Spanish, Chinese, and African.[82] "To Mexicanize Texas or Orientalize California," one nativist tersely wrote, "is a crime."[83]

The nativists' concern for preserving the racial vigor of the Nordic stock included the belief that too many southern European and Latin American foreigners were infected with Socialism, anarchism, and other anti-American radicalisms. When immigration restrictionists believed that biological arguments about the perils of race mixture and the decline of Nordic civilization were falling on deaf ears, they often resorted to the argument that Mexicans, like the "Slavs" of Russia, were "Bolshevists" and revolutionaries who stirred up trouble in this country. Nativists warned that many radicals from the Mexican Revolution of 1910 immigrated to the United States and took part in violent activity against the United States, as was revealed by the discovery of the *Plan de San Diego*. The plan, a revolutionary manifesto named after the south Texas town where it was supposedly drafted, had as its objective the establishment of an independent borderlands republic that would consist of Texas, New Mexico, Arizona, Colorado, and California. The irredentist plan called for a general uprising in February 1915 by the "Liberating Army of the Races and People," which was to be composed of Indians, Mexicans, Japanese, and blacks. A provision which called for all white males over the age of sixteen to be murdered caused a general panic in south Texas and led to the lynching and shooting of more than 200 Mexicans.[84]

Not surprisingly, then, a congressman on the committee worried that Mexican immigrants were mostly radicals who might share "this evil philosophy against capital and property that we find a good many Mexicans have."[85] The idea that Mexicans were revolutionaries (Carranzistas and Villistas, as they were often called) undermined Anglo confidence in the essential docility of Mexicans and aroused their fears that Mexican workers, like Russian Bolshevists, might suddenly turn violent. "The great mass of the Russian people were certainly a model of obedience," declared Congressman William Vaile of Colorado, but they had become among the most radical elements. He wanted to know if it were possible for Mexicans to go suddenly loco like the Mexican mustang and commit violence or organize like "the Negro . . . in some parts of the United States with armed violence."[86] It was a legal fiction, a Texas nativist wrote Congressman Box, "like the Apache Indian doctor's rattle and his mystic intonations," to believe that one could make "good citizens out of bandits and revolutionaries."[87] Despite the evidence of Mexican radical activity on both sides of the border, pro-immigrationist cotton farmers and fruit growers maintained, however, that Mexicans did not become citizens but came only because they wanted food and that, furthermore, if they were good cotton pickers, it did not matter whether they were Villistas or Carranzistas.[88]

Many Mexicans were, of course, good cotton pickers *and* revolutionaries, some of whom were in exile in Texas during the Mexican Revolution. In Texas they maintained an active interest in Mexican political affairs, which were extensively covered in such Spanish-language newspapers as *La Prensa* (San Antonio) and *La Crónica* (Laredo). Many Mexicans who lived and worked in Texas belonged to the PLM, the political party responsible for many of the armed uprisings in northern Mexico which launched the Mexican Revolution. One year after the outbreak of the revolution, working-class Mexicans met in Laredo and formed El Primer Congreso Mexicanista to build a regional federation of community organizations and to articulate a radical, working-class ideology that, according to one of the organizers, "would be socially significant here as well as in Mexico and would excite interest throughout the world."[89] In central Texas, Mexican sharecroppers and share tenants joined the Socialist Renters' Union, later the Land League of America, and demanded lower rents and better living conditions from their landlords.[90] In Dallas, Anglos feared that the growing population of Mexicans in the city would lead to radical organizing. One Dallas resident blamed agricultural and industrial "big interests" for the growing presence of "radical floaters" among the Mexican immigrant population. In 1926 Dallas Mayor Lou Blaylock ordered an investigation of a "red" organization, the Society of the Bolsheveki, which was allegedly composed mainly of Mexican workers from the Dallas *colonia*, where most Mexicans lived.[91]

Despite the copious testimony of cotton growers and chambers of commerce representatives that most Mexicans posed no threat either to white workers or to the "social or patriotic fabric of our government," Albert Johnson, chair of the House Committee on Immigration and Naturalization and president of the Eugenics Research Association, was not so easily convinced.[92] He worried that if Mexicans were able to organize a cotton-mill strike near Veracruz and convince nearly 40,000 laborers to threaten to walk out, "Is it not fair to presume," he asked, "that . . . they can soon organize in the United States?" Texas Congressman Eugene Black made the point more bluntly: If Mexican immigration continued unabated, he claimed, "Radicalism and discontent would . . . Samson-like . . . pull down the pillars of our whole economic structure on our heads."[93] Pro-immigrationists responded to this Cassandra-like portent that the majority of Mexican migrant laborers were peons who "do not meddle in your politics" and that, as mongrelized "half breeds," were simply incapable of posing a threat to white civilization. Asked whether he were not afraid that Mexicans might come to dominate the countryside, one cotton farmer replied: "Have you ever heard, in the history of the United States or in the history of the human race, of the white race being overrun by a class of people of the mentality of the Mexicans?" The prospect of Mexicans colonizing the United States and taking it over was to this grower "absolutely absurd."[94] A singularly nativist defense of unrestricted immigration thus rested on belief in the racial inferiority of Mexicans.

Many anti-immigration nativists, particularly eugenicists, believed that white women were the key to preserving the purity of Nordic civilization in America. Harry Laughlin, one of the leading eugenicists of the 1920s and an advisor to the House Committee on Immigration and Naturalization (chaired by fellow eugenicist Albert Johnson), testified that if white women were careful to select mates free of "colored blood," the white race would remain secure. "But if the time ever comes when men with a small fraction of colored blood could readily find mates among the white women," Laughlin warned, "the gates would be thrown open to a final radical race mixture of the whole population." White men, as the fathers of white women, must accept ultimate responsibility for their daughters' choice of mates for marriage. "Uncle Sam is not an old bachelor," Laughlin theorized, "he is a pater familias par excellence, and he should, therefore, look upon every immigrant as a prospective son-in-law." For Laughlin, mate selection was a question of racial as well as national patriotism because the survival of the white race depended on the "virtue and fecundity of American women."[95]

In the end, the labor needs of southwestern industry and agribusiness prevented labor interests, patriotic organizations, and eugenicist groups from imposing immigration restriction on Mexico similar to that on Europe and Asia. The expansion of industry and agriculture in the Southwest depended on Mexican labor and therefore outweighed nativist considerations that Mexicans would radicalize and mongrelize the Southwest. Texas Congressman John N. Garner, later the Speaker of the House of Representatives and vice president of the United States, spoke for many Texas cotton farmers when he told the Committee on Immigration and Naturalization that "Farming is not a profitable industry in this country" unless farmers can find cheap labor, and in Texas only landlords who can "get the Mexican labor" are able to make a profit.[96] An officer for federal reclamation projects employing Mexicans testified that he was opposed to hiring that class of Mexican who might compete for land with the American farmer. Instead, he argued that he was interested only in those laborers who "might not themselves, as a class . . . be able to direct themselves successfully." Congressman Box immediately countered: "What you really want . . . [is] a class of people who have not the ability to rise . . . , who do not want to own land, who can be directed by men in the upper stratum of society. That is what you want, isn't it?" To which the officer replied, "I believe that is about it."[97] Like the reclamation officer, cotton growers wanted a permanent class of peons to do farmwork. Clark Pease, a banker from Corpus Christi, offered a similar view of the kind of labor needed: "No. 1 laborers" occupying "No. 2 positions"—Mexicans who would not undertake to own land. Congressman Benjamin Welty of Ohio asked Pease whether he were concerned about the possibility of Mexican labor undermining the gendered roles of white men and women on the cotton farm by allowing women too much leisure: "Do you not think that is a dangerous attitude to take . . . to bring in a lot of laborers to work for us so that we can fold our hands and let the women take care of the poodle dogs, and after a while they will have a maid to take care of the poodle dog while they smoke cigarettes?" To which Pease responded: "I would rather my wife would have a poodle dog than pick cotton."[98] Welty wanted women kept busy on the farm, Pease wanted them to have some leisure to lessen the hardship of farmwork, but both wanted Mexican men and women on the farms.

The impact of Mexican immigration to Texas created divisions between newcomer immigrants and Texas Mexicans (tejanos). For Texas Mexicans who wished to become recognized as American and white, Mexican immigrants reinforced stereotypes that Mexicans in general were poor, dirty, and politically radical, especially since Anglòs rarely bothered to distinguish between Texas Mexicans and Mexican immigrants. One Texas Mexican declared that Texas-born Mexicans were "handicapped by the steady flow of immigration of the laboring peon class" because immigrants of that class were a "disgrace" and that Texas Mexicans "would get more wages if immigration were stopped."[99] Emilio Flores, a Mexican American from San Antonio and secretary of the Mexican Protective Association, a mutual-aid society, opposed Mexican immigration because too many Mexican immigrants were "the worst kind of anarchists" who read *Regeneración*, the anarchist newspaper published by the Magón brothers in Los Angeles, and were the cause of the "fatal division" that existed within Mexican American communities. Although Flores sympathized with "these poor unfortunates" because they were members of his own race, he maintained that Mexican immigrants had "their own ways of living in their own country," ways that were "absolutely different from ours."[100] Native Texan Manuel de la O favored immigration restriction because he wanted to see protected the "rights of native-born *American* working men." Like Emilio Flores, de la O embraced whiteness and shared some of the nativist prejudice against Mexican immigrants by implying that Mexican immigrants were criminals: "The first thing a Mexican does after he gets his first pay-check in this country is to buy a pistol."[101] That de la O was himself a Mexican, despite his newly constructed identity as an American working man, conferred more than a touch of irony on his racism, for white working men probably suspected de la O himself of carrying a pistol.

Since most Anglos presumed that Mexicans, especially immigrants, were nonwhite Indian Mexicans or peons, many Texas Mexicans, especially those of the middle class, wanted to claim whiteness in order to take advantage of the rights and privileges of being American. Being a Mexican was to Anglos, in other words, an issue less of nationality or citizenship than of race, however connected the two were in the minds of both Mexicans and Anglos. Johnny Solís, a tejano from San Antonio, told Taylor that the biggest obstacle Texas Mexicans faced was that "no matter how we behave or what we do or how long we have been here, we are still Mexicans."[102] Despite his U.S. citizenship, his English fluency, and his opposition to Mexican immigration, Solís complained that Anglos did not regard him as white, the essential requisite for becoming American. Texas Mexicans like Solís, Flores, or de la O might claim to be American and the law might regard them as American for the purpose of citizenship, but in everyday practice only whites referred to other whites as Americans. White Americans identified nonwhite Americans by their race—Negro, Mexican, Chinese, and so forth, or by their religion—Jewish or "Hindoo."

Some Mexican citizens reacted to the racism of white Texans with their own brand of racial invective. When Benito Rodríguez, the Mexican consul general in El Paso, was told at a San Antonio hotel that he could have a room only if he claimed to be a Spaniard, he replied: "I would rather be a dog than a Spaniard, a German, or a Jew," and added, apparently pleased with himself, "I think the landlady was a German Jew."[103] Rodríguez's disdain for Spaniards, Germans, and Jews reflected the long-term interaction among African, indigenous, and Spanish that became the foundation for the complex, hierarchical racial system of Mexico, a system whose racial categories were as complicated as those developing north of the border with the United States. After centuries of mestizaje, society in colonial New Spain was composed of multiple ethnoracial groups, although by the early twentieth century the Mexican government had created census categories for three racial groups: whites, Indians, and mestizos. The population of Mexico in 1920 consisted of about 14 million: 10 percent were classified as *raza blanca* (whites), 30 percent as *raza indígena* (Indians), and about 60 percent as *raza mezclada* (mestizos).[104] Mestizos had occupied an awkward position in this racial hierarchy, often hated by the Spanish for being part Indian and shunned by the Indians for being part Spanish. Those able to construct identities as Spaniards often regarded mestizos, Indians, and Africans with racial contempt. By the end of the nineteenth century, however, many urban mestizo elites claimed to be Spanish, or mostly Spanish, in order to establish racial and cultural distance between themselves and Indians. During the rule of Porfirio Díaz from 1876 to 1910, for example, many Mexicans sought to imitate Europeans, especially the French, in literature, arts, cuisine, and high fashion. Mestizo elites, like Porfirio Díaz himself, fostered the belief in the supremacy of European white culture over native Indian culture. Some Mexican Americans, one historian wrote, "were descended from exiled conservative elites, who had carried across the border as part of their 'cultural baggage' the Porfirian homage to white supremacy." [105] Some Mexicans had thus learned whiteness and "whitening" (*blanqueamiento*) before coming to the United States.

The identification of whiteness with Americanness throughout the nation, and particularly in the western South, made it especially difficult for Mexican Americans, who continually were treated as if they were racial foreigners. A white woman, Maud Burnette, whose people were "all Southern people," told two white men on a Dallas bus that she loathed all Mexicans, whether clean or dirty, U.S. citizens or immigrants, middle class or poor. A young tejana who had overheard the conversation told Burnette as the former was about to get off the bus, "I want you to know I am a Mexican girl." Burnette immediately replied: "And I want you to know that I have nothing to take back—I am paying taxes every year to build more school houses to educate just such as you, and you are occupying a seat right now that rightfully belongs to some nice white girl." Burnette also believed that some whites were not much better racially than Mexicans: "It just looks to me like the American people are 'trashy' enough without inviting the trash of all other nations to be dumped on our soil." The issue for Burnette, as for many whites, was not whether Mexicans were immigrants or U.S. citizens but that they were racial trash.[106]

White owners of cotton farms found themselves in the paradoxical situation of desiring cheap Mexican labor while deploring the settlement of Mexicans in their communities. They feared the threat Mexicans represented to established social and economic relations that governed their lives, as well as to the whiteness of their communities. Reliance on Mexican labor was not "altogether a blessing," wrote a University of Texas professor in 1916, because it introduced "another race into the social life of the already racially divided community."[107] Rural life in Texas was indeed changing in the opening decades of this century, and the arrival of Mexicans was but one of many consequences attendant upon the growth of cotton agriculture. Most whites did not like what they saw. Some wondered how the quality of the schools could be maintained if white schools were forced to open their doors to those whom the Texas rural researcher E. E. Davis called "biologically impoverished tribes of marginal humanity."[108] In 1925, for example, Davis wrote that farm communities of central Texas had become overrun by the "incoming tide" of Mexican immigrants and that once well-kept schoolhouses were now "crumbling monuments of vanishing white communities."[109] He lamented how "one of the most terrible chapters in all the annals of Texas was enacted by the apathetic, cotton-field Mexicans during the first two decades of the twentieth century." Mexicans, he continued mournfully, were destroying white rural culture:

Before the incoming hosts of Mexicans, Caldwell County's three basic rural institutions—the home, the church, and the school—fell like a trio of staggering tenpins at the end of a bowling race. White tenants could not compete with cheap Mexican labor. Prosperous owners moved to town, leaving the menial farm work for Mexicans to do. Rural dwellings, orchards . . . went to wreck . . . and the large rural schools packed with happy white children dwindled into sickly institutions for a few indifferent Mexican *muchachos*.[110]

The eugenicist Harry Laughlin warned in 1928 that Mexicans had destroyed healthy, vibrant white communities throughout the Southwest and replaced them with "alien centers" and "little Mexicos" that were "hard to dissolve."[111]

By the mid-1920s it was no longer clear in Texas that African Americans constituted the state's number-one race problem, as they had historically in other states of the South. In the West the threat to whiteness came principally from Asia and Latin America, particularly Mexico, not from Africa or African Americans. After all, many Texas whites had immigrated to Texas in the nineteenth century with their slaves, and, after emancipation, blacks and whites continued to live and work on cotton farms as owners, renters, and sharecroppers. Whites believed that they knew black people; and many blacks could boast of being fourth- and fifth-generation Baptists, like many whites, and of having shared the experience of being displaced by Mexicans on Texas cotton farms. Blacks, whatever else they might be to whites, were not "alien," a word reserved by nativists to describe nonwhite immigrants. And although many Mexicans had lived in the state for generations before the Austin colony was established in 1821, they were still regarded as alien culturally, linguistically, religiously, and racially. Their status as racially in-between, as partly colored, hybrid peoples of mixed Indian, Spanish, and African ancestry, made them suspect in the eyes of Nordicists, who feared that unless the back door of whiteness were closed to Mexicans, they would inevitably mix their blood with that of whites and defile the whiteness of Nordic civilization. Although there were laws against race mixing for whites and blacks, no such laws prevented the mixing of whites and Mexicans.

Despite the hardening of racial divisions heightened by Nordicism that hampered the efforts of whites, blacks, and Mexicans to organize against growers, owners, railroads, and logging interests, all of whom relied on a multiracial workforce, blacks and whites in east Texas joined the IWW-affiliated, biracial BTW and challenged the lumber lords, while Mexicans and whites in central Texas organized against King Cotton's landlords. Before we consider the radical responses to proletarianization in the countryside, we need to examine how white tenant farmers found themselves economically little better off than blacks and Mexicans, whom they feared as competitors and with whom they sometimes sought to form political alliances. In the next chapter we will explore the conflict between landlords and tenants in central Texas and the emerging notion that poor whites—the scourge of whiteness—were destined, like Mexicans and African Americans, to remain on the bottom rungs of the racial and economic hierarchy.

CHAPTER 3

The Whiteness of Cotton

Race, Labor Relations,
and the Tenant Question, 1900–1920

Around the turn of the twentieth century it was becoming clear to many tenant farmers that the achievement of farm ownership was becoming more difficult because of the sharp rise in land values, the high cost of credit, and the low price of cotton. Tenants in central Texas and elsewhere in the South fondly recalled the good old days before 1900, when, with a little hard work and thrift, a tenant could expect to own his own farm. In those days land was abundant and cheap, and, so the story went, tenants shared the same social and sometimes economic status as owners, frequently marrying into owner families. The owners' sons grew up doing farmwork, hired out as day laborers to neighboring farms, and then undertook to rent their own farms. Farm owners did not regard the labor they hired as belonging to a different class; often the laborer was a relative or the son of a neighbor. The owner and his family worked alongside the laborer, they ate at the same table, and, after a hard day's work, they all went to sleep under the same roof. Hired hands on family farms, the historian Cletus Daniel wrote, "were not a class apart, but were members in good standing of an undifferentiated rural class for whom arduous agricultural labor was a transcending fact of life."[1] After gaining farm experience, many of these laborers eventually rented their own farms and, depending on their farming skill, a few good crop years, and a strong market for cotton, were able to move up the agricultural ladder to full ownership.[2]

In 1890, however, the superintendent of the census made the famous pronouncement that the country's "unsettled area has been so broken into by isolated bodies of settlement that there can hardly be said to be a frontier line" left in the American West.[3] For many, the closing of the American frontier meant that American expansion into new land had been completed and that opportunities for many farmers to become proprietors of their own land for the cost of establishing a claim were dwindling fast. The West was no longer the secure harbor of free land or the safety valve for urban industrial unrest that pundits could invoke as a remedy for social problems in the East. The only place for farmers in the South and Southwest to go was down. Census data indicated a rapid rise in the percentage of tenancy throughout the South between 1900 and 1930, and in Texas the tenancy rate exceeded 60 percent in 1930 (see Tables 6 and 7). Agricultural economists began to question the conventional model of upward mobility on the agricultural ladder and gradually began to suggest that the problem lay with the ignorance and inefficiency of the tenant farmers themselves rather than with extortionate credit merchants, bankers, landlords, boll-weevil infestation, soil depletion, low cotton prices, floods, and droughts.[4] In central Texas the "white man's problem" thus began as a recognition of the fact that the majority of the tenants were whites but gradually came to mean that poor whites were destined to remain tenants, scarcely superior to black and Mexican sharecroppers and tenants (see Table 8).

As white tenancy increased in Texas and throughout the South, a class of poor whites permanently associated with the culture of cotton became the scourge of whiteness about which E. E. Davis was so concerned. Respected agricultural economists like William Spillman began

Table 6 *Percentages of Tenancy in Texas and the South, 1880–1940*

	Texas	The South
1880	37.6	36.2
1890	41.9	38.5
1900	49.7	47.0
1910	52.6	49.6
1920	53.3	49.6
1930	60.9	55.5
1940	48.9	48.2

SOURCES: U.S. Bureau of the Census, *Fifteenth Census of the United States, 1930: Agriculture*, part 2 (Washington, D.C.: Government Printing Office, 1932), 1360–61; idem, *Twelfth Census of the United States, 1900: Agriculture*, part 1 (Washington, D.C.: Government Printing Office, 1902), 5: 124–31; and idem, *Census of Agriculture: 1954* (Washington, D.C.: Government Printing Office, 1956), 2: 1040–49.

Table 7 *Texas Farm Owners, Tenants, and Croppers, by Race, 1900–1940**

	Total Owners	White Owners	Percentage of Owners Who Were White	Black Owners	Percentage of Owners Who Were Black
1900	174,639	154,500	89	20,139	12
1910	195,863	174,631	89	21,232	11
1920	201,210	177,671	88	23,539	12
1930	190,515	169,879	89	20,636	11
1940	210,182	190,067	90	20,115	10

	Total Tenants	White Tenants	Percentage of Tenants Who Were White	Black Tenants	Percentage of Tenants Who Were Black
1900	174,991	129,685	74	45,306	26
1910	219,575	170,970	78	48,605	22
1920	232,309	177,198	76	55,111	24
1930	301,720	236,321	78	65,399	22
1940	204,462	171,852	84	32,610	16

Table 7 (continued)

	Total Croppers	White Croppers	Percentage of Croppers Who Were White	Black Croppers	Percentage of Croppers Who Were Black
1900					
1910					
1920	68,381	40,382	59	27,999	41
1930	105,122	68,874	66	36,248	35
1940	39,821	24,949	63	14,872	37

SOURCES: U.S. Bureau of the Census, *Fourteenth Census of the United States, 1920: Agriculture*, part 2 (Washington, D.C.: Government Printing Office, 1922), 6: 4; idem, *Fifteenth Census of the United States, 1930: Agriculture*, part 2 (Washington, D.C.: Government Printing Office, 1932), 1362, 1384; and idem, *Sixteenth Census of the United States, 1940: Agriculture* (Washington, D.C.: Government Printing Office, 1943), 3: 188.

* Mexicans were counted as whites; Negroes, Indians, Chinese, and Japanese, as nonwhite. The numbers of nonwhites other than blacks were so small that I have chosen to substitute "Blacks" for "Nonwhites."

Also, the census classified all sharecroppers as "tenants" until 1920.

Table 8 *White and Black Tenant Farms in the Blackland Prairie and in the State of Texas, 1900–1940* *

	Blackland Prairie		
	All Farms	Percentage of Farms Operated by White Tenants	Percentage of Farms Operated by Black Tenants
1900	103,682	51.2	9.1
1910	106,488	51.8	10.2
1920	106,943	51.7	13.0
1930	111,119	56.7	14.6
1940	80,067	51.3	6.3
	Texas		
	All Farms	Percentage of Farms Operated by White Tenants	Percentage of Farms Operated by Black Tenants
1900	352,190	36.8	12.9
1910	417,770	40.9	11.6
1920	436,033	40.6	12.6
1930	495,489	47.7	13.2
1940	418,002	41.1	7.8

SOURCES: U.S. Bureau of the Census, *Twelfth Census of the United States, 1900: Agriculture*, part 1 (Washington, D.C.: Government Printing Office, 1902), 5: 124–31; idem, *Thirteenth Census of the United States, 1910: Agriculture* (Washington, D.C.: Government Printing Office, 1913), 7: 632–77; idem, *Fourteenth Census of the United States, 1920: Agriculture*, part 2 (Washington, D.C.: Government Printing Office, 1922), 6: 12–34; and idem, *Fifteenth Census of the United States, 1930: Agriculture*, part 2 (Washington, D.C.: Government Printing Office, 1932), 2: 1360, 1362–1401.

* All Mexican- and U.S.-born people of Mexican descent were included as whites. All farms whose tenants paid a share of the crop as rent or received a portion of the crop as wages (sharecroppers) were included. The Blackland Prairie counties are: Bell, Bexar, Caldwell, Collin, Comal, Dallas, Delta, Ellis, Falls, Fannin, Freestone, Grayson, Hays, Hill, Hunt, Kaufman, Lamar, Limestone, McLennan, Milam, Navarro, Rockwall, Travis, and Williamson.

to speak of the difference between "high-minded, self-respecting small proprietors" and the "discontented, thriftless, tenant class" who sank ever deeper into "poverty and unfitness for American citizenship."[5] Other analysts maintained, however, that the system of tenancy itself, for all the problems associated with it, represented "one of the normal stages on the way toward ownership."[6] To acknowledge too forcefully the systemic deficiencies in land-tenure arrangements and financial practices of banks and credit merchants, landlords feared, might stir up the radical Socialists in the region and would be tantamount to "hanging Thomas Jefferson in effigy."[7]

White tenants understandably resisted the idea that they were to blame for not being able to own their own farms. White tenancy was growing at the "bottom rung" of sharecropping rather than at the higher level of share tenants, suggesting that some share tenants were slipping into sharecropping and not simply that farm laborers were ascending into sharecropper status. Owners increasingly preferred sharecroppers because they could often, but not always, realize a higher profit from their land by hiring sharecroppers to grow cotton rather than by renting to share tenants. The increased value of the land, the absence of new land for cultivation, and the growing population of central Texas all combined to swell the ranks of tenancy, especially sharecropping. It became increasingly difficult for agricultural economists to continue to argue that sharecropping represented a rung on the ladder to ownership rather than a position to which many had fallen when they failed in the higher tenure stages.[8] One white tenant expressed his sense of disillusionment this way: "All I expect out of life is a living, and it is my opinion that 75 percent of us just get by."[9] The signs were unmistakable that the ladder no longer functioned as it was intended—if, indeed, it was functioning at all.

To complicate matters, the practice of subrenting often concealed the extent to which sharecropping was increasing in central Texas and masked the ethnic and racial composition of the sharecropping class. Share tenants, themselves renters, sometimes subrented or sublet their farms to sharecroppers. Although tenants who subrented realized fewer bales of cotton as profit, they did not actually have to farm the land, could exercise their authority as supervisors, and often spent most of their time in town. A survey of Travis County farms revealed how white tenants sometimes became absentee tenants, leaving the farms to be operated by Mexican or black sharecroppers. One investigator reported the case of "Mr. F.," who rented about 120 acres from a landowner living in

Austin and then subrented part of the farm to a black sharecropper "on halves." In another case, the owner of a large farm worked part of it himself and rented the rest to his sons on "the third and fourth," who in turn subrented to Mexican croppers.[10] The absentee tenant, according to the investigator, "stands around town, talks to his boss and others about his negroes or his mules and he feels himself very important."[11] Subrenting thus enabled share tenants to become overseers on their landlords' farms. Subrenting was also overlooked by census enumerators, whose task was to count the number of farms. Where the census saw one tenant-operated farm, the investigator saw two: one operated by a white tenant and the other often by a black or Mexican sharecropper. Subrenting thus concealed from census enumerators the actual extent of black and Mexican sharecropping on central Texas farms.

Increasingly the rhetoric of landlords suggested that white tenants were inherently flawed and lacked certain qualities of whiteness. One contemporary wrote: "We must take the tenant by the neck, if necessary, and force into him a little knowledge of real farming . . . and pump into him a sense of pride in appearance and achievement."[12] A planter who had begun to use Mexican and black wage laborers explained, "White tenants are . . . ignorant and lazy and seem to do as little work as possible to get along. . . . None of them ever accumulates anything. They move frequently and are generally very unreliable, rebellious, resentful, suspicious and unthrifty."[13]

Landlords frequently criticized tenant farmers for moving from farm to farm each year and attributed their poor standard of living to this "tendency to roam." Because migrancy was associated with Mexican agricultural workers in the state, it followed that roaming whites were hardly better—or better off—than Mexicans. Moreover, most tenants made few improvements on the land or property because the benefits, they rightly noted, accrued primarily to the landlords. Landlords, for their part, were reluctant to make improvements—fences, drainage, fertilization—because the cost reduced their profits, and they felt that peripatetic tenants would not take an interest in maintaining the property and soil. "One year a white man comes," wrote George S. Wehrwein, "the next year it may be a negro or Mexican."[14]

"Movin' time" for most tenants and their families, however, was not simply an aimless, annual rite but, rather, a quest for a farmhouse that was more than a shack, farmland whose soil was not already depleted, and a landlord who offered fair terms and could be trusted to keep accurate accounts of supplies obtained on credit. Rarely did they succeed in their quest. The Commission on Industrial Relations investigator Charles Holman described the "true psychology of the problem" in these words:

> We must picture a tenant living on his little strip of rented land, with no garden, rarely a cow, more rarely any hogs. . . . We must conceive of the house as ill-constructed, run-down, unscreened and more or less unsanitary. We must remember the meager income of the farm. . . . Perhaps a letter has come telling of unusual crops in another community. Perhaps a tenant has made a failure of his own crop. It is not surprising, therefore, that, at the end of the year, and sometimes even before, he should take stock of his situation in the world and counsel with his wife over the situation, only to come to the final decision, which he has probably made each time at the ends of 20 previous years, "Mary, I reckon we'll move."[15]

Each year thousands of tenants thus took to the road, some of whom unwittingly exchanged farms with one another, each in the hope of doing better than on the last. Few sharecropper families owned more than they could haul in the back of their wagon, which made moving an easy and attractive option to remaining another year in a dilapidated farmhouse. Moving was even less complicated for small families and single men. "Ain't no trouble for me to move," a white cropper claimed, "I ain't got nothing much but er soap gourd and er string er red peppers. All I got to do is ter call up Tige, spit in the fire place, and start down the road."[16] Sometimes, however, tenants fell into a pattern of moving each year without necessarily taking stock of their "situation in the world" or the counsel of their wives. One tenant's wife, asked why her family had left Texas, replied: "God only knows . . . 'cept my man is in a movin' mood."[17] Booker T. Washington told the story of how one family's chickens "regularly presented themselves in the dooryard at Christmastime with their legs crossed for tying up" in anticipation of the annual move to the next farm.[18] In 1920 nearly 150,000 families, or roughly 650,000 persons, representing about one-third of all farm families in the state, hit the road at the end of their lease to seek what had always eluded them, a higher standard of living.[19]

The annual ritual of playing musical chairs with tenant farms in Texas led to a variety of social and economic problems, according to a study of Travis County, for a state "interested as it should be in having a home-owning and home-loving citizenship." To remedy the situation, the author of the study, George Wehrwein, recommended that legislation be enacted to regulate contracts between landlords and tenants and that tenants be reimbursed for improvements made on farms. He made these recommendations in spite of his reservation that it might not be "wise to want 'permanency' as long as there are two non-white races in the midst of the white farmers."[20] For Wehrwein and his colleague Leonard Watkins, the presence of Mexican and black sharecroppers and tenant farmers was a "necessary element at present . . . on account of their cheapness," but these groups were socially undesirable as permanent residents in communities that were already racially divided. He singled out Mexican laborers as particularly undesirable because, in his view, they were "addicted to drink and observation goes to show that they are worse than the negro in this respect."[21]

Whites did not question the fundamental premise that Mexican and African American tenant farmers were less efficient than were whites. However, the investigator E. D. Penn showed in the same Travis County study that Anglo tenants were no more efficient producers of cotton than were either Mexican or black tenants. Penn pointed out that the average product of the Anglo tenant was 0.39 bale of cotton to the acre, compared with 0.38 bale for black and Mexican tenants, a difference of one-hundredth of a 500-pound bale of cotton, or five pounds of cotton per acre, a statistically insignificant difference. Penn used these data to refute the argument of bankers that they charged higher interest rates to Mexicans and African American tenants because, as inefficient farmers, these groups represented a greater financial risk than did white tenants.[22]

Had Penn consulted the U.S. Census of Agriculture for 1900, he would have discovered that black share tenants were actually *more* efficient cotton farmers than were white tenants *and* white owners. Based on averages from ten southern states, the census found that southern black tenants averaged 0.40 bale, whereas white tenants averaged 0.38 bale and white owners 0.39 bale of cotton per acre. Of course, the census was loathe to draw the conclusion that blacks, as a race, were more efficient farmers than were whites. The census therefore reasoned that because white owners were the most prosperous (not necessarily the most efficient) farmers and because the "negro share tenant . . . is more easily influenced, and cultivates his crop more nearly as directed by the owner than does the white tenant," the black tenant farmer "becomes more efficient than the white tenant who relies upon his own judgment." Black tenants were more efficient farmers, the census thus appeared to argue, because they were racially inferior.[23]

Despite evidence to the contrary, bankers continued to insist that tenants, particularly black and Mexican tenants, were not efficient farmers and therefore represented credit risks. Defending this policy, the president of the Texas Bankers' Association, Mr. Pondron, claimed that tenants were the "creators of their own bondage," from which they made no effort to escape. Defending tenant farmers against usurious lenders like Pondron, Texas Socialist leader Thomas Hickey put the practice of bankers and credit lenders in a different perspective, invoking the biblical account of Jesus banishing the moneylenders from the temple: "If Jesus were in Waco [central Texas] when the money-changers of Texas insulted the wealth-producers of the state and at the same time trampled upon the innocent women and children who are held in bondage by such as he [Pondron] . . . Christ would have taken a black-snake whip, laid it on their fat hides and driven the scum into the Brazos [river]."[24] Another Socialist, addressing Texas tenants, wrote: "My renter friend, you are poor and homeless, not because you are lazy and extravagant but because you have been and are being robbed by what our present society calls 'good managers.' They are robbing you with interest, rent and profit."[25]

While bankers and landlords continued to believe that inefficiency and thriftlessness were racial characteristics of mostly nonwhite groups, it became useful for landlords to regard white tenants as sharing some of those traits as an explanation for their permanent status as tenants. Thus, although Penn demonstrated that whites were no more efficient than were black or Mexican tenant farmers, the editor of the survey, the economist Lewis H. Haney, rejected the conclusion that tenants as a class were efficient farmers. The difficulty, it seemed, was that Penn did not emphasize strongly enough the "always shifting, often shiftless, sometimes unruly" nature of the average tenant. Throughout the 149-page study, which included eleven contributors (mostly economists and rural sociologists), Haney refrained from all but the most innocuous editorial interventions. In Penn's section on the relationship between race, bank credit, and efficiency, however, he disagreed with Penn's conclusions, despite their statistical soundness, and interposed his view that tenant farmers

have no business to borrow at all. The great evil in the situation is that men who are not fitted to be running farms, and who as a matter of fact are a sort of laborer, are made to go through the motions of running farms. It would be much better if the untrustworthy and incompetent "tenants" were encouraged to become farm laborers and paid cash wages at relatively short intervals to cover their living expenses.[26]

Although Penn demonstrated that one of the principal causes of poverty among nonwhite tenants was the high cost of credit the bankers charged them, Haney insisted that chronic indebtedness could be traced to basic deficiencies in tenants as a class, especially among Mexican and African American tenants. Haney had written elsewhere that the movement from tenancy to wage labor should not be cause for alarm because "tenancy is not desirable to the hopelessly inefficient," and in testimony before the Commission on Industrial Relations he singled out "negroes and Mexicans" as the "most thriftless sort of tenants."[27] Haney simply could not acknowledge that tenants, particularly black or Mexican tenants, could be efficient farmers, even after Penn empirically demonstrated that high interest rates were the price black tenant farmers were forced to pay for their efficiency.

For many landowners, the concept of upward mobility applied only to those who were preordained, like the religious elect, to become owners on the basis of superior character and sound business principles. That blacks and Mexicans lacked superior character was rarely questioned and served to justify high tenancy rates for these groups; increasingly, however, owners blamed white tenants for their own inability to achieve ownership, strongly implying that they were inferior whites. In the view of many owners, the growing class of permanent tenant farmers simply reinforced their conviction that laborers and many tenants, particularly sharecroppers, were not fit to become owners. The tenants themselves, however, told a different story. For some, the prospect of becoming an owner of a Blackland Prairie farm was sheer fantasy; for others, the hardships they would have to endure in order to become owners were not worth the advantages ownership was supposed to bestow.[28] They rejected the insinuation that they were "white trash" incapable of hard work and efficient farming practices.

Judge Brooks, a large landowner near Dallas, told the Commission on Industrial Relations that "90 per cent of the people don't want anything above today. They seem to proceed upon the peculiar economic conception that 'sufficient to the day is the evil thereof.'" For Brooks, "Every fool that follows the plow is not a farmer. He is just an agricultural clerk." If a tenant could not rise above tenancy, it was for lack of "business capacity" and a "boundless sense of frugality." Brooks gave as an example one of the seventy-five tenants who rented more than 5,000 acres of his land. He rented a farm to Henry "on the halves," the only way he rented. Henry had his own teams but agreed to farm on halves anyway because he needed a place. Brooks tried on two occasions to buy Henry's mules, but Henry refused. Later Henry sold his mules and a horse to someone else and with the profits from his sale purchased an automobile.

One day Brooks and his son were in their buggy trotting down the road when they heard an automobile behind them. Brooks said to his son, "Drive to the outside and let the gentleman have the smooth road." When Brooks saw that the driver was Henry, he became indignant. Henry's owning an automobile, Brooks testified, "epitomizes . . . the lack of frugality of those people." Henry asked to rent the farm for another year and announced his plan to build a garage on the place, but Brooks told him: "I don't rent land to people who own garages, because a fellow that owns a garage ain't got industry enough to burn." Henry was, by Brooks's own testimony, a successful tenant farmer. That Henry and his wife preferred an automobile and clothes to landownership apparently rankled Brooks more than did Henry's "lack of frugality." But the ultimate affront to Brooks's dignity was Henry's dressing like a landowner and driving a new automobile. Some tenant farmers, he complained to the chairman of the commission, "wear Stetson hats and fine shoes and just as good clothes as you and I."[29]

Judge Brooks believed that Henry's possession of an automobile indicated his prodigality, but if Henry had been a landowner, Brooks would have admired him for the economic success that ownership of an automobile symbolized. The possession of an automobile, however, transcended notions of frugality and prodigality, for "only in automobiles on public roads," noted Arthur Raper, "do landlords and tenants and white people and Negroes of the Black Belt meet on a basis of equality."[30] In this case, however, Judge Brooks had yielded the smooth road to his own tenant farmer, the "gentleman" automobile-owner Henry.

Even a successful tenant farmer like Henry most likely could not afford to purchase his Blackland farm, and even if he could, it would certainly mean that he would have to forego the automobile and fine clothing. Brooks, however, had claimed that he could go anywhere in the state without money and, "with his face blackened," buy a farm within ten years. He would accomplish by sheer hard work and determination what more than 60 percent of tenants with "white faces" had failed to do because of the low cost of cotton and the high price of Blackland Prairie land. The Socialist Tom Hickey countered "Babbling Brooks's" boast by reminding him that he had secured his large farm "not by sweat or toil and labor" but by the "magnificent fecundity" of his "paternal ancestor."[31] State Senator George B. Terrell also took issue with Judge Brooks's notion that anyone could own a farm:

He seems to think that because he bought land and paid for it when it was cheap, that he can do it again. I have bought my home and paid for it, but the land has advanced in price and I could not pay for it in fifty years by my own labor on the farm, and I am willing to wager that Judge Brooks can not pay for one hundred acres of his black land in Kaufman county in one hundred years by his own labor on his farm . . . yet these men who have no homes have nothing to pay with except their own labor. Judge Brooks has slandered the honest hard working tenants of this State.[32]

Most tenant farmers were not as prosperous as Judge Brooks's automobile-owning, Stetson-wearing tenant farmer Henry. More typical of the condition of many white tenants in central Texas was the case of Levi Thomas Steward and his wife, Beulah Hooks Steward. For eighteen years Steward moved from farm to farm in an attempt to support his family and improve their material condition. Steward started out a tenant farmer in Arkansas, bought a forty-acre farm from the railroad, but lost it after one year when he was short $40.00 to pay off his debts. In 1903 he moved to the Blackland Prairie region of central Texas and began to farm fifty acres on the halves. The landlord permitted him only five or six acres for the cultivation of corn, though Steward said he would have preferred to grow half corn and half cotton so he could raise hogs to feed his growing family of five children. Steward obtained supplies on credit from a merchant who held a mortgage for Steward's half of the crop. He stayed one year, then moved to another farm in Lamar County because, he said, "I thought I could better my position." He broke even. Next he moved to Joe Sisson's farm for two years. There he grew eleven bales of cotton and 500 bushels of corn, but came out $200 in debt as a result of medical bills and a bank note for supplies. The family moved to Donnegan's farm and made $200 at the end of the year, but they left because "the house was not very good; and it was down among the niggers, and no school nor nothing, and no convenience, and he would not fix anything." Steward then went to Drummond's farm for two years, where he worked seventy-five acres of cotton and twenty-five acres of corn—and broke even. On Kimball's 125-acre farm, he bought Kimball's team and tools for $750 and rented on thirds and fourths. He paid for the mules and broke even.[33]

Steward moved two more times over the next four years and finished off $700 in debt, which he secured with a lien on his workstock and implements. In eighteen years of farming, Steward and his family lived in no fewer than twenty houses, produced at least 450 bales of cotton and thousands of bushels of corn, and were homeowners for a brief period, but at the time of the hearings he was still looking for a place to rent for his wife and eight children and was $700 in debt. When asked whether his constant moving might have caused his "lack of success," Steward responded, "I never did have any roving spirit. I was always wanting to do the best I can." When sharecroppers made any money, he further testified, they had to move because if the landowners were not able to "get it all, they want you to go farther."[34] But the main reason Steward said he was dissatisfied was that he had little to say about what he planted. On each farm Steward's landlord required him to plant more cotton than Steward wanted, forcing him to purchase—on credit—what he was not able to grow; he also had to purchase his meat because he was not allowed sufficient acreage for corn and pasture to support livestock. Commission investigator Holman correctly noted in his field study that "from the individualistic point of view, the landlord has a right to insist upon his land being planted to any crop, but from the social point of view, this amounts in the end to an indirect form of eviction."[35]

Although planting cotton to the exclusion of other crops forced tenants to purchase on credit farm products they could have grown themselves, the root cause of their indebtedness was as much social as economic: Owners and merchants kept the books and often calculated whether their tenants would end up in debt or break even. Rarely did the books record a profit for sharecroppers. Steward claimed to break even for most years, but since he did not keep his own books, he had no way of knowing whether merchants charged him whatever his earnings would bear. One year he made $1,700 and owed money to two merchants. Mr. White claimed he was owed $600, leaving Steward a balance of $1,100. The other merchant, the son-in-law of Steward's landlord, claimed that Steward owed him exactly $1,100, which, of course, meant that Steward did indeed break even. The chairman, implying that the second merchant may have made his calculations based on his knowledge of Steward's remaining balance of $1,100, asked Steward whether he ever kept track of his accounts; Steward replied, "No; I never kept no track of it; I just thought it was all right, you know."[36] It is not likely that Steward wished to imply that he trusted merchants to keep accurate records or to pay him any profits that were his due after his debt was paid. For many sharecroppers, breaking even was "all right"—perhaps even like coming out ahead—when the usual alternative was carrying over debt into the next year, for debt, as one contemporary wrote, was a "dark place" in the life of a tenant farmer and his family.[37]

Of the sharecroppers who did keep records, few would have dared to dispute the word of the owner or the merchant, especially if the sharecropper was black and the owner was white. Sometimes it was the sharecropper's wife who attempted to settle with the landlord. The wives of black sharecroppers frequently handled the finances for their husbands because they often had more years of schooling than did their husbands. More important, however, it was safer for a black woman to confront a white owner, according to the historian Robin D. G. Kelley, because sometimes the landlord's wife would negotiate in his place. In this way, if a black male attempted to settle with the owner's wife and a dispute arose over the final agreement, the landlord could accuse him of "insulting a white woman." Thus "the presence of the sharecropper's wife or eldest daughter in his place," Kelley observes, "mitigated the landlord's desire to construe the dialogue as a violation of white womanhood."[38]

Beulah Steward's testimony of her unending hard work as a sharecropper's wife and their family's wretched living conditions had a powerful effect on the members of the commission. Commission investigator Holman described Mrs. Steward as a "shrinking little woman with faded eyes and a broken body." When it came time for J. Borden Harriman, the only female member of the commission, to question Mrs. Steward, a "look of relief passed over the little woman's face," Holman later recounted, "for already these two had become acquainted and had discussed matters that proved the universal sisterhood."[39] Mrs. Steward had worked in the cotton fields as a child, married when she was fifteen, had eleven children (three of whom died), made all of her own clothes and those of her family, sewed for "outsiders" in the evening to earn extra money, and sometimes went years without going to town. She made breakfast each morning at 4 o'clock and returned from the fields at 11 o'clock to prepare dinner. She went back into the fields until it was time to prepare supper, and then spent the evenings doing household chores and sewing. When Mrs. Harriman naively asked her if she had any help with the sewing, cooking, and other household chores, Mrs. Steward replied, "There ain't no one else to do it." Already worn from her heavy workload, Mrs. Steward continued to work in the fields until the sixth month of her pregnancies. She suffered from a skin disease and finally collapsed in a nervous breakdown from "overwork . . . and the strain." Asked whether she worried about the future, Mrs. Steward said: "I was told to not take any more in the head than I could kick out at the heels."[40]

Mrs. Harriman wrote later that, as she listened to Mrs. Steward's life of backbreaking toil, "my own back seemed to ache. . . . The misery of the tenant farmers made me feel that the social scheme of things had gone wrong at the root." She was so depressed by what she had heard at the Dallas hearing that "all the delightful company there seemed curiously unsatisfying when one knew of the land problem that was the skeleton-in-the-Texas-closet."[41] Mrs. Steward's testimony of punishing work on the farm may have spoiled the delights of Dallas's high society for Mrs. Harriman, but it drew an angry response from anti-landlord newspaper editor Tom Hickey, who wrote:

After reading her pitiable testimony of having only two hats in thirty years of married life, after raising a family of eight children, and after toiling into the night to make her own clothes and those of her children, to then have the charge of "shiftlessness" and "extravagance" thrown at them as it is customary with . . . scurvy grafting politicians and degenerate landlords, [it] stamps these gentlemen . . . as beings who have the morals of a crocodile, the heart of a hyena and the conscience of a Pontius Pilate.[42]

As for Mr. Steward, Hickey wrote simply that "It took 25 years of continuous exploitation to produce this hopeless man of the hoe."[43]

From the eugenicist perspective, the problem with the Steward family was that birth control was practiced least where it was needed most— among the poor whites and other "inferior stocks" who reproduced more prolifically than did Nordic whites. Charles B. Austin, head of the Division of Public Welfare at the University of Texas, who shared some of the assumptions of eugenicists, blamed the Steward family's physicians "who came year after year when the children came into that family . . . [and] did not get the father to one side and explain to him a fundamental principle in life." The problem with Levi and Beulah Steward, in other words, was that they had too many mouths to feed.[44] Eugenics without birth control, some whites believed, was powerless to solve the problem of poverty among indecently reproductive poor whites.

The publicity surrounding the hearings of the Commission on Industrial Relations brought the case of Levi and Beulah Steward and southern tenant-farmer families before the nation almost twenty-five years before John Steinbeck immortalized the Joad family during the Great Depression in *The Grapes of Wrath*. The printed testimony included numerous letters from tenants entered as evidence of their growing impoverishment as a class and, in some cases, their disillusionment with traditional political parties to solve their problems. A self-described "mother tenant" wrote that her tenant-farmer father had died when she was young, leaving her to work in the fields to help support the family. As a result, she had attended school for only three months. Married for twenty-three years to an "honest, hard-working" man and the mother of six children, she and her family had worked hard all their lives and did not have decent clothes to show for it: "At the present time we are in debt about $400. There are a few Socialists here and I wish that the whole State was Socialist."[45] Lewis Jones, a black tenant farmer from Smith County, wrote to the editor of *The Rebel*: "We are just alive, and that is all. . . . We make a very good crop every year, but do not get anything like a living out of it. We never get out of debt, no matter how we toil."[46] A tenant from Victoria County, northeast of Corpus Christi, worried because bankers and landlords were "pressing the tenants" and because some landlords planned to "let their lands lay out or hire Mexicans and negroes to cultivate it."[47] In most of the letters the tenants blamed landlords for charging high rent (a third and sometimes half the cotton, plus a "bonus") and merchants for charging too much for credit. Many share tenants lost their workstock and were reduced to sharecroppers or wage laborers. A white tenant farmer summed up his life in these words:

I have rented the most of my life. . . . I always kept up the place as I would my own, without any cost to the landlord. . . . I have lived in shacks that were not as good as the landlord's horse stable. I have dug wells, built houses, cow lots, hogpens, corncribs, horse sheds, grubbed out patches, repaired fences, cut ditches, all without cost to the landlord. . . . Our children grew up without education; and we are yet poor. . . . I will have to spend the rest of my days with broken-down health and pain and aches. . . . Shame, Shame on a system that will allow it.[48]

The material standard of living was lower for black tenants than for whites in Texas, and the historian Jacquelyn Jones has noted that throughout the South it "was considerably lower than that of midcentury western pioneer families."[49]

While most Mexicans kept a low profile in the "white-man's country" of central Texas, a growing number of Mexican sharecroppers and tenants in the region began to voice their discontent over breaches in their contracts, poor housing conditions, unfair credit practices, exploitative recruitment practices, and low wages. One missionary lamented that Mexicans were "always fooled with unkept promises" and, after months or years of working faithfully for some farmers, were told to leave "like an old horse no longer useful."[50] E. O. Meitzen, a prominent Texas Socialist and former member of the Farmers' Alliance and Populist Party, solicited letters from discontented Texas tenant farmers in preparation for his testimony before the Commission on Industrial Relations in 1915. He received a number of letters from Mexican sharecroppers in central Texas, all of whom expressed dissatisfaction with conditions on the farms. Mr. Campos, renting on thirds and fourths, complained that his kitchen "has no ceiling. There is one wooden window. The roof is not much good. . . . I have three sons and have to sleep in the crib, which has no battings. The water has to be gotten from the river, which is about 300 yards away." Mr. Medrano, a sharecropper, wrote: "I get $6 [in store credit] a month and we are starving on that. The horses are not good. I rent on halves. I get a piece of land for garden, but have to give half [of the garden's produce to the owner]." The sharecropper Manuel Longoria wrote that the "tools furnished by the landlord are not fit to work. I asked for credit to buy some clothing for my wife and children and he denied it, unless I would give a mortgage on my horse." In this way if Longoria could not pay back the debt on clothing from the proceeds of the cotton, the landowner could seize the horse. Without a horse, the Longorias would have to purchase one—on credit—from the new owner of the horse. Another Mexican tenant, Mr. Hernández, a DeWitt County tenant for fifteen years, complained: "The landlord would not let me have land for garden. He never has built a crib or . . . let me plant feed for my teams. . . . He does not want to fix the house for me. If a child walks across the floor the whole house shakes; the wind comes through the cracks. When it rains everything gets wet."[51]

The grievances of these Mexican sharecroppers and tenant farmers differed little from those written by Anglo renters. What is revealing is that by 1915 numerous Mexican renters, most likely Texas-born Mexicans, had been renters over a long period of time and resolved to write publicly—and in English—to a Socialist newspaper about the deteriorating conditions on the farms.

As some of these letters reveal, practically every cotton farmer, whether owner, tenant, or sharecropper—black, Mexican, or white—relied on credit for supplies needed to support the family until the cotton could be harvested and sold. The tenant's creditor was either his landlord, a bank, or the credit merchant, whose business it was to finance cotton farmers through the period of production. Interest rates for credit almost always exceeded the legal limit (10 percent a year), and goods purchased "on time" (vernacular for credit) always sold for a higher price than did goods paid for with cash.[52] The vast majority of farmers who borrowed year after year—"perennials," as bankers sometimes called them—did not borrow to invest but, as one analyst correctly noted, "to get a sort of circulating capital." In other words, "he borrows his wages and pays interest on them."[53]

At the heart of the credit system in Texas, as elsewhere in the cotton South, was the system of crop liens. Under the lien laws the landowner had a prior lien on the tenant's crop as payment for rent and any advances he had given. Laws enacted in the nineteenth century made the landlord's lien for both rent and advances superior to all other liens, except where tax liabilities were concerned. The landlord's prior lien increased the risk for other lenders, such as merchants or bankers, because the tenant might not have anything left over after paying the rent and repaying the landlord's advances. The chattel mortgage, though inferior to the crop lien, provided additional security for merchants and bankers; if the tenant could not repay the loan from the merchant or banker with proceeds from the crop, the lenders could seize his property, assuming, of course, that the landlord did not already have a chattel mortgage himself that he had obtained before the other lenders, in which case the landlord could seize the tenant's property to settle debts.[54]

Debt was no abstraction to the renter's family: It meant not only the loss, in some cases, of property but also, for example, little or no schooling for children who barely had clothes enough to wear and food to eat. A tenant from El Campo wrote that he had seen a family of six children picking cotton on a cold and muddy December morning: "Little girls not seven years old were standing in mud so deep that I could not see their shoes. When I got to town their landlord had on a $25 overcoat and was complaining about how cold it was."[55] A fifty-five-year-old renter and former wage worker from Van Zandt County expressed the sentiments of many Texas tenants who despaired of ever escaping the annual cycle of indebtedness when he told a contemporary investigator that "socialism is the only relief for farmers."[56]

As cash stores and banks cut into the credit merchant's share of business, there was also a widespread tendency to deny credit to a large class of farmers who possessed only a limited amount of livestock and farm implements and to those who had been unsuccessful as farmers, which usually was a reference to sharecroppers who failed to break even from year to year and thus were not able to pay their debts. These tenants, in all likelihood sharecroppers, were reduced to wage laborers once their credit had been cut off. One banker and owner of several farms operated by share tenants on thirds and fourths decided not to rent to sharecroppers over the age of forty "because if he has reached that age without getting ahead he has missed the ball too often for me to send him to bat."[57]

Small landowners often lost their farms if they were unable to pay back credit merchants. A black owner of 100 acres in Smith County reported that he was going to lose his farm because he could not pay his debt "at prices I must pay for supplies." Credit merchants at first told him to plant more corn, but, he added, "within the last few weeks their riders have demanded that we plow up corn and replant with cotton." A black tenant from the same county reported that the only way blacks escaped the power of credit merchants was to "walk out"—and many of them, according to the investigator, did just that and got along in the new place very well until they began to buy on credit again. The investigator also reported that credit merchants often refused to accept cash from a black tenant "in order to keep him in bondage" for the coming year.[58]

Some African American tenants did not walk out voluntarily to escape debt. One landowner made a practice of renting to black tenants, securing their notes for supplies, and then running them off his property just before the crop was gathered. "I ruther leave my crop than get shot," said one African American tenant from Dallas County. This landlord had been renting to African Americans and running them off as a standard practice for several years. The landlord would then seize possession of the crop "by legal means" and harvest it at his own expense. A county official acknowledged in 1911: "What chance has a negro tenant in such a situation? Who would take his word that the white man pulled a gun on him? It would be white man against negro, not landlord against tenant, and Texas juries would throw out the negro's testimony."[59] In another case, a black sharecropper from Lee County, Charlie Black, wrote to Governor Miriam Ferguson that his landlord, Dack Holman, took more cotton and seed than was owed him for debts. When Black protested, Holman "cocked his pistol in my face 5 or 6 times" while others watched. As a black high-school principal observed, for a "Negro to bring suit against a white planter is as hopeless as the government convicting a racketeer for murder."[60]

Banks provided another avenue of credit, but borrowing money from banks had its own risks, for they often seized property to pay for overdue notes. One African American owner in Rains County, described as a large landowner, owed a bank two notes on his farm. He had seventeen bales of cotton ginned and stored but decided not to sell them until the price of cotton had gone up, because at the going price he would not have earned enough to pay off his notes to the bank and still have enough to live on through the winter. When the bank demanded that he pay part of his debt immediately, he loaded seven bales of cotton on two wagons and went to Emory, the county seat, to sell the cotton and send the money to the bank. But the bank had other ideas. In the owner's own words:

When I arrived at the public square at Emory an agent of the bank roughly demanded immediate payment. I went into a store to see about selling my cotton and when I came out the agent of the bank had unhitched the mules from the wagon and in less than half an hour he sold them [the mules] for $225, although I had refused $350 for them and they were easily worth $400. The same day he went out to my farm and seized six head of cattle, including three fine milk cows, a two-year-old heifer and two two-year-old steers. He brought them to Emory and sold them the same day for $125, which was less than half their real value. I borrowed about $40 and paid the balance due on the notes to the bank and turned them over to a lawyer who sued the bank for usurious interest. An agent of the bank came to see me and tried to induce me to withdraw the suit. When I refused he threatened to put me in the penitentiary. As I had violated no law, I refused to talk compromise with him and he later settled with my lawyer for $200. The action of the bank "broke me up." I was left with a large family without a milk cow and have been compelled to go in debt again for living expenses.

The owner sold his remaining ten bales for $12.00 each. Had he been able to hold all seventeen bales for a short time until cotton fetched $12.00 per bale, he maintained, he could have sold them for enough to pay all he owed the bank and to support his family through the winter. Although he was forced to go into debt, he did not lose his farm, which was the case of many farm owners who could not pay their notes.[61] A farm analyst who studied the effect of credit on black tenants in east Texas wrote: "The mills of the credit merchant, like those of the Gods, grind slowly, but exceedingly fine, and so it was that with her citizenry largely held between the nether stones of these mills, east Texas for something more than a quarter of a century might have been said to have progressed backward."[62] Asked if there were any usury laws in Texas to protect tenants from banks that charged exorbitant interest, the director of the Farm Security Administration in Dallas replied: "Yes, sir, but just like our immigration laws and labor laws, when they break them no one pays much attention to them."[63]

Borrowing was not new to Texas farmers, and the debts imposed by the credit system had become a long-standing custom for tenants in Texas and elsewhere in the cotton South. "Many, perhaps most," wrote the Texas economist William Leonard, "have never known the time, either in their own lives, or that of their fathers, when the burden of debt did not press. It is looked upon as a natural kind of encumbrance."[64] That was certainly the case with most sharecroppers in Texas, but white share tenants on thirds and fourths, raised in the belief that they would one day be farm owners, still expected to come out ahead at the end of the year. They did not look upon debts that accumulated year after year, often forcing them into sharecropping arrangements, as a "natural kind of encumbrance." Yet that is what was increasingly taking place between 1900 and 1930, as banks and credit merchants continued to charge high rates for loans to farmers, claiming that risk and competition justified the rates. Tenants who dared to grow their own market-garden products to reduce their dependence on merchants for basic foodstuffs were quickly warned that they were jeopardizing their credit.[65] Under the existing form of credit and marketing arrangements, the tenant farmer could survive, according to one witness before the commission, only as "a peon and a serf."[66] The landlord, who often was the source of credit for sharecroppers, almost always had the upper hand: He owned the stock, the tools, the land, and "sometimes by an unwritten law, the cropper himself."[67] In William Faulkner's short story, "Barn Burning," Ab Snopes, a sharecropper who has agreed to work on Major DeSpain's land, says to his son, "I reckon I'll have a word with the man that aims to begin tomorrow owning me body and soul for the next eight months."[68]

A close correlation existed between race and tenant status in central Texas, with most blacks and Mexicans occupying the ranks of sharecroppers and wage laborers. White sharecroppers were stigmatized in Texas, as elsewhere in the South, as white trash, crackers, and rednecks, but even as marginal whites these sharecroppers came to enjoy, for a brief time, the social, psychological, and economical advantages of being white.[69] White tenants who had slipped into sharecropping were able, for example, to negotiate contracts as "half tenants" or tenants on the halves. If the cropper was black or Mexican, the white owner offered the standard contract: The cropper was hired "to make a crop," for which he was entitled to one-half of the proceeds of the cotton. The crop belonged to the owner, who sold it and paid the cropper any wages that were owed him and his family after settling debts accrued by the landlord or merchant for any supplies furnished on credit.[70] As a cropper his relation to the owner was strictly that of employee to employer; he did not own any part of the crop, and any attempt to sell it would have been considered theft of property.[71]

If the cropper was white, however, the owner made him a "half renter," whereby he was legally entitled to sell the crop and pay the landlord one-half in rent. As a half renter the white "cropper" was in actuality a tenant farmer because he had legal ownership of the crop.[72] Levi Steward, who farmed for most of his life on the halves, was actually a half tenant and not a true sharecropper.[73] The racial division in contract arrangements enabled owners to hire white sharecroppers when it seemed unlikely that black or Mexican sharecroppers could be found. The status of half renter was thus a temporary measure—a concession— to keep whites from abandoning farming, as were increasing numbers of African Americans. As half tenants, whites were entitled to use their share of the crop as a basis for obtaining credit independent of the landlord and, therefore, were guaranteed a minimal but symbolically important degree of autonomy that was not afforded black or Mexican sharecroppers.[74]

As increasing numbers of Mexicans settled in central Texas as sharecroppers, owners no longer felt the need to rent to whites as half tenants. Rather, owners hired them to make a crop as true sharecroppers, no different in status from Mexicans and blacks. Under this contract the sharecropper was not in any legal sense a tenant—he occupied the premises possessing only the right "to ingress and egress on the property"—and he could not sell the crop (because he did not own any part of it).[75] In effect, then, the white farmer on the halves without teams or implements slipped from the status of a half tenant *renting* land for a share of the crop paid to the landowner and became a true sharecropper *working* the land for a share of the crop paid to him as wages by the employer-landowner. The shift from renter to laborer had important implications for the white tenant whose primary identity was that of farmer and not farm worker. As a tenant he was accustomed to a certain degree of autonomy not generally accorded to sharecroppers. As a farm worker he was little different from a black or Mexican sharecropper who did not own his share of the crop and who generally worked under the supervision of the owner. The only difference now turned on race and not economic status.

In the Blackland Prairie counties, where there was no shortage of tenants to rent available farms, landowners began to ask for and frequently receive a rent bonus in addition to renting on the halves instead of thirds and fourths. There were so many tenants who would "undermine other fellows," wrote one tenant, "that it seems they are willing to do most anything in order to get shelter for wife and the babies."[76] The competition for farms meant that white share tenants were often reduced to half tenants even though they generally owned their own teams and tools. As white tenants contemplated their loss of status as independent farmers and thus the basis of their claim to superior whiteness, some tenants in Lamar County resorted to "night riding" to prevent share tenants from renting a place for one-half the crop, which would have forced all share tenants in the area to compete as half tenants. One share tenant who accepted a contract as a half tenant was taken out in the night and whipped.[77] Night riders also sowed a destructive weed called Johnson grass on the farms of offending landlords. Johnson grass had an extensive underground root system which required about three years to eradicate completely before cotton and corn could be safely planted. Federal investigator Holman noted that landlords of Texas feared the private vengeance that had been wreaked by the sowing of this seed in the fields.[78] Violence was also directed at Mexicans and blacks in the towns and the countryside, though rarely under the banner of the Ku Klux Klan, which had its strongest following in the cities, particularly Dallas and Houston. In 1922 a crowd of 300 whites marched through the black and Mexican districts of a town in Stephens County, west of Fort Worth, and drove out Mexicans and blacks by threatening to burn the homes of those who stayed. The group called itself the White Owls and organized for "bettering living conditions of white laborers."[79]

During the transition in status from tenant-renter to sharecropper-laborer, numerous conflicts arose between landowners and tenants over the exact nature of the contract, which was often a vaguely expressed, oral agreement.[80] Whether one was a cropper or a half tenant depended solely on the *intent* of the contracting parties—upon which, in the absence of a specific statement in a written contract, the courts decided. In negotiating an oral contract, for example, only a few words were necessary to establish time of payment, the amount of rent (cash, thirds and fourths, or halves), and sometimes the "furnish," or what the landlord intended to supply in addition to the land. The rest was implied by custom, which varied from region to region. In one case, J. E. Davis brought suit against his landowner, J. F. Tindel, for having seized Davis's cotton crop. Under the terms of the contract, according to Davis, landowner Tindel was to furnish the land, teams, feed, and tools, and Davis "was to make and gather the crop; and each to receive one-half of the crop." Did this contract make Davis a half renter or a sharecropper? The former had legal ownership of the crop; the latter did not.

Davis thought he was leasing the land for which he owed, as rent, half the crop; Tindel argued that he had hired Davis to "make a crop" and that Davis was therefore a sharecropper. The dispute arose when Tindel hired some hands to pick Davis's cotton against Davis's wishes. Davis claimed that he and his sons did not need extra help and were not willing to pay the cost of hiring extra labor and that, furthermore, Tindel had no right to make such a decision. When Davis refused to let the extra hands work, Tindel went before the county judge and obtained a court order forbidding Davis from interfering with his decision to have extra workers pick the cotton.[81] The judge ruled that the landlord, Tindel, did indeed possess the right to seize the crop and to enter the premises of Davis's farm because, according to the judge, Davis was not a true tenant but a laborer hired to make a crop—a sharecropper.[82] The ambiguity of oral contracts almost always favored landlords, for courts generally recognized that working on the halves constituted a sharecropping arrangement, not a tenancy, in which the cropper was simply a wage laborer paid in kind and in which the landowner-employer retained managerial control.[83]

The legal distinction between tenant and cropper created two classes of farmers who were not owners, but with important social and economic differences. Because the agreements were almost always oral, according to one observer, "the parties to these agreements often . . . forget or . . . deny their contractual obligations."[84] A tenant might think he was renting on the halves, as in the case of Davis, and discover later—usually in court—that he was hired to work as a sharecropper. The landowner only had to persuade the judge that he did not lease the land but, rather, hired someone to work it on the halves, and, in the absence of written contracts, the judge usually ruled on the side of the landowner. The distinction was important because ownership of the crop bestowed clear advantages in obtaining credit and meant that the tenant was not subject to supervision by the landowner. Whites had become accustomed to their status as semi-independent tenant farmers, and their reduction to sharecropping implied a loss of whiteness as well as of economic rank. As sharecroppers they had become, in effect, poor whites, who were little better off than were Mexicans and blacks.

Some Mexican sharecroppers who became tenant farmers insisted on selling their own cotton, as did white tenants, and refused to be treated like poor white sharecroppers. In another dispute over the issue of hiring extra labor to pick the cotton, an Anglo landlord wanted to hire pickers on Hernández's farm. Hernández, a Mexican share tenant in Karnes

County, southeast of San Antonio, objected because as a share tenant he was entitled to make decisions about whether or not to hire extra labor to pick *his* cotton. He argued that the landlord, by hiring pickers and charging the cost to him, violated his rights as a tenant and that, furthermore, paying for hired help would leave nothing for him and his family "to live on much less to pay the store bills and doctor and drugs." Hernández won his suit against the landlord because he was clearly a share tenant and not a sharecropper. The white landlord probably rented to Hernández in the first place on the assumption that a Mexican would not challenge a white landowner's authority or insist on his rights as a tenant farmer.[85]

The terms of contracts for renting the land were gradually changing as landlords sought to wrest control of the crop from share tenants and half tenants by renting to sharecroppers. Croppers, according to commission investigator Holman, were "popularly supposed to be tenants of the soil, but they are really not tenants. They represent a peculiar midstage between farm laborer and tenant. Laborers-in-fact, the croppers have not the status of the laborer. Tenants-in-fact, they have none of the rights of the tenant of the soil."[86] The courts in Texas and other southern states interpreted the sharecropper to be a wage laborer, which "legally casts him into the ranks of the casual laborer and the farm hand."[87] White sharecroppers were on their way to becoming full-fledged farm workers who, like Mexicans, migrated from farm to farm to pick cotton or became farmhands on large, corporate cotton ranches.

Although the majority of African Americans in east and central Texas continued to belong to the sharecropper class, as they had since the days of Reconstruction, white share tenants were thus losing ground legally and economically to landowners, credit merchants, and banks. Many were required to pay a bonus on top of the customary rent and to rent on the halves, even though they had their own workstock and tools. Those who did not have teams and tools saw their status as half tenants slip to that of sharecroppers. "This curtailment," wrote Holman in 1915, "is but another of the forces that tend to reduce the tenant from his present legal status of a halfway position between the peasant proprietor and the farmhand."[88]

In the Blackland Prairie of central Texas counties, where the percentage of tenancy was more than 60 percent, the Socialist Party attracted increasing numbers of tenants to its fold between 1900 and 1917, causing many owners to become alarmed at the growing class-consciousness of renters. One contemporary economist, Lewis Haney, observed that "unprogressive" tenants were particularly inclined to become Socialists who hoped to organize the discontent of the tenant "into the means of social revolution."[89] Haney believed, as did many landlords, that many poor white tenant farmers were becoming increasingly rebellious.[90] When white tenants began to organize renters' unions and join the Socialist Party, landlords responded by evicting Socialist tenants in droves and hiring in their places Mexican and black sharecroppers, whom they worked "for starvation wages under peonage conditions."[91] One absentee landowner from Waco complained bitterly that his white tenants had been ruined by Socialism:

White tenants are a worthless, lazy, lying, anarchist lot. I have kicked every one of them off my farm except one and replaced them with negro laborers, whom I can boss and who will do as I tell them. My experience with white tenants was disastrous. They will lie, steal, and cannot be depended on to take care of property entrusted to them. I do not know what is to become of the country so long as this class continues to increase, for they are socialists at heart—every one of them.[92]

A renter from Grandview, the father of nine children, wrote that all of his children were in need of shoes and school books and that he grew thirty bales of cotton, all of which he turned over to the landlord for rent and to the merchant for his store account. He ended his letter: "I am 50 years old and have always stood for peace, but I am now willing to shoulder a gun . . . [to] get justice."[93] A banker and landlord from Hall County warned that a growing number of tenants were imbued with "Socialism and Anarchy" and that a "dangerous state of opinion" existed in the region, especially among young tenants.[94]

The founding of the Socialist Renters' Union in 1911 marked the beginning of organized struggle against the decline in the social and economic fortunes of Mexican, black, and poor white tenant farmers. Significantly, the Commission on Industrial Relations had included the land struggle in the Southwest, particularly Texas and Oklahoma, in its nationwide inquiry into the causes of industrial violence because the struggle between landlord and tenant resembled the more violent industrial struggles in Colorado, Arkansas, and Louisiana.[95] Holman opened the hearings in Dallas with the warning that "the landlord and tenant struggle has reached its most acute state with the most open manifestations of discontent."[96] At the same time, in an attempt to arouse tenant farmers from passive acceptance of their immiseration by landlords, Socialist leader Tom Hickey issued a call to action to all Texas tenants, declaring: "Your clothes are shoddy. Your bacon is rancid. Your coffee is chickory."[97] In 1911 Hickey and the Socialist Party attempted to organize a biracial Renters' Union and Land League in central Texas, while Mexican tenant farmers organized their own locals within the Renters' Union. To Tom Hickey and other white Socialists, peon Mexican tenants best exemplified the manly courage that was supposed to be one of the defining characteristics of whiteness.

CHAPTER 4

Tom Hickey and the Failure of Interracial Unity

The Politics of Race, Class, and Gender in the Socialist Party of Texas, 1911–1917

When the Socialist Party of America was founded in 1901, the People's Party in Texas had largely lost its appeal to farmers, many of whom had drifted into the Progressive wing of the Democratic Party. But in Texas and throughout the South a growing number of tenant farmers found themselves without a party, for Populism, like the Democratic Party in Texas, was the party of small, landowning farmers who organized against monopolistic capitalism in the East.[1] Tenant farmers were rapidly becoming the dominant political constituency in the western South, although the Democratic Party was slow to recognize this fact. Texas Socialists, like E. O. Meitzen and "Red" Tom Hickey, immediately recognized the potential for organizing landless tenants against the tyranny of landlordism and endlessly declaimed that the number-one issue facing tenant farmers was the so-called land question. With more than 100 million idle acres of tillable land held for speculation by absentee landlords, Texas Socialists demanded that occupancy and use should constitute the only legitimate title to the land and that the full rental value of all idle land be taxed in order to force landlords to sell land that was not being tilled. "Land for the Landless—Homes for the Homeless" became the rallying cry for Hickey and the Texas Socialists. All other issues, such as Prohibition and the war in Europe, were denounced as machinations of the plutocracy to distract the working class from the oppression of landlords, bankers, politicians, and other "parasites."[2]

Tenants were growing weary of Democratic politicians who debated the perennial state issues, Baileyism and prohibitionism, to the exclusion of the land question. Baileyism referred to the anti-Progressive politics of Texas Senator Joseph Weldon Bailey, who achieved notoriety in the state for accepting fees from the Standard Oil Company and Kirby lumber interests.[3] In the gubernatorial election of 1914, however, Democratic nominee James E. Ferguson ignored the liquor issue and, calling himself "Farmer Jim," built his campaign around the land question. He promised to introduce legislation prohibiting landlords from charging a bonus in addition to the customary or "natural" rent of one-third the grain and one-fourth the cotton.

Hickey argued that the Ferguson law was "the damndest fake that was ever pulled off on a suffering people," since it did not inhibit "charging extra rent for dwellings, pasturage, barns or other improvements that the landlord may have on the land." Hickey was right to point out that there were numerous ways to charge a bonus and still remain within the law.[4] He also noted that Ferguson abolished tenancy on his own 1,000-acre farm in Bell County by hiring wage laborers: "He pays white men with families $1 per day and gives them a shack free, and has them in continuous competition with Mexicans and negroes and they work from sun to sun."[5] According to Hickey, if Ferguson was elected and his land plank adopted, "it would be a signal to all land owners to quit renting their land and have it worked by hired labor, particularly the vast mass of peon Mexican labor that has come into this state in multiplied thousands as a result of the Mexican revolution."[6]

Despite the enthusiasm generated by large turnouts at Socialist encampments throughout central Texas, which featured speakers Eugene Debs and Kate O'Hare, the Socialist candidate for governor, E. R. Meitzen, whose father, E. O. Meitzen, published the Socialist newspaper *The Rebel*, lost the election. By adopting the land question and promising to make it illegal for landlords to charge tenants a bonus to rent land, Ferguson had stolen the Socialist Party's thunder.[7] A year later "Farmer Jim" identified himself to the Commission on Industrial Relations as a "land-owner, lawyer, banker and governor of Texas." Angered by Ferguson's political duplicity, Hickey responded that the "first renter or small farmer who thinks that a governor so linked to the soft-handed graft of the professions mentioned is their friend should be first divorced from his wife and then starved until there is nothing left of him but a pair of suspenders and a wart."[8]

Despite the electoral victory of the Democrats, Socialism was gaining respectability in the state, largely through the efforts of Tom Hickey, who founded and edited *The Rebel*, the third largest English-language Socialist weekly in the United States.[9] Hickey and other Texas Socialists capitalized on the growing discontent of the Texas tenantry by forming the Renters' Union of America in 1911, which became the Land League in 1914.[10] The union called on all land renters and farm laborers to assemble in Waco in November 1911 to launch a statewide Union of Renters to abolish the bonus system, reduce rents, end the boycott by landlords against renters who had joined the Socialist Party, and give "a larger measure of legal and economic protection . . . to the men, women and children on the rented farms."[11]

Landlords, of course, had witnessed the rise and fall of agrarian organizations before, but this one was "socialistic," which worried a few and aroused the contempt of many. One wrote that the resolutions of the Renters' Union were "Socialistic, bordering on confiscation of property for the benefit of ne'er-do-wells, malcontents and disgruntled box-whittlers."[12] If the Renters' Union sought to provide legal and economic protection to these tenant "malcontents" and their families, the Land League that replaced it in 1914 sought to "emancipate" them by adopting a more explicitly militant strategy. In the preamble to the constitution Hickey and other Socialist leaders wrote: "To these slaves of the soil—men, women and children—we come as a militant organization, conscious of its inherent and destined power to strike the shackles from their limbs."[13] Hickey's rhetoric became increasingly militant after 1914 as he sought to rouse white tenants from their unquestioning loyalty to the Democratic Party, which tended to ignore class divisions in order to stress the solidarity of all Texas whites. On the issue of race, however, Hickey was not much different from the Democrat landlords he made a career of hating.

Black Americans had been disfranchised by poll-tax requirements shortly after 1900 and were subject to Jim Crow segregation throughout the state. At the same time, Socialist leaders like Oscar Ameringer and Covington Hall championed the principles of biracial unionism and economic equality based on shared class interests.[14] Even though the IWW and the BTW in east Texas and western Louisiana successfully organized blacks and whites into one union, Hickey reasoned that the Socialist Party had nothing to gain by including blacks because they had been disfranchised. Hickey also feared charges by the Democratic Party that Socialists were "nigger lovers" and stood for "social equality." He supported the idea of economic equality for African Americans and Mexicans, but he also nourished the illusion that such equality would be won by the efforts of white "rebels" of the South rather than by the militancy of nonwhite tenant farmers. The political pragmatism of the Socialist Party in the South, based as it was on the tenets of white supremacy and electoral politics, led to a "positive endorsement of the color line," wrote the historian David Roediger, "by making certain that its advocacy of the downtrodden was not mistaken for an appeal for racial justice."[15]

Tom Hickey nevertheless recognized that African American and Mexican sharecroppers and wage laborers were as much victims of land-lordism and capitalist agriculture as were tenants and small owners. But he and other Socialists, like E. O. Meitzen and W. S. Noble, were sensitive to charges by the Democrats that the tenant movement and Socialism in general stood for social equality for blacks and "mixing of the races." When the editor of an Oklahoma newspaper, Luke Roberts, declared that the "whole Socialist bunch" preached social equality, Hickey responded, in an article titled "Race Equality and Free Love": "Do you remember, Roberts, when the Populist Movement was strong in the South . . . [and] thousands of Democratic politicians . . . walked into the saloons with their arms around the negroes' necks and drank with them in spite of the smell in the good old summer time?"[16] Hickey accused the Democrats of privately fostering interracial sex while publicly denouncing the Socialists for the same thing. "There are five million mulattos in the South," Hickey wrote, "and I will give a $20 gold piece for each one that did not have a Democrat for a daddy."[17] The difference between the three parties was that "the Republicans, like Roosevelt, eat with the Negro; the Socialists will work with the negro and the Democrats mix with the negro." In the cities of Texas, white women worked alongside the "negress," Hickey pointed out, and black and white laborers drank out of the same cups. Thus "Capitalism has driven the workers into a social equality that would not be possible in Socialism," he declared, promising black workers economic equality, "and that is all."[18]

Hickey also was not fond of Mexicans, whom he referred to as peons and the "copper-colored sons of Montezuma." After the founding of the Land League in 1914, however, he became an ardent supporter of Emiliano Zapata and Francisco "Pancho" Villa and urged white tenants to launch their own revolution north of the border.[19] Texas Mexicans, however, had their own ideas about the best way to achieve equality and justice in the countryside and organized their own locals of the Renters' Union and the Land League. Many Texas Mexicans either belonged to or came under the influence of the PLM, the precursor to the Mexican Revolution, and therefore tended to be more radical to begin with than were their Anglo counterparts in the Socialist and conservative Democratic Party. Hickey at first was surprised by the radicalism of Mexicans, whom he had always regarded as docile, but soon extolled the "white-hearted" manliness of Mexicans who joined the Land League and tried to shame Anglo tenants into acting like "real men" instead of slaves and peons. By invoking manhood and whiteness, Anglo Socialists seemed to imply that Mexicans, if not African Americans, had become almost white through their manly opposition to exploitation by landlords, merchants, and bankers.[20]

Despite his reputation as a radical within the Socialist Party, Hickey at first envisioned a union that excluded black farmers, as he made clear when he wrote that the Renters' Union would "bring together a large number of the white men who as tenants are cultivating the farm lands in Texas." According to the original charter, membership in the new Renters' Union of America was limited to "all white persons" older than sixteen years of age who were farm renters or farm laborers.[21] Hickey, however, had come increasingly to admire the racial solidarity of the IWW-affiliated BTW, which offered the Renters' Union a model of militant industrial unionism broad enough to include tenants as well as timber workers, women as well as men, and blacks as well as whites. Socialists Covington Hall and Eugene Debs, as well as IWW leader "Big Bill" Haywood, also voiced their vehement opposition to segregated locals in IWW and Socialist-backed unions. At the second annual convention of the Renters' Union, Hickey and the Socialist "reds" thus moved to strike the word *white* from its membership clause and to add a clause that "persons of African descent shall be organized into separate local unions."[22] The founders of the Renters' Union remained optimistic during the first few years that they could forge a tri-ethnic coalition, employing rhetoric more hyperbolic than realistic:

When the Renters' Union was started there were many that said: "It won't succeed because the landlords will import Mexicans and negroes to break the union." But lo and behold the Mexican renters are flocking to our standard faster than the Americans, while the negro shows every sign of being ready for organization. If it has never done anything else the Renters' Union has already demonstrated that the exploited whites, browns, and blacks will stand together in defending and looking after their class interests.[23]

Although the constitution of the Renters' Union was amended to include African American farmers in separate locals, there is little evidence that black sharecroppers and tenants actually organized their own locals

1. Black sharecroppers near Dallas, ca. 1907. Prints and Photographs Collection, cotton file, CN #01281, Center for American History, University of Texas at Austin.

2. Mexican cotton pickers on the 500-acre Fall Family cotton ranch in McLennan County, central Texas, ca. 1937. Narciso Alderete, standing in the wagon, became one of the first Mexican sharecroppers to settle in McGregor, near Waco, in the 1920s. Teresa Palomo Acosta Collection, Benson Latin American Collection, University of Texas at Austin.

3. Narciso Alderete and his daughter, Lucía, in front of their 1929 Model-A Ford on the Fall Family cotton ranch in McLennan County, ca. 1935. Owning an automobile gave Mexican sharecroppers and cotton pickers the mobility to seek work at competitive wages. Teresa Palomo Acosta Collection, Benson Latin American Collection, University of Texas at Austin.

4. A white family on a Caldwell County cotton farm, 1939. Milton Schaefer and his family relax on their farm near Lockhart. Mrs. Schaefer sells cakes, eggs, canned chickens, dressed hens, fryers, and pecan pies to help pay the mortgage on their farm. Some white families were "hard-boiled southerners" who opposed the settlement of Mexicans in their communities. Agricultural Extension Collection, Special Collections and Archives, Texas A&M University, College Station.

5. Sign in a restaurant window in south Texas, ca. 1940. Russell Lee Photograph Collection, Center for American History, University of Texas at Austin.

6. The Alamo City Employment Agency, San Antonio, 1924. Private employment agencies contracted thousands of Mexicans and their families to work on cotton farms in central Texas. Photography Collection, Harry Ransom Humanities Research Center, University of Texas at Austin.

7. Mexican, black, and white sharecroppers on a Caldwell County cotton farm, ca. 1928. The sharecroppers, foremen, and townsmen (front right) gather for the funeral of the farm owner. The largest concentration of Mexican sharecroppers north of San Antonio during the 1920s was in Caldwell County, fifteen miles south of Austin. Courtesy Thad Sitton and the Caldwell County Oral History Project.

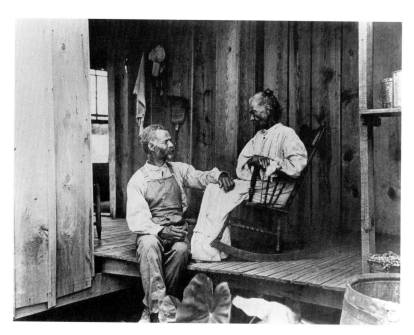

8. A black farm couple on their porch in east Texas, ca. 1910. East Texas Collection (gift of the Texas State Historical Association), CN #08851, Center for American History, University of Texas at Austin.

9. Black cotton pickers on a seventy-five-acre farm in central Texas, 1929. Rural Texas Blacks Photograph Collection, Agricultural Extension Collection, Special Collections and Archives, Texas A&M University, College Station.

10. Young combatant during the Mexican Revolution, circa 1914. Robert Runyon Photograph Collection, CN7206. The Center for American History, University of Texas at Austin.

11. "Hanged Negroes" in central Texas, ca. 1920. Texas ranked third among the states, after Mississippi and Georgia, in the total number of lynching victims. Prints and Photographs Collection, CN #02873A, Center for American History, University of Texas at Austin.

12. Thomas A. Hickey, the "Baby Blizzard" of Socialism in Texas, in 1911. He is holding a copy of *Theodore Roosevelt, the Public Dr. Cook: A Chronological Review of the Political Life of Theodore Roosevelt*, a pamphlet he wrote, probably after 1920, when he abandoned the Socialist cause. George and Grace Brewer Papers, Walter P. Reuther Library of Labor and Urban Affairs, Wayne State University, Detroit, Michigan.

13. Black and white timber workers in east Texas, ca. 1908. African Americans represented significant percentages of the labor force in Texas, from sharecroppers to timber workers. Although blacks and whites worked together, they ate and slept in segregated housing. East Texas Collection (gift of the Texas State Historical Association), CN #08850, Center for American History, University of Texas at Austin.

14. Mexican and black children on a cotton roller, ca. 1920. A Mexican boy and two African American boys sit together on a cotton roller at one of the Taft Ranch's six 1,000-acre cotton farms, which were operated mainly by Mexican wage laborers. May Mathis Green Watson Collection, CN #08836, Center for American History, University of Texas at Austin.

15. Sabina Palomo (mother of Teresa Palomo Acosta) and María Acosta (niece of Narciso Alderete) in front of Fall Family Ranch, near Waco, ca. 1934. During the 1920s Sabina Palomo and her family had picked cotton on the Taft Ranch for two years. Teresa Palomo Acosta Collection, Benson Latin American Collection, University of Texas at Austin.

16. President William Howard Taft (in the white hat) at the Taft Ranch, 1909. During a visit to his brother's corporately owned ranch, the president inspected one of the ranch's prized bulls. The journalists who followed the presidential entourage were impressed with the efficiency and profitability of supervising armies of wage laborers to grow cotton on more than 6,000 acres of ranch land. May Mathis Green Watson Collection, CN #08838, Center for American History, University of Texas at Austin.

17. The Oil and Gin Company on the Taft Ranch, ca. 1920. The Taft Ranch was actually a highly industrialized "factory farm" operated by hundreds of Mexicans from south Texas and Mexico. May Mathis Green Watson Collection, CN #08839, Center for American History, University of Texas at Austin.

18. Mexican wage laborers and their families pose in front of the huge barn of the Portland Farm, one of the Taft Ranch's six 1,000-acre cotton farms, ca. 1920. May Mathis Green Watson Collection, CN #08837, Center for American History, University of Texas at Austin.

19. Black and Mexican migrant cotton pickers at lunch time (Dorothea Lange). Robstown [near Corpus Christi]. Texas, August 1936. USF 34-9819-E, FSA-OWI Collection, Library of Congress.

20. Black farm women making rugs to sell, 1933. Ruby O. Phelps, a McLennan County home-demonstration agent (on the right) instructs members of the Harrison Community Club in making rugs. The cost per rug was about $0.30, but the women were able to sell them for $1.25 or more. Rural Texas Blacks Photograph Collection, Agricultural Extension Collection, Special Collections and Archives, Texas A&M University, College Station.

21. María and Consuelo Acosta, 1937. Like other Mexican women on cotton farms in central Texas, María and Consuelo worked as cotton pickers in the fields and also as domestics in the homes of farm owners. Teresa Palomo Acosta Collection, Benson Latin American Collection, University of Texas at Austin.

or that party members actively sought to recruit black farmers to their cause. Many white tenants regarded black sharecroppers as their competitors who supposedly entered into agreements with white landlords to push poor whites off the land.[24] For many whites, therefore, blacks and Mexicans were as much to blame for the immiseration of white tenants as were their landlord oppressors.

Hickey's politics were radical in practically every respect except when it came to the race question. Born in Dublin in 1869, he grew up loving the Molly Maguires and despising English landlords.[25] When he was ten years old, impoverished tenant farmers in western Ireland demanded lower rents in response to two successive years of massive crop failures and increased American agricultural imports. In 1879 they formed the Land League and sought the radical goal of wresting the land away from the few hundred aristocratic families that owned it and making it available to tenant farmers.[26] The Land League in Texas, which displaced the Renters' Union in 1914, descended—in name at least—from the Irish Land League of Tom Hickey's youth in Ireland.[27]

Hickey immigrated to America and settled in New York where, in the 1890s, he led a strike by Knights of Labor Machinists for a nine-hour day against the Sprague Electrical Works. After the strike he headed west and in 1903 organized lumberjacks in Washington and Oregon for the Socialist Labor Party. He later moved to the Southwest, joined the Western Federation of Miners, and took a job in Arizona, where he coedited the *Globe Miner*. He came to Texas in 1905 through El Paso and began to organize tenant farmers for the Socialist Party throughout the state and the South. When asked why he had come to Texas, Hickey replied with a droll, rhetorical question:

Don't you know that since Saint Patrick made the fatal mistake of driving out the snake that walked on his belly, and left the landlord snake that walks on his feet that a true Celt would sooner wield his shillelagh on the hide of a landlord than kiss a colleen or take a libation of poteen. Where then could one of my glorious stock cross the seas to find landlords more plentiful than in this glorious Lone Star State of ours?[28]

As an Irish immigrant, Hickey came to insist on his own whiteness and on white supremacy in his new identity as a Southern white worker, and he frequently appealed to the regional prejudices of white tenants by alluding to the myths of the Lost Cause and the glories of the Old South.[29] Like the Irish tenants who had risen up against their landlords a few decades earlier, the "new rebels of the New South," the white ten-

ants of central Texas, would rise again.[30] Tom Hickey's Irish back-
ground, coupled with his newly adopted identity as a white Southerner,
made him, according to Ruth Allen, "sympathetic to the already long-
standing obsession of Texans with the dream of the small family farm."
Variously described as a radical "baby blizzard," "the fighting Irishman,"
and "the exceedingly rebellious Texas Rebel," Hickey combined "the
militant agrarianism of the Sinn Feiner [sic] . . . with the romantic frontier agrarianism of the Texas farmers."[31] Irish tenants, however, did not
have to confront a race problem within their ranks, as did Southern
white tenants in the Populist and Socialist Parties.

Hickey was determined not to make the same mistake his Populist
forebears had made. Many Socialists had not forgotten how the Democratic Party in Texas during the 1890s successfully charged the People's
Party with being a "product of the North" and with being "too friendly
toward the Negro." Texas Populists actively sought the political support
of blacks, who had not yet been disfranchised by the enactment of poll
taxes, literacy tests, white-only primaries, and other barriers to the bal-
lot. Populists offered black voters, for example, the right to be called for
jury duty and recruited them to serve on local and state committees of
the Third Party. "With regard to most of these charges," wrote the historian Roscoe Martin, "the Populists could do naught but confess their
truth, though the confession admittedly alienated large blocks of white
voters."[32] Despite the failure of Populism and its interracial politics,
Hickey had nothing but contempt for those white Populists who returned to the Democratic fold. He described Populist leader Tom Watson, for example, as a "renegade populist who went back like a dog to
his democratic vomit."[33]

Some Socialist Party leaders favored interracial organization, although the most militant exponents of interracial unionism came from
members of the IWW and the radical BTW. Covington Hall, who belonged to both the IWW and the Socialist Party, believed with religious
fervor in the principles of interracial unity and biracial unionism, recognizing the oppression of women and children as well as men. He signed
his letters: "Yours for the liberty of man, woman and child, regardless of
creed, race or color."[34] He also waxed lyrical about a "miracle in Dixie,"
in which one "red day three Clans of Toil awakened from a hard superstition and the Anglo-Americans and the Afro-Americans and the Mexican-
Americans arose and gathered together . . . speaking . . . : 'Children of
Labor, wherein are we of different races? Why fight we each other over a
superstition, we who have all things in common and have a world to

gain by so recognizing?' "[35] Hall's choice of "Clan" for his vision of interracial working-class harmony betrayed a stunning insensitivity to language, for it would have required a true miracle to convince blacks and Mexicans to ignore the resemblance of Hall's clan to the Ku Klux Klan. The similarity was no accident: Hall perversely modeled the Clans of Toil after the "Great Klan of the Southern people," because he admired its "marvelous manner of organization" and romanticized its role during Reconstruction in protecting the South from "Northern capitalists and their Southern allies."[36]

Despite Hall's frequent call for interracial unity, he was unable to persuade Hickey to tone down his racist rhetoric, which did not go unnoticed by black members of the Socialist Party. Hubert Harrison, a black Socialist who wrote for the party journal in 1912, blasted Socialist Southerners for their racist "exhibitions of the thing called Southernism" and singled out "the recent dirty diatribes against the Negro in a Texas paper, which is still on our national list of Socialist papers." That paper was undoubtedly *The Rebel*, the largest and most influential Socialist newspaper in Texas. Harrison presented the issue squarely to southern Socialists like Hickey when he asked: "Southernism or Socialism—which? Is it to be the white half of the working class against the black half, or all the working class? Can we hope to triumph over capitalism with one half of the working class against us?"[37] Although the Socialist Party of the Progressive Era shared the racist assumptions of the larger society, which rested comfortably on the notion of Anglo-Saxon superiority, it nevertheless did not reject African American membership. African Americans were acknowledged in their economic roles as workers, but always in the context of racialized inferiors. The anarchist Emma Goldman claimed that Socialists treated blacks "like dogs" and that "the party consists chiefly of national and racial philistines, moral eunuchs, and religious soul savers."[38] Unlike Covington Hall, who actively supported biracial unionism, Hickey barely paid lip service to the principle of interracial solidarity: The all-white Renters' Union followed the segregated racial pattern of the South in a way that the integrated BTW did not. Thus blacks could hardly be blamed for their coolness toward the Texas Renters' Union, the principal spokesman for which was the race-baiting Tom Hickey and the membership of which, according to James Green, consisted mainly of "Southern-born poor whites who feared and often hated their 'colored competitors.' "[39]

When Hickey was not denouncing "coons," he was busy exposing the sex crimes of the Catholic clergy.[40] Texas Socialist leaders insisted, however, that their party was not opposed to organized religion, in part because they were sensitive to charges that Socialists stood for free love, atheism, and social equality. As one Socialist visitor to Texas asked: "Have you swallowed the bunc . . . that Socialism would break up your home, destroy your religion, and put you on a level with the 'nigger'?"[41] Socialists sometimes criticized the sanctimonious ministries of wealthy Protestants but recognized the importance of religion and revivals to poor folks in the countryside. Forgetting that poor Catholics, many of whom were Mexicans, depended on the Church for many reasons, including protection from racist Anglos, Hickey resorted to classical Know-Nothing attacks on Catholicism, singling it out as a symbol of the landed oligarchy, secrecy, superstition, and antidemocratic politics.

Hickey broke from the Catholic Church decades before publishing *The Rebel* and was ostracized by his own family, including two sisters who were nuns in a Canadian convent. Nevertheless, as an Irish-Catholic immigrant, he was probably responding to anti-Socialist nativists who charged that he wore "a Roman Bridle."[42] He claimed, for example, that the editor of the *Dallas-Galveston News*, which generally represented the interests of landlords and bankers, was "run by a pink-whiskered Catholic dago named Lombardi."[43] Evidently Hickey was not too fond of Italians, either. Covington Hall called him not only "the uncrowned king of Texas Socialism" and "its despot" but also, somewhat ironically, given the ethnicity of the Vicar of Rome, its "pope" as well.[44]

Hickey and other Texas Socialists often invoked whiteness and manhood to shame white tenants into joining the Land League and reserved labels like "white trash," "slave," "peon," and "menial" for those who sheepishly followed their landlords to the voting booth to elect Democratic landowners, merchants, and bankers to office. Bankers, editors, and landlords, Hickey wrote, "desire the tenant to be a nice subservient menial who will meet the landlord cap in hand and confer with him as to how much of his hide shall be taken and under what conditions shall the skinning be done."[45] A few months before the Democratic primary in 1916 the Socialist Henry M. Tichenor visited Texas and wondered how white tenants could work "like galley slaves year in and year out." "How under the sun can a . . . real man," he wondered, "look his wife and children in the face and vote for the thing to continue?"[46] Real men, white men, stand up against their oppressors because whiteness, if anything, compels the defense of women and children.

While Hickey and others in the Land League deployed the manly language of whiteness to forge class unity on cotton farms, racialized discourse also served to strengthen the color line between whites and blacks. One white tenant wrote that the only way he could avoid "becoming a slave" was to join the Socialist Party and "build up an army of emancipation."[47] Here it is instructive to note Roediger's proposition that white Southern workers were not just manipulated into racism; rather, "their consciousness was a double one that constantly pulled them toward urgent insistence on their whiteness and toward a questioning of whether their class grievances did not outweigh their racial privileges."[48] Many poor whites on the farms found it increasingly difficult to discern any racial privileges deriving from their nominal status as whites, for their status as sharecroppers stigmatized them as white trash and segregated them from other whites in the countryside.[49]

Tenants who joined the Socialist Party to reclaim their manhood and reassert their status as free white people often found themselves let go by landlords who refused to rent to any Socialists. Tom Hickey was particularly incensed by the actions of one landlord in Coleman County, J. Tom Padgitt, who rented land to about fifty tenant families on his 20,000-acre Day Ranch near the town of Leaday.[50] Padgitt made his home in Dallas, some 288 miles from the ranch, and hired an overseer, C. A. Rives, a former "wood hauler" from Oklahoma, to supervise the tenants. Padgitt and his brothers in Dallas formed Padgitt Brothers, Co., for the purpose of manufacturing saddlery and harness and other leather goods. As an absentee landowner he authorized Rives to represent him in all matters concerning the tenants and "when anything came up to use his own judgment and not write me . . . but to act for himself." In 1912, three years after Rives was hired, something came up: At least seven of the tenants on the Day Ranch became active members of the Socialist Party, which had been organized in the county in 1909.[51]

Rives and a few companions rode around parts of two counties asking tenants to join an anti-Socialist league to "upbuild Christianity," and Rives took it upon himself to inform the Socialist tenants of the Day Ranch that "they must get off the part of the earth that he controlled." Rives had written to a prospective tenant from Oklahoma named Leach that "Leaday is having war" between the Socialists and anti-Socialists and that the latter are "fighting socialists at every corner for the sake of peace in the community." He informed the Oklahoman that he intended "to let all Comrads [*sic*] take a walk after Jan. 1st" and that "on account of peace in the community" he could not "rent to my brother if he was a socialist." If Leach were not a Socialist, Rives promised that he would do his best to "fit you and your people up with good places" on the Day Ranch. Rives then fired the ranch merchant and hotel keeper, Mr. Flynn, for his involvement in the Socialist Party and placed an advertisement in the *Coleman County Herald* offering the position to the "right party." Lest there be any doubt about who constituted the wrong party, he added: "Calamity howlers need not apply." The ranch blacksmith was also dismissed when Rives discovered that he was secretary of the Socialist local. "This un-American puppy called Rives backed by Mr. Padgitt," Hickey wrote, "decided upon wholesale extermination."[52]

Rives's attempt to control the politics of the tenants split the community of Leaday wide open. The dispute was carried into the schools, the churches, and the fraternal lodges. "Like dragon's teeth," Hickey wrote, "the seeds of hatred were sown." Some owners suggested that they would "allow the Socialists no more privileges on the Colorado river, such as fishing and hunting, on their land." Others posted signs: "No Socialists allowed any privileges here."[53] In response to these initiatives, fifty-eight Socialist renters, some of them from the Day Ranch, as well as a few Socialist landowners, signed a petition to Padgitt in Dallas requesting that Rives be removed from his position as manager of the Day Ranch for dismissing tenants who supported the Socialist Party or its policies and for attempting to "dominate their views and personal liberties." The petition asked that Padgitt return to Leaday to hear their complaints and to resolve the issue personally. Padgitt and his wife traveled from Dallas to a schoolhouse in Leaday to meet with a committee of tenants elected by the petitioners. After three hours of hearing from both sides, Padgitt issued his ultimatum: "These people who are quarreling with my superintendent . . . must leave. I have appointed him to attend to my business and I shall continue him to attend to my business."[54]

The majority of the tenants who signed the petition did not rent from Padgitt, but they understood that their own personal and political liberty was at stake, since other owners might become emboldened to engage in similar restrictions and intimidations. Hickey gave examples of landlord prohibitionists in Caldwell County who compelled their renters to sign a cash bond for $100.00, "said sum to be forfeited if they take one drink of liquor in a year." In McLennan County some landlords forced renters to move because they refused to vote for Prohibition. And in Milam County tenants had been "ordered out of the jury box because of their political views."[55] W. S. Noble, in a letter to E. O. Meitzen, secretary of the Renters' Union, warned that if landlords could force renters to abstain from alcohol, vote a particular ticket, or belong to a particular political party, then it would not be long before they would say: "You must allow me to sleep with your wife or daughter or move."[56]

Padgitt admitted to the Commission on Industrial Relations that Rives dismissed the tenants not for any charge of inefficiency, negligence, or destruction of property but for their "political agitation" on behalf of the Socialist Party. Moreover, Padgitt steadfastly maintained that he was not opposed to renting to Socialists as long as they did not give him any trouble. When the chairman of the commission asked him what he meant by "trouble," Padgitt explained that he objected to tenants who "agitate and stir up trouble and talk at the store and keep everybody stirred up all the time." Who would judge, the chairman wanted to know, whether a renter was expressing "certain principles that he held were beneficial to mankind" or if he was stirring up trouble? Padgitt's immediate response was that his agent, in this case Rives, would be the sole judge of whether "a man was attending to business or not." Asked what sort of political agitation constituted "trouble," Padgitt replied: "A man that would go around and would talk to the other men and cause them to become dissatisfied, and poison their minds as to their landlords." Padgitt went on to explain that, as a businessman, he believed that any renter who engaged in political activity of any sort—whether Socialist, Democrat, or Republican—was "stirring up trouble" and had no place on his ranch. "We want men to attend to business," he told the chairman, "and make the farm pay."[57]

Although Padgitt maintained that the basis for dismissing Socialist tenants was one not of politics but of business expediency, his wife recognized the trouble for what it was, namely, a clash of both economic interests and political ideologies—a class struggle in which one had to choose sides. She said to the assembled tenants at Leaday: "Your community is split wide open but the same thing is going [on] everywhere. This is not only a Coleman county fight but it is a state-wide fight, a nation-wide fight, in fact it is going on in all parts of the civilized world. And I agree with my husband that the best thing to be done is to have all of you who do not agree with us leave the places, get off, and we will put others in your place."[58] The trouble in Leaday was not an isolated incident.[59] The Commission on Industrial Relations came to essentially the same conclusion after its hearings in Dallas in 1915: "In some cases tenants are oppressed by landlords . . . by eviction without due notice, by discriminations because of 'personal and political convictions.'"[60]

Hickey, incensed by the imperious manner of the "leather man of Dallas," called upon all tenants to boycott Padgitt's goods:

We have purchased your stuff direct from Dallas and we have bought from retailers that handle your ware, but so help us God[,] Mr. Padgitt[,] if you don't call off your dog [Rives] at Leaday, and allow these men and women to have the freedom of the press, speech and assemblage that the American citizen believes in[,] then we will never buy another piece of harness from you. Your leather goods will rot on the shelves before we will purchase them. . . . In other words, if you boycott white Americans because of their political beliefs, then we'll boycott you until the cows come home.[61]

Padgitt might forbid nonwhite tenants from joining the Socialist Party, Hickey implied, but white Americans demanded that landlords treat them as fellow white men.

Increasingly, white tenants associated work on these business plantations or corporate cotton ranches as "nigger work" or "peon work," while they complained of their displacement on large-scale farms by African American sharecroppers who were "almost peoned."[62] Hickey seemed perplexed by the census returns of 1910, which indicated that black farmers were actually making faster progress than were whites in entering the ranks of tenancy from wage labor and sharecropping and even in ascending in rank from tenancy to ownership. The rate of white tenancy increased faster than the rate of black tenancy between 1900 and 1910, while the percentage of black owners increased faster than that of white owners. Texas whites, who historically had been owners and tenants, were slipping down the agricultural ladder, while some African Americans were inching up from wage laborers to croppers, tenants, or owners. Hickey actually applauded white tenants for refusing to ascend the ladder as quickly as black tenants, who "half starve their children and half clothe their wives and half house themselves" in order to buy land, "as white men bred to a superior civilization cannot bring themselves to do."[63] However, Hickey usually blamed avaricious merchants and oppressive landlords for the growth of white tenancy. When a landlord named Bailey Turner, owner of an 800-acre blackland farm in Milam County, notified his white tenants to get off his land so he could replace them with black sharecroppers and wage workers, Hickey editorialized that Turner would have preferred the "Aryan to the Ethiopian [except] . . . that the sons of Ham are as easily exploited as the sons of Montezuma so between the stove polish and copper-colored brethren the white man is being ground to dust."[64]

Hickey was not always consistent in his racism. On one hand, he made it clear that whites who did not organize or join the Land League were worse than "coons," while, on the other hand, he lambasted whites who would not join unions that accepted "colored men" into their ranks. He encouraged the view that blacks and unorganized Mexicans were the competitors of white tenants and the pawns of landlords and urged white tenants to join Socialist unions by pandering to their racial prejudices. When, for example, he learned that white farm laborers earned only $6.00 per day, Hickey asked: "Why do you see the negro boot-blacks of Ft. Worth, Dallas and Houston organized and you refuse to carry a card? Aren't you as good as a shoe-shining coon? Don't tell me the negroes have brains and you haven't?"[65] He then proceeded to rebuke "muttonhead white Lumberjacks and Working Farmers" in east Texas for not joining the BTW simply because it admitted "colored MEN" to its membership.[66]

Socialist leaders like Covington Hall and Eugene Debs avoided any criticism of the ideology of white supremacy but stressed the common economic interests of workers regardless of race—unions in which there were only "white *men*, Negro *men*, and Mexican *men*" but "no niggers, greasers or white trash." Hickey, however, could not seem to move beyond the crude racism of the "muttonhead lumberjacks" who did not see any difference between a "coon" and a "colored man," whether unionized or not.[67] He utterly failed to recognize that the BTW derived much of its strength from its African American membership and that its white members might learn about worker loyalty and strategies of resistance from its black members. Nor was he able to see that the Land League derived much of its radical ideology and oppositional strategies from its Mexican membership and their ties to the PLM.

The contradictions of Hickey's racist rhetoric did little to promote the view that the Land League was a biracial union or that he was willing or able to adopt Covington Hall's clever use of gender as the meeting ground of all men of all races—men who were bound by common class interests that made them superior to "niggers," "greasers," and "rednecks" if not equal to one another. Nevertheless, he maintained, despite his highly racialized vocabulary, that race was not an issue on the Socialist agenda and that, in fact, solving the land question would automatically solve the race question. Taxing the idle 117 million acres of tillable land in the possession of speculators and large landowners, he argued, would cause them to sell the "manless land" to the "landless man." Then there would be "two places for one man instead of two men for one place." He told the story of a northern man who visited Texas and asked a former slaveholder about the race question, to which the Texan answered: "When the white man owned the 'nigger,' there was no race question; if the 'nigger' owned the white man, there would be no race question; but when the 'nigger' and the white man both want the same job at the same time, then there is a race question." Hickey concluded: "The race war in the last analysis is but a minor symptom of the class war."[68] He wanted it both ways: to ignore the race question as a minor symptom of the class war and, at the same time, to characterize class struggle as essentially a race war. "Despite his revolutionary rhetoric," noted James Green, "'Red Tom' was fairly yellow when it came to facing the challenges posed by the race question."[69]

Hickey was beginning to learn that his all-white Land League lacked the revolutionary fervor, and therefore the manly whiteness, of the independently organized Mexican locals of the Land League, locals that were more imbued with the radicalism of magonismo than the electoral politics of the Socialist Party. The more Hickey read about revolutionaries in Mexico seizing land from large landowners and redistributing it, the more he advocated revolution on this side of the border.

After the outbreak of the Mexican Revolution in 1910 and increased immigration of Mexicans to Texas and other states of the Southwest, many owners in central Texas began to hire them as sharecroppers because they often had larger families than did white or black sharecroppers and were constrained to accept living conditions unacceptable to Anglo tenants. Unless Mexicans were brought into the union, one member warned, your "Mexican neighbor . . . will compete you out of house and home."[70] More important, however, the Mexican Revolution, which was taking place just a few hundred miles away, led Tom Hickey to revise his view of Mexicans as docile peons or border bandits. The uprising had revealed to Socialists like Hickey the radical potential of Mexican revolutionaries engaged in a national struggle to reclaim land from owners who had consolidated their holdings under the regime of Porfirio Díaz. For Hickey, Mexican "greasers" and "peons" had suddenly become fellow revolutionaries in the struggle to overthrow capitalism.[71]

Although many Texas Anglos believed that the peon class of Mexicans constituted a degraded mongrel race, Texas courts maintained that the social construction of "white" included Mexicans, at least for the purpose of securing citizenship through naturalization.[72] In 1896, for example, two Anglo politicians in San Antonio, worried that Mexican immigrants could become citizens and exercise the franchise, filed suit against Ricardo Rodríguez, who wished to become a naturalized citizen, on the grounds that he was "Indian Mexican" and therefore not "white." Because Indians and Asians were barred by law from becoming U.S. citizens, the lawyers hoped to prove that Rodríguez, a dark Mexican who freely admitted he was probably of Indian descent, was racially unfit for citizenship. In one of the many briefs filed in the year-long case, one of the attorneys opposed to granting citizenship to Rodríguez cited, as evidence, the findings of the French anthropologist Paul Broca, who compiled a "scientific classification" of race according to the variety of human skin color "from the fairest hue of the Swede, and the darker tint of the Provençal, to the withered leaf brown of the Hottentot, the chocolate brown of the Mexican, and the brown black of the West African." Since it was impossible to distinguish between the race of Indian Mexicans, African Mexicans, and Spanish or white Mexicans, the attorneys essentially argued that the boundary of whiteness be drawn on the basis of skin color, for Rodríguez was undeniably a "chocolate-brown" Mexican.

Citing Article VIII of the Treaty of Guadalupe Hidalgo, in which the United States granted citizenship to Mexicans in the conquered region of the Southwest after 1848, the court rejected the suit on the grounds that Rodríguez was eligible for citizenship on the basis of his Mexican nationality, thereby circumventing the issue of his race. The ruling was significant because it meant that all Mexican citizens, regardless of race, were entitled to become U.S. citizens. Had the Anglo politicians succeeded in their suit, thousands of Mexicans in south Texas would have been disfranchised, as were the Chinese in California who, the courts ruled, were judged not to be white.[73] Though Anglos still did not consider Mexicans white and often discriminated against them in the highly segregated society of central and south Texas, most Anglos also did not consider them black, which, for Southern whites, implied a whole set of complicated interactions going back to antebellum times.

When the Renters' Union became the Land League in 1914, it made special efforts to organize Mexicans in the region between Austin, San Antonio, and Corpus Christi, where Mexican tenant farmers and Socialists, such as José Ángel Hernández and F. A. Hernández, risked violence and imprisonment for organizing their own locals of the Land League and the Socialist Party. Hickey and other Anglo Socialists credited them with a degree of manliness that they felt too often was lacking among white tenant farmers. In one of many comparisons between Anglo and

Mexican tenants, the secretary of the Land League, W. S. Noble, wrote: "One of the strange things to me is that the American renter who boasts that he is one of the freest of the free is so afraid of his boss he cannot be induced to join a union for his emancipation while the Mexican tenants not only join the League but will starve before they will submit to a higher rent than the League and law says is just under the present system. You men that claim you have a right to be the father of white American children, what is the matter with you? Did your wife marry a satisfied peón?"[74] Noble described the white "American renter" as a slave who would not struggle for his own emancipation and thus had lost the right to call himself the father of "white American children." Mexicans, he implied, were usurping that prerogative by their manliness in seeking to protect their wives and children from exploitation. Nonunion Anglo tenant farmers had thus been transposed into "satisfied peons" by the revolutionary fervor of "docile" Mexicans.

Many of the Mexicans who joined the Socialist Party in Texas maintained close ties with the PLM, which led armed uprisings in northern Mexico in the early years of the Mexican Revolution. Many Mexicans entered the Socialist Party in Texas through their association with the PLM, which, in 1911, the year the Socialist Renters' Union was founded in Texas, publicly embraced the radical tenets of anarchism and adopted as their motto *tierra y libertad* (land and liberty). U.S. officials arrested magonistas and Mexican Socialists in Texas for violating neutrality laws, but their real concern was that Mexicans were radicalizing local labor struggles. Landowners in Austin, for example, more than 200 miles from the border, worried that the revolution was spilling over the border into the state and influencing Mexican tenant farmers to join the Socialist Party. In fact, however, many Mexicans who joined the Socialist Party in Texas were already members of the PLM and IWW and served as valuable links between the Mexican Revolution and radical movements throughout the Southwest. Anglo organizers of the Land League and Socialist Party thus began to recruit Mexicans when it became clear to them that Mexicans and Mexican Americans were in the vanguard of radical protest in central Texas.[75]

Texas Mexicans, however, did not wait for Anglo-American Socialists to organize them: They drew on their prior experience with the PLM and began to organize their own locals of the PLM, the Land League, and the Socialist Party. José Ángel Hernández and others, like F. A. Hernández and Lázaro Gutiérrez de Lara, were important and highly visible Mexican stump speakers and backwoods organizers who belonged to both the PLM and the Socialist Party in Texas. José Ángel Hernández was a PLM organizer before he came to Houston in 1910 and became a member of the Socialist Party and Land League. He read Mexican Socialist newspapers and *Regeneración*, the newspaper published by the Magón brothers in Los Angeles, and spent a brief period in Indianapolis, where he married an English-speaking Mexican American woman who also appears to have been active in the PLM. He quickly learned English and addressed crowds in both English and Spanish. He was arrested in Houston in 1913 for attempting to raise funds for the defense of Jesús María Rangel, an organizer and military leader of the PLM, and Charles Cline, an IWW organizer and BTW veteran. Rangel had led a group of about twenty Mexicans, accompanied by Cline, toward the border with Mexico in order to join forces with the Zapatistas. They were ambushed by a sheriff's posse but managed to escape, although one of the deputy sheriffs was killed in the attempt. The group was later captured and charged with murder. José Ángel Hernández came to the defense of the "Texas martyrs," because, in his words, they were "merely trying to aid the Madero revolution for the good of Mexico."[76]

Increasingly, Anglo authorities came to view Mexican immigrants as dangerous radicals who sought to import the Mexican Revolution to the Southwest. In 1915 José Ángel Hernández was arrested again, this time in San Antonio for "inciting to rebellion" about 1,000 Mexican laborers who had congregated at Market Place to hear various speakers. Hernández was attempting to convince the Mexican tenants who lived on the outskirts of town to join the Land League and vote for Socialists in the upcoming city election. Chief Brown, a federal officer with the Secret Service in San Antonio, called Hernández a "rabid Socialist" who was "attacking our institutions." During the campaign to raise funds for Hernández's defense, Noble observed that Hernández was arrested "for no other purpose than to intimidate the growing sentiment among the Mexican tenants for decent rental contracts and houses for the tenants to live in."[77] Before his arrest Hernández had been invited to attend the Socialist Party and Land League conventions in Waco, where his "American brothers" gave him a welcome that would "convince him that the work he is doing to lead his Mexican brethren into the light of truth and out of the grip of the rotten Southwest Texas political rings is appreciated."[78] Noble, like Hickey, could not help but be impressed with the courage and conviction of organizers like Hernández, who risked arrest and imprisonment to organize tenants and workers and exhorted white tenants who continued to vote for "land-hog" Democrats: "Show our Mexican brothers that you have at least as much nerve and spirit of liberty in your breast as they have."[79]

Covington Hall, who viewed the militancy of Mexican Socialists with growing admiration, frequently praised the land reforms enacted by the revolutionary government in Mexico and contrasted the radicalism of Mexican revolutionaries with the apathy of American tenant farmers, who lacked "the common decency to quit referring to the Mexicans as a lot of 'Damned Greasers.'"[80] Tom Hickey ran a lengthy feature headlined "The Great Mexican Revolution," in which he eagerly championed the "tremendous steps toward Land and Liberty the embattled peón-revolutionists are taking on the west side of the Rio Grande." He then impugned the manhood of Texas tenant farmers in order to shame them into joining the Socialist Party, complaining that

the land slaves of Mexico have displayed more manhood, more real love for their wives and children than have the peóns [white tenants] on this side of the line [border with Mexico] that meekly walk into the primary trap and vote the usurer-landlord politicians back into power so they and their filthy tribe may walk over the slaves that boost them into power.[81]

Manhood, which formed a tight orbit around the nucleus of whiteness, separated the slave from the free, the white man from the Mexican peon. Without the courage to fight for one's rights that manhood was supposed to safeguard, one's claim to whiteness faltered. W. S. Noble wrote that "Mexican renters will live on boiled corn to win a just contract but the average American is so afraid of his boss he fears to join the league for fear he won't have the privilege of enslaving his wife and children another year."[82] Gendered notions of whiteness thus played an important role in whitening Mexicans and in complicating whiteness for Anglos like Hickey and Noble, who wondered aloud how Anglo-American tenant farmers could claim to be white if they acted like peons.

More than a thousand Mexican tenant farmers and sharecroppers joined the Land League in south-central Texas, mostly in segregated locals organized by a few Mexican Land League organizers who traveled from county to county setting up new locals and distributing constitutions and other literature in Spanish. The most successful of these organizers was F. A. Hernández, the "live wire Mexican organizer" from De-Witt County, southeast of San Antonio, who was also referred to as the "Mexican-English organizer" because of his fluency in English.[83] A member of the Renters' Union from its inception in 1911 and elected to the Land League's executive committee in 1914, F. A. Hernández organized more than a dozen locals from Austin to Corpus Christi. He was elected assistant state organizer, with authority to organize anywhere in Texas because of his ability, according to E. O. Meitzen, to "make things warm for the landlords."[84]

Hernández invited Meitzen to speak at an encampment organized by the Mexican local of the Renters' Union in DeWitt County in the fall of 1915. Meitzen spoke to the white tenants in English and to the German tenants in German; S. C. Cárdenas, a Mexican organizer from Karnes County, addressed the Mexicans in Spanish. Meitzen, himself a German American, noted that the trilingual encampment, which spanned several days, was well attended and that among the Anglos, Germans, and Mexicans could be felt "a spirit of solidarity not often met with." That solidarity was not simply one of shared class interests; it also included the notion, "not often met with," that these three groups represented different cultural constituencies of whiteness that made them more alike than different, particularly in the southern context of black–white race relations. Just as many Texas Germans maintained a cultural identity separate from that of other white Southerners, the boundaries of whiteness sometimes included Texas Mexicans like F. A. Hernández, who, like immigrant Germans, belonged to a kindred domain of liminal whiteness.[85]

Like other tenant farmer organizers, whether Mexican, German, or Anglo-American, F. A. Hernández ran into trouble with landowners and merchants because of his union activity. The difference, in the eyes of Anglo-American Socialists, was that Mexican tenants were not afraid to confront landlords to defend their interests. The furnishing firm with which Hernández had been doing business for more than a decade refused to advance him credit for groceries as a result of his union activity. An association of landowners brought suit against him for an overdue note of $160 when, according to Hernández, "they knew it was impossible to be paid." The manager of his small farm also hired extra day laborers to pick Hernández's cotton and then charged the cost to Hernández. Since Hernández's share of the crop was insufficient to cover his debt, the manager tried to seize his corn crop to cover the cost of picking his cotton. Hernández wrote to *The Rebel* that "It can't be justice and right to leave a family to face starvation" and declared: "I will be shot before they touch my corn."[86] Anglo leaders of the Land League admired Hernández's willingness to take up arms in defense of his family and his Socialist principles and began to call him "Brother Hernández," as if to welcome him into the family of all white people. Mexican organizers like José Ángel and F. A. Hernández, Hickey observed, were furnishing "an inspiration to the American renters and actual farmers who have less difficulties to overcome but have until lately done less for the freedom of their wives and children than have those strangers in a strange land, that certainly are of a better metal than the poor fools that call them 'greasers.'"[87] The "copper-colored sons of Montezuma" had become an inspiration for Hickey and other poor white farmers whose assumed superiority foundered as Mexicans "unmanned" their whiteness.[88]

Central Texas landlords made it clear they would "rent them out" if Mexican tenants joined the Renters' Union or the Socialist Party. Antonio Valdés, an organizer for the Renters' Union near Austin, reported that revolutionary activity south of the Rio Grande made his job as organizer more difficult because landlords were wary of hiring Mexicans suspected of harboring Socialist ideas imported from Mexico. He also complained that, in some areas, landlords harassed Mexican organizers and threatened Mexican renters to such an extent that "Travis, Hays and Caldwell counties [near Austin] are infested with the worst kind of [Mexican] tenants, all cowards and scared on account of the Mexican war, the landlords tell them not to join us . . . and that they will take land from them if they organize."[89] White landowners rarely made any distinction between white Mexicans and nonwhite Mexicans or between immigrants and Texas Mexicans; the only distinction that mattered to them was whether their Mexican tenants were influenced by the Mexican Revolution, the PLM, the IWW, or the Socialist Party.

Although Anglo Socialist leaders like Hickey, Meitzen, and Noble acknowledged Mexican Socialists as their brothers in the struggle against high rents and absentee landlords, Hickey never printed any articles in Spanish in *The Rebel* and, in fact, frequently printed letters from white tenants expressing their racial animosity toward Mexicans just as he was growing more enamored of their revolutionary fervor and courage. One white tenant, unwavering in his belief that Mexicans represented a menace to white racial and demographic superiority, wrote that he had seen over the last few years

diseased, lame, halt, blind, illiterate, syphletic [*sic*], leprous, idiot, and degenerate Mexicans coming across the border and permanently locating in Texas . . . apparently the border is open to this scum of scums. They have no education, no money, and no morals, and yet they are welcomed and given jobs and shelter, to the great detriment of the white laborer. . . . In five years more there will be one million Mexicans of the class above described in Texas; then we will have a constant gangrene upon our social body and our moral atmosphere will be so rotten that it will require oceans of carbolic acid to disinfect it.[90]

Although seasonal Mexican labor was desired by some tenants as well as owners to harvest the cotton crop, tenants began to worry—not without grounds—that landowners were beginning to recruit more and more of these laborers to settle on central Texas farms as year-round wage laborers and sharecroppers. These newly recruited Mexican laborers sometimes undermined the efforts of Anglos as well as Mexican Americans, like José Ángel and F. A. Hernández, to organize tenants, because landlords could and did "rent out" politically active renters and replace them with newly arrived Mexican immigrants.

Hickey and other Texas Socialists began to regard Mexican radical Socialists, like José Ángel Hernández, as different from peon Mexicans, whose stolidity, they believed, was no worse than that of sorry whites. Texas whites, particularly in central Texas, rarely viewed Mexicans as white, yet Hickey and others came to regard radical Mexicans as almost white and in some ways whiter and more manly than poor whites who refused to join the Land League or struggle against landlords. The construction of this intermediate racial status for Mexicans made life easier for Socialist white tenants who hoped to include Mexican tenants in their union, because even if not-quite-white Mexicans were still regarded as inferior to Anglos, they were accorded slightly higher status than were blacks, which, in the South at least, counted for something. Mexicans organizing Mexicans, in other words, was not as politically risky as whites organizing blacks in a state that had once belonged to Mexico and to the Confederacy.[91]

The segregated locals of the Land League became a convenient way for magonistas and Socialist Mexicans to operate in Texas while Anglo Socialists gradually changed their perception of Mexicans as submissive peons.[92] Yet although Hickey and other Anglo Socialists made room in the Texas Socialist Party for these "strangers in a strange land," they were unable or unwilling to recognize Mexicans as militant leaders in their own right and thus deprived whites in the Socialist Party and Land League of models established by Mexican militancy and resistance. The only way they could understand the radicalism of Mexican Socialists was through the filter of their own subjectivities, which viewed Mexican militancy as a measure of gendered whiteness. While they praised Mexican Socialists for acting with the manly courage of white men, they tried to shame Anglo tenant farmers for lacking the "white-hearted manliness" to join the union. The frequent invocation of common manhood was not enough to transcend the racial boundaries between Anglo and Mexican tenant farmers; however, militant opposition to landlords constituted at least one measure of manhood that, for a brief time, expanded the boundaries of whiteness to construct Mexican tenant farmers as almost white through their radical politics.[93]

With the entry of the United States into World War I, Socialists all across the country were harassed and imprisoned for conspiracy against the government, and without the leadership of the Socialist Party, landowners and county councils of defense easily undermined and discredited the Land League and other Socialist unions.[94] Patriotic council members kept a keen eye out for citizens who were less than enthusiastic about the war and bullied them to buy their quota of liberty bonds; they also volunteered as "enforcers" who conducted raids to round up "slackers" as well as "idlers, vagrants, and other non-effectives."[95] In the aftermath of the "red scare" in the fall of 1917, the Land League and other Socialist Party organs soon collapsed. Some Texas Socialists drifted into the Farm Labor Union; others, like Hickey and E. O. Meitzen, joined the short-lived but radical Nonpartisan League in North Dakota, which escaped the severe repression that had swept through Texas and Oklahoma.[96] Hickey wrote his comrades in 1917: "I believe the Socialist Party cannot function in any agricultural state in the nation while the present unpleasantness is on."[97]

At the beginning of World War I, Hickey's career as editor of *The Rebel* came to an abrupt end. On May 17, 1917, federal officers and Texas Rangers arrested him at his wife's farm in Stonewall County and charged him with conspiracy against the government for his alleged membership in a secret organization known as the Farmers' and Laborer's Protective League (FLPA). Agents of the government contended that the organization pledged to oppose conscription even by resorting to force.[98] George Bryant, an FLPA organizer and a defendant in the case, informed the federal agents and Texas Rangers that Hickey could not possibly belong to the FLPA because he was neither a farmer nor a laborer.[99] But the agents had their orders, and Hickey was arrested anyway. He recounted: "I was surrounded by four men and told to climb into an automobile. . . . The leader . . . who said that he was a Texas ranger, said to me, when I asked him for a warrant, that no warrant was necessary, that I had to 'climb in. . . . ' Under the persuasion of the guns I got in the automobile."[100] His final words appeared in the Dallas *Times Herald* and were printed in the last edition *The Rebel* was to publish: "I am writing all this under a sort of censorship that my readers will understand; however, I can definitely promise that the real story will appear in the next Rebel unless I am killed or kidnapped again."[101]

The next edition of *The Rebel* was never published. The postmaster general of the United States, Albert Sydney Burleson, used the provisions of the newly legislated Espionage Act to ban "seditious" literature from the mail. The law forbade the publication of material calculated to foster disloyalty or to sabotage the war effort, such as urging young men to avoid duty in the military service. Hickey charged that *The Rebel* had been singled out for persecution not simply for its "radical utterances against militarism" but, more directly, for having "incurred the enmity of the large banking and landed interests in the state." Texas politicians serving in Washington, like Burleson and Colonel E. M. House, "took advantage of a national crisis," he wrote, "to crucify a political opponent they could not bribe or control."[102] Burleson interpreted the law broadly to mean that no publication could say "that this Government is the tool of Wall Street or the munitions-makers" because "that kind of thing" is a lie and "breeds disloyalty."[103] Since all Socialist newspapers held the view that the government was the tool of Wall Street, they were barred for making false statements.

The Rebel was the first Socialist newspaper Burleson barred from the mails, but not merely because he believed that it violated the law or espoused radical ideas. Rather, Burleson despised Hickey and *The Rebel* for having made him front-page news when he evicted all of the tenant families on his 4,000-acre cotton farm in Bosque County, Texas, and replaced them with convict labor. Hickey frequently alluded to the Burleson plantation as one of the worst cases of landowner greed and indifference to the suffering of tenant farmers that he had ever encountered. In his autobiography Oscar Ameringer pondered how one Christmas morning prison guards and convicts arrived at the Burleson plantation and "threw the group of tenant farmers and their belongings, along with their old, sick, halt, lame, blind, and babies, out in the festive, frosty Yuletide air."[104] Burleson retaliated by personally barring *The Rebel* from the mail and by having Hickey arrested on charges of sedition.

Within a few years, however, the "the fighting Irishman" and "baby blizzard" of Texas Socialism had decided that it was more effective and profitable to cooperate with capital than to seek its overthrow, although he left no clues to explain his sudden change of heart.[105] In the early 1920s Hickey moved to the south-central Texas county of McMullen, sixty miles south of San Antonio, and became the secretary of the Chamber of Commerce and booster for the oil industry in the county. He wrote columns for the *Independent Oil and Financial Report* and other industry magazines and rhapsodized about the future prospects of his new home: "[Texas] Rangers and skyscrapers. Think of it. And oh, Lord, how I love the Rangers and all they have stood for in the dear days that are passing when derricks will take the place of derringers and danger, and the coyote will sing his evening song no longer to the gibbous moon."[106] It did not seem to bother Hickey that only a few years earlier he had been kidnapped at gunpoint by the Texas Rangers.

In 1925 he moved to Fort Worth and championed the construction of a railroad line from there through the Texas Panhandle to Tucumcari, New Mexico, an area that was quickly becoming the leading cotton-producing region in Texas. Large-scale, irrigated cotton ranches, highly capitalized and mechanized, like those of the Coastal Bend area of Corpus Christi, came to dominate the High Plains of west Texas, which lay beyond the traditional cotton belt where small tenant farms prevailed. The railroad would play the role of the "great emancipator" to this "new empire" which, Hickey proclaimed, would become the "great cotton belt of the world." In one of his last pronouncements before disappearing from the historical record, he wrote: "Eventually labor and capital will find it more profitable to lock arms than lock horns."[107]

While I cannot explain Hickey's conversion from radical Socialist to businessman booster, we can draw some important conclusions about the partial success and/or failure of radical movements in the countryside in the opening decades of the twentieth century. Biracial unionism had succeeded in east Texas with the BTW in large part because more than half of the timber workers were blacks. The mostly white Renters' Union and Land League, on the other hand, chose not to include blacks and were little involved in organizing Mexican tenants, since Mexican tenants themselves undertook to organize their own locals. Although both unions included nonwhite members, neither challenged the assumptions of white racial superiority, choosing instead to emphasize common class interests among Mexican, black, and white tenants and timber workers. Just as importantly, however, the Land League was not simply a local development that arose out of the conflict between landowners and tenants; it had its origins in land and labor disputes in Ireland in the late nineteenth century and sought to create in Texas a revolution not unlike the one the Mexicans had begun in northern and central Mexico to redistribute land among the dispossessed. The diffusion of radical ideas about land distribution and ownership was thus a transnational and global phenomenon brought about by the geographical mobility of workers like Tom Hickey, E. O. Meitzen, and José Ángel Hernández from Ireland, Germany, and Mexico, respectively. Although it chose not to organize blacks, the Land League represented the cross-fertilization of rural union movements of Mexican, Irish, German, and native whites who traveled between states, countries, and continents in search of land they could call their own. The growing industrialization of agriculture throughout parts of the world created new challenges for these displaced farmers, who in some areas were becoming proletarianized workers on large-scale tenant plantations and corporate cotton ranches.

Not until the New Deal would a new generation of Socialists, under the leadership of H. L. Mitchell, Howard Kester, and Norman Thomas, organize the STFU and fight against evictions and political repression on sharecropper farms in the western South, particularly in Arkansas, Oklahoma, and Texas. During the 1920s the widespread adoption of the tractor and massive immigration from Mexico gave rise to industrial cotton farms in parts of Texas that were similar in size and organization to the enormous cotton ranches of California. Mechanization and "Mexicanization" accelerated the growth of industrial cotton ranches in south-central Texas and laid the foundation for the creation of a multiracial agricultural proletariat.

CHAPTER 5

The Scientific Management of Farm Workers

Mexicans, Mechanization, and the Growth of Corporate Cotton Culture in South-Central Texas, 1900–1930

In chapter 4 we saw how some tenants were asked to leave the 20,000-acre Day Ranch because they joined the Socialist Party. These tenants were not independent farmers working on small family farms they hoped one day to own. Rather, they worked under the close supervision of the overseer, C. A. Rives, who determined who was hired and fired, made decisions about how much cotton and corn to plant, and when to plant it, and even decided which political affiliations and activities were acceptable for ranch tenants. Furthermore, on this tenant plantation individual tenant farms were operated as a single large farm, and tenants were managed like employees rather than treated as independent farmers. Whether called tenant plantations, neoplantations, or business plantations, agricultural economists argued that these centrally managed, large-scale cotton ranches were more efficient producers of cotton than were small, undercapitalized family farms.[1]

Although the Day Ranch was not corporately owned, a number of large cotton ranches under corporate ownership developed in the Corpus Christi area shortly after 1900. One of the first of these was the approximately 200,000-acre Taft Ranch, where Mexicans, blacks, and whites labored under the direction of a new class of professional farm managers sometimes recruited from state or federal agricultural agencies as well as from agricultural and mechanical colleges. Trained in the principles of "scientific management," these managers sought to control most aspects of the workers' lives—their housing, their stores, their children's schools, and their churches were all built and owned by the company; and the teachers and pastors were hired and fired by Taft management. Managers even instructed company employees how to vote in local and national elections, especially since the principal owner of the Taft Ranch, Charles Phelps Taft, was the brother of President William Howard Taft.

The region of south-central Texas near Corpus Christi was an ideal place for the Taft Ranch to develop its experiment in scientific farming and the management of a triracial workforce, for Corpus Christi lay in the cultural and economic borderlands between the plantation South and the semiarid Southwest with its history of cattle ranching and Mexican communities. The presence of white tenants and African American sharecroppers linked this region to the South, while the employment of increasing numbers of Mexican laborers on large-scale cotton ranches at the turn of the century foreshadowed the rise of the irrigated agribusiness empire in California and other parts of the West, including West Texas.[2] Thus, while plantations in the traditional South relied on African American sharecroppers, cotton ranches on the far-western rim of the New South pioneered the use of Mexican wage laborers.[3]

The consolidation of small farms into plantations and industrial farms went practically unnoticed by many historians who believed that the major social, political, and economic struggles of the postemancipation South had taken place during the latter half of the nineteenth century. By the century's end, according to conventional wisdom, the economic contours of southern agriculture had been established, and they remained essentially unchanged until the New Deal. On one level, not much *had* changed: The majority of African American and white farmers, owners and tenants alike, still used horse-drawn plows to plant and cultivate, and hoes to chop the cotton on mostly small family farms. Subtle and significant changes, however, were gradually taking place in the *organization* of the farms throughout the South.[4] The 1910 special census report on plantations revealed what many agricultural economists had long suspected: Individual tenant farms were often part of a single, larger unit of production. Tenants were not so much independent farm operators as farm workers subjected to an unprecedented degree of supervision—a sharecropper, essentially, with a mule. In forty-one selected counties of central and south Texas, according to the 1910 census report, there were 3,468 tenant plantations comprising 32,658 tenant farms, which represented 20.2 percent of all farms in those counties.[5] In 1914 the journalist O. C. Payne, who visited the Taft Ranch, wondered: "Will the small, one-family farm give way eventually to the mammoth farm under corporate ownership and management? Is the man who actually tills the soil to be reduced to a day-laborer and the mule and turning-plow to be displaced generally by the powerful tractor and deep-tilling gang [plow]?"[6]

In the area around Corpus Christi, where there were no cotton plantations and the land was cheaper than in the Blackland Prairie of central Texas, businessmen and corporations bought enormous tracts of land and set out to organize cotton farms and cattle ranches along corporate lines. Others inherited large tracts of land or used their positions as bankers and ranchers to purchase land at rock-bottom prices. *The Rebel* reported that Henrietta Chamberlain King of Corpus Christi owned 1,400,000 acres, adding that it was "just 50 miles from her front porch to her back gate." Charles P. Taft owned 167,000 acres, and "C. W. Post of breakfast food fame owned 200,000 acres" on the plains. Reporting on the growth of the Taft Ranch, which occupied 39 percent of the land area of San Patricio County, Tom Hickey wrote that "great syndicates are buying up and holding millions of Southern and Western lands" and that the time was not distant when all the farmers would be employed on "immense farms of the most powerful landed oligarchy the world has ever seen."[7] Even at the peak of industrial cotton ranching during the 1920s, Texas agricultural industrialists hardly formed the world's most powerful oligarchy, but Hickey's exaggerating the size of the problem perhaps owed as much to his having become a Texan, as his rancorous fulminations against landlords derived from his being Irish.

The impact of consolidation on the small farmer was devastating: Individual farmers, with little or no capital, could not possibly compete with corporate cotton ranches and often lost their farms through fore-closures. "What's the poor devil in Texas going to do with two mules, a broken-down plow, a bum cultivator, four kids and a sick wife?" Tom Hickey wondered.[8] One possibility was to become a tenant farmer on an industrial cotton ranch or tenant plantation. Absentee landlords and corporate owners hired farm managers, like C. A. Rives of the Day Ranch, to tighten control over tenants and day workers who were rapidly becoming "industrial operators" of the new agricultural proletariat. "From the standpoint of farm organization," wrote one U.S. Department of Agriculture (USDA) economist, on large farms "the relationship is virtually that of employer and employee rather than that of landlord and tenant."[9]

The development of industrial agriculture was hailed by many as an indication of the progress that could be expected from the application of scientific management to agricultural production. Farm analysts Edward

Mead and Bernhard Ostrolenk wrote in 1928 that for every hundred workers in manufacturing only three worked for themselves, whereas in agriculture, for every hundred farm workers, sixty-five worked for themselves, and thus the latter's work was not performed under the "same expert supervision as in manufacturing industry." Mead and Ostrolenk concluded that farmers would be more productive "if placed under skilled supervision."[10] Another analyst, Lynn W. Ellis, wrote that the "farmer has no more right to be independent in the present sense than the laborer in the city. Some day he must be content to be one of the rank and file, working with his neighbors under the direction of those best equipped, if he is to continue his work at a profit."[11] In the new farm order, tenant farmers, regardless of ethnoracial status, had lost their right to be independent farmers. It was not only desirable but necessary, these analysts argued, for them to be transformed into proletarians on industrial farms, not unlike wage laborers in the urban industries, and to submit to those "best equipped" to handle them. Scientific management thus ordained that Mexicans, blacks, and poor whites must learn to accept the close supervision of businessmen farmers as their gifted white superiors.

The owner of the Chapman Ranch near Corpus Christi, John O. Chapman, for example, divided more than 18,000 acres of his land into roughly 160-acre plots and rented them to 124 "white Americans" and their wives and children. All 124 farms were operated as a single unit under one management, with well-defined and uniform standards for each of the farms. "That is to say," wrote one journalist, K. C. Davis, "all of these farms are virtually alike." Each farmer was required to use the same seed and to prepare the soil under the general management of the company expert. The management had each farm treated for boll-weevil infestation and ensured that harvesting would be "pushed diligently at the proper time." Each tenant was given "such independence as he desires," Davis declared, "providing, of course, that he produces in the right way."[12] Since Chapman Ranch tenant farmers and their families were not entitled to any more independence than ranch management was willing to bestow, Davis allowed that there might be some "theoretical dangers" lurking in any system of large-scale farming that might lead to a kind of feudalism, but he insisted that any reduction in a tenant's independence was a fair trade-off for the advantages of increased efficiency, profits, and better living conditions.

None of Chapman's white tenant families was able to harvest 160 acres of cotton without the help of local and seasonal Mexican workers.

There was no shortage of seasonal labor, for Corpus Christi had served for decades as a major gathering point for Mexicans from the border counties of South Texas on their annual migration to central and east Texas to pick cotton.[13] The economist Paul Taylor reported that the local labor supply in Nueces County—the Corpus Christi area—in 1929 was 97 percent Mexican, 3 percent black, and "practically no whites." Of those who migrated to Nueces on a seasonal basis to pick cotton, 65 percent were Mexicans, 20 percent were blacks, and 15 percent were Anglos. In Nueces County, where Mexican laborers facilitated the development of large-scale farming, the number of bales of cotton produced between 1900 and 1927 increased from 6,000 to more than 250,000, making it the leading cotton-producing county in the state. In 1923 more cotton was being produced on corporate cotton ranches west of the Mississippi than on cotton farms in the plantation South, where sharecropping still prevailed.[14] By 1930, Nueces led the counties of the entire United States in the production of cotton.[15]

On their ranches some corporations built so-called company towns in which the company owned everything from the hospital to the hotel, giving owners unprecedented control over workers. Owners erected schools on the ranches to attract and hold a year-round labor force. Chapman, for example, built two schools—one for the children of the white tenants and one for the children of the Mexican laborers—and donated two buildings for churches. In addition to the cotton farms, Chapman operated the Chapman Motor Company, which supplied and repaired automobiles and tractors, and the Chapman Mercantile Company, under whose 36,000-square-foot roof were housed the motor company, hardware store, grocery store, implement store, and dry-goods stores. No matter what any of Chapman's employees needed, there was no other place to buy it. The most successful ranches monopolized industries related to agricultural production and thus came to form the prototype of industrialized agribusiness farms.[16] The Commission on Industrial Relations concluded in 1915 that a disturbing new tendency existed to develop huge, corporation-owned, industrial-type agricultural operations based on extremely low wages, paid partly in scrip, with arbitrary wage deductions for various reasons, and company-owned housing areas where regulation of employees' lives was possible "to almost any extent."[17] In the Corpus Christi area corporate farming achieved its highest degree of centralization in the operations of the Taft Ranch, the ne plus ultra of industrial agriculture.[18]

The Taft Ranch began as a partnership during the era of Reconstruction, when San Patricio County, just north of Corpus Christi, was home to more cattle than people. The company was formed in 1879 and incorporated under the laws of Texas in 1880 for the purpose of raising stock for domestic and foreign markets. The rapid turn to cotton in the county began during the 1890s, when prospective immigrants found on the ranch a stalk of cotton containing eighty bolls that had grown, so the story went, entirely without culture from an accidentally dropped seed.[19] Joseph Green, one of the principal stockholders in the Coleman-Fulton Pasture Company and later the superintendent of the company ranch, began to call the Pasture Company the Taft Ranch at about the same time, ironically, that the ranch was switching over from cattle to cotton. In making the change Green may also have wanted to ingratiate himself to President William Howard Taft, who visited the ranch in 1909, as well as to Charles Phelps Taft.[20]

Railroad links to Corpus Christi from San Antonio, Fort Worth, and Saint Louis stimulated population growth and the sale of new lands, and its location on the Gulf Coast made it possible to ship cotton to domestic ports in the East. Green hired hundreds of Mexicans to clear the land and began renting to farmers who agreed to cultivate 50-acre tracts in cotton. By 1909 a total of 2,300 acres had been planted in cotton and grain. Six years later approximately 12,000 acres were under cultivation, about one-third of which were rented to tenants on a thirds-and-fourths basis.[21] Invoking the rhetoric of Manifest Destiny, Green explained the high purpose of industrial agriculture in a speech to Taft Ranch tenants, reminding them that God "had given us this good climate, this fertile soil and a good road on the sea almost at our door to carry our cotton cheaply to all the markets of the world."[22]

Marketing cotton to the world demanded that it be done cheaply, and to this end Green envisioned white tenant farmers and Mexican wage laborers working the land under company supervision, occupying company-built homes, and purchasing supplies in the company store. There the experiment in company farming began: The company erected three small houses to shelter Mexican laborers and installed a cotton gin.[23] By 1912 the Taft Ranch was the focus of national attention for its application of industrial organization to agricultural production.

The company recognized early on the advantages of utilizing the available Mexican labor in the region. Before Green was named superintendent of the company, Charles Phelps Taft inaugurated a plan in 1897 to replace Anglo cowboys with Mexicans because the company could pay Mexicans lower wages. Three of the Anglo cowboys had worked for the ranch for fifteen years. A. Ray Stephens, the historian of the Taft Ranch, noted that it was a difficult task for the superintendent "to replace three of the most valued employees" with Mexicans, but he added, unflinchingly, that "out of courtesy for their fifteen years of service to the company he gave them thirty days' notice." Green continued the policy of hiring Mexicans because he understood "how to handle them." Mexican laborers cleared out the mesquite and live oaks so that powerful tractors could break the sod and put the land in cultivation. The company cleared 5,000 acres of land, built comfortable cottages and barns, and rented to tenants under the crop-share plan.[24]

The company operated six 1,000-acre cotton farms, each employing more than 25 Mexican wage workers. Green estimated in 1915 that the six farms employed between 150 and 200 Mexican laborers year-round and about 25 white tenants. A number of African American laborers worked for the Taft Company's oil mill, eight gins located in six towns, machine shop, grain elevator, mixed-feed plant, and cottonseed-oil refinery or were wage workers on the cotton farms. The Taft Ranch encouraged African Americans to immigrate to the area by providing houses near the plant site practically rent-free, with no charge for wood and water. Mexican and black laborers were originally required to live at the company boardinghouse and to trade at the company store.[25]

As the superintendent of the Taft Ranch from 1900 until his death in 1926, Joseph Green exercised almost complete control over all of the ranch's farming and industrial operations. During that time he instituted a number of changes to accommodate the company's gradual shift from cattle to cotton. In oral contracts with tenants, Green made it clear that he expected them to purchase their supplies at the company store and not from independent merchants. Company tenants were also expected to have their cotton ginned only at company gins. The penalty for violating these provisions was almost always dismissal. George Rhodes, a "negro preacher" and company tenant, was "stopped" by Taft management when he attempted to gin his cotton at the independent gin of Dale Walker, although the Walker gin charged slightly more than the Taft Ranch gin. According to Rhodes, when a white tenant also attempted to let Walker gin his cotton, the company "got rid of him." T. D. Williams, a carpenter for the company, was dismissed because his wife traded at an independent store. His supervisor told him that his work was satisfactory and there was enough work to retain him but that he had orders to dismiss him.[26] From the start Taft managers insisted on conformity and compliance with company policy, even if it meant that employees had to forfeit basic freedoms.

Although the company dominated business in the three towns of Taft, Gregory, and Portland, independent merchants and gin operators competed with the company for the business of independent farmers in the region. The company lowered its ginning price in 1913 in an effort to attract as many independent farmers as it could and, in the process, drove some of the smaller gins out of business. Walker refused to sell his cottonseed to the company, as had other independent gins, because he could realize a higher profit by selling to an agent. Green retaliated by proposing to E. C. Hodges, a prominent independent farmer, that Hodges enter into a partnership with the company gin to drive Walker out of business. The Taft management was especially eager to ruin Walker's ginning business because numerous independent tenant farmers chose Walker's gin over the Taft Ranch gin despite Walker's slightly higher prices. According to one report, these tenants "regarded Taft as a standing menace to their liberty."[27]

Walker spoke freely about his problems with the Taft Ranch during his interviews in 1914 with David J. Saposs, an investigator for the Commission on Industrial Relations. Saposs personally investigated the Taft Ranch, interviewed many of the workers, and compiled a highly critical report of how the ranch's progressive techniques were transforming cotton agriculture into "factory farming" and family farmers into company employees who were denied basic liberties. When Walker appeared before the commission during its hearings in 1915, however, he avoided any direct reference to the company's efforts to drive him out of business and merely noted that the company had lowered its ginning price to below what he was able to offer, which, he confessed, affected him "a little bit." Green's presence in the hearing room no doubt caused Walker to choose his words carefully. Thus when Chairman Frank P. Walsh urged Walker to speak frankly "as to the competitive conditions" on the Taft Ranch, he responded: "Well, Mr. Chairman, it is a sort of hard proposition to make them [complaints]. I have them, but it is . . . a hard matter for a man . . . to go into it. It is this way: I have never ginned a bale of cotton for the pasture company's farm."[28] This was Walker's circumspect way of telling Walsh that Green had forbidden Taft Ranch tenants from bringing their cotton to his gin. Like independent merchants and other independent gin owners, Walker was reluctant to make public his complaints against the company for fear that Green would retaliate with even more drastic economic measures.

Green was also a member of the Board of Directors of the First National Bank of Gregory, which was owned by some of the principal stockholders of the Taft Ranch and was also the bank that provided loans to tenant farmers in the area. Not surprisingly, therefore, the bank refused Walker's application for a $100 loan when he opened another gin in Portland, a few miles from Gregory. Green immediately opened a gin near Walker's and warned Taft Ranch tenants to gin their cotton only with the company gin. After the season was over, Walker was forced to withdraw his operation from Portland.[29] Walker was in "great dispair [*sic*]" in 1914 at the time of the interview and feared "he would not be able to bear it any longer." Saposs likened the tactics of Green and the Taft Ranch to those of a boxer delivering steady but relentless blows to the body: Walker's case, he wrote, was "an admirable illustration how the powerful combatant, not being able to down his weaker adversary with one stroke, wears him out gradually all the time waiting for a chance to get in his knockout punch."[30] In a separate report on industrial communities, or company towns, Saposs characterized the strategy of corporate farming as one designed "not so much to drive out non-submissive businessmen, as to keep them within bounds by constantly harassing them. Of course, they would prefer to oust them altogether, but sometimes find it necessary to follow a less drastic policy. In that event they inaugurate various tactics by way of a reminder of their power and as an indirect warning as to what might be expected if an aggressive opposition manifests itself."[31]

The power of the company extended into most of the affairs of its tenant-employees, but it especially affected those who showed independence by questioning or challenging company policy. The often vague nature of oral contracts, for example, resulted in conflicts between the company and the tenant in which the tenant's only choice was to accede to company authority in all matters or be forced to leave the farm. George Rhodes, the black preacher, agreed under an oral contract to rent on the halves. Rhodes told Saposs in 1914 that the Taft people had agreed to clear the land at no expense to him. When the company learned at the end of the season that Rhodes had a surplus after paying all of his expenses, it deducted $3.50 per acre for the cost of clearing the land. Rhodes protested to the company, to no avail. Another black tenant, J. H. Woods, told Saposs that he rented from the company under an oral contract with the understanding that the company would clear the land for $1.50 per acre. When Woods also showed a surplus at the end of the season, the company charged him $3.50 per acre. Rhodes left after one year because he expected to be put off for having "shown his independence." Woods had heard a rumor that the company would not renew contracts with other black tenants because they were "manifesting too much independence" and that Mexicans would be substituted for black tenants "for they are more subservent" [*sic*].[32]

Tenants (mostly Anglos and African Americans) and wage laborers (mostly Mexicans) were required to purchase supplies from the company store as a condition of the oral employment agreement. Tenants as well as wage workers were issued coupon books for the sums of $1.00, $2.00, $5.00, and so forth, which they used to purchase goods at the store. Charles Alvord, the manager of the cotton farms, explained in testimony before the Commission on Industrial Relations how the coupon system saved the company and the customer money: "a Mexican will come in and buy 5 cents' worth of potatoes and 5 cents' worth of sugar, and 10 cents' worth of flour, and if we would have to make a 5-cent charge for each one of those items, it would take a force of bookkeepers to keep their accounts." But the principal use of the coupon system was to make salary advances to the Mexican laborers, who could purchase food and supplies only at the company store with company coupons. It was not so much store credit as a form of currency issued as wages that could only be redeemed at the Taft Ranch's two stores or at smaller commissaries located on the 1,000-acre farms. To hear Alvord explain it, the coupon system was devised simply to serve the needs of the workers: "if a man wants anything, he [the foreman] gives him a book."[33] The store manager kept a record of the total cash sum for the coupon books issued to each tenant or laborer, which was then deducted from his wages at the end of the month, in the case of the laborer, or at the end of the season, in the case of the tenant. The primary role of the store manager was thus to monitor debt, the chief purpose of which was to hold labor on the farms.

Charles Holman, a commission investigator, was not persuaded by Alvord's salutary description of the coupon system. He told Green during the 1915 Dallas hearings that he had heard statements that "the use of the coupon-book system was for the purpose of concentrating the trade of the people on your place at your store and to prevent trade with competitive stores." Green responded simply, "I don't know much about it." The chairman of the commission, Frank Walsh, skeptical that Green could be ignorant of the operations of the company store, pursued Holman's line of questioning and asked Green what he thought the purpose of the coupon system was, to which Green again replied: "Well, I don't really, to tell you the facts, know anything about it."[34] This was flagrant deception: Green knew all about how the coupon system worked, as he did every other operation of the company. In fact, he delighted in explaining each operation in great detail to a succession of prominent visitors: Serefino Domínguez, known as the "corn and cotton king of Mexico"; A. Brill of Palestine, who represented the Rothschild family; Theodore H. Price, owner of the Campbell experimental cotton-picking machine; Don Von Simpson, a large landowner from Prussia; and various agricultural representatives from Cuba, Brazil, Austria, and Africa.[35]

Texas journalists also flocked to the Taft Ranch to report on the operations of these new corporate cotton ranches, and Green himself explained to them in detail the operations of the company. The journalists wrote articles extolling the efficiency and fairness of Taft management, often failing to investigate the veracity of the claims made by the company.[36] Green especially liked to accompany writers from Texas magazines and farm journals in order to showcase the benefits of corporate farming, including how to manage a triracial workforce without running the risk of race mixing. The company constructed three schoolhouses—one for Anglos, one for African Americans, and one for Mexicans; separate churches for each group—Presbyterian, Baptist, and Catholic; and segregated housing areas for the different classes and races of laborers. The Taft Ranch also paved roadways, built modern gins, operated commissaries, and established a hospital with separate dormitories for Mexicans and blacks.[37] Racial segregation was thus carefully preserved on the ranch, even as the company established educational, religious, and economic control over the lives of its employees.

Corporate farms were not merely large in scale; they constituted a particular set of beliefs, sometimes called "Taylorism" or scientific management, which sought to organize work and workers according to scientific principles that would increase efficiency and profits. Company gins, schools, commissaries, and churches, Green explained, were all crucial to maintaining an efficient labor force. Farm efficiency, he further explained, was measured by bales of cotton to the acre, which also depended on soil type, climate, weevil infestation, capital equipment, and, of decisive importance, the availability and cost of Mexican labor at harvest time. Weevil infestation was a problem, he admitted, but with chemical treatment not insuperable, and Mexicans could generally be counted on to arrive in large numbers and to work for low wages. Magazine and journal writers took the bait and earnestly reported that large-scale farming was the solution to the problem of too many inefficient tenant farmers clamoring for their own land, even if the majority of those tenant farmers were whites.[38]

The Taft Ranch operated a string of fifty 100- to 200-acre tenant-operated farms with fields tilled by tractors pulling multiple-row cultivators and plows. Mexican laborers were assigned to each tenant farm, and hundreds of other Mexicans were hired for the labor-intensive tasks of chopping and picking the cotton. Of the fifty tenants, two were Mexicans, a small number were African Americans, and the rest were "Americans." As an incentive to bring tenants to the ranch, the company arranged for them to purchase nearby unimproved rangeland with their profits from tenant farming. White tenants who purchased land hired Mexicans to clear the land and then farmed it in addition to their rented acres on the Taft Ranch. On each tenant farm the ranch also built a four-room house equipped with a bathroom, a spacious barn, and two or three two-room cottages for the Mexican day laborers—and offered the "whole outfit . . . to any good man." Upon observing the quarters built for the Mexicans, one visitor rhapsodized, "The Mexican laborers must look upon their little cottages as elegance itself." And perhaps they did, for the cottages were outfitted with screens and wooden floors.[39]

To ensure uniformity and efficiency in the management of tenant farms, the Taft Ranch laid out some farms in 200-acre tracts, grouping four tenant houses at a single crossroad that divided the 800-acre quadrant. This series of contiguous quadrants, separated at mile intervals, each with its cluster of four tenant houses, were collectively called "spiderville" because the fields formed a weblike pattern around the nucleus of tenant houses at the crossroads. This carefully designed pattern enabled the Taft Ranch to provide water to four farms from a single well and to supervise white tenants and Mexican laborers more efficiently.[40]

In addition to the tenant farms of spiderville, the Taft Ranch operated six 1,000-acre cotton farms worked primarily by Mexican wage laborers under the close supervision of foremen. Of these wage workers, Green estimated that 90 percent were Mexicans, 5 percent were blacks, and 5 percent were Anglos. Some of the foremen were Mexicans. In addition to the year-round Mexican laborers, the company recruited hundreds of Mexicans from Laredo, a border city about 100 miles west of Corpus Christi, to pick the cotton during harvest. In 1912 *The Rebel* reported that "originally the land on the Taft farm was cultivated by white tenants, but that has been almost altogether abandoned and the work is now done by Mexican wage laborers."[41] However, the idea was not simply to replace white tenants: The Taft Ranch hoped to replace tenancy itself. The management realized a larger profit from using low-paid Mexican wage laborers than from renting to Anglo tenant farmers on thirds and fourths, who paid as rent only one quarter of their cotton. These six farms thus represented the Taft Ranch experiment in the use of Mexican wage laborers instead of less profitable tenant arrangements. Paying Mexican laborers only $0.80 per day was an attractive feature of the experiment. To increase efficiency and profits further, the Taft management switched from paying Mexicans monthly wages of $25.00 to day wages of between $0.80 and $1.00, which effected a savings of more than 12 percent to the company by shifting the wet-weather risk to the workers.[42]

One journalist described the corporate configuration of the 1000-acre farms operated by Mexican wage laborers:

At each farm is a large, finely built, commodious house for the farm superintendent and family and his foremen. Down one side of the big inclosure is a double row of two-room, well-built cottages for the Mexican laborers.

There is a large barn . . . equipped on modern methods . . . silos . . . power equipment . . . great sheds for machines and wagons and a garage with repair outfits.

Each farm is a complete unit in itself, operated under a number, and its accounts, debits and credits, are kept at headquarters in as systematic a manner as an expert accountant can devise.[43]

Each 1,000-acre farm thus operated as a self-contained unit that consisted of a white superintendent, Anglo or Mexican foremen, and Mexican laborers. A 1934 survey of the western cotton area reported that on the Taft Ranch the little cottages for Mexican farm laborers, the barns, the commodious house for the superintendent and foreman, and the farm equipment all "huddle together in little communities."[44]

Until the 1930s, few Anglos hired themselves out as farmhands even at slightly higher wages than those paid to Mexicans because of the stigma attached to farm labor—in the Corpus Christi area only Mexicans were supposed to "grub" the land and work under Mexican foremen. Thus there was some truth to Charles Alvord's testimony before the Commission on Industrial Relations that the Taft Ranch hired Mexican laborers not simply because they worked for lower wages than did Anglos but because in the Corpus Christi area there was a shortage of "white labor" willing to do Mexican work for poor white wages.[45] White employers were sometimes reluctant to hire whites even if they were willing to work for so little. One white tenant from Nueces County, in describing poor whites who picked cotton for a living, told

Paul Taylor that "A sorry white man is about the sorriest person there is."[46] The economist Ruth Allen wrote in 1930 that since farm workers were forced to endure squalid living conditions as well as low wages, many owners in Texas preferred to hire Mexicans for the simple reason that "the American landowner and his wife dislike to see 'white people living that way.' "[47]

For eugenicists like Madison Grant, however, wages were not the issue: White people were inferior to Mexicans and blacks in their ability to survive in a climate where the sun's "actinic rays . . . affect adversely the delicate nervous organization of the Nordics." "In the south," Grant claimed, "men of the Nordic race . . . grow listless and cease to breed."[48] Poor whites in the South, however, did not claim to be Nordics and encountered less difficulty in breeding than in surviving on $0.80 per day.

Despite Alvord's contention that the Taft Ranch hired Mexicans because of a shortage of white labor, the principal reason was their willingness to work for lower wages than whites or African Americans, but not always, however. Alvord told the commission that in 1914 a "bunch of Mexicans," about fifteen or twenty, struck the ranch. They wanted $0.75 for a hundred pounds of cotton picked instead of $0.60, or they would go "where they could get it." "My man told them to go," Alvord testified, "and they went."[49] Mexicans throughout the cotton belt of Texas often exercised their displeasure at low wages by simply walking off, unless, as was sometimes the case, they were arrested and deported for unspecified crimes or guarded until they worked off any debts.[50]

For some farm analysts, however, the degree of profit was not as important as the enormous value of the lesson that Green intended the Taft Ranch to teach the farmers of the Southwest and the American agricultural world—that on the Taft Ranch agriculture had become as "thoroughly commercialized and . . . as business-like as any manufacturing concern."[51] On corporate cotton ranches King Cotton was subject to a board of directors, and his retainers were now mostly Mexican wage laborers.

The gradual shift to Mexican wage labor also enabled Taft management to replace Anglo and African American tenants who exercised too much independence, such as voting for political candidates in county elections who had not been endorsed by company management. During election time ranch officials "rounded up" their Mexican workers, issued them completed ballots, and took them to the polls. Anglos and African Americans on the ranch were expected to vote for the candidate supported by Taft management, who included William Howard Taft, the

Republican candidate in the 1912 presidential election. Charles Alvord and the division foreman, Mr. Tolman, visited a number of tenants and other employees and instructed them not to " 'make up their minds on politics' until they had heard from the management." Before the election, moreover, all "Negroes and Mexicans were caucused, their ballots were marked and they were voted for as President, etc." Investigator Saposs noted that, as a rule, tenants did not "dare express their political views when they differ[ed] from those of the company."52 Green tried to coerce O. A. Brown, the manager of the Taft store at Gregory, to vote against Prohibition because "it was not good politics." Green further tried to impress upon Brown "that all employees were expected to vote according to the wishes of company." Brown lost his temper and "raked Green over the coals" for trying to tell him how to vote. Three months later he was discharged without reason. A resident of the town of Sinton, adjacent to the Taft Ranch, confirmed the company's practice of "herding Mexicans" and noted that the company also paid the poll tax for its employees and then deducted it from their wages. An owner of a boardinghouse in Sinton told Saposs that "the general feeling of renters is that a man cannot be independent politically . . . if he wishes to remain on Taft land."53

The churches in the Taft Ranch towns served the social and economic aims of the company: They were built with company funds, and the company contributed to their maintenance and to the salaries of the pastors. According to Saposs, one clergyman acknowledged that "it would be indiscreet to at least actively and openly antagonize the company or its interests." Another clergyman told Saposs that the company would withdraw its financial support and "demand the parsonage if the clergyman advocated Socialism or unionism or in any way differed from the company and opposed it openly." Clergymen either refrained from asserting their independence or sought transfers to other churches. Spanish-speaking Catholic priests were either appointed by the bishop or, in the case of missionary priests, by a member of the missionary order. While such an arrangement did not give the company the same degree of control that it exerted over Protestant pastors, nevertheless it could learn from its Mexican American foremen, who spoke English and Spanish, whether priests were engaged in organizing activity of any sort. Furthermore, some large cotton ranches also continued to care for Mexican workers who were too old or infirm to farm, and in return the disabled workers served as "watchmen" and, as one Anglo tenant put it, told " 'em what's going on . . . sort of undercover stuff."54

As part of its effort to win the goodwill of its employees, the Taft Ranch sponsored holidays: for Mexicans, June 24, Saint John the Baptist Day; for African Americans, "Juneteenth" (June 19), the date Texas blacks celebrated their emancipation in 1865; and for "Americans," the Fourth of July, which Green proclaimed was a holiday for Mexicans and blacks as well as for whites. The company furnished food and refreshments (alcohol was strictly forbidden at any time on company property), music, and transportation. On Christmas Day Joseph Green sponsored a party at his mansion, La Quinta, in which Mexicans, blacks, and whites congregated at separate places on the grounds. Green or one of the foremen visited each group separately and distributed candy to the children. Music was provided by the Taft Ranch Band, which was made up of company employees furnished at company expense with instruments, uniforms, and music instruction. The band, under the direction of Charles Weyland, the company gardener, took its show on the road as a "cheerful advertisement" for industrial agriculture at regional gatherings as far north as Dallas.[55]

The infatuation of the Taft Ranch and other cotton ranches with Mexican labor diminished somewhat in the Corpus Christi area after the outbreak of the Mexican Revolution in 1910, and clashes between Mexicans and Anglos in the border counties were reported with increasing frequency. In the years just prior to America's entry into World War I, the Texas border area became the site of frequent raids by Carranzistas, Villistas, and other revolutionary factions maneuvering for domination of northern Mexico. On the U.S. side, conflict escalated between Mexican ranchers and Anglo commercial farmers. Texas authorities viewed the discovery of the irredentist *Plan de San Diego* in 1915 as yet another example of Mexican lawlessness and banditry, since few believed that Mexicans were capable of mounting an insurgent movement in Texas.[56]

Fearing an armed Mexican uprising, the Taft Ranch took the precaution of hiring only Mexican men with wives and children, on the assumption that they would be less likely than solos to engage in political activity or armed revolt. The Taft Ranch went a step farther than most cotton ranches when it organized a so-called rifle club for its Anglo employees and supplied them with .30–.30 caliber rifles and .38 caliber pistols. Ranch managers permitted the home guard, as the rifle clubs were called, to hold target practice on company farms. Superintendent Green also recommended that the company obtain a mounted machine gun "as a future precaution." At a company meeting in the summer of 1916 he explained that "there is practically no danger of any disturbance now, but if we should get a cotton crop and have a thousand or two Mexican pickers here, then there might be some danger of some one trying to get them to make an uprising of some sort and . . . it would be good policy for this reason to have a gun of this kind and have some of the men trained so they understand using it."[57] Green's readiness to supply the Taft Ranch with a machine gun flatly contradicted his assertion—made while on tour in the East to encourage investors—that the "so-called revolution [in Mexico] was a mere farce, and that no one need have any hesitancy in coming to the Southwest or going into Mexico."[58]

By all accounts the Taft Ranch succeeded in organizing cotton production according to the principles of corporate management, which included the racial division of the workforce. Mexican wage workers and Anglo tenants alike were employees of the company and subject to its authority, which was vested in Green, his superintendents, and their foremen. Theodore Price had observed the operations of the Taft Ranch and concluded in 1913: "Taft Ranch is daily demonstrating that, in the hands of competent executives, agricultural development and enterprise are legitimate subjects of capitalistic exploitation on a large scale." But perhaps the company superintendent himself, Joseph Green, best summed up the new business orientation toward agricultural production when he explained in 1919: "We're in this for business. We're giving nothing away." Corporate farming was thus not a way of life in which Nordic planter-aristocrats fulfilled certain responsibilities of noblesse oblige to their poor white tenants and Mexican laborers but rather a business enterprise in which profits and efficiency became the new creed.[59]

Although many large farms began to mechanize in the 1920s and 1930s, tractor power did not wholly displace Mexicans, blacks, and whites—or, for that matter, mules. Nevertheless, the use of tractors increased dramatically in Texas between 1920 and 1930, when their number soared from 9,000 to 37,330, or an increase of 314 percent. The Midwest and the West accounted for the largest increases in tractor use, while the South lagged far behind the rest of the country until after 1945. By 1930 Texas was home to more tractors than were the combined states of South Carolina, Georgia, Florida, Alabama, Mississippi, Louisiana, and Arkansas.[60] In 1940 Texas and Oklahoma were the only states in the cotton belt of the South with more than twenty tractors per hundred farms, which was four times the average of the eight principal cotton states of the Old South. The ratio of tractors to farms was highest in the

Corpus Christi area, where some estimates showed that there were more tractors than farms.[61] Although most preharvest tasks (such as planting and cultivating) could be done by machine, human hands were still required on cotton farms, large and small, to pick the cotton. Not until the 1950s was an efficient and economical picking machine marketed in large numbers.[62]

Between 1910 and 1930 some corporate farms began to invest in experimental models of cotton-picking machines, and some farms, like the Taft Ranch, paid the developer of the picker, Theodore Price, $500 per week to keep one of his machines in the field in order to discourage cotton pickers from striking for higher wages and better working conditions. As early as 1912 the Taft Ranch Board of Directors decided to rent a Campbell Cotton Picker despite its high cost and uneven performance because its mere presence in the field, according to the minutes of a board meeting, "made the Mexicans work and pick more when they could hear the sound of the machine that threatened to take their places."[63] In 1929 an African American laborer told Paul Taylor, "The cotton picking machine will knock the Negroes and Mexicans out of good jobs." Mexicans who had seen the machines, Taylor reported, were "loathe to make any comment upon it."[64]

However, experimental picking machines were not as prevalent or threatening as were tractors and multiple-row cultivators. An advertisement for a new model tractor asked, "How many hands can YOU replace with a Model G?" The advertisement showed a picture of a field of farm workers juxtaposed with a picture of a solitary farmer on his Model G tractor.[65] Charles Fisher, a white tenant farmer from Refugio County on the Gulf Coast, observed in 1912 that "while going to Marina the other day, I met a big gasoline tractor with 8 large plows behind it and I decided that we had best get ready for these machines [because] if we were organized we could adopt them to our own use. Otherwise, we are 'gonners.'"[66] Growers, on the other hand, regarded mechanization as a powerful tool in controlling workers' wages. For example, a cotton weigher in Nueces County told Taylor in 1929: "This spring the Mexicans struck on us for 10 cents a row in cotton chopping. Then we began to cross-plow and they came and told us they would do it for 8 cents." He then added, "It would be a good thing to have some of these [picking] machines to keep the pickers in line." A large landowner told him, "I keep a plow going to keep Mexicans in a frame of mind to do it at a reasonable price. . . . Not that we want to beat the Mexicans out—but if we have machines, the pickers would be satisfied with $1 instead of $1.25 a hundred pounds."[67] Taylor himself was hardly neutral in his attitude toward mechanization. He wrote a colleague in 1940 that tractors "mowed down people with the same efficiency as tractor-drawn combines cut wheat."[68]

Mexicans realized that experimental picking machines could not pick cotton nearly as well or as cheaply as they could themselves. They further understood that it was their cheap labor that kept them employed and their families fed and that growers would invest more money in developing efficient picking machines to displace them if and when the cost of hiring seasonal laborers became unprofitable. Like industrial laborers everywhere, Mexicans felt threatened by mechanization, and the idea of displacement through technology was dramatically symbolized by the early prototypes of cotton-picking machines that some ranches deployed.

Cotton ranches in the Corpus Christi area reflected the racial and class divisions found elsewhere in the cotton-growing South where black sharecroppers worked for predominantly white owners; but the steady substitution of Mexican wage labor for Anglo and African American tenant farmers throughout central and south Texas represented a dramatic break from the southern pattern and mirrored changes taking place throughout the West and Southwest in the composition of the agricultural workforce. Charles Alvord preferred Mexican laborers to African Americans. As he explained it, Mexicans "are as sensitive as children and must be handled as such. They are very different from the negro, who too often will take advantage of your good nature and accept your praise as a signal to indulge himself in a protracted loaf."[69] Fred Roberts, a Corpus Christi rancher, told a congressional committee in 1920 that he could not operate a large cotton farm without ready access to Mexican labor and that many owners had difficulty recruiting Anglos and African Americans from cities and towns to the north. Labor recruited from northern cities, he maintained, would not work on the farms because white workers could not tolerate the heat of the sun during the summer picking months and that "only . . . Mexicans and niggers can stand it."[70] One owner claimed that the low altitude in Corpus Christi made white people lazy and "draggy-like."[71]

Most owners of cotton ranches continued to rely on Mexican migrant laborers until well into the 1950s, when the introduction of efficient mechanical pickers dramatically reduced the demand for migrant cotton pickers.[72] In Texas and California large-scale cotton ranches became increasingly dependent on Mexican labor, and during the 1920s growers successfully opposed numerous bills in Congress to impose immigration restriction on Mexicans. One disgruntled Texas nativist tersely wrote: "Our Southern states are being Mexicanized."[73] But owners of cotton ranches argued that the entire cotton industry in Corpus Christi was "absolutely and unconditionally based upon Mexican labor."[74] W. W. Walton, the owner of a 2,560-acre cotton ranch in Nueces County, informed the immigration committee that he was so pleased with Mexican tenants that he decided to put wooden floors in their houses. Roy Miller, representing the Rural Land Owners' Association in Corpus Christi, testified that housing with floors for Mexicans was really unnecessary because "The Mexican is a primitive man. I have known of instances where they have torn the floor out of the house in order that they might live on the ground as they do at home." Many tenants, it was said, "could study astronomy through the openings in the roof and geology through holes in the floors." On large farms in San Patricio County, the administrator for the Texas Relief Commission reported, Mexicans lived "in shacks that a white person would not put a dog in." But perhaps the greatest advantage of using Mexican sharecroppers was the large size of their families. Fred Roberts put it most directly: "when I am speaking of Mexicans I am speaking of everything from 3 years old up, because they all work."[75]

Many Anglo owners hired Mexican "patch croppers," so-called because the Mexican cropper received a cash wage in addition to the cotton grown on a four- or five-acre patch. This quasi-sharecropping arrangement fulfilled the owner's need for year-round wage labor by giving the wage hand a few acres of land to grow his own cotton and vegetables.[76] Other owners of cotton ranches from the Corpus Christi area testified that they hired Mexican sharecroppers to work year-round because of the uncertainty of the migrant flow into their area during planting, chopping, and picking. W. M. Clarkson, who ran a 1,985-acre cotton ranch near Corpus Christi, permanently employed about sixty Mexicans, "grown ones and small ones."[77] Another landowner employed a Mexican man named Pancho to supervise Mexican cotton pickers because "he knows them and I don't." His only complaint was that in general the Mexican laborer was the "damndest thief." "He figures . . . it's just like the nigger: 'Massa's nigger, Massa's watermelon,' so it can't be stealing," though the farmer did not specify what the Mexicans were stealing. He clearly believed that he treated Mexicans fairly and that, for the most part, Mexicans were fairly treated in Nueces County; he told Taylor: "You can come down here and talk of subjection, but he's as free as a bird of the air. Don't come down here from the north and describe the poverty of the Mexicans at the back door of the white man's high civilization. . . . All his work is by contract, no one drives him, he can stop any time and roll his shuck cigarette and Lobo tobacco, and his pay is by the weight at the scales."[78] Mexican sharecroppers, like sharecroppers elsewhere in the cotton South, were burdened with debts and crop liens that belied the notion that they were "free as a bird of the air," but Anglo owners of cotton ranches almost uniformly agreed that Mexicans made better croppers than did Anglos. As one county agricultural agent explained, "When Mexicans come to your house here they come to the back door just like the colored people."[79] A representative of the Pima Cotton Growers' Association explained that "a Southerner can handle a Negro . . . [but] we of the Southwest—we are neither North nor South; we are Westerners—we know the Mexican; we know how to please him and how to get him to please us."[80]

Despite the growth of corporate cotton farming in Texas and other parts of the West, white tenants continued to believe with religious fervor that only on small family farms could one acquire "self-reliance and Yankee ingenuity, a pastoral simplicity and a character-building respect for the fruitfulness of Nature." But it was Yankee ingenuity that had engineered the factory farm and the huge profits it produced for the owners and managerial class.[81] Superintendent Green, who was also a part owner of the Taft Ranch, owned a fancy car and lived in grand style on his estate home, La Quinta. Visitors to the Taft Ranch could see that Green belonged to a new class of corporate cotton farmer—part owners and superintendents who met payroll, purchased tractors, managed banks and commissaries, owned schools and churches, and generally presided over the company towns they built and the workers who lived in them.[82]

Corporate farming was transforming the entire pattern of land tenure in the South and West, in effect employing farm workers in place of tenant farmers. Tom Hickey foresaw in 1915 that tenancy was "but a transitional state in America because it comes together with another revolutionary change in agriculture—the application of mechanical power on the farm." Early on he understood that the appearance of the tractor would make it possible for the landlord "to take the next step and transform his tenant into a wage worker."[83] When Henry Ford announced that the tractor would establish a six-hour day for the farmer, Hickey responded: "Verily capitalism is upside down. Just when the time comes that the inventive genius of man lifts the load from the backs of the farmer—just at that moment the farmer becomes a nomad, a pariah sitting at the landlord's gate without a home or a chance of founding a home of his own, tractor or no tractor."[84]

Gradually agricultural analysts saw the productive merit of corporate farming as it emerged in some areas of the Southwest and West—particularly in Texas and California—and, however reluctantly, began to give it their approval. The experts could not deny the efficiency of these corporate farms, but they also knew that the era of independent family farms, whose cherished ideal had been championed by Thomas Jefferson more than a century earlier, was drawing to a close. Some farm specialists argued in the 1920s that family farms might be the most desirable farms socially but that economically they were not as efficient as the industrialized farm where farmers worked under skilled supervision, as did industrial laborers in the cities.[85] Industrial farms thus also changed the ethnoracial composition of the local population from white family farmers to a highly mobile rural proletariat of mostly nonwhite farm workers. Having lost their status as family farmers, poor whites lost their claim to the status of, or aspiration to, independent yeoman manhood and the wages of whiteness that went with it.

Most agricultural economists recognized—and still do—the politically perilous consequences of challenging the heritage of small, family-owned farms. Since most farms in the South were family-operated by tenants (including sharecroppers) but were not family-owned, farm analysts foresaw large-scale farming as the solution to what they believed lay at the root of the South's tenancy problem: inherently inefficient and improvident tenant farmers—poor whites as well as African Americans and Mexicans. The large-scale farm, wrote one analyst, "makes a financial success out of an otherwise poor shiftless producer who starves his family and markets his crop often without profit because he is attempting to operate on too little capital. In a word, it is . . . the final and complete solution of the American farm problem because it is economically sound, socially safe, and scientifically efficient."[86] The era of small farms, which had sustained the centuries-old dream of the landless to own their own farms, was gradually yielding to the modern era of centralized, corporation farming, a development that spread from west to east at the same time that cotton production was shifting from south to west. Mechanization and Mexicans accelerated this shift to large-scale cotton production in the West and western South. Cotton ranches unarguably offered greater efficiency in cotton production, but tenants and wage workers paid a high price as they slowly found themselves, in the words of an old song, owing their souls to the company store.

Indeed, the rapid transformation of tenants to supervised wage work-ers took place in the 1930s all over the South in response to the acreage-reduction program of the AAA. During the first seven years of AAA pro-grams the South lost more than 30 percent of its sharecroppers and 12 percent of its tenants.[87] At the same time, the consolidation of small farms into larger, more efficient units operating with expensive farm ma-chinery resulted in the displacement of thousands of southern tenant farmers, only a fraction of whom could be absorbed by the new com-mercial farms. The hardships endured by displaced white farmers be-came the focus of national attention in the 1930s. Destitute and homeless white farmers took to the highways in multitudes to find work as sea-sonal agricultural workers, much as Mexicans had been doing for decades in the Southwest, the Midwest, and the West.

By World War II some farm analysts could still be heard singing the praises of family farming, even as they praised the efficiency of corporate farms, but fewer voices were heard on the subject of ascending the agri-cultural ladder from tenant to owner. The growth of corporate cotton ranches in Texas had rendered obsolete the notion of rising up from farm laborer to farm owner. For the first time in American history, large numbers of displaced black and white southern farmers were reduced to wage laborers who, along with Mexican migrants, provided the seasonal labor required on cotton ranches. The prototypes of modern agribusi-ness farms throughout the South and the West, corporate cotton ranches revolutionized the employment and management of a multiracial agri-cultural workforce.

CHAPTER 6

The Whiteness of Manhood

Women, Gender Identity, and "Men's Work"
on the Farm

For the "forgotten man" of the rural South—the white tenant farmer—the transition from family farm to industrial farm was a hard one, but for women on cotton farms in central Texas life had become an unrelenting routine of fieldwork, child rearing, and endless household chores. Modern labor-saving devices such as tractors and multiple-row cultivators often eased the burden of work for white male farmers who could afford them, but white women were often the last to benefit from technological advancements on the home front, such as electric washing machines, canning steamers, and kitchen appliances, and nonwhite women often not at all. Whether on small tenant farms or large cotton ranches, farm women had little good to say about the virtues of living and working in the country. As women increasingly crossed the boundary between men's and women's work on central Texas cotton farms, their overlapping identities as mothers, wives, wage workers, and farmers often were in conflict with local, state, and federal agricultural policies—and the agrarian ideology that engendered them. Also, as more white families entered the ranks of sharecroppers and tenant farmers, the relationship between women's work, manhood, and whiteness changed, for farm ownership defined the boundaries of yeoman manhood and served as the master trope for agrarian whiteness.

Whether central Texas farm women worked on rented farms, owned their own farms, or joined the migrant workforce, their labor played a crucial role in the farm family's survival and in the standard of living they could sustain through their mostly unpaid labor. Anglo, African, and Mexican American women stood, in the words of the contemporary economist Ruth Allen, "where economic struggle is fiercest."[1] They determined the size of the labor force and indirectly the tenure status of the family, and therefore the family's living conditions. Yet although the importance of women as reproducers of the labor force made the farm woman "an indispensable adjunct to a farm," it tended to place her "in a subordinate position as a means to an end" and degraded "the mother to the position of a breeder of a labor supply."[2] Nonwhite farm women in Texas, moreover, were virtually ignored by the middle-class Country Life Movement, which sought to extol the virtues of rural life, while agricultural extension agents sought to impose middle-class standards of household efficiency on women who often worked in the fields as much as they did in the homes.[3]

The agrarian ideology of Thomas Jefferson eloquently addressed the virtues of farm life for white men. Since the democratic principles that yeoman culture was supposed to engender and sustain did not apply to women, and especially not to black or Mexican farm women, little attention was paid to the role of white women in the construction and maintenance of this agrarian whiteness. The complete economic independence of the white yeoman farmer lay at the heart of this rural creed, and the implicit corollary of the creed was that women were expected to be dependent on and subordinate to their husbandmen, whose labor on the earth made them, in Jefferson's view, "the chosen people of god."[4] A woman raised the children, tended the garden, helped in the fields, and ran the household, which included cooking, cleaning, washing, sewing, canning, and a multitude of other tasks. Her role as man's helper was understood to be as natural as for a white man to own the land he farmed. Her subordinate position within the household was taken for granted, her happiness assumed, and her aspirations for herself and her children largely ignored.[5]

The maintenance of agrarian whiteness nevertheless required that women occupy an exalted place on the farm as the benefactors of white civilization, with white women themselves sometimes participating in the elaboration of this gendered ideology of farm life. Numerous bulletins of the Texas extension service carried photographs of women happily engaged in domestic farmwork, from cooking and ironing to raising children and chickens, while state demonstration agents, trained in domestic economy, carried the "gospel of right living" to white, black, and Mexican women farmers.[6] Yet the paeans glorifying women's roles on the farm too often conflicted with the endless hardship, poverty, isolation, and demoralization many women experienced. Increasingly, farm women in Texas objected. The celebration of motherhood on the farms, wrote the anthropologist Deborah Fink, thus "obscured the economic connection by representing motherhood as a sacred calling that existed apart from the economic calculus of the market." In other words, "agrarian ideology failed mothers except as a sentimental sop."[7]

Regardless of race, virtually all farm women spent time working with the men in the fields and contributed to the farm economy through food production and preservation. During the Progressive Era, however, government policies sought to transform her role as producer and laborer into that of homemaker and consumer. At the same time, government programs and extension agents would teach her husband scientific farming and transform him from a vacuous hayseed to a progressive farm manager or businessman farmer. The gendered ideology of the "new agriculture" sought to impose rigid boundaries between men's work and women's work, the separate spheres of middle-class urban life, with women working principally in the home and men running the farm. However, the division of labor on central Texas cotton farms was never rigidly observed, and women—especially Mexican and black women—frequently performed men's work. And while most farm women wanted kitchens equipped with modern conveniences, many resisted the government's attempts to curtail their role as farm producers and laborers by defining their sphere as essentially domestic and consumer oriented.[8]

Recent studies recognize the centrality of gender as the most important variable in examining the unequal partnership between men and women of all classes and races on the farms. As these women often remarked, "Man works from sun to sun, but woman's work is never done."[9] Most farm women, it must be remembered, doubled as both farmers and homemakers, and many worked for wages either in or outside the home. They canned, made quilts and rugs, took in laundry, and hired out as domestic servants and cotton pickers.[10] Bearers of the "double burden," wrote Ruth Allen, struggle "in a no man's land between being a helpmate for her husband wherever her labor is needed and being a homemaker and relieving her husband of responsibility for that section of his domain."[11] Men, by contrast, rarely crossed over gendered boundaries to engage in household work or the care of children, a gendered domain that unerringly remained a no-man's-land. According to one study of farm homemakers, fathers and sons contributed only a few hours a week to assisting with household chores, mainly carrying wood for fires and pumping water. Only 25 percent of the men with children under the age of six spent any time caring for them, and then only for an average of two and a half hours per week. Daughters of high-school age and female relatives living in the home provided the highest degree of aid to homemakers, and therefore it was the number of daughters and other women old enough to share the work—not the amount of household work to be done—that determined how much help farm women received. Men, especially sons, contributed the least amount of time performing domestic chores.[12] Since childcare and household work were culturally devalued on the farms as well as in the cities, "flexibility," observed the historian Mary Neth, "usually meant women doing the work of men, not the reverse."[13]

Life on the farm had never been easy for women, but while improvements in farm machinery made life somewhat easier for men, at least for those who could afford them, women's work was becoming progressively more demanding. As wives of owners, renters, and sharecroppers they were working in the fields in greater numbers and for longer periods of time, even as their workload in the home remained the same or increased. The nation would be inundated with images of impoverished rural families during the Great Depression, but the burden of poverty had rested on the shoulders of women on tenant farms for decades in the South. A journalist observed in 1918: "Show me a housewife with eight or ten children, all of them ragged and dirty, with her own dress drabbled and frayed, with her back bent over with toil, with children sick or unhealthy . . . and the chickens on the front porch—and nine times out of ten you are showing me the wife of a tenant farmer."[14] After chopping or picking cotton for fourteen hours, and in some instances using single cultivators, these women were too bent over with pain and exhaustion to devote themselves full-time to running the household.[15] A University of Texas researcher claimed in a 1915 survey of a central Texas county that "big stout men with stiff fingers and 'slow joints' are actually at a disadvantage when compared with the more nimble women and children."[16] Both boys and girls often began picking when they were five years old, and many boys developed stiff fingers and slow joints from a life of picking. One elderly tenant farmer from Caldwell County recalled that he had picked so much cotton in his lifetime, beginning when he was a child, that he could not bring himself to "pick the cotton out of an aspirin bottle."[17]

Children represented between one-third and one-half of the available labor supply in central Texas. As early as 1898 the Texas farm magazine *Farm and Ranch* reported that "60 percent of the labor devoted to the cotton crop of Texas is rendered by women and children. Without this labor . . . the cotton industry in Texas would go to pieces in a single year."[18] In central Texas, children worked an average of more than nine hours per day in the fields for all tenure and race categories, and in some communities they worked eleven or twelve hours per day—from "dark to dark," or as African American women in Burleson County used to say, "from can't to can't" [can't see in the morning to can't see at night]. Though reported by the census as unpaid family workers, farm women and children were, in reality, wage hands who determined in large measure the size of the cotton crop and thus the cash income of the farm.[19] As one central Texas farm owner put it, "This land wouldn't pay if my wife [and children] didn't help."[20]

Planters determined how much land to rent to a tenant or sharecropper based on the number of children in his family, because the amount of cotton that could be planted was limited to the number of hands that could pick it. Therefore the first question a landlord posed to a prospective sharecropper was "How much force have you got?"[21] Landlords in Texas were not likely to rent to newly married sharecropper couples without children or with children too young to work. One landlord in central Texas remarked that he never rented to a man who did not have at least eight children and a wife who "worked like a man."[22]

Texas landlords often chose to rent to Mexican sharecroppers because they tended to have larger families than did either Anglos or blacks. One study of central Texas tenant farmers reported that "Among the Mexicans . . . families of six, seven and eight working children and more were relatively more common among this class than any other."[23] A study of Williamson County in 1934 noted that "the Mexicans do not practice birth control to any great extent" and "whole families of Mexican men, women, and children . . . under 10 years old are seen picking cotton."[24] In fact, however, Margaret Hagood's famous study of southern white women on tenant farms, *Mothers of the South* (published in 1939), found that few women practiced birth control, even though their families tended to be slightly smaller than Mexican and black families.[25] One white mother of nine children condemned the practice: "Many a soul is going to fry in hell for that very thing [birth control]. . . . We are put here to do the Lord's will and He says in His Book to multiply and susplenish [*sic*] the earth."[26] One of the women who practiced "withdrawal" as a form of birth control told Hagood, in metaphorical if not exactly euphemistic language, "when you chew tobacco, it don't make so much mess if you spit it out the window." Another tenant mother explained, "If you don't want butter, pull the dasher out in time!"[27] White families nevertheless tended to be smaller on average than Mexican or black families not because of any deftness with the dasher but because nonwhite families often included cousins, uncles, aunts, and husbands and wives of married children. One study of African American, Mexican, and "American" (white) women on Texas cotton farms in the 1920s showed that Mexican extended families "tend to stay together in a way almost unheard of in the American [white] group."[28]

A high correlation existed between the class position of farm women and the likelihood of their working in the fields. In a 1923 study of six cotton-producing counties in Texas, one of every three women on owner farms, one out of every two on tenant farms, and four out of every five on sharecropper farms spent part of the year tending to the cotton crop. However, an even stronger correlation existed between race and fieldwork: Almost nine out of every ten African American farm women did fieldwork, compared with two out of every five white farm women in all class categories.[29] Another study conducted in central Texas a few years later reported similar findings: Of 207 African American women on cotton farms, 87 percent performed fieldwork, compared with 46 percent of the white women. The proportion of Mexican women working in the fields, 57 percent, was considerably less than that of African American women but higher than that of white women. Thus although the conditions of work varied for different classes and races of farmers, women's work differed mainly in the amount of fieldwork required of them, with white women spending less time in the fields than either Mexican or African American women.[30]

Most women on sharecropper and tenant farms were expected to care for small children while they worked in the fields. Some mothers were able to leave their young children under the care of aging and often ailing grandparents or an older daughter. Mothers without help brought their babies with them to the fields, where they placed them in makeshift cribs at the end of a cotton row. One African American tenant mother worked 95 days in the field, seven hours a day, and took her two children, a three-year-old and a fourteen-month-old, to the field with her. Another African American tenant mother of eight children worked 60 days a year. The three oldest worked with the mother, while her six-year-old took care of the four younger brothers and sisters. A white mother in a landowning family with five children, whose ages were twelve, ten, nine, six, and three, spent twelve hours in the field 150 days a year.[31] Mothers of young children were able to avoid fieldwork only when some of their children were old enough to take their place in the fields.[32] For some farm men, however, women and children were expected to take *his* place in the fields. During the picking season in one Texas county, the field investigator came across an able-bodied white tenant sitting in the shade of a tree, puffing on a corncob pipe, while his wife and five children, aged thirteen, eleven, nine, seven, and five, were in the field picking cotton. He explained to the investigator that it was not hard work and that, besides, "they need the exercise."[33]

Many farm women working in central Texas cotton fields had others to help with the housework, usually one of their children and especially a daughter old enough to be pressed into service as a substitute mother. But whether or not one had help at home depended mainly on tenure status: One-half of owner women, one-third of tenant women, and less than one-fourth of cropper women had someone to help with housework.[34] Some white women were able to hire African or Mexican American women to do laundry and perform other household tasks.[35] In Karnes County some Anglo landlords required that the Mexican tenant's wife do the washing for the landlord's wife at no charge. A landlord in the same county demanded that the wives of two Mexican tenants work in the fields even though the wives were "ready to be confined" for childbirth. When the tenants refused, they were "put out of the place and got nothing for their work."[36] An onion buyer from south Texas told Paul Taylor that he knew a man who hired Mexican families to work on his farms and "if there was a daughter he liked he would tell the mother that he expected her daughter 'to keep house' for him. If she objected he told them no work; and he has as nice a wife as you ever saw."[37] Regardless of race or class, however, most tenant farmers could not afford to hire outside help, and most of those who could were white owners or tenants who hired Mexican or African American women and children.[38]

To increase household income during the slack season, some black and Mexican farm women who lived near towns and cities worked off-farm as domestics in the homes of whites.[39] The larger cities, such as Houston, San Antonio, Austin, and Dallas, provided many farm women with opportunities to work as maids and cooks. Mexican women were handicapped in this market, however, because many did not know how to prepare "American" food for southern white families unaccustomed to tortillas, tamales, and frijoles. In addition, many Mexican women were unfamiliar with the new electrical gadgetry of modern households. By performing most household chores by hand, however, Mexican domestic workers saved many households from having to purchase new appliances.[40] Still, Anglos complained that Mexican domestic workers rarely stayed very long and were apt to leave homes where they felt they were mistreated or where they were not shown the proper degree of respect. A white superintendent of schools who had employed three Mexican women as domestics said he preferred black domestics: "You can back up and bawl out a Negro. To one [Mexican woman] my wife said simply, 'You are late this morning,' and she left." He wondered how "a Mexican can live on a dirt floor for $3.00 a week and then if you say anything to them they are independent as a millionaire. But a Negro," he added, "thrives on words and battle."[41]

Despite their shared experience of child rearing and domestic work under the domination of their husbands, an enormous social and economic gulf existed between white women on owner farms who did not work in the fields and poor white farm women on tenant and sharecropper farms who did. African American and Mexican women on sharecropper farms had even less in common with white women on owner-operated farms. Many white farm women in Texas, for example, joined the Women's Bureau of the Farmers' Congress to discuss strategies for increasing household efficiency, and in their presentations on domestic work and home decoration they saw themselves as little different from the wives of bankers and merchants.[42] They frequently exchanged ideas on the latest labor-saving devices, such as washing machines, and on ways to make their kitchens more efficient work spaces. White women who worked in the fields did not have the leisure of non-field-working women on owner farms to pursue educational and cultural interests. One farm woman bitterly resented the position of women on tenant farms and wrote: "A [tenant] farmer's wife toils like a slave from before dawn until far into the night trying to do her housework and be a field hand too, and while she is doing it she knows that she and her children are being robbed of the product of their toil." She called for the government to provide low-interest loans directly to tenant farmers so they could purchase their own farms. In this way, she wrote, the farmer's wife and her children would cease to be "slaves" and would have time for "education, culture, sociability, and refinement." A poor white farm woman from Texas, however, more realistically observed that on cotton farms it did not much matter whether one slaved on a farm that was owned or rented: By age fifty-five the farm owner was "practically a physical wreck," and his forty-nine-year-old wife was "stooped and wrinkled," with the appearance of a seventy-five-year-old grandmother.[43]

After spending hours in the hot sun chopping or picking cotton, many women returned to their two-room tenant shacks to perform chores without the aid of domestic appliances or, in many cases, the convenience of running water. A Texas farm woman wrote the Department of Agriculture that the condition of farm women in the South in general was deplorable, in large measure because her "liege lord" thought it more important to purchase for himself labor-saving machinery, without a thought given to her back-breaking workload.[44] Women's work on the farm was rapidly becoming more manly in the sheer amount of physical toil than men's work. One advertisement for washing machines depicted an indignant husband in an apron carrying a basket of laundry while his smiling wife waves to him from her tractor. The advertisement read: "If your husband did the washing, he would insist on having a new Maytag, for the same reason he buys power machinery for his field work."[45] It was no secret that riding a tractor required less physical strength than doing the laundry. Yet most farm men complained that they could not afford washing machines and other mechanical aids for the home even as they purchased the latest power machinery to lighten their own workloads in the barns and fields.

What must have truly rankled, however, was that town women who succeeded in reducing family expenses for a week or a month were able to invest the savings in a new chair or to combine them with their husbands' earnings and together purchase other household furnishings that added to the attractiveness and comfort of the home. When country women managed to reduce their household costs below what had been allocated for a week or a month, their savings were more likely to be used to pay for "long-needed repairs to the barn, for a new attachment for a machine, or an addition to the chicken house."[46] Thus, while men traded in their hoes for expensive steel plows, farm women continued to haul water from the wells in pails, "just as Rebecca did in the Old Testament Days."[47]

Piped or running water was considered a luxury on most cotton farms in central Texas. In one study, only 36 percent of white women had running water, the majority of them from the owner class of farmers. Only one African American woman of the 207 surveyed had running water, and none of the Mexican farm women.[48] Mrs. E. M. Barrett, addressing the Woman's Division of the Texas State Farmers' Institute, asked of the mostly white women present: "Have you running water? No? Well, the pigs and calves have, and why not mother and the girls?"[49] Mary Gearing, director of the Department of Domestic Economy at the University of Texas, told the story of how a mother and her daughters on one farm had asked repeatedly for running water but were told each time that the family could not afford it. The women were suddenly called away by illness, and the housekeeping was left temporarily to the father and sons, who experienced firsthand, perhaps for the first time, the inconvenience of operating a household without plumbing. When the women returned, they found running water in the kitchen. "If all the country women would band themselves together and go on a general strike for a month," Gearing admonished, "I have an idea that most of them would find running water in their kitchens on return—and other labor-saving devices as well."[50]

If men ignored the need for running water and other facilities for women, they also paid little attention to designing houses, especially kitchens, that would make women's work a little easier. One woman complained in 1915: "Farmers give more or less study to the architecture of barns, granaries, stables, drainage, water supply—in short, to all farm mechanics except that of the woman's workshop, the kitchen." Farmers built kitchens with shelves that were too high and narrow for convenient use and, inexplicably, built one or two steps at the entrance to the kitchen that, for women who must climb and descend them innumerable times each day, "sap her vitality . . . and are a menace to her health." Reflecting on the poor design of houses and kitchens, one woman wrote: "The farmer's wife wears her life out in a weary tramp about an inconvenient kitchen cooking for the men who have their barns conveniently arranged." Another farm woman observed that "the number of miles a woman races around the kitchen and dining room would leave a professional hiker far behind in a journey. But few women design a house. Most of them are not even consulted." One man admitted that for men who build farmhouses, the kitchen was an "afterthought," while another farm woman's husband thought well-designed homes and kitchens would "help them to be more contented and therefore more human."[51] For most African American and Mexican farm women, however, a poorly designed kitchen would have been an extravagance, for the majority of the one- and two-room hovels they rented had neither kitchens nor running water, much less dining rooms.[52] As for running water, one African American woman said of her two-room tenant shack: "It leaks outside and rains in the house."[53]

In the division of labor between men and women on the farms, it was generally assumed that women were responsible for the household and men for the crops, a division that was sometimes viewed as indoor and outdoor work. Many farm women, however, were growing weary of the increasing amount of outdoor work required of them, from working in the fields to tending the garden. "This is my question," wrote one farm woman, "When I have cooked, and swept, and washed, and ironed, and made beds for a family of five (two small children), and have done the necessary mending and some sewing, haven't I done enough?" She added, "In any fair division of labor between the farmer and his wife the man would take the outdoors and the woman the indoors. That would drop the chickens on the man's side, with the probable result that on most farms there would be no chickens."[54] Although it was true enough that women were dissatisfied with the amount of work they were expected to perform, farm women were more interested in "technological parity" with farm men—households equipped with labor-saving appliances—than in redefining the boundaries of indoor and outdoor work, since many of them preferred outdoor work to housework.[55] Indeed, many farm women intended to use these technological conveniences to broaden their functions as farm producers rather than to relinquish their outdoor life for the comfort of the kitchen.

Texas farm women made it increasingly clear to state and federal agencies during the Progressive Era that while urban households benefited from modern technology—washing machines, telephones, automobiles—"We women are doing much of our housework after the manner of *prehistoric* women." "In fact," the same woman wrote, "many of our mothers and sisters are doing the work of a *gasoline engine*."[56] African American and Mexican American women, who most often lived on sharecropper or tenant farms, were lucky to have roofs that did not leak and wooden floors in their shacks, much less the conveniences of modern home appliances. Besides, these women traditionally had engaged in outdoor work to a much greater degree than had white, middle-class farm women who were wedded to the Progressive ideal of separate spheres for men's and women's work. In fact, the entire reform effort of the Country Life Movement was aimed at predominantly middle-class white women farmers who were likely to have the resources to acquire labor-saving devices for their household work.

Going to town on Saturdays, attending church on Sunday, and visiting friends periodically formed practically the only occasions on which farm women could get away from the farm and off the treadmill of everyday chores. But most farm women rarely had time to visit friends or the opportunity to go to town, which made farm life for many women "disgustingly lifeless."[57] To the average tenant farmer's wife, farm homes were "prisons," and the women, prisoners—"trusties, of course, but nevertheless prisoners." Yet for those who were able to go to town on

Saturdays, the trip was often not a time of leisure and relaxation, as it usually was for men. Many white farm women complained that there was nothing for them to do in town while their husbands and sons purchased supplies. There was "no place to stop at or get warm, or write a letter." Most ended up congregating on street corners, nervously waiting for their husbands to finish their business. "I am haunted now by the faces of the women I find myself looking for on the street corners," wrote one farm woman, who saw the specter of women waiting for their husbands "pathetic." When they arrived home, "tired, cold, and hungry," they were faced with "extra work to do after dark on account of the half day off."[58]

White women on owner farms were able to visit towns and cities more often than were women on tenant farms, in part because they worked less in the fields and because as a class they owned automobiles in greater percentages than did other classes and races of farmers.[59] However, one study found that "negroes as a class" visited more frequently than did either whites or Mexicans, mainly because the whites in this central Texas county were divided along ethnic as well as class lines: The "native American" whites regarded the national customs of the Swedes and Germans in their community as "distasteful" and "immoral." The "carousing Germans" danced and drank and, like other "European foreign classes," visited among themselves more than did the socially conservative native whites. Thus although nationality lines were not drawn as tightly as was the barrier of race and color in the county, the study concluded, "yet they induce a spirit of clannishness among whites" that prevented them from visiting across ethnic lines.[60]

In Travis County, where African Americans and Mexicans came to occupy the same geographical space as immigrant whites and native whites, one native white owner claimed that "we have no more free-for-all barbecues, picnics and old-time camp meetings" because, as one woman explained, "Mexicans and negroes have come into the land and ruined the social life." These native whites expressed fear of the growing number of Mexicans and blacks "on the roads" and said that they no longer "felt safe anymore" and would "have to move." Native whites kept clear of barbecues and picnics because of carousing Germans and the increasing presence of African Americans and Mexicans in their communities.[61]

Mexican families often left the farms to visit friends and families in neighboring farms or towns, despite the risk of encountering hostile treatment by native whites, such as refusing them service in restaurants or refusing to allow them to use rest rooms. Some of the poorest Mexicans, however, lacked the clothing or the transportation to visit towns like Waco or Austin. One Mexican tenant in Travis County complained: "We never go anywhere, for we have no clothes, no money. We go to church on Sunday to pray the Lord to help us, but he doesn't help anybody."[62] Most Mexicans took advantage of the various forms of entertainment available in the county or in nearby Austin—motion pictures, circuses, fairs, picnics, barbecues, holiday celebrations, and other community gatherings. But they did not have to leave the countryside to enjoy the festive dances held at someone's home, usually on Saturdays, which featured the musical talents of Mexican tenants playing the accordion in a style of music popularly called *conjunto* among Texas Mexicans.[63] At these dances, in the privacy of their homes, Mexicans were able to imagine themselves back in Mexico or south Texas, with all its comforting familiarity, if only for one evening a week.

Black families, according to one study, celebrated holidays more often than did either whites or Mexicans. One of the biggest holidays for blacks in Texas was "Juneteenth"—June 19, 1865, the day on which Union General Gordon Granger arrived in Galveston and proclaimed, two years after Abraham Lincoln issued the Emancipation Proclamation, the end of slavery in Texas. In 1865 a Galveston newspaper reported that in observance of the first Juneteenth, there were hardly any blacks to be seen, "giving the streets quite the appearance of a northern city."[64] In one county 62 percent of African American tenants celebrated holidays, compared with only 16 percent of white tenants who, as a class, the study showed, rarely take a day off to celebrate holidays.[65] It is not clear to what degree women were able to relax on these days since they were still responsible for preparing holiday meals and performing other necessary household chores.

Churches were also important venues for establishing social relations in the countryside. In Travis County, African American farm families attended church more regularly than did either whites or Mexicans, and women attended more regularly than did men of all classes and ethnoracial groups. The author of the study attributed high church membership among African American families to the "tendency of emotional folk to manifest their religious feelings in a socially approved way."[66] A more convincing reason was that African Americans, of all classes and races of farmers, had the highest percentage of resident pastors, many of whom were tenant farmers themselves. Thus even as tenant farmers moved from farm to farm every few years, the farmer-preachers moved with them and provided religious services for the itinerant faithful.[67] Black churches also provided safe space for the expression of African American culture and may have substituted for formal political gatherings and the risks they involved.

Automobiles provided farm families with the quickest escape from farm drudgery, but farm women whose husbands owned Fords were often no less isolated than were those farm women without automobiles. Social life in the countryside often depended on the distance between farms as well as the length of time it took to complete farm chores. Thus one farm woman complained that she and her husband put in sixteen-hour days and were too tired in the evenings to drive to the nearest neighbors, five miles away, whom they had not visited for five years.[68] Moreover, the work of hosting neighborly visits remained chiefly the responsibility of women. Women had to prepare extra food for the visitors, clean up after they left, and still finish their own work for that day and the following day. Automobile ownership, according to one farm woman, revitalized a man's social instincts in such a way that he was constantly inviting people from town to "Come out and spend the day; bring your wife and family." However, if for some reason his wife was not at home or was ill and he was doing his own cooking, then "he never solicits visitors, either singly or in carloads."[69] Nevertheless, for many farm women the automobile altered the social geography of rural life, shrinking the cultural distance between town and countryside and, by enabling them to cover greater distances in shorter periods of time, enlarged their network of friendships beyond their immediate farm neighbors.[70]

By the late 1920s the majority of farm families in central Texas owned automobiles. A study found that of 207 African American farm families in central Texas, none owned a radio, only 2 had telephones, but 112, or more than half, owned automobiles. Among Mexican families in the central Texas study, a few had telephones, none a radio, but 45 percent owned automobiles; and among white farmers more than half had telephones, 8 percent owned radios, and fully 85 percent owned automobiles.[71] In some cases, automobiles may have curtailed the farm men's liberty while enlarging that of farm women and children. Allen noted that

Under the old carless regime, the masculine members of the household got out their horses, saddled them, and rode away unquestioned. There was no room to take the wife, daughter, or sister; and there was no room for argument or protest. There is room in the car, and when the car goes the wife and daughters get in. . . . The man has lost his liberty. No longer is "going to town" the open sesame to a few hours of absolutely uncensored life.[72]

More frequent visits to towns and cities exposed farm women, often for the first time, to motion pictures, the latest clothing styles, popular music, new consumer products, and other features of mass culture. Mexican American children were especially quick to adapt to current fashions and to abandon the traditional dress of their Mexican-born parents. A school official in Lockhart told Paul Taylor in 1929 that Mexican American girls had begun to bob their hair and that they rarely could be seen with shawls over their heads.[73] In some Mexican farm families traditional musical instruments, like the accordion, had "been displaced by the cheap graphophone" and the classic Mexican song "La Paloma" by the popular hit "My Man."[74]

As part of a nationwide program to improve efficiency on the farms, the federal government created the Extension Service in 1914, which provided home demonstrations for farm women in order to "lessen her heavy burdens."[75] The Texas Agricultural Extension Service, established in the same year, began to address issues affecting women on farms under the rubric of Home Economics. Agents visited numerous rural communities to demonstrate improved methods of food preservation, better gardening techniques, and more efficiently planned kitchens. One of the main concerns of extension agents was to demonstrate improved canning techniques, which would increase the amount of food preserved from home gardens for home consumption. A steam canner lessened the work of canning, but few farm women were able to afford one. Those who did, however, sometimes canned for their neighbors "on the halves," splitting equally the proceeds of the goods canned, and sometimes they canned in return for other labor.[76] Since most African American women could not afford their own canning equipment, a pressure cooker and a steamer, some African American women canned at community canning centers, which they built and supplied with the necessary equipment. The first such center was built in 1931 in Anderson County. By 1933 black extension agents reported that 63 black canning centers in 21 Texas counties owned 278 canners and 276 sealers, valued at more than $17,000.[77] Nevertheless, although 69 percent of white women canned in one study, most African American and Mexican women relied more heavily on commercially canned foodstuffs than did white farm women. As poor farm women, often working long hours in the fields or off-farm for wages, they often had nothing to preserve. More than 76 percent of Mexican women on tenant farms in Texas had no garden, according to one study, none had an orchard, and only 3.7 percent were able to preserve food for family use.[78]

Farm women all over the nation made it clear enough to county home-demonstration agents that they were overworked and underpaid, and many confided that they had not spent a night away from the farm in as many as seven or eight years, much less gone on vacation. "I have been a farmer's wife for 30 years," wrote one farm woman, "and have never had a vacation."[79] Extension agents conceived of the idea of vacation camps, where women could spend a few days of rest, recreation, and learning. The idea was not new. Women themselves had written to the Department of Agriculture urging it to support efforts to improve the social opportunities of farm women. As one woman wrote in 1915, "A playground for the grown-ups is as important as for the children."[80] Most of these women, the white wives of farm owners, had become increasingly dissatisfied with the social isolation of farm life. The first camps were established in Montana, Tennessee, West Virginia, and Texas in 1921–1922. By 1927 more than 200 camps operated in thirty states, and almost 20,000 women attended them. In Texas the women brought their own provisions and prepared their own meals to help defray the cost of attending the camp, which varied from $3.00 to $9.00 depending on the length of stay. A southern farm woman summed up her experience at the camp: "No family, no chickens, no debts for three whole days."[81]

More than simply time-outs for overworked women, these camps sought to strengthen an agrarian ideology that consistently viewed women as helpmates, whose primary task was to run households and create a pleasant environment for their husbands and children. Thus, in addition to instruction in food preparation, canning, and the latest sewing techniques, women were also instructed in the aesthetics of farm life: flower growing and arranging, the proper application of beauty products, hygiene and personal appearance, music appreciation, and, in general, the "relation of food, clothing, and living habits to health."[82] The gendered ideology of new agriculture failed to acknowledge the economic importance of women's work in the successful operation of the farm and essentially ignored the roles that African American and Mexican women played in doing fieldwork and hiring out for wages. Although the vacation camps were open to all farm women in a county, the report gave no indication that African American or Mexican women were enrolled at the camps. It also did not make clear whether these farm women were the wives of owners, tenants, or sharecroppers. Given the heavy demands on women working on tenant and sharecropper farms, and often the family's indebtedness to merchants and landlords, it is not likely that many tenant mothers had either the time or the money to attend the camps. For those mostly white women who were able to attend, however, the camp experience was purposefully designed to inspire them to return to their homes "happy and rested, having renewed old acquaintanceships . . . gained helpful information, and absorbed a bigger and finer outlook on life."[83]

Men, of course, were as constrained by the gendered ideology of farm life as were women. Manhood and home ownership were inextricably linked, in much the same way that craft workers viewed skilled work as a measure of manhood. Owners who lost their farms from indebtedness consequently suffered a loss of manhood. White tenants and sharecroppers were implicitly less manly—and less white—than were owners. Home ownership, according to one contemporary, required that a white man make sacrifices necessary to "make a man of yourself" and liberated the tenant from feminine dependency as a "mere hewer of wood and drawer of water, to do somebody else's bidding all the rest of your life." Landownership gave one control over one's life and, in the context of Jeffersonian agrarianism, formed the basis of a democracy among white men. Working as a farm laborer or tenant on a large-scale industrial farm or tenant plantation was thus unmanly "nigger" and Mexican peon work that ran counter to the principles of individualism and self-rule at the heart of agrarian whiteness. "We don't like to see boys who . . . have the right stuff in them," wrote one male farm analyst, "become mere wheels or cogs in somebody else's big machine."[84]

Ownership was also a measure of a white man's worthiness in the eyes of his wife and daughters. A land speculator from Erath County, for example, linked the moral value of home ownership with the "worth and love of the wife and children."[85] Home ownership in the white patriarchy was synonymous with manhood and provided the basis for controlling women's behavior as well as their labor. "Homes," wrote J. S. Daugherty, "would rescue your daughters from the pitfalls of factory, store and office, and maintain them in the ways of moral rectitude, and prepare for them the way to fill the divinely approved functions of wife and mother."[86] Confining women to homes would prevent them from crossing borders between men's work and women's work—gendered borders that men, sometimes by choice or purposeful exclusion, themselves did not cross.

But if ownership conferred manhood on men, it also gave women a purpose in life other than the drudgery of washing, cooking, sewing, and picking cotton: Ownership was supposed to open up the women's world to the possibilities of beauty and refinement. Noting that nothing in the biblical account of Genesis indicated that Eve had a shelter she could call a home in the "plantation of Eden," Kate Alma Orgain, in a speech before the Texas Farmers' Congress, reflected that if Eve had possessed a "tiny bit of Oriental carpeting, a picture or two, a harp and a home, she would have joyously busied herself in their artistic arrangement and the serpent would never have found her wandering idly and aimlessly round the farm, a ready victim to temptation." But central Texas was not the Garden of Paradise, and wives of owners, tenants, and sharecroppers hardly wandered aimlessly around the farm. The idea was that farm women would somehow lead more wholesome and fulfilling lives and could resist temptation to leave the farm if their husbands owned their own homes. The Fall of Adam and Eve from the prelapsarian bliss of the Garden, Orgain argued, began with Adam's failure to provide Eve with a "harp and a home" to ward off the temptation to sample the fruit of urban ease and prosperity.[87]

Farm women increasingly voiced their dissatisfaction with the economic place and cultural space assigned to them by custom and tradition. In 1913 the Secretary of Agriculture wrote to 55,000 farm women asking them to suggest ways in which the department could render more direct service to them. The idea for the inquiry itself came from a farm woman in North Carolina who had written the *Progressive Farmer* that the "farm woman has been the most neglected factor in the rural problem, and she has been especially neglected by the National Department of Agriculture."[88] Women from all over the country responded in letters that farm life was unbearably tedious and exhausting.

The almost complete absence of any form of entertainment for farm women formed an important source of their dissatisfaction. Unable to attend movies or join clubs in town, some women immediately recognized the entertainment value of the new "talking machines" that were being marketed in 1915. One woman wrote that she saved $0.69 on 98 pounds of flour and announced with great glee that it was almost enough to buy a record. Most of the women respondents were wives of owners, and though no data exist on the race or ethnicity of the writers, it is fairly safe to assume that the vast majority of them were therefore white women. One owner's wife, for example, recommended that each school district own a phonograph and a supply of records that women music lovers could use without cost. She added, "I do not mean coon songs or rag time, but real music." Finally, one farm woman informed the Department of Agriculture how it could best help her and other farm women deprived of entertainment: "I would rather have moving pictures than free seeds."[89]

The letters by farm women revealed the depth of their anger and resentment toward a government agency that appeared to be more concerned with plants, animals, and machinery than with the welfare of women farmers or the rearing of children. A woman from Texas wrote to denounce the formation of the Boys' Pig Club, claiming that prize farming was an "insult to any intelligent farmer." "Prize farming reminds me of when we were children when they used to blow us up on Santa Claus to get us to kill ourselves picking cotton." She enclosed a newspaper photograph of a boy giving up his milk to feed it to his pig, an act of self-sacrifice perversely abetted by the messages of department bulletins that placed the welfare of pigs and chickens above the health and well-being of women and children. "I was much impressed with the fact that the fundamental principles in raising fine chickens were much the same as those pertaining to rearing fine children," declared one woman at a Texas farmers' congress, "but how few mothers are as well informed in the business of rearing children as are the experts on raising chicks and calves."[90] One woman told an assembly of Texas farm women: "I have seen kindergartens for colts, but never a home garden for the children, a kitchen garden for the mother or playground or nursery for the baby."[91] A woman from the Texas Department of Agriculture accurately noted that even when the farm woman loaded the dinner table with nutritious vegetables and meats, she was not feeding her "man child" as well as her husband fed his baby pig.[92] Many women on tenant farms were not able to provide nutritionally balanced meals for their families, much less their pigs, and children suffered the most from malnutrition. During one difficult year a doctor asked a tenant farm woman what she had been feeding her twelve-year old son, who suffered from pellagra and rickets. She told him that "she was glad none of her family had glass stomachs so people could see what had gone in them."[93]

One of the concerns of farm demonstration agents and the home economics program was that poor diets and heavy workloads degraded white farm women to the level of nonwhite and off-white immigrant women. Mary Gearing appealed to the racial pride of white farm men by beseeching them to better conserve their women from poor diets and strenuous farmwork because "the woman is the mother of the race and only in proportion to her strength will the race be strong." Farm women and girls, she continued, worked too long and too hard in the fields and warned that white farm women would come to resemble the "flat-breasted, heavy-faced, splay-footed" country women of Europe, who "work with no more hope or ambition than dumb, driven beasts. God forbid that America should produce such a race at such a cost!"[94] The standards of new agriculture and home economics, according to the historian Sarah Elbert, called for a new "pseudoprofession" to preserve white women, not unlike the pseudo-science of eugenics, but a profession that was unpaid and unlicensed—in other words, housewifery.[95] Housewives did not do fieldwork or produce for the market; they worked in their modern kitchens and left the business of farming to the men. But since farm men would continue to be more interested in the health and attractiveness of their livestock than of their wives and daughters, farm women were enjoined to take an interest in their personal appearance, and, as a consequence, farm magazines began to devote columns to beauty tips for farm women. One such column advised: "Keep the tint of your fingertips friendly to the red of your lips, and check both your powder and your rouge to see that they best suit the tone of your skin in the bold light of summer."[96] Few white farm women were able to take advantage of beauty fashions, and the only powder on the faces of Mexican and black farm women was likely to be dusty loam.

Long hours of wearisome work made many farm women wish they could live in town, where they could join clubs and enjoy the company of other women. Mothers were frequently torn between wanting their daughters to stay on the farm to assist in the housework and desiring them to seek better opportunities in the towns and cities, where, as one report put it, advances in the "ease of living" were drawing away both men and women.[97] Daughters often left the farms at the encouragement of their mothers, whose isolation from female kin and friends made life dreary and solitary.[98] To eliminate the "intellectual barrenness" of their lives and the scarce opportunities to form friendships with other farm women, one Texas woman wrote that farm women should establish women's unions, or clubs, in order to get out of the home and "get ideas from the outside world."[99] Some farm men, however, saw little need for women to develop their friendships or their minds. One male writer, opposed to women getting ideas, declared that "these are the days in which women kill with clubs."[100]

As the nation braced itself for entry into World War I, farmers were expected to increase their production at a time when the labor supply had decreased as a result of the draft and the demands of industry. Employing women from the cities on the farms was one solution to the farm-labor shortage, and programs were instituted to train women in farmwork. Women who had experience driving automobiles, for example, could be taught with a little additional training how to operate tractors. Farm women would train nonfarm women to milk cows, drive harrows, hoe crops, kill and dress poultry, and perform other tasks that would serve to "harden them physically," so that when they actually began working on the farms, farmers would have respect for their ability. If a hundred thousand women could be trained to work on farms, "the agricultural labor problem of this country," one contemporary wrote, "would be largely solved."[101]

During World War I many women volunteered to work on farms as part of the Women's Land Army, in which farmers found them especially well adapted to picking apples and other fruit because they were "more accurate and efficient than men."[102] One farmer hurt by the labor shortage hired five "farmerettes" to harvest and mow hay: One farmerette mowed with a two-horse mower, two worked with oxen, and one mowed with a tractor drawing a seven-foot mower. Together they harvested between 150 and 200 tons of hay. "But for the women," this farmer confessed, "we farmers would be ruined."[103] Not all male farmers were pleased with the increasing role of women as paid agricultural laborers and home demonstration agents during the 1920s and 1930s. College-educated female demonstration agents drove automobiles and drew large salaries, threatening the gendered hierarchy of farm life, in which women generally had neither independence nor freedom of movement. The manager of a 3,300-acre plantation bitterly complained that female demonstration agents "sit on their teddybares [*sic*], chew gum, draw their breath and salaries and are not worth a tinker's dam."[104] Indeed, it is likely that few men on tenant farms earned the income or enjoyed the freedom of most female demonstration agents.

During the depression years of the 1930s, when many tenants were forced off the land by acreage reduction and mechanization, many farm women joined the migratory workforce in Texas that had previously been dominated by Mexican families. When conditions of white farm workers were exposed by New Deal photographers—unsanitary shelters, no toilets in the fields, no drinking water, and poverty wages— many expressed shock that white farm workers could live that way. The nation viewed with disfavor the idea of whites living like Mexican migrant workers.

Fewer black families than Mexicans worked as migrant pickers, and most blacks regarded migrant white "road trash" with bitter contempt.

One black woman from central Texas, "almost barefooted" and picking cotton, commented in 1929: "You don't never see no colored person livin' that way. Bringin' up dey children in the middle of the road."[105] Yet despite the harsh conditions of migrant life, many poor white farm women preferred the life on the road even when their husbands sometimes did not. "Comparing their lives with that of the wife of the cotton cropper, with its deadly monotony, its grinding poverty and ceaseless toil," Allen wrote in 1930, "who shall say that they do not choose wisely?"[106] A few years later, however, farm families would have little choice in the matter, as the New Deal acreage-reduction program led to the displacement of tens of thousands of tenant families throughout the South, especially the western South of Oklahoma and Texas, where tractors, dust storms, grasshoppers, drought, and Mexican farm workers accelerated the collapse of cotton tenancy and opened a new chapter in the struggle and survival of poor white, Mexican, and black agricultural workers.

CHAPTER 7

The Darker Phases
of Whiteness

*The New Deal, Tenant Farmers,
and the Collapse of Cotton Tenancy, 1933–1940*

The system of sharecropping and tenancy that prevailed in
the South since the Civil War provided a sense of security and subsistence for most farmers, even those who moved from farm to farm every
year or so. Sharecroppers lived with the certainty that they could always
make a crop, if not always profitably. The system was far from perfect,
and landlords everywhere were prone to exploit their tenants. But even
H. L. Mitchell, one of the founders of the STFU, conceded that many
landlords in the South were often not much better off than most tenants,
like "paupers trying to bargain with paupers."[1] Nevertheless, tenancy,
both as a system of control and a way of life, allowed for a certain fluid-
ity which the poetically minded have called the agricultural ladder. Life
may have been hard and crude, but it was secure. "There was that element of hope and promise in the system," wrote one historian during the
Great Depression, "that people could describe as a preparation for 'better things to come.'"[2] The promise, after years of backbreaking work,
could be found just over the horizon, where the farm family would eventually own their own farm.

Although the rate of tenancy had been steadily increasing in Texas
and elsewhere in the cotton South since 1900, the hope and promise of
a better life vanished quickly for most tenant farmers during the depression years of the 1930s. A letter from a farmer's wife, Mrs. M. M. Clayton, to President Herbert Hoover captures the despair of many farmers
throughout the country: "For thirty-nine years myself and husband have
farmed, worked from 4:30 a.m. until 9:30 p.m. and . . . never in our life
have we faced such a time as your administration has thrust upon us.

Now with old age creeping upon us, my husband and I are losing every-thing."[3] In an effort to remedy the plight of farmers, newly elected Pres-ident Franklin Roosevelt persuaded Congress to enact the Agricultural Adjustment Act of 1933 to reduce the supply and raise the prices of cer-tain farm commodities. Few agricultural analysts could have foreseen the profound changes the acreage-reduction program of the New Deal would have on already destitute tenant farmers and farm laborers.[4]

Agricultural experts in the 1930s looked favorably on the trend to-ward large-scale, mechanized farming in Oklahoma, Texas, Arizona, and California. As preharvest operations, such as clearing the land, planting, and cultivating, were increasingly performed by tractors and new farm implements, landowners required fewer tenants and sharecroppers as resident laborers, relying instead on an army of nonresident, seasonal la-borers to chop and pick the cotton. "Soap-box orators may decry [me-chanical] cotton pickers, tractors, two- and four-mule machinery," mused one agricultural expert who favored the growth of large-scale farming, but "they and other modern farm machines are just as essential to farmers . . . as are linotypes to printers . . . [and] modern spinning and weaving machines to textile manufacturers." In the new farm order of the New Deal, tenants and sharecroppers had become anachronistic and inefficient producers, while migrant cotton pickers, like "other modern farm machines," were essential to more profitable and efficient agricultural production.[5] White tenants, in short, were forced to join the ranks of Mexican sharecroppers and migrant workers as off-white Okies and Arkies. Capitalist transformation in the countryside during the New Deal thus restructured class hierarchies and racialized group relation-ships, especially as poor white tenants were systematically excluded from the rights and privileges accorded the higher class of white landown-ers—their whiteness having waned with the cotton they once produced.

Tractor plowing and a reduced labor force increasingly came to char-acterize the new style of cotton production, particularly in south-central and west Texas, where many farms were foreclosed by banks and con-solidated into large units operated by professional farm managers. J. H. Youngblood, a manager for several bank-owned farms totaling 12,000 acres near Waco, let go of all but a few of the tenant farmers and ran most of the farms with wage laborers. On one 1,000-acre farm he used three wage workers and a four-row general purpose tractor, whereas the old style of production had required twenty sharecroppers or tenants and their families, a one-row cultivator, and about forty teams of horses and four mules.[6] According to one estimate, between 1935 and 1940 each tractor displaced from three to five families, or about 10,000 families a year.[7] O. D. Britton, a sharecropper from Rains County, in central Texas, wrote to President Roosevelt that large-scale farmers were no better than the "tyrants of industry" the president frequently criticized and that these "reckless gamblers" were taking "the meat and gravy away from honest hard working share-croppers."[8]

The efficiency of power farming came with the social costs of a throng of homeless and underemployed farm laborers. In Bell County an agricultural investigator reported that 200 farms were foreclosed and sold to insurance companies; the companies then rented the farms to large-scale operators who farmed the land with tractors and wage laborers.[9] One STFU member observed that society, "instead of benefiting from the social value of the machine, finds itself burdened with a new and more serious economic problem. The machine thus drives out the men."[10] The rapid increase in the use of all-purpose tractors during the 1930s thus accelerated the growth of large-scale cotton ranches throughout the Southwest.

The so-called Dust Bowlers who left Texas and Oklahoma for California in the mid-1930s were not simply "burned out, blowed out, eat out"—the victims of drought, windstorms, and grasshoppers. Rather, mechanization of cotton farms in the western South, particularly in Texas, Oklahoma, and Arkansas, expelled more farmers from the land than did drought or dust storms. Increasingly, the common explanation of refugees to California was "tractored out."[11] One tenant from Clay County, in north-central Texas, wrote that in his community a single landlord had evicted seventeen tenants and that other large farm owners in the county were driving tenants into the cities and towns by the thousands, "making serfs, slaves or peasants of them."[12] Mechanization was not simply a technological advance over animal power but a transformation that had to be recognized, according to one analyst, as a "social as well as an economic revolution."[13]

Mechanization and scientific management began the process by which tenants were transformed into wage laborers, but the depression of the nation's economy in the early 1930s let loose forces that undermined the relationship between landlord and tenant. Many landlords refused to furnish tenants during the winter months, forcing many of them to go on relief. Low cotton prices, acreage reduction, and government payments all offered specific monetary incentives to landlords to reduce the number of tenants and croppers on their farms and to convert those who remained into wage laborers. Landlords often used rental and parity payments to purchase tractors, forcing many displaced tenants to become roaming agricultural workers. The restructuring of southern agriculture, in part through the AAA's acreage-reduction program, hastened the industrialization of agriculture and the attendant decline of tenancy—without, however, providing jobs or security for the tenants its policies were directly responsible for displacing.[14]

The centerpiece of the early New Deal's farm policy was the establishment of acreage-reduction programs, which were designed to raise the market value of agricultural commodities, particularly cotton, to parity with the level of purchasing it had enjoyed during the "golden age" of 1909–1914.[15] The Agricultural Adjustment Act of 1933 called for federal payments to farmers to plow under 10 million acres of cotton, or one-fourth of the crop, in order to raise the price of cotton by cutting back the supply. A processing tax levied on ginners provided the funds for these payments, which were inducements made primarily to large growers to participate in the reduction program. A reduction in cotton acreage, however, obviously implied a reduction in the number of tenant farmers needed to grow the cotton. Many landlords evicted their tenants rather than support them during the winter months or share with them the government checks, as required by the terms of the cotton-reduction contract. Thus one of the consequences of reducing the surplus of cotton through government payments was the creation of a surplus of sharecroppers and tenants (see Table 9).[16]

The cotton contract devised by the AAA was fraught with ambiguities that enabled landowners to reduce their tenants, both in number and in status, as well as their cotton acreage. Payments were made to the landlords, who were obligated to divide them with share tenants and sharecroppers according to a formula. There were two types of payments: rental and parity. Rental payments went to owners, cash renters, and "managing share tenants," who rented land to the government that was then taken out of production. Cash tenants received all of the rental check. A managing share tenant was entitled to one-half the rental. Following the rule that rental payments went with the land, sharecroppers and nonmanaging share tenants were not entitled to any share of the rental payments. Parity payments, on the other hand, were divided according to the tenant's share in the crop. Cash tenants therefore received all of the payment, managing and nonmanaging share tenants generally received three-fourths, and sharecroppers half. The proportion of rental and parity payments received by the tenants thus depended on their class position. Owners and cash tenants stood to benefit the most from cot-

Table 9 *Numbers of Sharecroppers and Tenants in Texas after 1930, by Race**

	Whites		
	Tenants	*Sharecroppers*	*Percentage of Tenants Who Were Sharecroppers*
1920	177,198	40,382	22.8
1930	236,321	68,874	29.1
1940	171,852	24,949	14.5
	Blacks		
	Tenants	*Sharecroppers*	*Percentage of Tenants Who Were Sharecroppers*
1920	55,111	27,999	50.8
1930	65,399	36,248	55.5
1940	32,610	14,872	45.6

SOURCES: U.S. Bureau of the Census, *Fourteenth Census of the United States, 1920: Agriculture*, part 2 (Washington, D.C.: Government Printing Office, 1922), 6: 4; and idem, *Fifteenth Census of the United States, 1930: Agriculture*, part 2 (Washington, D.C.: Government Printing Office, 1932), 2: 1362, 1384.

* All Mexican- and U.S.-born people of Mexican descent were included as whites.

ton reduction, while sharecroppers could only hope for half the parity payment, which amounted to half a cent per pound of cotton.[17] Many whites suddenly found their status reduced from "managing" share tenant to "managed" share tenants, a reduction that further eroded their status from semi-independent white tenant farmers to semi-white farm workers.

Many landlords dismissed their tenants and sharecroppers in order to receive all of the rental and parity checks. Other landlords who kept their tenants peremptorily reduced them to "managed" in order to keep the rental checks for themselves. Since county cotton committees almost exclusively comprised white landowners, they could be counted on to rule in favor of landlords when tenants complained to them. Gardner Jackson, fired from the AAA for his protenant views, asked a county agent why no sharecroppers or tenants sat on county committees. The agent replied, "Hell! You wouldn't put a chicken on a poultry board, would you?"[18] It would also not do to have Mexican and African American sharecroppers sit in judgment of white landowners.

Without representation on county committees, many sharecroppers were forced to work for monthly wages and received no share of the parity payments, while landlords and county committees narrowly construed the meaning of "managing" to exclude numerous white share tenants from the category entitled to rental payments. According to the contract, a managing share tenant was "one who furnishes the work-stock, equipment and labor, and *who manages the operation of the farm.*"[19] Landlords seized upon the ambiguity of "who manages the operation of the farm" to declare that their share tenants were managed, not managing, and that they were therefore ineligible to execute cotton contracts to receive their share of the rental payment.

Confusion over the meaning of managing share tenant prompted the USDA to issue a memo addressing some of the ambiguities inherent in the term *managing*. By custom, a share tenant was one who paid as rent one-fourth of the cotton and one-third of the grain and who supplied his own labor and equipment. But some share tenants were subject to more, or less, supervision than were others. It was never the intention of the AAA to create a subcategory of share tenant based on the degree of supervision received, but that was what resulted, in effect, from the wording in the contract.

Various county cotton committees had different ideas about what constituted a managing tenant. For some, any contact the tenant had with the landlord indicated that the tenant was not a managing share tenant. The AAA, however, indicated that share tenants still managed the farm even though the landlord visited it periodically to discuss the time and place of ginning and marketing the cotton or other farming matters. Only those tenants who did not make basic decisions about planting and harvesting and whose landlords oversaw the operation of the farms could not be considered managing share tenants. Tenants on large-scale cotton farms, like the Taft Ranch in south-central Texas or the large cotton ranches in west Texas, were not managing share tenants because they were supervised by farm managers and superintendents and therefore did not themselves "furnish the actual management of the farm."[20] However, the majority of tenants in the Blackland Prairie of central Texas north of San Antonio were independent, managing tenants on nonplantation farms.[21]

It was already too late to clarify the language in the contract when tenants began to flood the AAA with complaints that landlords and county cotton committees had interpreted the contract to exclude many tenants from signing contracts and therefore to deny them their share of rental payments. Mordecai Ezekiel, economic advisor to Secretary of Agriculture Henry Wallace, wrote in a confidential memo:

We are in a bad situation because we permitted the contract to go out in the form it is in. Having done so, however, I think all we can do now is to stand by our guns . . . and not attempt to remodel it (even though that would be highly desirable from the point of view of fairness to the tenants to give them a better break than under the contract as written).[22]

The loophole was allowed to stand, and landlords made good use of it to deny thousands of share tenants their portion of rental payments on the grounds that they were not managing the operation of their farms. What the AAA unwittingly accomplished, in other words, was to enable landlords to create a distinction among nonplantation share tenants where none had existed before. Senator Joseph Robinson called the Cotton Section of the AAA to ask what a managing share tenant was, because, as far as he could tell, nobody in the South had ever heard of it. The section chief, C. A. Cobb, wondered, "If there was no fundamental difference between a share tenant and a managing share tenant, then we are confronted with the fact of having provided for a difference of privilege . . . [for] if one is entitled to sign a contract . . . then why not the other?"[23] Equally as significant, the division in tenure status reified the difference of privilege into managing whites and nonmanaging poor whites, Mexicans, and blacks.

Texas tenants complained bitterly that landowners refused to keep them on the farms unless they signed a side agreement in which the tenant waived his share of the rental and sometimes even the parity check. If the tenant refused to sign, the landlord rented to someone else, often to a Mexican sharecropper.[24] Tenants who did sign the waiver were often warned that if they reported the action to the county AAA agent their leases would not be renewed. Mrs. Lillie Harthcock, a tenant's wife from Limestone County, wrote to the USDA that her landlord, a medical doctor, lived in town while she and her family managed and operated the farm with their own tools, teams, feed, and labor. Nevertheless, her landlord refused to allow them to sign a contract entitling them to a share of the rental payment. She was writing to the USDA because her landlord was chairman of the county cotton committee that approved the contracts and "everything goes as he says go." When she took her complaint to the county agent, T. B. Lewis, he refused to talk to her. She left with the impression that Lewis "was being paid by the landlords to ignore tenants that complain of such contracts." When the landlord found out that she had made a formal complaint against him, he told her that they would have to move at the end of the year. Mrs. Harthcock warned that unless some action were taken, "thousands of dollars that belong to tenants will be paid to landlords in Limestone County."[25]

From the start, Texas tenants were at the mercy of county committees made up of white owners who in some cases made rulings on the status of their own tenants. D. M. Allen, a share tenant from Lamb County, wrote to the USDA that his landlord refused to share the rental check with him, offering only to give him his share of the parity check. Allen made it clear that he owned his own equipment and paid one-third of the grain and one-fourth of the cotton, the traditional rent for share tenants in Texas. The problem, Allen wrote, was that his landlord was also a member of the county cotton committee, which had determined that Allen was not a managing tenant. How was a tenant to expect a fair ruling from a committee on which his own landlord sat? The USDA, as was its routine in such cases, referred his complaint to a local field representative, who offered the absurd suggestion that Allen "discuss the matter with the County Cotton Committee."[26] This was less a bureaucratic mix-up than a purposeful evasion by the AAA to avoid enforcement of its own flawed cotton contract, which left interpretation, implementation, and enforcement to local committees. "The complaint machinery," wrote the historian Pete Daniel, "fed the victim to his oppressor."[27]

Since county AAA agents, as well as members of county cotton committees, were chosen primarily from the ranks of white landowners, tenants rarely stood a chance, even when they protested directly to Washington. Walter Sanders, a share tenant from Navarro County, had been renting from the same landlord for more than twenty years, when his landlord suddenly decided that he was not a managing share tenant and would not renew his lease unless he agreed to forfeit his half of the rental check. Sanders at first complained to the USDA, telling the department not to advise him to consult with the AAA county agent, Morris, because Morris and his landlord, Allison, had been making speeches throughout the county that there were only two or three tenants in the county who could be called managing share tenants. Sanders, however, clearly was a managing share tenant who furnished his own tools and equipment and hired and paid for all labor "without the consent of anyone." Infuriated by the complicity of the county agent with his landlord, Sanders circulated a petition asking the Commissioners Court to remove Morris from office and collected more than nine hundred signatures. The court, however, took no action, claiming that it had no jurisdiction over the implementation of the cotton contract, and Sanders was evicted on the grounds that he was a "nuisance."[28]

At the county level the judicial system operated in nearly the same way as the complaint machinery of the USDA, which is to say, as Sanders learned, not at all. The assistant director of the Commodities Division of the AAA, D. P. Trent, acknowledged that the administration had been "inclined to pussy-foot and dodge responsibility" by telling tenants to take their complaints to local cotton committees even when those committees were the subject of the complaints. And since the committees were composed of landlords, one journalist observed in 1936, "the average tenant gets exactly what the planter wants to give him—no more and no less."[29]

County committees sometimes ignored the cotton contract altogether or flagrantly lied to tenants about its meaning. In the case of one absentee landlord, for example, the committee allowed an agent for the landlord to sign the contract and therefore to receive the rental check instead of Alvin and Frank Rose, the actual share tenants on the farm. When the Rose brothers protested that only managing share tenants like themselves could sign contracts with the owners, the county committee advised them that "the statement on the contract applied to Oklahoma and not to Texas." Frustrated by this blatant violation of the contract, Rose then wrote to the AAA regional supervisor, who correctly advised him that "there is no difference in the application of this contract in Texas, Oklahoma, or any other State" and authorized him to appeal the decision of the county committee to the state committee. Incredibly, the district agent for the AAA then wrote to the regional supervisor that, as far as he understood the contract, the county committee always had the final say in these matters and that no appeal process was in place. The fact that the county committee had made up its own rules did not seem to matter to him. The district agent felt only that the regional supervisor ought to uphold the decision of the county cotton committee even when the committee explicitly violated the terms of the contract it was sworn to enforce.[30]

The "forgotten man" in the cotton-reduction contract, however, was the half-tenant or sharecropper who furnished only his own labor, especially if the sharecropper was black. L. B. Archer, a black sharecropper, wrote to Secretary Wallace: "Us poor farmers that farms on the halves don't get any cash rental at all . . . and can't make ends meet but we are . . . still living in hopes that sometime we will get a fair deal."[31] Sharecroppers like Archer were entitled only to parity payments, which amounted to half a cent per pound, compared with the two and a half cents per pound paid the managing share tenant who furnished both the mule and the labor. The share tenant thus received five times as much in benefit payments as did the sharecropper. The division of benefits in the cotton contract, according to one USDA consultant, rated "the labor of a mule four times as deserving as the labor of a man in reducing the production of cotton."[32]

A black sharecropper on the Nesbiett plantation in Fort Bend County wrote to the secretary of agriculture that Nesbiett required the sharecroppers to pay $5.00 per acre to grow corn on land leased to the government, even though the cotton contract clearly stipulated that sharecroppers and tenants were permitted to grow food and feed crops for home use on land leased to the government at no charge to them.[33] Nesbiett also refused to share the parity checks with all his croppers. The "coloreds" on the Nesbiett plantation, he complained, "aint gettin the money you put out for us no way." He asked the secretary to "please help us out" but would not sign his name because the owner "don't allow us to write up there, so I am writing any way." Another black sharecropper, who mailed his letter from a train, was afraid to sign his name because "they are hard on us about writing Washington, D.C."[34] C. A. Walton, an African American extension-service agent for Dallas County, reported that many black sharecroppers had been put off the farms because of acreage reduction and that "in Dallas County there is no place for a sharecropper as far as the negro is concerned."[35] These sharecroppers risked eviction and possibly violence against them and their families by writing to the secretary of agriculture because they believed that the government, once informed of these contract violations, would intercede on their behalf. What they received instead was a form letter directing them to their local all-white cotton committee.

The cotton contract also prohibited landlords from reducing the number of tenants on their farms and from reducing tenants to the status of sharecroppers and wage laborers in order to secure a larger share of the benefit payments. When sharecroppers complained to county committees and AAA agents that some landlords had evicted them in violation of the contract, these landlords argued that the complainants were not sharecroppers at all but hired labor and therefore not entitled to the security afforded sharecroppers and tenants by the cotton contract. Other landlords reduced their sharecroppers to laborers in the middle of the growing season simply by refusing to provide them with credit at the commissary, which forced them to work for wages or starve.[36] The cotton contract thus fundamentally served to transfer government money to landowners, who often evicted unprofitable and expendable tenant farmers and their families.

Even before the acreage-reduction programs tempted owners to discharge their tenants, landlords were not required to renew leases. Requiring landlords to keep their tenants would have constituted a serious intervention into the traditional relationship between owner and renter; the AAA therefore chose a middle ground, one that was filled with loopholes. The contract called for landlords to maintain the normal number of tenants on their farms insofar as possible, unless "any such tenant shall so conduct himself so as to become a nuisance or a menace to the welfare of the producer." Landlords could technically maintain the same number of tenants while ridding themselves of any who had become a nuisance, which often meant those who refused to waive their share of the rental payments. In actuality, however, many owners did not even bother to maintain the same number of tenants, because only in rare cases were the provisions of the contract enforced.[37] In many instances landlords evicted white tenants and replaced them with African Americans or Mexicans who, desperate for work, agreed to side agreements with owners waiving their rental and parity payments.[38] The cotton contract thus contributed to the racialization of the rural workforce in which Mexicans, already regarded as nonwhite, cheap labor, became even more desirable as sharecroppers and wage workers.

White tenants and sharecroppers in Texas resented competition from Mexicans, who had been immigrating in large numbers since 1910. The immigration debates of the 1920s highlighted the division between growers, who opposed immigration restriction, and white tenants and day laborers, who favored restriction. The Great Depression once again focused attention on Mexicans, for they continued to pick the cotton for low wages and became wage laborers on farms previously operated by white tenants. A tenant from Lamb County in central Texas wrote to President Roosevelt that owners would not pay more than $0.50 per hundred pounds of cotton and would rather let the cotton rot in the fields than pay more. "Some farmers have brought in hundreds of mexicans to pull their cotton at even less," and he bitterly observed that owners who hired Mexicans "take the bread of life from our wives and children."[39] Displaced white tenants could not easily compete with Mexicans and African Americans in picking cotton. A tenant farmer from Fort Bend County complained that "This county is literally overrun with Mexicans. . . . I am an up-to-date cotton and truck farmer and a good gang foreman, but as I am not a mexican, there is no work for me."[40] According to one report, "Wages of the Mexicans and negroes will almost certainly remain low for some time to come due to the large numbers of men, women, and children, especially among the Mexicans, who compete intensively for what seasonal work is offered in the cotton fields."[41]

Landlords took particular advantage of Mexican sharecroppers who did not speak English or who were unfamiliar with their rights under the provisions of the cotton contract. Mexican sharecroppers who sought help from county officials or the Mexican consular office faced retaliation from their angry landlords. Domingo Laureles, a Mexican tenant of a landlord-sheriff named Ellison in Caldwell County, reported to the Mexican consul general that Ellison would not pay him his share of the parity check, which amounted to one-half. When Ellison learned that Laureles had lodged a complaint against him, he and another party drove to Laureles's house and, according to the consul general, "struck Laureles' daughter-in-law, who lived there, and her infant child, the child dying as a result of the blows." Shortly afterward, Ellison evicted the family from the farm and appropriated the balance of the crop belonging to Laureles. The Mexican consul general, de la Colina, wrote two letters to the Caldwell County attorney requesting an investigation, but the county attorney refused even to answer his letters. De la Colina then wrote to Governor Miriam Ferguson to ask assistance in obtaining a reply. He received the standard bureaucratic response from the governor's secretary that he should direct his inquiry to the county agent. The secretary never once referred to Sheriff Ellison's attack on the Laureles family or to the death of the child.[42] Years later a deputy sheriff told Paul Taylor: "Sheriffs here treat the Mexicans the same as white men as long as they can, but if there is provocation," he added with a touch of understatement, "they will hit him a little quicker." Southern whites were never able to treat Mexicans like whites for very long, however. "Over there it is 'señor,'" observed one white farmer, "Here it is 'hombre,'" which meant that in Mexico a Mexican man at least could command respect, whereas in Texas a Mexican was just an hombre, and a nonwhite one at that.[43]

Almost fifty Mexican sharecropper families worked the 6,000-acre Martindale Ranch in Caldwell County, and not one received a parity check from the government. The Mexican overseer explained to them that the checks belonged to Martindale and not to them. One of the sharecroppers journeyed twenty-five miles to Austin to ask a lawyer whether they, and not the owner, were supposed to receive the checks. The lawyer informed him that, according to the cotton contract, the sharecropper was entitled to the parity check but that the owner retained the right to replace any tenants whom he felt had become a nuisance. He told the Mexican sharecropper that the law was on his side if he wanted to take Martindale to court but that by challenging Martindale he would almost certainly be asked to leave the ranch. The Mexican sharecropper decided to take no further action. According to Fidencio Durán Sr., one of the sharecroppers on the Martindale Ranch, none of the sharecropper families thought it was worth losing their place on the cotton ranch over a small parity check. "What could we do?" asked Mr. Durán, exemplifying the predicament of many Mexican sharecroppers in central Texas during the 1930s.[44]

By the end of the decade only ten Mexican tenant families were left on the Martindale Ranch, the rest having been let go because of acreage reduction and mechanization. Durán stayed on as a patch cropper and tractor driver; the other Mexican families joined the growing surplus of agricultural laborers who were forced to seek work elsewhere. Many of them migrated out of the state for the first time to seek work as beet-field workers in Michigan and Ohio.[45] Others were deported by immigration officials to ease the burden of relief in the state, while many Mexicans chose repatriation over relief or starvation. Those who stayed were often barred by local discriminatory practices from obtaining relief work through Civil Works Administration (CWA) and WPA programs. Between 1929 and 1939 an estimated 250,000 Mexicans and Mexican Americans returned—or were deported—to Mexico from all parts of Texas.[46]

The problem of displaced tenants was most acute in west Texas, where acreage reduction, rapid mechanization, and the growing use of Mexican migrant labor accelerated the shift to large-scale production and the attendant decline in the system of tenant operators on small farms. The west Texas Chamber of Commerce, however, claimed that it had no tenancy problem if by that phrase was meant the existence of an "under privileged and under benefitted group of agricultural workers." D. A. Blandon, author of the report, believed that the only tenancy problem in west Texas was that there were too few farms for too many tenants. He acknowledged that landowners had discharged their tenants in record numbers but blamed the AAA for disturbing the relationship between the landlord and tenant by allowing the tenant to receive half the rental payments, which Blandon claimed was discriminatory to the landlord. As a consequence, Blandon wrote, the landlord "has dismissed the tenant and is farming his own land by tractors and by day laborers in order to get all the crop and benefit payments." In effect, the Chamber of Commerce washed its hands of any responsibility for the problem of displaced tenants in west Texas, claiming that the AAA's own discriminatory provisions for sharing benefits with tenants led to their displacement and that it was now the government's problem to find them farms or provide them with relief.[47]

Landowners as well as tenants blamed the AAA for the plight of evicted tenant farmers, while the AAA in turn blamed the "effects of the depression on industry." As a result, many tenants, who had left their farms to work in industry during previous years, returned to the countryside, where they were unable to find farms to rent and thus were forced onto relief. This explanation enabled the USDA to rationalize that the rise in the number of displaced tenants was in no way the result of the cotton acreage-reduction program. The AAA boasted that it had not interfered with the landlords' right to replace undesirable tenants and that evicted tenants were often replaced "with better ones." "Even allowing for some evasion of our cotton contract," the USDA argued, "the net result . . . is to make for a better situation on the part of tenants, in general, in the South than would have been the case if there had not been the A.A.A."[48] The AAA suggested that some white share tenants, the better ones, were more desirable than poor whites, while many central Texas landlords noted, from both an economic and a racial perspective, that Mexicans were more desirable as tenants than were "sorry whites."

In response to mounting criticism in the press, the AAA repeatedly stressed that it was committed to protecting the tenant farmer from abuses in the administration of the cotton contracts, even as it informed its district agents that many of the complaints of tenant farmers were probably without foundation.[49] AAA administrators, moreover, made it clear to county agents that it was not the AAA's purpose to "undertake to dictate the usual and normal relationships and tenure arrangements between landowners or landlords and their tenants." As far as the USDA was concerned, it was never the intention that the AAA deal with "deep-seated social problems" which had existed for decades. Agents were instructed to deal with disputes between landlords and tenants "in such a manner as not to unduly disturb . . . the relationships between landowners and their tenants."[50] It was unfortunate if the usual and normal relationship included fraud and exploitation, but the AAA adopted the stance that such disputes were a family matter in which the federal government ought not to intervene.

Thus on one hand the AAA's acreage-reduction program provided the economic incentives for owners to hire wage laborers to replace tenants, while on the other it adopted a hands-off policy in dealing with complaints from tenants that they were being evicted or reduced to wage laborers. The USDA instructed its local AAA agents to investigate complaints in such a way as not to reflect unfavorably upon the work which had already been done by local leaders who made up county committees: "Nothing must be done which might cause them to feel that their actions are being questioned and nothing must happen which might create an impression that the committeemen and others have not been fair and just." The work of the agents was supposed to be "as much for the protection of committeemen, county agents, landowners and others who have been unselfish . . . as it [was] for the protection of tenants or of the Agricultural Adjustment Administration."[51] The AAA refused to acknowledge that its program had created the very incentives owners needed to switch from tenants to wage labor, along with the bureaucratic control owners required to bring about such a change. As one historian wrote, the AAA "was innocent of displacing tenants, favored programs that displaced tenants, and it washed its hands of the conflicting results."[52] Secretary Wallace and the prolandlord AAA were not about to challenge the political and economic hegemony of southern planters. Gardner Jackson observed that it would be political suicide for the Roosevelt administration and the AAA to go against the planters because they were all Democrats "who have the real power in the South."[53]

The displacement of tenants during the 1930s exacerbated the problem of too many people seeking work on too few farms in the South.[54] Thousands were forced to leave the countryside or face starvation. Fuller Jones, a forty-eight-year-old tenant from central Texas let go by his landlord during the first year of the cotton-reduction program, was one of numerous Texas tenants who had no means of support or shelter for his family. "I must winter those eight girls and wife somehow somewhere," he wrote to the USDA; "I have no money and no credit, only the courage to keep going."[55] And keep going they did. The rural South lost 2,275,000 people through migration between 1930 and 1940. During the same period the number of Texas farmers decreased by 83,000, the majority of whom were tenants and sharecroppers from central Texas and the lower Panhandle, where multiple-row farm machinery was introduced on a large scale. Most migrated to nearby cities. Oklahoma suffered the worst out-migration, followed by Texas, Georgia, and South Carolina. Many of the migrants of Texas and Oklahoma ended up destitute in California, where they competed for agribusiness jobs with native Californians and Mexican immigrants.[56]

In Texas many of the displaced Anglo sharecroppers were replaced by Mexican patch croppers, who received wages in addition to the cotton grown on a small patch of the owner's land.[57] Quasi-share labor was used by planters who had mechanized preharvest operations and no longer required a large resident workforce of sharecroppers. As an intermediate status between sharecropping and wage labor, patch croppers represented a temporary adaptation to retain preharvest laborers and was useful only in the beginning stages of mechanization.[58]

After the New Deal acreage-reduction programs took effect, the number of tenant farms in Texas between 1930 and 1940 in Texas decreased by 32 percent, while in the Blackland Prairie the number of tenant farms was reduced from 79,169 to 46,051, a decrease of 42 percent. The rest of the cotton South also showed a decline in the number of sharecroppers and tenants in the 1930s.[59] During the same period the number of tractors in Texas increased from 37,000 to 99,000, reflecting the trend toward large-scale, mechanized production in the newer cotton area of west Texas. By 1939 cotton acreage in Texas had been cut from 17 million acres to 8 million, and nearly 50 million dollars was paid annually by the government to Texas farmers not to grow cotton, the bulk of federal money having gone to large landowners. J. R. Butler, president of the STFU, acknowledged in 1936 that tenants and sharecroppers, who benefited minimally from cotton reduction, would not be able to own their own homes under "conditions as they exist now" and blamed the economic system that worked for most farmers like a "constant stairstep downward from farm ownership, to renter, to sharecropper, to day laborer, and to 'get on relief if you can.'"[60]

The New Deal relief programs in Texas served the socially vital function of providing a safety net for unemployed farm workers and displaced tenants. At the bottom of the stairstep downward, former tenants and sharecroppers lined up to receive relief from the Federal Emergency Relief Administration (FERA), which was designed to meet the needs of the destitute throughout the nation during the early years of the New Deal. A survey in 1933 revealed that the rural South exceeded all other sections of the country in its dependence on relief, reflecting the profound structural changes wrought by cotton-acreage reduction, drought, and mechanization.[61] However, various work-relief programs, administered locally by all-white county committees, often excluded Mexicans and blacks, maintaining that "this work is for whites only."[62]

One of the criticisms that particularly provoked AAA officials was that the cotton-reduction program swelled the ranks of white tenants forced to go on relief, the contemporary equivalent of welfare. L. P. Gabbard, chief of the Division of Farm and Ranch Economics for the Texas

Agricultural Experiment Station, answered one critic by arguing that most of the displaced farmers on relief were Negroes and Mexicans, a class of farmers, he maintained, that had always been on relief of some sort: "It requires no difficult psychological adjustment for 'Rastus' to get his groceries from Uncle Sam instead of 'Massa John.'"[63] Gabbard's response to the growing numbers of people seeking relief in the South and the Southwest echoed the argument made by some agricultural economists a few decades earlier that high tenancy rates in the South were not a problem because they reflected the large number of mostly black sharecroppers swelling the ranks of tenancy. For Gabbard and others, relief, like tenancy itself, became a serious problem only when it affected whites.[64]

Although many owners took advantage of relief programs to provide subsistence for their tenants during slack seasons and thus avoided the expense of furnishing their tenants year-round, others believed that the federal government was spoiling farm laborers by providing relief work at wages higher than the going rate for agricultural labor. In San Patricio County, for example, landlords who relied almost exclusively on Mexican laborers feared that the racialization of relief efforts would upset the labor situation because it would increase "labor costs beyond the Mexican level" and therefore serve as a blow to profits. South Texas citrus growers complained that government wages represented a 140 to 175 percent wage increase over "Mexican wages." In a letter to the Texas relief director, the secretary of the Texas Citrus League, W. R. Gwathney, wrote: "We fail to see why the welfare of unskilled Mexican field labor should be promoted at the expense of American growers and tax-payers." For Gwathney, the issue of relief involved one's race more than one's citizenship, for he assumed that Mexicans and Mexican Americans were neither American (read white) nor taxpayers. In response, the editor of the *Hidalgo County News* pointed out that Mexican Americans were taxpaying American citizens who were free to choose whether to work for the growers at starvation wages or for higher-paying federal projects.[65] Of course Gwathney's point was that the interests of nonwhite, unskilled Mexican field labor—regardless of citizenship—should never be put before the interests of white people, the "American growers and tax-payers."

White farm owners continued to complain that relief was bad for business. Sam Crow, an owner of 250 acres in Madison County, wrote that relief programs, staffed by "tax eaters" and "cigarette sucking soda jerks," had "taken all our labor" and that owners like himself could not compete with government wages at the prevailing prices they received for their products. "There has always been a class who never owned property or tried to. It seems that our Government has taken this class under its special care, while to the small home owners it says Root hog or die." The government was undercutting the ability of Crow and owners like him to make a profit by directly competing with them through public-works projects and by siphoning off Mexican and African American laborers from the farms. While owners were going bankrupt, Crow claimed, the government was feeding and clothing "a lot of folks that will be hollering for free soup when Christ comes again." Taking their cue from owners like Crow, local relief committees, composed of white landowners, denied relief work to Mexicans, blacks, and poor whites who refused farmwork.[66]

In addition to providing relief programs for the South's rural poor, the New Deal established a credit program through the Bankhead-Jones Farm Tenancy Act to furnish low-interest loans to tenants to purchase their own farms. Dan Dove, a tenant farmer from Limestone County, in central Texas, urged the President's Committee on Farm Tenancy to enact such legislation because "unlike our fathers in days of old," Dove wrote, farmers could no longer move west in search of free land on a new frontier.[67] The Bankhead-Jones Farm Tenancy Act, approved by Congress in 1937, authorized the secretary of agriculture to make loans to tenants, farm laborers, and sharecroppers to enable them to purchase their own farms. The terms of the loan required payment of interest on the unpaid balance at 3 percent and for amortization of the principal over a period of forty years. As indicated in the act, however, preference was given to married applicants with families, to those who were able to make a down payment, or to those who already owned livestock and farm implements, and to an applicant whose "character, ability, and experience indicate that he is likely to succeed." These criteria made it difficult, if not impossible, for most farm laborers and sharecroppers to obtain loans, because they were least able to make a down payment and generally did not own livestock or farm implements; the fact that they were farm laborers or sharecroppers, moreover, stigmatized them as belonging to a class that was not "likely to succeed." Since Mexicans and African Americans were most heavily represented in the lower ranks of sharecropping and day labor, they were least able to take advantage of the loan program.[68]

Even the most enthusiastic supporters of the Bankhead-Jones Farm Tenancy Act believed that the program would not be able to assist all or even most of the sharecroppers and tenants of the South; nor, they reasoned, would it be desirable to do so. Any plan to transform all tenants into owners, according to L. C. Gray, chief of the Land Policy Section of the AAA, was unfeasible, given the differences that existed within the tenant class with respect to "personal integrity, dependability, energy, thrift, managerial ability, age, race, and general capacity for independent ownership." Race figured prominently in Gray's assessment because he and others linked whiteness with the general capacity to become owners. Not all whites, however, were possessed of equal degrees of whiteness. For Levi Thomas Steward and his wife Beulah Hooks Steward and their family, who were unable to escape the impoverishment of tenancy after eighteen years and 225,000 pounds of cotton (and whose plight I discussed in chapter 3), the quality of whiteness was strained. Gray emphasized that this class of tenants, along with black and Mexican sharecroppers, was better adapted to a permanent system of tenancy that would be "benevolent rather than exploitative in intent."[69] Expressing a similar view, an owner and banker from Dallas who rented to white tenants explained that these tenants, the "worthless, the shiftless, the dead-beats," should be dealt with in a gentle manner but as a class ought to be dealt with as "charity patients" rather than as potential farm owners.[70] As the racial detritus of whiteness, poor whites were incapable of becoming owners, many believed, and efforts to help them escape tenancy were doomed from the start.[71]

Tenants in all forty-eight states received a meager 6,094 loans under the Bankhead-Jones Farm Tenancy Act between 1937 and June 30, 1939. Mississippi tenants received the largest number, with 629. Georgia received 566, Alabama 538, and Texas 537. In Texas almost 15,000 loan applications had been received as of October 31, 1939, of which an estimated 542, or fewer than 4 percent, were approved.[72] There were far more applicants for loans than there was loan money available, and only tenants in selected counties in each state were eligible to submit applications. Tenants from all over Texas wrote to the USDA seeking information on how to obtain a home-purchase loan. Many of these letters reveal the desperate situation of families evicted by their landlords. For many tenants, the prospect of moving to town was no solution at all, not only because jobs in the cities were scarce but also because they had their hearts and minds set on living in the country, where they could raise their children the way they themselves had been raised.[73]

Criticism mounted from tenants and their supporters in state and federal government who believed that the Bankhead-Jones Farm Tenancy

Act provided too little too late and that it sought primarily to repair damage done by the AAA and its crop-control program. The Socialist leader Norman Thomas opposed the Bankhead bill because he believed it would create "subsidized peasants" on cotton farms. A better solution, according to Thomas, and one that took into account the steady transformation of tenants and sharecroppers into wage laborers, was to organize sharecroppers and farm laborers into unions. Such a union would have to be different from the Farmers' Educational and Co-operative Union of America, founded in 1902, which ultimately failed, according to Theodore Saloutos, because of the "lack of a common bond of interest between the poorer and more substantial farmers" and because benefits of cooperative farming were intended for whites and "only incidentally for the Negroes." A union of agricultural wage laborers could tap an already shared "community of spirit" based on years of struggle for existence on plantations throughout the South.[74]

The founding of the STFU in 1934 represented an effort to bridge the racial divide between whites and blacks on the farms of the South. In attempting to forge a biracial union, however, the STFU overlooked the often conflicting class interests of owners, tenants, and farm workers. In central Texas, at least, the line had already been drawn between farm worker and tenant farmer, and it paralleled the color line dividing whites from nonwhites. Meanwhile, in the newer cotton areas of west Texas, Arkansas, and California, wrote the Socialist Party organizer Martha Johnson, "you will find the true proletariat; here you will find inarticulate men moving irresistibly toward revolution and no less."[75]

CHAPTER 8

The Demise
of Agrarian Whiteness
*The Southern Tenant Farmers' Union
in Texas and the Racialization of Farm Workers*

The collapse of cotton tenancy in many ways signaled the collapse of agrarian whiteness and the rural way of life that was supposed to nurture the values necessary to sustain the life of the white republic. The idea of white yeoman farmers and their families tilling the soil, dependent only on themselves and their hard work for survival, was never really the reality in the cotton belt of the southern states, where owners, tenants, and sharecroppers—whites, blacks, and Mexicans—were subject to high interest rates, rising land values, low cotton prices, liens, and other hardships that made a mockery of yeoman independence and self-reliance. The 1930s marked a downward spiral in their fortunes and resulted in the creation of a racialized, rural workforce of off-white Okie and Arkie migrants and Mexican farm workers. Although some blacks joined the growing army of migrant farm workers, most headed for the cities and towns, where they hoped to find work.

By 1940 the nation continued to pay lip service to the notion of family farming even as cotton agriculture was entering a stage of mechanized, large-scale production that would revolutionize the countryside. Many white Americans viewed the transformation from white family farmers to a throng of nonwhite and poor white farm workers as a "menace to the very life of American institutions."[1] If small family farms engendered values of self-reliance, the proletarianization of farmwork fostered values of collective action that led to the largest agrarian protest in the nation's history. The formation of Communist and Socialist-backed unions of agricultural workers emerged in some parts of the South and the West on plantations and factory farms, where agrarian whiteness was as anomalous as it was anachronistic.

As wage-earning rural workers, many began to organize unions to bargain for better pay and working conditions. In southern California, Mexican farm workers organized the Confederación de Uniones Obreras Mexicanas (Confederated Union of Mexican Workers), and the Communist Party organized the Trade Union Unity League (TUUL). TUUL brought together many indigenous unions and was the first nationwide agricultural union to be established since the demise of the IWW. In Alabama, black sharecroppers organized the Sharecroppers' Union in 1931, and in 1935 12,000 members went on strike for higher wages in six cotton counties of southern and eastern Alabama. In Arkansas, twenty-seven white and black sharecroppers founded the STFU in 1934 to protest the government-sponsored crop- and acreage-restriction programs that led to the eviction of many tenants.[2] In Texas, however, no cotton strikes occurred in the 1930s, and most union-organizing activity took place in south Texas citrus and vegetable agroindustries. The STFU attempted to organize blacks, Mexicans, and whites in west Texas and blacks in central Texas, but overall the STFU failed dramatically in the Lone Star State. Texas, where the Socialist Renters' Union and Land League had flourished twenty years earlier, experienced relatively little strike activity compared with sharecroppers in Alabama and Arkansas and farm workers in California. In order to explain why the farm-labor situation was, for the most part, all quiet on the southwestern front of Texas, we need to compare the structure of cotton agriculture in Texas and these other states, their different class and racial hierarchies, and the strategies pursued by both cotton growers and cotton workers.

The 1930s witnessed a rise of labor unionism among agricultural workers, particularly in California, where 140 strikes involving 127,176 farm workers took place between 1930 and 1939. Texas farm workers, on the other hand, organized only 6 strikes involving 4,057 farm workers during the same period, and none of the strikes in Texas occurred on a cotton ranch.[3] Major strikes in cotton agriculture took place in only three states, Arkansas, Alabama, and California. California was the home of factory farming; and in Alabama and Arkansas major changes took place during the early 1930s that reduced large populations of white and black sharecroppers to farm laborers on large-scale cotton plantations, sometimes called neoplantations or business plantations. On these plantations, croppers were worked "through and through," a phrase that in local usage referred to a system of working tenants and croppers "in gangs like wage hands without regard for any individual's crop, but each tenant or cropper having a claim on the crops produced on a certain tract of land."[4] No longer accorded the status of farmer, they had become, in effect, proletarianized farm workers who worked under the direction of farm managers.

The pattern of agriculture in the most fertile cotton-producing regions of Texas and Oklahoma did not, for the most part, conform to the plantation model of the Arkansas Delta and the other plantation areas of the South. On large plantations in Arkansas, for example, most tenants and croppers, whites and blacks, coalesced around issues of wages and working conditions, not "rent," whereas most tenants in the Blackland Prairie of Texas lived mainly on nonplantation family farms and had a long history of aspiring to become farm owners like many of their late-nineteenth-century ancestors.[5] These mostly white share tenants on thirds and fourths thought of themselves as farmers rather than as farm workers, even when they were reduced to sharecroppers. They were therefore reluctant to organize or join unions of farm workers.

Even in south-central Texas and in west Texas, where large-scale cotton ranches more closely resembled the California model of industrial agriculture, no organized strikes were recorded during the 1930s. There are a number of possible explanations. Agrarian protest during the decade was more pronounced on large-scale farms in Alabama, Arkansas, and California than in Oklahoma or Texas, in part because of the influence of trade unionism that flourished in industrialized urban centers, like Birmingham, Memphis, and Los Angeles. The only industrial center in central Texas, Dallas, lay at the northern fringe of the cotton belt and, like San Antonio at the southern fringe, was not a site of mining, smelting, or the production of iron and steel products, as was Birmingham, where heavy industry and aggressive urban unions recruited both black and white laborers.[6] The proximity of large industrial cities to plantation areas in Arkansas and Alabama thus facilitated trade and commercial connections between town and countryside and led to the rapid commercialization of plantation farming by absentee owners and corporate investors. Relations between owners and tenants/sharecroppers grew less personal, and plantations there, unlike in more traditional plantation areas of the South, were operated as business enterprises to be run for profit, rather than as estates to furnish a way of life for country gentlemen.[7]

Displaced tenant families left the farms and migrated to the cities, competed with other tenants for the smaller number of high-rent farms in the Blackland Prairie, or, as a last resort, dropped into the migrant workforce. White tenants did not organize roadside demonstrations and strikes, as had evicted white and black sharecroppers in Missouri and Arkansas: In Texas they often chose to leave the countryside altogether rather than acknowledge their quasi-racialized status as poor white farm workers.[8] Finally, efforts to organize against white landlords in the cotton South often met with fierce suppression, often violent, by hooded and unhooded members of the community, often including the local officers of the law. Poll taxes and Jim Crow laws ensured that neither blacks nor poor whites would be able to protect themselves and their interests through political channels.

On cotton ranches in south-central and west Texas Mexican farm workers expressed their dissatisfaction with wages and working conditions by walking off in groups and seeking higher wages and better conditions on another farm or ranch. These cotton ranches, like the Taft Ranch near Corpus Christi, relied heavily on Mexican laborers, mostly immigrants, for both seasonal and year-round labor. Their proximity to the border made organizing difficult, however, because employers could usually rely on fresh supplies of immigrants to serve as strike breakers. In addition, Texas growers had not established a firm network of employer associations, as had California owners of cotton ranches, which eliminated competition among the numerous large-scale growers by establishing standardized wage rates. Wages were more variable in Texas, as was the structure of cotton agriculture, and farm workers in Texas could choose to pick cotton on small farms in east and central Texas or on large ranches in west and south-central Texas. They could also seek higher wages working in other crops in south Texas, or they could leave the state to harvest sugar beets or work in industries in Michigan and other states of the Midwest.[9] For these reasons, unions organized by Mexican farm workers in south Texas were usually small and conducted only local and usually brief strikes against growers.

Despite the variation in cotton production from small farms to cotton ranches and the multiracial composition of the workforce, Texas was a major producer of cotton, and the STFU decided that it should make an attempt to organize tenants there. Founded in 1934 in Arkansas, the STFU represented the aspirations of its members rather than the reality of their situation, for none of the east Arkansas sharecroppers was actually a "tenant" in the sense of renting a farm and operating it with little or no supervision by the farm's owner. This "tenant farmer union" was actually a union for supervised wage workers on large plantations who could only euphemistically be called farmers. To be a farmer implied the manly yeoman virtues of independence, individualism, and political equality—virtues supposedly fostered by the operation and ownership of family farms. Nevertheless, by targeting wage workers and plantation sharecroppers, the STFU successfully organized 328 locals and more than 16,000 members in Arkansas, whereas in Texas it barely managed to organize 8 locals with a total union membership of fewer than 500. Most of these were located in the new, large-scale cotton farms in west Texas—where wage laborers outnumbered share tenants—and among black sharecroppers in a tiny town in central Texas.[10]

The structure of agricultural production, whether large-scale enterprises or individual tenant-operated farms, and the formation of interracial unions thus played a key role in the willingness of farm workers to organize strikes. The west Texas locals of the STFU were principally located in the Lubbock area of the Panhandle, where large-scale cotton production had been established in the 1920s using tractors and wage laborers, mostly Mexicans and blacks. During the 1930s cotton production increased dramatically in the High Plains counties of the Panhandle, mainly as a result of the larger cotton acreages, which were better suited to mechanized farming, and of the rapid increase in the number of irrigated farms. More than 10,000 farm wells watered more than a million acres of cropland in the High Plains, most of which was planted in cotton. The increasing cost of hand labor, the presence of root-rot and Johnson grass, eroded and nutrient-depleted soils, boll-weevil infestations, and the prevalence of small farms ill-adapted to large-scale cotton production all contributed to the shift of cotton production to west Texas.[11] In counties such as Lynn, Garza, Dawson, Hockley, and Lubbock, small owners could not compete with larger, mechanized farms. Between 1930 and 1936, about one-third of the farmers in Lynn County had been evicted and rehired as day laborers. Owners kept wages low by hiring blacks and Mexicans to pick cotton for $0.40 per hundred pounds. Large-scale cotton farms in west Texas and the Corpus Christi area came increasingly to rely on Mexican wage labor during the 1930s.[12]

The STFU initially attempted to organize tenants, croppers, and day laborers in west Texas with the help of a white landowner, Fred Matthews, who joined the union and offered to be its principal organizer in the Lubbock area. Matthews, who rented to four tenants, at least one of whom was black, often talked about the plight of homeless and displaced tenants. He wrote to Mitchell that it would be a good idea to organize the Mexican cotton pickers and wage workers in the area, although he acknowledged that he had little understanding of Mexican culture. Alluding to the large number of men, women, and children traveling together and living in one-room shacks or in the open, near streams, he noted in a letter to Mitchell, "Gosh, but there is a bunch of moral laxity among these Mexicans." J. R. Butler, a white sharecropper and president of the STFU, visited the plains area of Lubbock to investigate the slow progress of organizing and reported that the union needed "an intelligent Mexican to commission for organizer." He did not seem optimistic about the prospect of organizing Mexicans; as he put it, "Mexicans have always been used to low wages and many of them do not seem to want anything better than they have always been used to. Even at that they are not much behind a lot of white people." Mexicans, however, did not need the STFU as much as the growers needed their labor; when Mexicans demanded higher wages and did not receive them, they walked off the job in unison to seek better wages elsewhere. With no way of communicating in Spanish their goals or objectives, STFU organizers like Matthews could not offer Mexicans anything they were not already capable of doing on their own.[13]

The STFU was a little more effective in organizing blacks in central and west Texas. Despite its success in Arkansas in forging interracial cooperation through its integrated locals, in Texas the locals remained segregated.[14] Matthews frequently worked with Charles Deo, the president of the all-black local of the STFU in Tahoka, near Lubbock, to organize African American pickers in the area. Matthews described Deo as "the leader of the Negroes of the Plains" and a "Black African type and colored Negro" who spoke Spanish, German, Portuguese, and French. Matthews and Deo called a meeting of the segregated locals of the STFU in the area to stress "cooperation of the broke farm laborers of the two races." The problem with organizing whites, Matthews reported, was that many "lazy minded poor white trash" needed to "soak some of this race prejudice out" in order to cooperate with black and Mexican sharecroppers and wage workers. As a white landowner, Matthews's class prejudice extended to "poor white trash" farm workers whose race prejudice he denounced. In the meantime, however, Matthews and Deo organized two locals, one for whites and one for blacks. Together they would decide how to organize Mexicans and whether to include them in white or black locals or to form another local just for them.[15]

The segregated locals of the STFU in Lubbock voted to bring Mexicans into the union, but in yet another segregated local because many

Mexicans did not speak English. Thus although Mitchell boasted of the interracial locals of the STFU in Arkansas, in west Texas the union was segregated in three ways. Communication among the segregated locals took the form of joint meetings after each of the locals had met separately: "The three races will meet in the negro church next sat. night and then meet at the court house with the whites the following sat. then meet in Mexican town the following sat. after meeting with the whites." In a letter, Mitchell told Deo to continue his efforts to organize Mexicans because they were a "factor in the state that we have never reached," who were "not altogether hopeless by any means." He asked that Deo arrange to have some Mexicans attend the STFU conference in Muskogee, Oklahoma, in January 1937, especially because he had invited Mexicans from Laguna, Mexico, to send delegates from "old Mexico" to the conference. At least one Texas Mexican attended, "round faced Mexican cropper Acacia Zosa Olguin," who pleaded "in fluent, accent-tainted English, for unity of all nationalities. Next day he plucks guitar-strings and sings Mexican love-songs to delighted delegates."[16]

Mitchell himself attended a labor conference in Laguna in 1939, where he was impressed that black and white STFU delegates were welcomed everywhere in Mexico. "Jim Crowism begins and ends at the American border," he wrote. Echoing the progressive racial ideology of Covington Hall and the IWW, Mitchell declared that "Mexicans are not 'greasers,' no more than our American Negroes are 'niggers.' We are all members of the same human family no matter what color we are or what language we speak."[17] But despite these pronouncements, neither Mitchell nor the STFU made serious efforts to organize Mexicans in Texas. Biracialism in the STFU, in Texas at least, was mostly top-down rhetoric rather than rank-and-file union practice.

Fred Matthews was himself a strange choice to lead the STFU's efforts to organize cotton pickers; he was the owner of a 160-acre cotton farm and employed both sharecroppers and cotton pickers. Although the STFU did not represent the class interests of owners, Matthews joined the STFU because, he claimed, he sympathized with tenants, sharecroppers, and wage workers. Matthews saw himself as the "good owner" who would lead tenants and laborers to the promised land of the STFU, but gradually he revealed his antipathy to the class he hoped to organize. He wrote Donald Henderson, leader of the newly formed United Cannery, Agricultural, Packing, and Allied Workers of America (UCAPAWA), that the average tenant farmer was "an ignoramus at heart . . . without a social thought in his whole make up." Matthews continually complained about the improvidence and drunkenness of four of his own tenants and added that "we can't turn these wild savages loose." Yet in true paternalist fashion he believed that he knew "what is best for them," understood their weaknesses, and was prepared "to do one thousand times as much to bring this class out from under our present system."[18]

Before long, however, Matthews's sympathy for tenants and wage workers ran out, and he began to disengage himself as an STFU organizer. In a long and rambling letter to Mitchell, Matthews complained that the "negro pickers" on his farm required too much of his time. He had to take one to a surgeon in Lubbock for removal of a knife blade from his nose, a wound inflicted by a woman. Incidents like this, he wrote, cost him time and money, so he could no longer afford to spend time organizing in west Texas.[19] Matthews had realized, in effect, that organizing farm workers and sharecroppers into a union of tenant farmers was incompatible. Farm owners like Matthews, as well as independent tenant farmers, often *hired* farm workers; higher wages for farm workers meant less profit for farm owners and tenants. The STFU could more easily bring together different races of farm workers and sharecroppers in Arkansas than it could different classes of farmers in Texas.

The only other activity of the STFU in Texas was organized through the initiative of a black teacher and minister, J. E. Clayton, who founded and operated a small school for black children in Littig, a tiny town in Travis County, about twenty-five miles east of Austin. Clayton corresponded frequently with Mitchell over the necessity of organizing Mexican and black sharecroppers in certain parts of central Texas counties. "These Mexican share-croppers and day laborers are worrying me daily about being organized." He also told Mitchell that a white man could organize Mexicans in his area, but only a "Colored Organizer" could reach black farmers in Texas with any degree of success because the Negroes of Texas had been trained to follow "Race Leaders." Clayton's all-black locals paid their dues, and the Littig local also made a contribution to the striking pecan shellers in San Antonio, most of whom were Mexican women.[20] The regional director for the Committee for Industrial Organization (CIO), Barney Egan, wrote to Mitchell that he had visited a "fine meeting of negro farmers" in Littig under Clayton's sponsorship. He found Littig's African American farmers "quite intelligent and fairly well educated," a "remarkable community . . . of negroes which has come down from Reconstruction days." Unfortunately, Mitchell and the STFU were unable to commit funds to organize Texas farmers despite

Clayton's repeated appeals that his efforts would be in vain without more support from the STFU.[21]

Clayton warned Mitchell in a series of letters that black farmers in central and east Texas were being scattered by the enemies of the CIO who, recognizing that most Texas African Americans were deeply religious, claimed that the CIO was atheistic. "My people are an emotional and group conscious people," Clayton wrote, "and 98% of them can be reached in churches." To counter the anti-union propaganda of white owners, Clayton proposed once more that Mitchell hire him as a regional organizer for Texas who could take the message of the STFU and the CIO into all of the black churches. Mitchell wrote Clayton that he could not raise the necessary funds to put more organizers in Texas, or even to pay Clayton for his expenses, but he urged Clayton to continue his organizing efforts anyway. Anticipating Clayton's disappointment, Mitchell explained that "an organization as poor as we are does not have the financial standing of a capitalist business interprize [*sic*]. . . . These banks and business houses realize which side they are on if the ordinary worker does not."[22] But in a letter to Egan, Mitchell confided that "Clayton has only one weakness, that being his desire to go on the road with expenses."[23] In view of the fact that the STFU did not have a single paid organizer in Texas, a state with one of the highest percentages of tenancy in the South and producing more than one-third of the nation's cotton, it is puzzling that Mitchell, despite the financial frailty of the STFU, regarded Clayton's offer to become the only paid organizer in the state a personal weakness.

The STFU was far more successful in building a biracial organization in Arkansas than it was in Texas, in part because there was little difference between black and white wage laborers and sharecroppers on plantations in Arkansas. Both groups were essentially employees on centrally managed neoplantations whose main concerns were contract terms, wages, and working conditions. The election of E. B. McKinney, a black preacher, as the union's first vice president also sent a clear signal to blacks and whites that the STFU intended to cross the color line in representing the class interests of tenant farmers. In Arkansas and Alabama, blacks and whites recognized that they shared the common experience of proletarianization, and although whites did not shed their racism entirely, "hard times," STFU president Butler recalled, "makes peculiar bedfellows sometimes."[24]

In Texas, however, white tenant farmers aligned themselves with white owners on the basis of class as well as racial solidarity, because most blacks and Mexicans were not true tenants but sharecroppers. Poor white sharecroppers in west Texas tried to have it both ways by establishing segregated locals of the STFU and by emphasizing that class solidarity did not imply "social equality" for African Americans and Mexicans. In central Texas, however, most tenants were white, nonplantation share tenants who themselves rented to black, Mexican, and poor white sharecroppers; they would not be interested in joining a "tenant" union that would require them to pay higher wages to cotton pickers and to share parity checks with sharecroppers to whom they may have subrented, particularly when a growing number of those sharecroppers and laborers were drawn from the ranks of Mexican migrant laborers.

Fred Matthews came to the same conclusion when he informed Mitchell that he was withdrawing from the union; the time simply was not ripe, he wrote, "to organize Farm Workers and actual farmers into one organization in this vicinity."[25] Indeed, the time had never been ripe for organizing competing classes of farm workers and actual farmers into one union. The constitution of the union specified, in Mitchell's own words, "that only workers who receive wages, or part of the crop as wages, may be members of the Union."[26] Actual farmers, which included owners and share tenants, did not receive wages—they *paid* wages. Share tenants paid owners a share of the crop as *rent*, but they also paid wages to the workers they hired during the chopping and picking season. And although tenants may have engaged in wage work on nearby farms part of the year, especially during the harvest, their identity was primarily that of renters, not workers. In attempting to be a truly interracial union, the STFU mistakenly sought to be interclass as well, and it failed to see the class difference between farm workers and nonplantation farm tenants in Texas.

A dispute erupted between Mitchell and the Communists, led by Donald Henderson, precisely over this contradiction of organizing tenants and farm workers within the same union. The disagreement reached its peak during the short-lived merger of the STFU and the Communist-supported UCAPAWA. The fundamental difference was that UCAPAWA correctly viewed agricultural workers and sharecroppers as little different from industrial workers and not as actual farmers ascending the ladder to share tenant and owner. The STFU insisted on a single union for both tenants and farm workers (including sharecroppers), on the grounds that all nonowners were essentially laborers. The distinction may not have been meaningful in the plantation region of Arkansas, where most tenants were actually sharecroppers who went on strike for

22. Young black farm couples enjoying themselves, 1925. Rhone Family Papers, CN #08852, Center for American History, University of Texas at Austin.

23. Mexican family members on an outing, ca. 1936. On the Fall Family cotton farm, Andrés Acosta holds a bouquet of flowers that his two sisters, Consuelo and María, and his cousin Lucía had brought him. Teresa Palomo Acosta Collection, Benson Latin American Collection, University of Texas at Austin.

24. Black farm women at a community canning center in east Texas, 1934. Rural Texas Blacks Photograph Collection, Agricultural Extension Collection, Special Collections and Archives, Texas A&M University, College Station.

25. A Texas farm woman operating a tractor, 1943. Rural Women in Texas Photographic Collection, Agricultural Extension Collection, Special Collections and Archives, Texas A&M University, College Station.

26. "Migrant Mother with children" (Russell Lee). Weslaco, Texas, February 1939. USF 34-32086-D, FSA-OWI Collection, Library of Congress.

27. "Woman of the high plains [Nettie Featherston, Childress, Texas]"
(Dorothea Lange). USF 34-18294-C, FSA-OWI Collection, Library of
Congress. "We made good money a pullin' bolls, when we could pull.
. . . The worst thing we did was when we sold the car, but we had to sell
it to eat, and now we can't get away from here. . . . This county's a hard
county. They won't help bury you here. If you die, you're dead, that's
all."

28. "Native Texan" (Dorothea Lange). Hall County, Texas, June 1937. USF 34-18277-C, FSA-OWI Collection, Library of Congress. "Well, I know I've got to make a move, but I don't know where to. . . . I've eat up two cows and a pair of horses this past year. Neither drink nor gamble, so I must have eat'em up. . . . One man who had six renters last year kept one. Of the five, one went to Oklahoma, one got a farm south of town, and three got no place. . . . But them men that's doing the talking for the community is the big landowners. Them's the only ones that's got the money to go to Washington. . . . A letter I would write would sound silly up there."

29. Black sharecroppers hauling cotton, ca. 1935. Prints and Photographs Collection, CN #03022A, Center for American History, University of Texas at Austin.

30. The Landa family, Mexican sharecroppers in McLennan County, ca. 1936. Teresa Palomo Acosta Collection, Benson Latin American Collection, University of Texas at Austin.

31. Cristina and Vicente Mendoza, central Texas sharecroppers during the Great Depression. Teresa Palomo Acosta Collection, Benson Latin American Collection, University of Texas at Austin.

32. Resettled white farmer and his wife (Arthur Robstein). Ropesville Farms [Hockley County], Texas, April 1936. A U. S. Resettlement Administration rural rehabilitation project. USF 34-2948-E, FSA-OWI Collection, Library of Congress.

higher wages, as did their counterparts in industry. However, share tenants in nonplantation areas of central Texas were not wage workers.

At the STFU convention in Muskogee, Oklahoma, in 1937, the Communist Party delegates recognized the inherent contradiction of a union composed of farm workers and farm tenants and therefore proposed that the STFU dissolve and that its membership join separate unions: Its tenants would become members of the National Farmers' Union, and farm workers would become members of newly chartered AFL labor unions. The proposal, recognizing the opposing interests of farmers and farm workers, was defeated. The delegates next proposed that the STFU be a union that consisted only of small farmers, tenants, and sharecroppers. Farm workers, including plantation sharecroppers, would join AFL unions, because most farm workers were employees of industrialized farms and agribusiness plantations. Mitchell rallied the STFU delegates to defeat this proposal as well.

Mitchell stubbornly refused to concede any class distinction between tenant and farm worker and informed Henderson that "we do not look with favor upon the introduction of 'craft unionism' in the cotton fields." Henderson then criticized the STFU for being neither "fish nor fowl" because it attempted to represent the opposing class interests of farm workers and "actual farmers."[27] Although class lines between tenants and sharecroppers were constantly being crossed in both directions, fundamental differences nevertheless existed between the owner-tenant class and the sharecropper–farm-worker class—differences that eventually required the STFU to change its name to reflect its true constituency.

While Mitchell no doubt understood these differences, he nevertheless chose to think of all laborers in cotton agriculture as tenant farmers belonging to a single class of actual farmers, because he was not ready to concede that tenants would most likely never own their own farms. In this sense Mitchell was a conservative in the face of radical changes brought about by New Deal government programs. His heart was with the displaced tenants, but he could not accept the irrevocable transformation of tenant farmers into a rural proletariat. He was also opposed to the proposals to separate farmers from farm workers because he feared that the Communists might take over the union or dissolve it, and he particularly disliked Henderson, the Communist president of UCAPAWA.

At the time of the proposals' defeat in 1937, Mitchell rationalized that the STFU delegates were "deeply religious" and held the STFU constitution, which was patterned after the constitution of the Socialist Party's

Renter's Union, "in just about the same reverence as the Holy Bible." The STFU constitution maintained that all "working farmers," tenants, sharecroppers, and farm workers "who shared in the proceeds of the sale of the crop" were eligible for membership in the union. By this definition even owners could join the STFU since they received their income from the sale of cotton. What was lost in the phrase "working farmer" was the notion that some worked for wages whereas others paid wages. Owners and working farmers like Fred Matthews in west Texas, who rented to black sharecroppers and hired Mexican and black cotton pickers, could thus join a union that represented the class interests of those to whom they paid wages.[28]

In 1939 Mitchell acknowledged in a STFU report that the union had begun in 1934 as an organization for tenant farmers and sharecroppers but had become "more than ever the organization of migratory farm laborers." Seven years later, in 1946, the STFU changed its name to the National Farm Labor Union (NFLU), became affiliated with the AFL (as the Communists had originally urged it to do), and moved its operations from Arkansas to California, where it organized mostly Okie and Arkie grape pickers against the DiGiorgio Fruit Corporation. The NFLU also organized California cotton pickers, mostly Mexicans and Mexican Americans (including a young man named César Chávez) in the San Joaquin Valley.[29]

In 1942 the federal government inaugurated the Bracero Program, which authorized the introduction of thousands of Mexican farm workers from Mexico, further demonstrating the need for a union of farm workers as opposed to tenant farmers. Only a few years later the NFLU underwent yet another transformation, and in 1952 it became the National Agricultural Workers' Union (NAWU). The shift from a union of "tenants" to a union of "agricultural workers" demonstrated the soundness of the Communist delegates' insistence more than ten years earlier that tenants and farm workers ought to belong to separate unions. In Texas, where racial lines more clearly paralleled class lines and manly whiteness was inextricably tied to farm ownership, white tenants never fully embraced agricultural workers, mostly Mexicans and blacks, as class allies.[30]

White tenants in Texas were especially resistant to the idea that they had become proletarianized farm workers. Even as sharecroppers and half tenants they still thought of themselves as "actual farmers" whose status was only just below that of owners. Land owners, on the other hand, began to acquire an employer consciousness and viewed themselves as business farmers who regarded all classes of tenants as farm workers requiring supervision. After 1940, however, the number of tenant farmers in the South declined dramatically as a result of the restructuring of agriculture brought on by the cotton-reduction program, mechanization, and the trend toward large-scale, industrial farming. When cotton-picking machines began to displace agricultural workers from the cotton fields of the West during the 1950s, the very idea of a tenant farmers' union, like the STFU, became truly anachronistic. Yet even as late as 1939 Mitchell maintained his belief that the main goal of the STFU ought to be the "restoration of land to the landless," echoing Tom Hickey's slogan for the failed Land League more than twenty-five years earlier: "Land for the Landless and Homes for the Homeless." At least Hickey understood in 1915 that the tractor would someday make it possible for the landlord "to take the next step and transform his tenant into a wage worker."[31]

Although during the 1930s the STFU could not keep its class lines straight, or failed to acknowledge distinctions among classes of rural workers, it nevertheless succeeded, in Arkansas, at least, in creating a biracial union of black and white sharecroppers and farm workers. The STFU also eventually recognized the centrality of women in sharecropper communities, including black women, although largely as a result of the women's own demands for equality within the union leadership as well as in the rank and file. Women, black and white, challenged the men-only union culture and the consciousness that engendered it. Evelyn Smith, the first office secretary to work for the STFU, pressured the executive council into electing two women to serve on the council as representatives of sharecropper women. At first, Mitchell confessed, "none of us males knew what to do," so he suggested that the "woman problem" be referred to the all-male executive council. The women, including sharecroppers as well as wives of sharecroppers, won their demands: Marie Pierce, a black woman, and Myrtle Moskop were elected to the council, despite Mitchell's admission that he tried to use his "not inconsiderable powers of persuasion with the opposite sex to forestall any further action." He called Pierce and Moskop "token representatives" on the council, but their influence and their usefulness as union members belied his patronizing assessment of women sharecroppers.[32]

George Stith, secretary of an all-black STFU local, claimed that farm women were not just silent partners but "had a voice when it came down to talking or voting." In some locals the women were more active than the men because, according to Stith, "men were afraid." Union men had good reason to be afraid. Owners often kidnapped and assaulted male union members, but Stith recalled that "they was a little bit slow about bothering women." All of the officers in one of the locals were women.[33] The violence that touched the lives of most of the male membership may have persuaded the STFU to overcome its gender biases with fewer protests than might ordinarily have been expected from a traditionally all-male organization.

Women also took on the work of regional organizers and fundraisers for the STFU. An African American widow and sharecropper, Henrietta McGee, traveled throughout the western South making speeches for the STFU and raising funds wherever she went "because she got right down to earth with the things she had to say." She traveled to New York and Washington on union business and attended the first convention of the CIO, in Atlantic City. George Stith recalled an episode that he believed illustrated the kind of person she was. McGee and her party entered a restaurant in Washington and took a table, but the waiter refused to serve them. Eleanor Roosevelt, who was sitting at a table nearby and observed the affront, signaled to McGee to join her at her table. When the waiter arrived, Mrs. Roosevelt apologized to McGee in the presence of the waiter: "You know, a while ago, I didn't know that you were a Puerto Rican." McGee replied, "Well, I'm not. I'm a nigger, a nigger sharecropper from down in Arkansas." The waiter served her anyway.[34] By refusing to be served as a Puerto Rican, even at Mrs. Roosevelt's polite suggestion, McGee insisted on her own status and identity as a black woman sharecropper from down in Arkansas.

Mitchell tape recorded the stories of some of the women sharecroppers and wives of sharecroppers who were active in the STFU. These stories, like those of McGee, provide a glimpse of the courage of black women who stood up for their rights and dignity as blacks, as women, and as workers. Deacy Real, a black woman and the wife of a plantation sharecropper named Edward, tried to teach her husband to read and write so that he could demand the parity checks their landlord routinely withheld from them. Edward continued to endorse his check over to the landlord by marking it with an X despite his wife's objections. Deacy, who understood the terms of the AAA contract better than her husband did, told him: "If you put your X on the next parity check, I am going to leave you, because that's our money." Thereafter Edward cashed his own parity checks. Later Deacy worked as a domestic for Mrs. Moore, a white woman, who once rebuked her in these words: "Deacy, the next time you go out of here and don't leave dry wood in this kitchen, I am going to slap your face." Deacy recalled how she had felt such a surge of anger that she had to take a drink of water to prevent her from saying "too much." Later, after she composed herself, she found Mrs. Moore in the kitchen and politely began: "Mrs. Moore, I want to tell you one thing. I am a full grown woman and the mother of five children. . . . I love my husband better than I do you [and] I ain't going to take no slaps off him either." Then, shaking her finger in Moore's face, she continued, her anger returning in full force: "The day you slap me, that's the day I am going to slap you until I get tired. Then when I get through slapping you, I am going to choke you to death." She worked for Mrs. Moore for six more months and "never had no more trouble."[35]

For all its organizational shortcomings, the STFU brought the plight of the tenant farmers of Texas, Oklahoma, Arkansas, Missouri, and Mississippi to the attention of the nation. The union's activities had provoked governmental investigations, both state and national, into conditions in the cotton industry and had given southern sharecroppers a voice, a "cry from the cotton." Perhaps most important, it laid the foundation for the unionization of farm workers whose only claim to the land would be little different from the industrial workers' claim to the factory. The Socialist concept of a cooperative commonwealth no longer applied where farmers had been transformed into wage laborers. Perhaps for this reason the STFU and later the NFLU during the 1940s harbored no illusions about returning to some agrarian Eden. The leaders of that union concentrated their efforts on securing higher wages and better working conditions for the growing numbers of farm workers and sharecroppers on absentee-owned neoplantations and industrial cotton ranches.

In places like central Texas, where tenancy was primarily a "white man's problem," labor militancy was never as great as it was in other places in the South and West with greater numbers of African Americans and Mexicans. In California, for example, the Okies were less inclined to organize and join unions than were the Mexicans and Filipinos who, organized by the TUUL and its affiliated Cannery and Agricultural Workers Industrial Union (CAWIU), struck repeatedly in 1933 and 1934. The 1933 cotton strike in California involved more than 12,000 farm laborers, more than half of whom were Mexicans.[36] When between 300,000 and 500,000 Okies arrived in California between 1935 and 1938, John Steinbeck predicted that farm labor in California henceforth would be "white labor, it will be American labor, and it will insist on a standard of living much higher than that which was accorded the foreign 'cheap labor.'"

The *San Francisco News*, which hired Steinbeck in 1936 to write a series of articles on the Okies and "little Oklahomas" of rural California, editorialized that Dust Bowl migrants are "Americans of the old stock" and "cannot be handled as the Japanese, Mexicans and Filipinos."[37] But the unionizing drives of the largely Mexican farm workers in 1933 and 1934 were far more successful than were those organized by American-born Okies in 1938 and 1939 under UCAPAWA leadership. CAWIU led twenty-three strikes in 1933–1934 involving 42,000 farm workers, whereas only the San Joaquin Valley cotton strike of late 1939, involving mostly Okies, approached the size of earlier strikes.[38]

Okie strikes tended to be spontaneous outbreaks arising over specific conditions on the farms rather than union-sponsored actions. These displaced white tenants still thought of themselves as independent farmers rather than as proletarianized farm workers like Mexicans, Filipinos, and African Americans. Throughout 1938 and 1939 UCAPAWA labored in California, wrote the historian Walter Stein, "and brought forth a mouse."[39] Indeed, some union organizers left the fields entirely when they realized that Okies, with their nativist hatred of Mexicans and Filipinos and their patriotic hatred of union "agitators," were not their allies as much as their potential enemies.

Many of the strikes involved violent clashes between strikers and vigilante groups hired by the growers to break the strikes. The La Follette Committee held hearings in California to investigate the growers' use of violence to suppress farm-worker organizing and discovered, almost by accident, it seemed, the industrial revolution in agriculture that had put so many former farmers into migrant camps on the outskirts of huge factory farms. In the six years from 1933 to 1939, more than 140 agricultural strikes had taken place in thirty-four of the fifty-eight counties in California.[40] Although California produced only 3 percent of the nation's cotton, the state had within its borders approximately 47 percent of all large-scale, industrialized farms in the country.[41]

African Americans also engaged in more militant union activity than did white tenants. One of the first attempts at collective action took place in Alabama in 1931, with the founding of the Share-Croppers Union. Led by Communists and composed mainly of black sharecroppers, the union was most active in Tallapoosa and Lee Counties in Alabama. The union program called for continued store credit between cultivating and picking, for the right of croppers to sell their crops for cash, for cash settlements at picking time, for black schools that were open for nine months a year, and for the right of croppers to have their own truck farms. The struggle soon developed into a miniature civil war as landlords responded with violence and vigilante tactics: "Nigger hunts" were organized, night raids conducted, and some fifty croppers were arrested. One was killed, and four "disappeared" from a local jail. In 1932 in Reeltown, Tallapoosa County, black croppers and tenants forcibly resisted efforts by sheriffs to seize a black tenant's livestock as payment of a debt. The deputies opened fire, shots were exchanged, and in the foray one black cropper was killed and four deputies were wounded. Heavily armed posses descended on the black cropper communities, and black families were driven into the swamps and countryside, terrorized by the violence. Twelve farmers were arrested, two died from their wounds in jail, and five were brought to trial and sentenced to prison for from five to fifteen years. In 1934 the Share-Croppers Union successfully struck on Alabama plantations for higher wages and shorter days, and in 1935 it completed a cotton-choppers' strike involving thousands of black and white pickers. By the spring of 1935 its membership had grown to 12,000, mostly black croppers, and was confined largely to Alabama.[42]

In Texas, however, not a single cotton strike took place during the entire decade. The only strike in Texas agriculture involving more than 500 persons was a Mexican-led onion strike in Laredo. Although their strikes were small in scale, Mexican agricultural workers in south Texas formed their own unions in order to confront the organized citrus and vegetable growers. They formed the Catholic Workers' Union of Crystal City to improve working conditions and demand higher wages in spinach fields. In Laredo the Asociación de Jornaleros included agricultural workers in onions, and the South Texas Agricultural Workers' Organizing Committee was formed in 1937 in Corpus Christi to organize cotton pickers into unions affiliated with the AFL.[43] These unions, including the UCA-PAWA and the CIO, organized Mexicans who worked mostly in vegetables and citrus in south Texas border areas.[44] Mexican ranch workers, however, like those on the Taft and Chapman Ranches in San Patricio and Nueces Counties, were "conspicuously absent from these organizations," according to the historian Emilio Zamora, "because of their isolation and the more effective methods of control that ranch owners used on them."[45] In any case, most of these unions failed within a few years, as workers found themselves unable to pay union dues and as growers continued to replace strikers and union activists with Mexican immigrants.

Clearly, the racial structure and organization of cotton production and labor relations in the South and the West were not the same. Neither were the patterns of resistance that emerged from highly proletarianized California farm workers and those of central Texas tenant farmers, Mexican patch croppers, and migrant laborers. The formation of a racialized agricultural hierarchy that included white farmers and non-white laborers, particularly Mexicans, came to characterize industrial agriculture in parts of Texas and California during the 1920s and 1930s. Racial hierarchies in agricultural production, whether of large-scale enterprises or family-sized tenant farms, thus also played a key role in the susceptibility of farmers and farm workers to unionization. Texas, the state that was the birthplace of the Farmers' Alliance, the Farmers' Union, and the Socialist Party's Renters' Union and Land League, produced no radical farm movements in the 1920s or 1930s for farmers or farm workers engaged principally in the production of cotton.[46] It was mostly in the newer areas of industrialized agriculture, like the Arkansas Delta during the 1930s, that African American and white sharecroppers organized under the banner of the STFU or in the Central Valley of California, where Mexican farm workers in cotton, peaches, sugar beets, cherries, apricots, and other crops struck for higher wages, often under the leadership of Communist trade unions.[47] Nonwhite farm workers pointed the way to unionization for whites who had to learn that farmwork did not make one a farmer.

Almost twenty years earlier, in Texas, the Socialist Party's Renters' Union and Land League declined in part because of co-optation of the Democratic Party and the repression by the state and federal governments during World War I. Virulent racism and reactionary politics of the Ku Klux Klan in the 1920s tended to mute agrarian protest.[48] Less conspicuous but ultimately more devastating to farmer movements generally was the gradual change in the structure of agriculture from a network of tenant- and owner-operated small farms to larger units of production that relied on wage labor and power farming. For many displaced tenants, the STFU offered no solution and no relief. White tenants in Texas wanted more than their share of parity and rental payments; they wanted their own farms. And when they realized that the agricultural ladder to ownership had utterly collapsed in the wake of industrial farming, tractors, and Mexican labor, their response was to abandon farming altogether or seek new opportunities farther west.

The impoverishment and homelessness of displaced tenants were captured in photographs that Dorothea Lange, Walker Evans, and Russell Lee took for the Farm Security Administration. The photographs—and works such as Caldwell's *Tobacco Road*, Steinbeck's *Grapes of Wrath*, and Agee and Evans's *Let Us Now Praise Famous Men*—put southern poor whites in the national spotlight during the 1930s. Only when whites were reduced to living like Mexicans and blacks did the nation take notice. Although there had always been poor whites, like the Jeeter Lester family in Erskine Caldwell's popular novel *Tobacco Road*, the existence of such a large army of migrant whites was unsettling to white America.[49] The nation was inundated with images of white men, women, and children living in the most abject poverty, little different from the poverty of Mexican and black sharecroppers and cotton pickers. Whereas blacks had gone by the millions to city ghettos, displaced whites were drawn by the illusory promise of California's agribusiness farms. They would not all go gently into that corporate domain, and they only reluctantly surrendered their identities as white farmers for off-white farm workers, at least until World War II, when other opportunities opened up for them. For the poor white farmers of central Texas, the cotton culture of the New South had gone west.

Conclusion

On June 9, 1996, the New Light House of Prayer, a black church in the central Texas town of Greenville, in Hunt County, was heavily damaged by fire. In the early morning hours of the following day, another black church in Greenville, Church of the Living God, was set ablaze. In the previous eighteen months more than thirty black churches had been torched throughout the South, and the work of racist arsonists was suspected in these two cases, as well as in the others. Greenville lies in the northern end of the Blackland Prairie, where for many years a banner stretched across the main street, and later a neon sign, that read: "Welcome to Greenville: blackest land, whitest people." Hunt County Judge Steve Shipp, president of the local historical society, said that the slogan referred to the rich fertility of its black soil and to the "purity of its people."[1] Although it is possible that "whitest people" also alluded to the purity of the town's black folk, it is not likely, and Judge Shipp said he understood how blacks were offended. Whitest people, after all, suggests the campaign of terror of the white supremacist Ku Klux Klan against black people throughout the South. But the assertion of whiteness in the Greenville slogan also belies the insecurities of white people in rural central Texas whose parents and grandparents often failed to achieve the status of yeoman manhood that farm ownership conferred. They insisted on their whiteness against the economic and racial pressure of New Deal agricultural policy, Mexican labor, mechanization, corporate agriculture—and, more recently, the competing claims of Mexicans to whiteness.

Between 1900 and 1940 the immigration of Mexicans into the black-and-white economy of central Texas cotton ruptured whiteness along ethnoracial as well as class lines into whites and poor whites, reflecting the increasing social and economic distance between white owners and white tenants. The landholding class held itself aloof from tenants and, as a class, according to one report, thought "that their children should not go to school in the same company with the children of the tenant class." The author of the report alluded to the large and "inferior type of white tenant population" and described them as "noted for thinness of neck and shoulder, narrowness of face, and a general stooping from the shoulders."[2] White landowners increasingly regarded these perennial tenant farmers as off-white landless "road trash" whose shiftlessness and innate lack of business sense made them sorry whites. The white scourge was thus not simply an allusion to the immiseration of thousands of white tenants on cotton farms in Texas but also to the menace of poor whites—the trash of whiteness—to what the contemporary eugenicist Lothrop Stoddard called "white-world supremacy." During the 1930s and 1940s, the ethnoracial identities of whites as well as Mexicans thus continued to be forged against kaleidoscopically changing backgrounds of economic structures, nationality, and shifting class alignments.

The Great Depression undermined the eugenicist notion that Nordic whites were inherently more successful than poor whites and nonwhites because it affected the biologically fit as well as the unfit. Yet those who suffered least in the rural areas of the South were in fact those who best fit the eugenic description of Nordic whites—the successful owners of cotton farms, large and small, who were able to take advantage of government programs to purchase more land and tractors as they rid themselves of superfluous tenant farmers. In their places they hired poor white, Mexican, and black sharecroppers whom they could "scientifically manage" in a fashion not unlike the way in which the eugenicists hoped to manage the "germ plasm" of the white race. The application of business methods to the production of cotton, the rising value of the land, and the high cost of credit changed the way farmers worked on farms, creating hierarchies of labor stratified or split along both race and class lines: white owners and share tenants, African American and Mexican sharecroppers, and mostly Mexican migrant workers. Meanwhile, the white belt of central Texas became noticeably brown between 1900 and 1940, leaving many poor whites to recall with nostalgia the pristine whiteness of Texas before the Mexicans came, when the whitest people could be found on the blackest land.

During the New Deal many share tenants were reduced to wage laborers who worked under the direction of farm owners and managers, while thousands of others were "tractored off" the land. The presence of a large, nearby reservoir of Mexican laborers in south Texas and Mexico facilitated the transition from small agricultural production on independent farms to large-scale production utilizing a combination of tenants, sharecroppers, and wage workers. At the same time, the STFU failed to be an effective organization of nonplantation tenant farmers in central Texas. Its evolution into the NFLU and then the NAWU reflected the transformation in cotton agriculture from small farms operated by white tenants to the new industrial agribusinesses that employed thousands of mostly nonwhite farm workers.

The beginning of World War II marked the decline in the public's concern with the Joads, the Jeeter Lesters, and their real-life poor-white counterparts. Wartime industry created a labor scarcity in agriculture that formalized the bilateral agreement between the United States and Mexico to provide Mexican "guest workers" in the United States—the Bracero Program. The Bureau of Agricultural Economics reported a loss of 2.8 million agricultural workers between 1939 and 1943, mostly to the armed services and war-related industries. In Texas there were approximately 200,000 fewer farm workers in the state in 1943 than there had been in 1941.[3] Aggressively recruited in the 1920s, repatriated and deported in the 1930s, and imported as contract laborers in the 1940s, transborder Mexicans continued to cross and recross the international boundary while state and federal governments attempted to control their movement in both directions.

The Bracero Program was inaugurated as part of the Emergency Farm Labor Program in 1942. Given congressional approval in 1952 by the enactment of Public Law 78, the Bracero Program continued until 1964 and oversaw the temporary importation of hundreds of thousands of Mexican farm workers. As a wartime emergency measure between 1943 and 1947, the program raised no objections from nativist groups, organized labor, or even the Communist Party. The Emergency Farm Labor program was put under the jurisdiction of state extension services, which imported more than 220,000 braceros from 1942 to 1947. The program required that growers provide adequate housing, sanitary facilities, and compliance with the wage scale set by state wage boards appointed by the secretary of agriculture.[4]

Many growers objected to the Bracero Program, preferring instead the arrangement made during World War I under which they recruited laborers directly from Mexico with little government interference. Growers especially disliked the imposition of a mandatory $0.30 minimum wage, claiming that this was the first step toward government regulation of farm labor. Texas had decades of experience in hiring undocumented workers from Mexico and viewed the Bracero Program as an infringement on their "free-market" rights. In 1943 members of the National Grange, the American Farm Bureau Federation, and the National Council of Farmer Cooperatives submitted a joint statement to the House Committee on Appropriations in which they strenuously objected to the Emergency Farm Labor Program's provision for establishing a minimum wage and regulating maximum hours and other conditions of employment. These organizations wanted the government to supply them with Mexican labor, as it had done with the World War I temporary-admittance program, without intervening in the contract between employer and bracero. "Under the guise of the war effort," they wrote, "a social revolution is being perpetrated upon the American people."[5]

Despite their objections to the program, Texas growers formally asked for braceros in 1943. However, the Mexican government refused to allow braceros to work in Texas until the state guaranteed their fair treatment and an end to de facto segregation and overt discrimination against all Mexicans. Although most of the labor demand came from agribusiness enterprises in California, Texas cotton growers nevertheless desired braceros to keep wages low and the labor supply abundant. In an effort to persuade the Mexican government that Texas no longer regarded Mexicans as targets for racial discrimination, Governor Coke Stevenson persuaded the state legislature in 1943 to pass the so-called Caucasian Race Resolution. This clever resolution was intended to convince Mexico that discrimination against Caucasians would not be tolerated in Texas, the assumption being that Mexicans were, of course, members of the Caucasian race, which they were only in some legal, pseudo-scientific, and ethnographical sense; but practically no Texan regarded Mexicans, particularly bracero farm workers, as white.

The resolution stated that since "our neighbors to the South" were cooperating in the effort to "stamp out Naziism and preserve democracy" and in order to "assist the national policy of hemispherical solidarity," the state of Texas resolved that "all persons of the Caucasian Race . . . are entitled to the full and equal accommodations, advantages, facilities, and privileges of all public places of business or amusement." Whoever denied to any person these privileges "shall be considered as violating the good neighbor policy of our State."[6] This disingenuous resolution thus sought to reassure Mexican officials that the state of Texas, if not its citizens, recognized Mexicans as fellow Caucasians. In the same year Governor Stevenson established the Good Neighbor Commission of Texas to promote better understanding between Texas whites and Caucasian Mexicans. With so much official recognition of the whiteness of Mexicans in Texas, the Mexican government finally relented in 1947 and permitted braceros to enter Texas.[7]

For the next seventeen years the government functioned as a national labor contractor for southwestern growers at taxpayers' expense. Although, technically, growers were not permitted to request braceros where domestic labor was plentiful, in actuality they were able to set wages low enough to discourage domestic workers from applying and thus created a labor shortage for imported bracero laborers. Not only did growers prefer Mexican braceros in order to avoid paying wages at domestic levels, they also used braceros as a reserve labor supply to undercut attempts at farm unionization, especially by the NFLU and the NAWU. In one sense, the growers were biding their time until the mechanical cotton picker, introduced in the 1950s, could be perfected and thereby eliminate the need for braceros. Growers had always sought a solution to the labor problem, including one Louisiana grower's failed experiment to import Brazilian monkeys to pick cotton.[8] By the end of the decade approximately 8 percent of U.S. cotton was machine harvested. In 1964, the final year of the Bracero Program, the figure had risen to 78 percent.[9]

The Bracero Program had also stimulated massive immigration of undocumented Mexican workers, which presented major obstacles to Mexican Americans who were pursuing their own civil rights agenda and economic objectives. Mexican American organizations were outspokenly critical of the Bracero Program. They argued that braceros lowered wages for domestic workers, which included many Mexican Americans, served as strike breakers, and reinforced negative stereotypes of Mexicans as uneducated, unskilled farm workers. Others, like Ernesto Galarza, himself a Mexican immigrant and former migrant worker, argued that braceros were abused, exploited, and denied basic rights by their employers. He sought to end a program of federally sponsored labor contracting that left braceros without the protection of either the U.S. or the Mexican government. In some ways the 1940s recapitulated the debates over the desirability of importing Mexican labor for agricultural work, with growers and employers on one side and organized labor on the other. More important, the debate over the Bracero Program reawakened racialist arguments about Mexicans in general; and Mexican Americans, fearing a backlash against all Mexicans regardless of citizenship, sought to put ethnoracial distance between themselves and braceros.

While Anglos were learning to distinguish between "wetback" Mexicans and Mexican Americans, in central Texas, where Mexican sharecropper families were relative newcomers to the western South, Anglo parents and children resented their presence and often refused to attend schools that admitted Mexican children.[10] Children of black farmers, whether of owners or tenants, were never allowed to attend the same schools as whites. In parts of central and south Texas, where the population of African Americans was too small to warrant a separate school, black children were simply not able to attend school at all.[11] Some black men and women sought to marry Mexicans in order to claim whiteness for their children, especially if they produced a "white Mexican" with "straight hair." One black woman would not let her daughter marry a white Mexican because he had a "little colored blood in him" but permitted her to marry a "dark Mexican" who, though he treated the daughter "like a dog," was neither a black Mexican nor a white Mexican.[12] Intermarriage had created whole new ways of describing and classifying black Mexicans or Mexican blacks in such a way that it was possible to talk about a half-black, white Mexican.

Miscegenation laws forbade the marriage of blacks with whites, but because Mexicans were often regarded as nonwhite, even if they were legally white, they were rarely, if ever, prosecuted.[13] In one particular case the law was applied for entirely different reasons than that of intermarriage. During the 1920s a jury indicted Bob Lemmons, an African American married to a Mexican woman, for violating the law forbidding miscegenation. He would not have been prosecuted were it not for the fact that he and his wife attempted to send their children to the white school instead of the black school. Mexican children in this township attended the white school in separate classrooms for the first two or three years; afterwards, only a token few, usually the ones Anglo teachers singled out as being "clean" and "not like the others," were permitted to continue their education. A judge from Dimmit County, where the case was tried, told Paul Taylor: "The Negroes with Negro-Mexican children and the Mexicans wanted to send their children to the white school, so when that started . . . they just indicted and tried them for violating the law against intermarriage. Then they tipped off the women that if they had nigger blood they could not put the men in jail."[14] Lemmons's Mexican wife confessed that she must be part black in order to have charges dropped against her husband for marrying a white person. This "proved that all the Mexicans were black," reported one county resident, "so we put the Mexicans and Negroes together in school and employed a part Negro to teach them."[15] The judge solved the problem of segregating Mexicans from whites in a town that had only two schools for three ethnoracial groups by changing the racial classification of Mexicans to black.

Members of the so-called Mexican American generation, the offspring of Mexican immigrants, had come of age in Texas during the 1930s and 1940s and began insisting on their status as whites in order to overcome the worst features of Jim Crow segregation, restrictive housing covenants, employment discrimination, and the social stigma of being Mexican, a label which, in the eyes of Anglos, designated race rather than citizenship. Mostly urban and middle class, a group of Mexican Americans founded the League of United Latin American Citizens (LULAC) in 1929 in Corpus Christi to foster the goals of Americanization in Texas and other states of the Southwest, restricting membership to U.S. citizens and emphasizing English-language skills and loyalty to the U.S. Constitution. LULAC members constructed new identities as Latin Americans in order to arrogate to themselves the privileges of whiteness routinely denied to immigrant Mexicans, blacks, Chinese, and Indians. As Mexican Americans sought acceptance as white Americans, they created tensions not only between themselves and Mexican immigrants but also with the black community.[16]

In order to become white, many Mexican Americans adopted the American discourse of what Cornel West has called "negatively-charged Blackness."[17] To claim whiteness fully and convincingly, LULAC emphasized the importance of maintaining the color line between its members and African Americans and urged members not to associate with Negroes. Mexican Americans began to object strenuously to being labeled as "colored" or forced to share facilities with African Americans. During the 1930s and 1940s Texas Mexicans increasingly began to call themselves white. One Mexican American cotton picker, whose "Indian ancestry was evidently strongly prominent," told Paul Taylor that "It does not look right to see Mexicans and Negroes together. Their color is different. They are black and we are white." A member of one of the LULAC councils explained that the organization expelled one of its own members for having "married a Negress" and that both she and her husband were shunned by other Mexicans. He then added, "An American mob would lynch him. But we are not given the same opportunity to form a mob and come clean."[18] While most LULAC members did not go to these extremes to assert their whiteness, at least one regretted that he was not white enough to lynch one of his own with impunity.

LULAC members also fought vigorously against the U.S. census when it established a separate category for Mexicans. Until the 1930 census, Mexican Americans were counted simply as white, but the 1930 census included a new category of Mexican, with instructions to place any person of Mexican descent "who is definitely not white" into the category. No instructions were given to enumerators on how to determine which Mexicans were white. A few years later, in 1936, LULAC took on the El Paso city registrar, Alex K. Powell, and the city health officer, Dr. T. J. McCamant, when they announced that El Paso would begin classifying Mexicans as "colored" in its birth and death records, although previously they had been classified as white. Powell stated that he was merely following a ruling by the Census Bureau, which had reclassified Mexicans, and that other cities had already done the same: Dallas, Fort Worth, Houston, and San Antonio.[19]

The main issue, however, was infant-mortality rates, which were embarrassingly high in a city that was attempting to market itself to the rest of the country as a major health resort. By classifying Mexicans as colored, city officials could realize a dramatic improvement in their white infant-mortality rates. Led by Frank Galván, president of LULAC, and Cleofas Calleros, a member of El Paso's National Catholic Welfare Conference, Mexican Americans protested the reclassification scheme, arguing that the Mexican American was "recognized by law as belonging to the white race." M. A. Gómez, president of the Mexican American unit of the Veterans of Foreign Wars in El Paso, blamed the growing prejudice against Mexicans on the recent influx into Texas of "white trash," to whom all Mexicans, regardless of citizenship or somatic differences, were colored. The Veterans of Foreign Wars hired an attorney to file suit on behalf of twenty-five Mexican Americans, naming El Paso city officials Powell and McCamant as defendants.[20] LULAC nevertheless credited McCamant for bringing the classification scheme to its attention and thanked him for pointing out "the nigger in the woodpile."[21] Mexicans had come a long way from the 1850s, when they freely associated with slaves and free blacks, often helping slaves escape to Mexico and thereby earning the hostility of white slaveowners.

The majority of Mexican Americans, especially among the working class, did not seek to define themselves as Caucasian or to achieve racial parity with whites at the expense of blacks. One working-class member of the Mexican American generation who resisted the lure of whiteness was Emma Tenayuca, a labor organizer and leader of the Pecan Shellers Strike in San Antonio, Texas, during the 1930s. As a woman Tenayuca defied the gendered boundaries of both Anglo and Mexican culture when she assumed the role of labor activist; she also crossed the ideological divide between patriotic Americans and traitors when she joined the Communist Party.[22] While many Anglos regarded Tenayuca as a stereotypical Mexican who had suddenly gone *loca*, the largely Catholic, anti-Communist, and middle-class Mexican American community of San Antonio, which included LULAC leaders and the Catholic Church, opposed Tenayuca along ethnoracial fault lines as well as those of religion, gender, and politics. Tenayuca identified herself as an Indian like her father and was fond of saying that she did not have a "fashionable Spanish name like García or Sánchez."[23]

Mexican identity, like whiteness itself, fissured along lines of class, nationality, language, and culture. Few of their immigrant parents identified themselves as whites; they were always mexicanos. Many middle-class Texas Mexicans, however, were moving out of the ethnoracial borderlands between blackness and whiteness by constructing identities as Americans and embracing whiteness. The ethnoracial position of African Americans did not change substantially throughout this period, even though as a group they continued to add to their ethnic makeup through intermarriage. By the so-called one-drop rule, persons of African descent, however slight, were racially marked as black. But whiteness and Mexicanness, like slow-moving tectonic plates, shifted over time, slipping over and under one another and creating a new ethnoracial terrain on which Mexican Americans could forge identities as white citizens in order to benefit from what the historian George Lipsitz has called "the possessive investment in whiteness."[24]

For more than a century the South has been the historians' laboratory for analyzing race relations between blacks and whites. But the West, with its multiplicity of races and ethnic groups encountering each other for the first time on ranches, farms, and railroads—and in the cities, mines, and forests—continues to raise questions about the ways in which whiteness itself is discursively constituted in relationship to blacks, Mexicans, Indians, Chinese, Japanese, and other racialized groups. "In race relations," Patricia Limerick has perceptively written, "the West could make the turn-of-the-century Northeastern urban confrontation between European immigrants and American nativists look like a family reunion. Similarly, in the diversity of languages, religions, and cultures, it surpassed the South."[25] But we need to remember that ethnoracial and class conflict also inheres in whiteness and that white family reunions in the South and West were often rancorous affairs.

Still, the West exerts a powerful hold over the imagination of scholars as well as laypersons: For many the white West represents the metaphorical cradle of American democracy and the prelapsarian garden of the world. It is the place where manly white men, like Theodore Roosevelt, fought the "righteous war" between civilization and barbarism, between the Nordic race and dark-skinned others. Attempts to view the West through less romantic lenses continues to meet spirited resistance.[26] Yet gradually the history of the American West is being rewritten, and in tone if not substance it has begun to share certain commonalities with the historiography of the South. Nowhere is this more evident than in the increasing number of scholarly works on race making and race relations in general in the American West and Southwest. Of particular importance will be histories that examine how the experience of whiteness as normative and racially unmarked masked the privileges and advantages of a group that defined who they were in terms of who they were not.

Another task before us is to write histories that transgress the regional boundaries of South and West, to study the migrations of people from the Southwest to the South, as well as from the South to the West. Today, for example, Mexicans work in tobacco and melon fields in Virginia and North Carolina and have formed communities in virtually all southern states where they are recruited to work in agriculture for low wages. Chicanos born in the South often speak English with a southern accent and are as accustomed to eating grits as tortillas. These communities form networks that link Mexicans in the South with their ancestral homes in the West and Southwest and shape the social and economic culture of the rural and urban South as much as they are shaped by it.

Whether southern or western, many Mexican Americans, often identifying themselves as Hispanics, are as worried today about the large presence of Mexican immigrants in the Southwest as were whites in 1930, when a Texas congressman told the House Immigration Committee that the American people must decide whether "to preserve the Southwest as a future home for millions of the white race or permit this vast region to continue to be used, as it is now being used, as a dumping ground for the human hordes of poverty stricken peon Indians of Mexico."[27] While not sharing some of the racist assumptions of Anglo-Americans, these Mexican Americans recognize that policies aimed at

Mexican immigrants continue to affect their own social and ethnoracial status in American society. Such concerns, however, should not obscure the fact that English-only laws, propositions that deny medical, educational, and other benefits to undocumented workers and their families, and increasing physical violence against Mexican immigrants are nothing less than the nativist reassertion at the close of the twentieth century of the primacy of whiteness and therefore, as David Roediger reminds us, of the "empty and terrifying attempt to build an identity based on what one isn't and on whom one can hold back."[28] The problem of the color line is the scourge of whiteness that will continue to shape race relations into the twenty-first century.

Notes

Introduction

1. James C. Cobb, *The Most Southern Place on Earth: The Mississippi Delta and the Roots of Regional Identity* (New York: Oxford University Press, 1992). For a small sample of the literature that both shaped and was shaped by these images, see William Faulkner, *Snopes: The Hamlet, The Mansion, and The Town* (New York: Random House, Modern Library Edition, 1994); Erskine Caldwell, *Tobacco Road* (1934; reprint, New York: Signet, 1962); and John Steinbeck, *The Grapes of Wrath* (New York: Viking Press, 1939). For two revealing memoirs, see Theodore Rosengarten, *All God's Dangers: The Life of Nate Shaw* (New York: Alfred A. Knopf, 1975); and William Alexander Percy, *Lanterns on the Levee: Recollections of a Planter's Son* (New York: Alfred A. Knopf, 1941). See also commentaries and photographs in Erskine Caldwell and Margaret Bourke-White, *You Have Seen Their Faces* (New York: Viking Press, 1937); James Agee and Walker Evans, *Let Us Now Praise Famous Men* (Boston: Houghton Mifflin, 1941); and Dorothea Lange and Paul S. Taylor, *American Exodus: A Record of Human Erosion* (New York: Reynal & Hitchcock, 1939). On the early years of the New South, see C. Vann Woodward, *Origins of the New South, 1877–1913* (Baton Rouge: Louisiana State University Press, 1971); and Edward L. Ayers, *The Promise of the New South: Life after Reconstruction* (New York: Oxford University Press, 1992).

2. On interactions between Mexicans and Anglos in Texas, see David Montejano, *Anglos and Mexicans in the Making of Texas, 1836–1986* (Austin: University of Texas Press, 1987); Américo Paredes, *"With His Pistol in His Hand": A Border Ballad and Its Hero* (Austin: University of Texas Press, 1958); and Arnoldo de León, *The Tejano Community, 1836–1900* (Albuquerque: University of New Mexico Press, 1982). On slavery in Texas, see Randolph B. Campbell, *An Empire for Slavery: The Peculiar Institution in Texas, 1821–1865* (Baton Rouge: Louisiana State University Press, 1989); Paul D. Lack, *The Texas Revolutionary Experience: A Political and Social History, 1835–1836* (College Station: Texas A&M University Press,

1992), 238–52; and Eugene C. Barker, *The Life of Stephen F. Austin: Founder of Texas, 1793–1836* (1926; reprint, Austin: University of Texas Press, 1985), 201–25.

3. Terry D. Jordan, John L. Bean Jr., and William M. Holmes, *Texas: A Geography*, Geographies of the United States Series (Boulder, Colo.: Westview Press, 1984), 5, 91.

4. Robert A. Calvert, "Agrarian Texas," in *Texas through Time: Evolving Interpretations*, ed. Walter L. Buenger and Robert A. Calvert (College Station: Texas A&M University Press, 1991), 197.

5. Oscar Lewis, *On the Edge of the Black Waxy: A Cultural Survey of Bell County, Texas* (Saint Louis, Mo.: Washington University Studies, New Series, 1948), 2.

6. On the reluctance of many white Texans to identify with the Texas of the South and the Confederacy, see Campbell, *Empire for Slavery*, 1. For a long-overdue discussion of the burden of Western history, see Patricia Nelson Limerick, *The Legacy of Conquest: The Unbroken Past of the American West* (New York: W. W. Norton, 1987), esp. 17–32. On the connection between southern and western regional identities, see David M. Emmons, "Constructed Province: History and the Making of the Last American West," *Western Historical Quarterly* 25 (Winter 1994): 437–59, and, in the same issue, the responses by Joan M. Jensen (pp. 461–63), A. Yvette Huginnie (pp. 463–66), Albert L. Hurtado (pp. 467–69), Charles Reagan Wilson (pp. 470–73), Edward L. Ayers (pp. 473–76), and William Cronon (pp. 476–81). See also Edward L. Ayers, "What We Talk about When We Talk about the South," and Patricia Nelson Limerick, "Region and Reason," in *All over the Map: Rethinking American Regions*, ed. Edward L. Ayers et al. (Baltimore, Md.: Johns Hopkins University Press, 1996), 62–104.

7. Paul S. Taylor, "Opportunities for Research in the Far West," *Publication of the American Sociological Society* 29 (August 1935): 103–4. Reflecting the duality of contemporary Texas culture, the *Austin American-Statesman*, December 2, 1992, carried the front-page headline: "Is Texas in Dixieland or Cowboy Country?" See also Frank Vandiver, *The Southwest: South or West* (College Station: Texas A&M University Press, 1975). On the historical links between Texas and the West, particularly California, see Howard Lamar, *Texas Crossings: The Lone Star State and the American Far West, 1836–1986* (Austin: University of Texas Press, 1991). The convergence of the South and the West represented by the settlement patterns of Anglos, African Americans, and Mexicans in Texas is explored in Terry G. Jordan, "A Century and a Half of Ethnic Change in Texas, 1830–1986," *Southwestern Historical Quarterly* 89 (April 1986): 385–422.

8. Testimony of W. B. Yeary, U.S. Congress, Senate Commission on Industrial Relations, *Final Report and Testimony*, 64th Cong., 1st sess., 1916, S. Doc. 415, 10: 9166 (hereafter cited as *Final Report and Testimony*).

9. Between 1850 and 1980 the proportion of Mexicans in Texas increased from 6.5 percent to 22 percent, while that of blacks in the population declined from 27 percent to 12 percent (Jordan, "Ethnic Change in Texas," 418).

10. Work Projects Administration, *WPA Guide to Texas* (New York: Hastings House, 1940; reprint, Texas Monthly Press, 1986), 5.

11. See Devra Weber, *Dark Sweat, White Gold: California Farm Workers, Cotton, and the New Deal* (Berkeley: University of California Press, 1994); Camille

Guerin-Gonzales, *Mexican Workers and American Dreams: Immigration, Repatriation, and California Farm Labor, 1900–1939* (New Brunswick, N.J.: Rutgers University Press, 1994); and Carey McWilliams, *Factories in the Field: The Story of Migratory Farm Labor in California* (Boston: Little, Brown, 1939).

12. Max Sylvius Handman, "Economic Reasons for the Coming of the Mexican Immigrant," *American Journal of Sociology* 35 (January 1930): 609–10; and idem, "The Mexican Immigrant in Texas," *Southwestern Political and Social Science Quarterly* 7 (June 1926): 37.

13. For the growing literature on working-class constructions of whiteness, see David Roediger, *The Wages of Whiteness: Race and the Making of the American Working Class* (London and New York: Verso, 1991); idem, *Towards the Abolition of Whiteness: Essays on Race, Politics, and Working-Class History* (London and New York: Verso, 1994); Eric Lott, *Love and Theft: Blackface Minstrelsy and the American Working Class* (New York: Oxford University Press, 1993); Theodore W. Allen, *The Invention of the White Race*, vol. 1, *Racial Oppression and Social Control* (London and New York: Verso, 1994); Noel Ignatiev, *How the Irish Became White* (New York and London: Routledge, 1995); and Alexander Saxton, *The Rise and Fall of the White Republic: Class Politics and Mass Culture in Nineteenth-Century America* (London and New York: Verso, 1990). On the legal construction of whiteness, see Ian F. Haney López, *White by Law: The Legal Construction of Race* (New York: New York University Press, 1996); and Cheryl I. Harris, "Whiteness as Property," *Harvard Law Review* 106 (June 1993): 1709–91. On racial formation and the gendered construction of racial ideologies, see Howard Winant, *Racial Conditions: Politics, Theory, Comparisons* (Minneapolis: University of Minnesota Press, 1994); Evelyn Brooks Higginbotham, "African-American Women's History and the Metalanguage of Race," *Signs* 17 (Winter 1992): 251–74; Peggy Pascoe, "Miscegenation Law, Court Cases, and Ideologies of 'Race' in Twentieth-Century America," *Journal of American History* 83 (June 1996): 44–69; Ruth Frankenberg, *White Women, Race Matters: The Social Construction of Whiteness* (Minneapolis: University of Minnesota Press, 1993); and Vron Ware, *Beyond the Pale: White Women, Racism, and History* (London and New York: Verso, 1992). See also Barbara J. Fields, "Ideology and Race in America," in *Region, Race, and Reconstruction: Essays in Honor of C. Vann Woodward*, ed. J. Morgan Kousser and James M. McPherson (New York: Oxford University Press, 1982), 143–77; Thomas C. Holt, "Marking: Race, Race-Making, and the Writing of History," *American Historical Review* 100 (February 1995), 1–20; and Ronald Takaki, *Iron Cages: Race and Culture in 19th-Century America* (Seattle: University of Washington Press, 1979).

14. On eugenics and scientific racism, see Daniel J. Kevles, *In the Name of Eugenics: Genetics and the Uses of Human Heredity* (New York: Knopf, 1985); Edward J. Larson, *Sex, Race, and Science: Eugenics in the Deep South* (Baltimore, Md.: Johns Hopkins University Press, 1995); Nicole Hahn Rafter, *White Trash: The Eugenic Family Studies, 1877–1919* (Boston: Northeastern University Press, 1988); Stephen Jay Gould, *The Mismeasure of Man* (1981; reprint, New York: W. W. Norton, 1993); H. H. Goddard, *The Kallikak Family: A Study in the Heredity of Feeble-mindedness* (New York: Macmillan, 1912); Donald K. Pickens, *Eugenics and the Progressives* (Nashville, Tenn.: Vanderbilt University Press, 1968); J. David Smith, *The Eugenic Assault on America: Scenes in Red, White, and*

Black (Fairfax, Va.: George Mason University Press, 1993); Thomas F. Gossett, *Race: The History of an Idea in America* (Dallas: Southern Methodist University Press, 1963); Elazar Barkan, *The Retreat of Scientific Racism: Changing Concepts of Race in Britain and the United States between the World Wars* (Cambridge, England: Cambridge University Press, 1992); Thomas G. Dyer, *Theodore Roosevelt and the Idea of Race* (Baton Rouge: Louisiana State University Press, 1980); and Alan M. Kraut, *Silent Travelers: Germs, Genes, and the "Immigrant Menace"* (New York: Basic Books, 1994).

15. On the doctrine of Nordicism and the writings of the eugenicist Madison Grant, see Gossett, *Race*, 353–57, 466 (Coolidge), and 155–63 (eugenics). C. Vann Woodward (*The Strange Career of Jim Crow*, 3rd rev. ed. [New York: Oxford University Press, 1974], 94) notes that racialist literature in the early twentieth century reflected the deterioration in race relations that accompanied the white-supremacy movement and the "flourishing cult of Nordicism." See also Andrew Baker, "Recent Trends in the Nordic Doctrine," *Journal of Psychology* 2 (1936): 151–59; and Franz Boas, "This Nordic Nonsense," *Forum* 74 (October 1925): 502–11. The notion that poor whites or "white trash" were believed to be hybrid or "moronic" whites, biologically inferior to Nordic whites, was not uncommon during the 1920s. In 1916 Grant wrote in his popular work, *The Passing of the Great Race, Or the Racial Basis of European History* ([New York: Charles Scribner's Sons, 1916], 77), "Where two distinct species are located side by side history and biology teach that but one of two things can happen; either one race drives the other out, as the Americans exterminated the Indians and as the Negroes are now replacing the whites in various parts of the South; or else they amalgamate and form a population of race bastards in which the lower type ultimately preponderates." Four years later Lothrop Stoddard published *The Rising Tide of Color against White World-Supremacy* (New York: Charles Scribner's Sons, 1920), which popularized the idea that the Nordic race was in danger of being inundated by inferior races. These works were sufficiently popular that they appeared in F. Scott Fitzgerald's *The Great Gatsby* ([New York: Charles Scribner's Sons, 1925], 13): The wealthy industrialist Tom Buchanan, worried that the "white race will be utterly submerged," asks if anyone has read "The Rise of the Colored Empire" by someone named "Goddard," a conflation of the names Grant and Stoddard. See Gossett, *Race*, 397; and Richard Slotkin, *Gunfighter Nation: The Myth of the Frontier in Twentieth-Century America* (New York: Harper Perennial, 1993), 198–200, 698.

16. Anthropologist John Hartigan Jr. has written that poor whites historically have been "marked off as racial detritus—the trash of whiteness" (quoted in "Trash Talk," *Lingua Franca* 5 [April 1995]: 9). See also his article, "Name Calling: Objectifying 'Poor Whites' and 'White Trash' in Detroit," in *White Trash: Race and Class in America*, ed. Matt Wray and Annalee Newitz (New York and London: Routledge, 1997), 41–56.

17. Edward Everett Davis, in *The Cotton Crisis: Proceedings of Second Conference Institute of Public Affairs*, ed. S. D. Myres Jr. (Dallas: Southern Methodist University, 1935), 42.

18. Edward Everett Davis, *The White Scourge* (San Antonio: Naylor, 1940), ix–x; and Davis, *Cotton Crisis*, 42.

19. E. E. Davis to John C. Box, February 24, 1928, Oliver Douglas Weeks Papers, box 2, folder 8, LULAC Collection, Benson Latin American Collection,

University of Texas at Austin (hereafter cited as Weeks Papers); and idem, *White Scourge*, 131.

20. Larson, *Sex, Race, and Science*, 100; Roediger, *Wages of Whiteness*; and David T. Wellman, *Portraits of White Racism*, 2d ed. (Cambridge, England: Cambridge University Press, 1993), 58–62.

21. See, for example, Texas Applied Economics Club, *Survey of Southern Travis County*, ed. Lewis H. Haney and George S. Wehrwein, University of Texas Bulletin 65 (Austin: University of Texas, 1916), 132; and Edward Everett Davis, *A Report on Illiteracy in Texas*, University of Texas Bulletin 2328 (Austin: University of Texas, 1923).

22. Matt Wray and Annalee Newitz, eds., *White Trash: Race and Class in America* (New York and London: Routledge, 1997); and Michele Fine et al., eds., *Off White: Readings on Race, Power, and Society* (New York and London: Routledge, 1997).

23. On the Irish and white racial formation, see Roediger, *Wages of Whiteness*, 133–63; and Ignatiev, *How the Irish Became White*. On relations between Germans and blacks and Mexicans in Texas, see Dorothy Grace Redus Robinson, "Seed Time and Harvest: A Story of the Redus Family," typescript, 1966, 24, Robinson Papers, Center for American History, University of Texas at Austin; and "Renters' Union," *The Rebel*, May 10, 1913, 3. Historian Walter Buenger shows how the nativist planks of the Know-Nothing Party of the 1850s cemented political relations between Texas Germans and Mexicans who formed Democratic clubs to defeat the Know-Nothings. See his *Secession and the Union in Texas* (Austin: University of Texas Press, 1984), 91–93. See also Terry G. Jordan, *German Seed in Texas Soil: Immigrant Farmers in Nineteenth-Century Texas* (Austin: University of Texas Press, 1966).

24. See Reynolds R. McKay, "Texas Mexican Repatriation during the Great Depression" (Ph.D. diss., University of Oklahoma, 1982); Abraham Hoffman, *Unwanted Mexican Americans in the Great Depression: Repatriation Pressures, 1929–1939* (Tucson: University of Arizona Press, 1974); and Francisco E. Balderama and Raymond Rodríguez, *Decade of Betrayal: Mexican Repatriation in the 1930s* (Albuquerque: University of New Mexico Press, 1995).

25. Another problem with the category of "Mexican" and "Mexican American" is that, like "Anglo," it also masks the ethnic diversity of a people who have undergone centuries of *mestizaje* (race mixing) and who continue to intermarry with Irish, German, Italian, Asian Indians, Chinese, Japanese, Native Americans, African Americans, and other groups.

26. Despite these intra-ethnic differences, I nevertheless use the term "Mexicans" to denote both Mexican Americans and Mexican immigrants, primarily because Mexicans themselves often ignored the distinction and referred to one another simply as *mexicano*, sometimes using the phrases *de este lado* or *de otro lado* (from this side or from the other side of the border) when it was necessary to distinguish between the American-born and the Mexican-born. When it is important to distinguish between those born in the United States and those in Mexico, I use "Mexican Americans" and "Mexican immigrants," respectively. For a fine study of the commonalties and divisions between Mexican Americans and Mexican immigrants in the Southwest and the important ways in which these "walls and mirrors" shaped ethnic identity and identity politics, see David

G. Gutiérrez, *Walls and Mirrors: Mexican Americans, Mexican Immigrants, and the Politics of Ethnicity* (Berkeley: University of California Press, 1995).

27. Werner Sollors, ed., *Invention of Ethnicity* (New York: Oxford University Press, 1989), 228. According to the historical geographer Terry Jordan ("Ethnic Change in Texas," 400), nearly 16,000 blacks in Texas claimed Hispanic ancestry in the 1980 census.

28. For an interesting anecdote about the conflicting constructions of what constitutes racial categories of white and black, see Fields, "Ideology and Race," 146.

29. For discussions of tenancy and the notion of the agricultural ladder, see LaWanda Fenlason Cox, "Tenancy in the United States, 1865–1900: A Consideration of the Validity of the Agricultural Ladder Hypothesis," *Agricultural History* 18 (July 1944): 97–105; and Shu-Chung Lee, "The Theory of the Agricultural Ladder," *Agricultural History* 21 (January 1947): 53–61.

30. A problem in terminology inevitably arises in any discussion of tenancy in the South because of the complex and changing relationship between landlord and tenant over time and from region to region. In this study I will use the term *tenant* to encompass the many forms of tenancy (cash, share, mixed, standing) as well as sharecropping, although sharecroppers, strictly speaking, were not tenant-renters but laborers. I will use the term *sharecropper*, or *cropper*, when it is important to distinguish between this class of "tenant" and other forms of tenancy. For a discussion of the legal, social, and economic implications of these distinctions, see Harold D. Woodman, "Post–Civil War Southern Agriculture and the Law," *Agricultural History*, 53 (January 1979): 319–37; and, especially, Woodman's fine study, *New South—New Law: The Legal Foundations of Credit and Labor Relations in the Postbellum Agricultural South* (Baton Rouge: Louisiana State University Press, 1995), 67–94.

31. See, for example, Remson Crawford, "The Menace of Mexican Immigration," *Current History* 31 (February 1930): 902–7; E. E. Davis, "King Cotton Leads Mexicans into Texas," *Texas Outlook* 9 (April 1925): 1–3; and Handman, "Mexican Immigrant in Texas," 33–41.

32. "Land League," *The Rebel*, October 23, 1915, 4. David Roediger (*Towards the Abolition of Whiteness*, 152–53) shows how black timber workers in east Texas demonstrated their "white-hearted manliness" to whites when they walked off their jobs rather than "scabbing."

33. Gerda Lerner, "Reconceptualizing Differences among Women," *Journal of Women's History* 1 (Winter 1990): 110.

34. Faulkner, *Snopes*, 12.

35. See James N. Gregory, *American Exodus: The Dust Bowl Migration and Okie Culture in California* (New York: Oxford University Press, 1989).

36. See L. P. Gabbard and H. E. Rea, *Cotton Production in Texas*, Texas Agricultural Experiment Station Circular 39 (College Station: Agricultural and Mechanical College of Texas, 1926).

37. Donald W. Meinig, *Imperial Texas: An Interpretive Essay in Cultural Geography* (Austin: University of Texas Press, 1969), 116, 123. South Texas in this study refers to the transnational region south of a line drawn from Laredo to Corpus Christi, where the majority of Mexicans historically have resided in the

state. The largest region, west Texas, extends from San Antonio to El Paso and includes the Panhandle. Central Texas, the broadly defined region between east Texas and west Texas that includes the Blackland Prairie and the coastal bend area near Corpus Christi, is the site where, according to Jordan (*Texas: A Geography*, 5, 91), "a large European population of Germans, Slavs, and Scandinavians is thoroughly mixed with lower-Southern whites, Blacks, upper Southerners, and Hispanos."

38. Studies of Mexicans in Texas include Montejano, *Anglos and Mexicans in the Making of Texas*; de León, *Tejano Community*; and Mario T. García, *Desert Immigrants: The Mexicans of El Paso, 1880–1920* (New Haven, Conn.: Yale University Press, 1981). Among the histories of blacks in Texas are Alwyn Barr, *Black Texans: A History of Negroes in Texas, 1528–1971* (Austin: Jenkins, 1973); Lawrence D. Rice, *The Negro in Texas, 1874–1900* (Baton Rouge: Louisiana State University Press, 1971); James M. Smallwood, *Time of Hope, Time of Despair: Black Texans during Reconstruction* (Port Washington, N.Y.: Kennikat Press, 1981); and Ruthe Winegarten, *Black Texas Women: 150 Years of Trial and Triumph* (Austin: University of Texas Press, 1995).

Chapter 1

1. An *empresario* was a contractor who agreed to settle families of colonists in exchange for a grant of land.

2. Gabbard and Rea, *Cotton Production in Texas*, 7.

3. Ibid. See also Karl E. Ashburn, "The Development of Cotton Production in Texas" (Ph.D. diss., Duke University, 1932), 63–65.

4. In 1824 the Mexican provinces of Coahuila and Texas were united as one state. A *labor* was a Spanish land unit that measured 177 acres. Ron Tyler, ed., *The New Handbook of Texas* (Austin: Texas State Historical Association, 1996), 2: 171 and 3: 1180.

5. Reuben McKitrick, *The Public Land System of Texas, 1823–1910*, University of Wisconsin Bulletin 905 (Madison: University of Wisconsin, 1918), 31.

6. Tyler, *Handbook of Texas*, 4: 75–76 and 2: 846.

7. Barker, *Austin*, 178–230. Jordan ("Ethnic Change in Texas," 394) suggests the term *wetnecks* for white illegal aliens.

8. Austin to Wily Martin, May 30, 1833, quoted in Barker, *Austin*, 223–24. See also the discussion of Austin's wavering on the slavery issue in Campbell, *Empire*, 30. José Antonio Navarro, an elite tejano landowner and a close friend of Austin, joined Anglo Texans in opposing Mexico's antislavery laws. See Buenger, *Secession*, 90–91.

9. Quoted in Campbell, *Empire*, 46–47.

10. Ibid., 2; and Lack, *Revolutionary Experience*, 250–52.

11. Reginald Horsman, *Race and Manifest Destiny: The Origins of American Racial Anglo-Saxonism* (Cambridge, Mass.: Harvard University Press, 1981), 208–28.

12. Commissioner's Court Minutes, November 19, 1860, Refugio County, reel 1012469, 222, Local Records Division, Texas State Library, Austin. On the

disposition of public lands in Texas, see Thomas L. Miller, *The Public Lands of Texas, 1519–1970* (Norman: University of Oklahoma Press, 1972).

13. For a penetrating analysis of the historical and legal development of whiteness as property, see Harris, "Whiteness as Property," 1709–91; and George Lipsitz, "The Possessive Investment in Whiteness: Racialized Social Democracy and the 'White' Problem in American Studies," *American Quarterly* 47 (September 1995): 369–87.

14. Quoted in Horsman, *Race and Manifest Destiny*, 217.

15. Saxton, *White Republic*.

16. Quoted in Thomas R. Hietala, *Manifest Design: Anxious Aggrandizement in Late Jacksonian America* (Ithaca, N.Y.: Cornell University Press, 1985), 30.

17. On Texas annexation and the "black peril," see ibid., 10–54 (quotation on p. 48). Hietala notes that the shape of Texas, not merely its location, suggested "its potential for funneling blacks into Latin America" (p. 31, n. 43). One contemporary analyst, D. R. Hundley, wrote in 1860 that the poor whites of the South continued to move westward "in search of their New Atlantis" until the "half-civilized mongrels" of Mexico would swallow them up. "Good riddance," he concluded. Quoted in Donald W. Walden, "No Way for White People to Live: Travellers' Visions of Poor Whites in the Nineteenth Century" (M.A. thesis, University of Texas at Austin, 1992), 19–20. See also Horsman, *Race and Manifest Destiny*, 215; David M. Pletcher, *The Diplomacy of Annexation: Texas, Oregon, and the Mexican War* (Columbia: University of Missouri Press, 1973); and Frederick Merk, *Slavery and the Annexation of Texas* (New York: Knopf, 1972).

18. Quoted in Hietala, *Manifest Design*, ix. See also Frederick Merk, *Manifest Destiny and Mission in American History: A Reinterpretation* (1963; reprint, New York: Vintage Books, 1966); Albert K. Weinberg, *Manifest Destiny: A Study of Nationalist Expansion in American History* (1935; reprint, Chicago: Quadrangle Books, 1963); and Bernard DeVoto, *The Year of Decision, 1846* (Boston: Little, Brown, 1943).

19. D. W. Meinig, *The Shaping of America: A Geographical Perspective on 500 Years of History*, vol. 2, *Continental America, 1800–1867* (New Haven, Conn.: Yale University Press, 1993), 145. Works on the War with Mexico include Gene M. Brack, *Mexico Views Manifest Destiny: An Essay on the Origins of the Mexican War* (Albuquerque: University of New Mexico Press, 1975); Ramón Eduardo Ruiz, ed., *The Mexican War: Was It Manifest Destiny?* (New York: Holt, Rinehart and Winston, 1963); and, for a cultural history of the war, Robert W. Johannsen, *To the Halls of the Montezumas: The Mexican War in the American Imagination* (New York: Oxford University Press, 1985). On the history of the western boundary of Texas, see William C. Binkley, *The Expansionist Movement in Texas, 1836–1850* (Berkeley: University of California Press, 1925).

20. Quoted in Horsman, *Race and Manifest Destiny*, 235; and in Anders Stephanson, *Manifest Destiny: American Expansionism and the Empire of Right* (New York: Hill and Wang, 1995), 38. Walt Whitman, editor of *The Brooklyn Eagle*, wrote at the beginning of the war: "Let our arms now be carried with a spirit which shall teach the world that, while we are not forward for a quarrel, America knows how to crush, as well as how to expand!" (*The Brooklyn Eagle*, May 11, 1846, quoted in Archie P. McDonald, *The Mexican War: Crisis for American Democracy* [Lexington, Mass.: D. C. Heath, 1969], 47).

21. *New York Herald*, January 30, 1848, quoted in Weinberg, *Manifest Destiny*, 90; and Hietala, *Manifest Design*, 166. John O'Sullivan, author of the phrase "manifest destiny" and Jacksonian exponent of territorial expansion, wrote that America was "destined . . . to establish on earth the noblest temple ever dedicated to the worship of the Most High—the Sacred and the True" (quoted in Stephanson, *Manifest Destiny*, 40).

22. Quoted in Richard Slotkin, *The Fatal Environment: The Myth of the Frontier in the Age of Industrialization, 1800–1890* (1985; reprint, New York: HarperCollins, 1994), 230–31.

23. The literature on these racial encounters is vast and growing. On white racial ideology in the nineteenth century see, in addition to Horsman, *Race and Manifest Destiny*; Takaki, *Iron Cages*; and idem, *A Different Mirror: A History of Multicultural America* (Boston: Little, Brown, 1993). Other studies of racial conflict in the West include Tomás Almaguer, *Racial Fault Lines: The Historical Origins of White Supremacy in California* (Berkeley: University of California Press, 1994); Douglas Monroy, *Thrown among Strangers: The Making of Mexican Culture in Frontier California* (Berkeley: University of California Press, 1990); Montejano, *Anglos and Mexicans*; Ricardo Romo, *East Los Angeles: History of a Barrio* (Austin: University of Texas Press, 1983); Sucheng Chan, *This Bittersweet Soil: The Chinese in California Agriculture, 1860–1910* (Berkeley: University of California Press, 1986); Alexander Saxton, *The Indispensable Enemy: Labor and the Anti-Chinese Movement in California* (Berkeley: University of California, 1971); and Quintard Taylor, "Blacks and Asians in a White City: Japanese Americans and African Americans in Seattle, 1890–1940," *Western Historical Quarterly* 22 (November 1991): 401–30.

24. Quoted in Horsman, *Race and Manifest Destiny*, 241. See also Richard Griswold del Castillo, *The Treaty of Guadalupe Hidalgo: A Legacy of Conflict* (Norman: University of Oklahoma Press, 1990).

25. Hietala, *Manifest Design*, 162, 163.

26. Ibid., 162–66.

27. Santiago Tafolla, "Nearing the End of the Trail: The Autobiography of Rev. James Tafolla, Sr., A Texas Pioneer, 1837–1911," typescript, 11, 15–16, Santiago Tafolla Papers, Benson Latin American Collection, University of Texas at Austin.

28. Ibid., 15–16, 22, 31, 46–48.

29. From Austin and San Antonio newspaper accounts quoted in Paul D. Lack, "Slavery and Vigilantism in Austin, Texas, 1840–1860," *Southwestern Historical Quarterly* 85 (July 1981): 6, 9.

30. Letters to various Texas newspapers reproduced in a "statistical appendix" to Frederick Law Olmsted, *A Journey through Texas: Or, a Saddle Trip on the Southwestern Frontier* (1857; reprint, Austin: University of Texas Press, 1978), 503–4. On restrictions placed upon freed persons of color in antebellum Texas, see Harold Schoen, "The Free Negro in the Republic of Texas," *Southwestern Historical Quarterly* 41 (January-April 1937): 83–108. See also William W. White, "The Texas Slave Insurrection of 1860," *Southwestern Historical Quarterly* 52 (January 1949): 259–85.

31. Olmsted, *Journey through Texas*, 503–4.

32. Ibid., 456.

33. Ibid.

34. Ibid., 456, 502.

35. Ibid., 456.

36. Texas slaves themselves were aware of the relatively short distance that lay between them and freedom in Mexico. Tom and Esau, for example, the personal servants of Sam Houston, president of the Texas Republic, escaped across the Rio Grande to Matamoros and freedom. Houston's reaction reveals as much about his attitude toward Mexicans as about his regard for Tom and Esau, who, he wrote, "were smart and intelligent fellows . . . [and] would help to civilize and refine Mexico" (quoted in Rosalie Schwartz, *Across the Rio to Freedom: U.S. Negroes in Mexico* [El Paso: Texas Western Press, University of Texas at El Paso, 1975], 26, 28). Other reports of runaway slaves in Texas can be found in "Runaway Negroes," typescript, 13, folder "Southern Texas, General History," Z–R4, Paul S. Taylor Collection, Bancroft Library, Berkeley, California (hereafter cited as Taylor Papers, immediately preceded by a reference to the appropriate subcollection of the Paul S. Taylor Papers). For a discussion of fugitive slaves in Mexico and planter efforts to retrieve them, see Ronnie C. Tyler, "The Callahan Expedition of 1855: Indians or Negroes?" *Southwestern Historical Quarterly* 70 (April 1967): 574–85; and idem, "Fugitive Slaves in Mexico," *Journal of Negro History* 57 (January 1972): 1–12.

37. Maurine M. O'Banion, "The History of Caldwell County" (M.A. thesis, University of Texas, 1931), 171; Byron Porter to Lt. J. L. Kirkman, AAA General, August 19, 1867, vol. 60, Letters Sent, series 3659, Bastrop, Texas Subassistant Commissioner, Bureau of Refugees, Freedmen, and Abandoned Land (BRFAL), Record Group 105, National Archives, Washington, D.C.; and *Statesman*, January 24, 1874, quoted in Rice, *Negro in Texas*, 161.

38. Elmer Harrison Johnson, *The Basis of the Commercial and Industrial Development of Texas*, University of Texas Bulletin 3309 (Austin: University of Texas, 1933), 16.

39. Edward Everett Dale, *The Range Cattle Industry: Ranching on the Great Plains from 1865 to 1925* (1930; reprint, Norman: University of Oklahoma, 1960), 3–5.

40. Joseph Nimmo Jr., *Report in Regard to the Range and Cattle Business of the United States* (1885; reprint, New York: Arno Press, 1972), 24, 31–37. See also Ray Allen Billington and Martin Ridge, *Westward Expansion: A History of the American Frontier*, 5th ed. (New York: Macmillan, 1982), 611–28. Classical economic studies of the range-cattle industry are Ernest S. Osgood, *The Day of the Cattlemen* (Minneapolis: University of Minnesota Press, 1929); and Louis Pelzer, *The Cattlemen's Frontier* (Glendale, Calif.: Arthur H. Clark, 1936). For a discussion of the origins of the Anglo and Hispanic cattle and farming frontiers in central and south Texas, see Montejano, *Anglos and Mexicans*, 13–99; Meinig, *Imperial Texas*, 66–69; and Terry G. Jordan, *Trails to Texas: Southern Roots of Western Cattle Ranching* (Lincoln: University of Nebraska Press, 1981), 125–57.

41. The captain may have also been incensed that wire fences reduced the number of wage hands or cowboys required to care for the herds. For most large, fenced ranches in the 1880s, only one man per 800 or 1,000 head of cattle was required, whereas in former times on the open range three men would have been needed. James W. Freeman, ed., *Prose and Poetry of the Live Stock Industry of the United States* (Kansas City, Mo.: National Live Stock Historical Association,

1905), 685–86 (quotation); R. D. Holt, "The Introduction of Barbed Wire into Texas and the Fence Cutting War," *West Texas Historical Year Book* 6 (June 1930): 65–79; and Wayne Gard, "The Fence Cutters," *Southwestern Historical Quarterly* 51 (July 1947): 1–15. For a brief discussion of the role of barbed wire in transforming the range to ranches and farms, see James Cox, *Historical and Biographical Record of the Cattle Industry and the Cattlemen of Texas and Adjacent Territory* (1895; reprint, New York: Antiquarianism Press, 1959); and Henry D. McCallum and Frances T. McCallum, *The Wire That Fenced the West* (Norman: University of Oklahoma Press, 1965).

42. In 1870, for example, the eastern counties showed a gain of 140,000 head of cattle; between 1870 and 1900 the number of cattle in twenty key western counties rose from 154,433 to 906,424, and cattle in eight Panhandle counties increased from none to 256,673. See John S. Spratt, *The Road to Spindletop: Economic Change in Texas, 1875–1901* (Dallas: Southern Methodist University Press, 1955), 87–88; Johnson, *Commercial and Industrial Development of Texas*, 87; Freeman, *Live Stock Industry*, 538, 741–42; and Nimmo, *Range and Cattle Business*, 60–66, 164–65.

43. William Bennett Bizzell, *Rural Texas* (New York: Macmillan, 1924), 169–79, 233–34; and Spratt, *Road to Spindletop*, 25–26, 29–30, 32–33. See also Charles S. Potts, *Railroad Transportation in Texas*, University of Texas Bulletin 119 (Austin: University of Texas, 1909); and S. G. Reed, *A History of the Texas Railroads and of Transportation Conditions under Spain and Mexico and the Republic and the State* (Houston: St. Clair, 1941), 127–87.

44. U.S. Bureau of the Census, *Report on Cotton Production in the United States; Also Embracing Agricultural and Physico-Geographical Descriptions of the Several Cotton States and of California*, part 1, *Mississippi Valley and Southwestern States*, Vol. 5, *Cotton Production of the State of Texas* (Washington, D.C.: Government Printing Office, 1884), 707 (hereafter cited as *Report on Cotton Production*). The U.S. census of agriculture for 1890 supports the prediction. See cotton-production figures for various west Texas counties in the Panhandle in U.S. Census Office, *Report on the Statistics of Agriculture in the United States at the Eleventh Census: 1890*, vol. 5 (Washington, D.C.: Government Printing Office, 1895), 396–97.

45. During the 1880s, for example, railroads linked the fruit orchards of southern California with the markets of the Midwest and the East, until citrus fruits and later cotton displaced "King Wheat" (Cletus E. Daniel, *Bitter Harvest: A History of California Farmworkers, 1870–1941* [Ithaca, N.Y.: Cornell University Press, 1981], 34).

46. Don H. Biggers, *From Cattle Range to Cotton Patch* (Abilene, Tex.: Abilene Printing, circa 1908), 85. Micropublished in *Western Americana: Frontier History of the Trans-Mississippi West, 1550–1900* (New Haven, Conn.: Research Publications, Inc., 1975), microfilm 512, reel 54.

47. Meinig, *Imperial Texas*, 55.

48. An 1880 U.S. census report on cotton production in Texas noted that the composition of the labor force in the Blackland Prairie or the Black Waxy region of central Texas was predominantly white, except in McLennan, Fannin, Collin, Falls, Rockwall, Dallas, Travis, Williamson, and Caldwell Counties, "where the proportion of whites and negroes is about equal." After 1880, however, whites began to outnumber blacks in each of those counties. The report also noted that

Mexican laborers were found in Bexar (San Antonio) and Caldwell Counties. See *Report on Cotton Production*, 819.

49. On the growth of the population in central Texas, see Mattie Bell, "The Growth and Distribution of the Texas Population" (Ph.D. diss., Baylor University, 1955), 134; *Report on Cotton Production*, 772; U.S. Census Bureau, *A Compendium of the Eleventh Census, 1890: Population* (Washington, D.C.: Government Printing Office, 1892), 508; U.S. Bureau of the Census, *Twelfth Census of the United States, 1900: Population*, part 2 (Washington, D.C.: Government Printing Office, 1901), 557. See also Victor S. Clark, "Mexican Labor in the United States," *Bulletin of the Bureau of Labor*, no. 78 (September 1908), 519. County lines do not neatly follow geographical regions, so any partition of Texas into discrete regions by counties is somewhat arbitrary. I used the regional divisions in Bell, "Texas Population," to which I also turned for population data based on aggregate regional figures (p. 72).

50. Scholars have shown that the census figures underestimated the number of people of Mexican descent in the United States before 1900 by as much as 300 to 400 percent. The census included U.S.-born of Mexican descent in the category of "white" until 1930, when a separate classification for "Mexican" was created. The total number of Mexican-descent people was therefore much greater than that given by the census. See Arnoldo de León and Kenneth L. Stewart, *Tejanos and the Numbers Game: A Socio-Historical Interpretation from the Federal Censuses, 1850–1900* (Albuquerque: University of New Mexico Press, 1989); Arthur F. Corwin, "Early Mexican Labor Migration: A Frontier Sketch, 1848–1900," in *Immigrants—and Immigrants: Perspectives on Mexican Labor Migration to the United States*, ed. Arthur F. Corwin (Westport, Conn.: Greenwood Press, 1978), 34–35; and Oscar J. Martínez, "On the Size of the Chicano Population: New Estimates, 1850–1890," *Aztlán* 6 (Spring 1975): 43–67.

51. Cited in de León, *Tejano Community*, 65. Mexican labor may have been used by black tenant farmers in Wharton County, where African Americans constituted 80.7 percent of the population in 1890 (U.S. Bureau of the Census, *Compendium of the Eleventh Census, 1890: Population*, 511).

52. Paul S. Taylor, *An American-Mexican Frontier: Nueces County, Texas* (1934; reprint, New York: Russell and Russell, 1971), 102.

53. *Beeville Bee*, August 17, 1894; and de León, *Tejano Community*, 65. In Gonzales County, for example, the landlords Stewart and Fisher refused in 1911 to rent to the Anglo tenant Jack Robinson "because Mexicans were more profitable" (*The Rebel*, September 9, 1911, quoted in Charles W. Holman, "Preliminary Report on the Land Question," reel 13, I48–A2–H [p. 125], no. 52, unpublished reports of the Division of Research and Investigation, U.S. Commission on Industrial Relations, State Historical Society of Wisconsin [hereafter cited as "Land Question" (draft)]). On the economic reasons for the migration of Mexicans to Texas, see Elliott Gordon Young, "Twilight on the Texas-Mexico Border: Catarino Garza and Identity at the Cross-Roads, 1880–1915" (Ph.D. diss., University of Texas at Austin, 1997), 278–353.

54. Davis, "King Cotton," 1–3. On Mexicans who became landowners in central Texas after 1920, see author interview with Andrés and Sabina Palomo Acosta, March 16, 1993, McGregor, Texas. The superintendent of schools for Lockhart, in Caldwell County, reported that there were about twelve Mexican

landowners in the county but that most of the county's Mexicans were croppers on large farms (interview with Caldwell County superintendent of schools, n.d., folder "South Central Texas," no. 196–367, 74–187c, Taylor Papers; and interview with Felix Enriquez, n.d., folder "Nueces County," no. 105–695, 74–187c, Taylor Papers).

55. *Final Report and Testimony* 10: 9203; *The Rebel*, October 10, 1914; and Lewis H. Haney, ed., *Studies in the Industrial Resources of Texas*, University of Texas Bulletin 3 (Austin: University of Texas, 1915), 47–48. Dallas and Harris Counties, where the cities of Dallas and Houston are located, gained 21,765 blacks between 1900 and 1910 (Bell, "Texas Population," 120).

56. For a study of region as community in northern New Mexico and southern Colorado, see Sarah Deutsch, *No Separate Refuge: Culture, Class, and Gender on an Anglo-Hispanic Frontier in the American Southwest, 1880–1940* (New York: Oxford University Press, 1987), esp. 9–12.

57. William Owens, *This Stubborn Soil: A Frontier Boyhood* (New York: Charles Scribner's Sons, 1966), 40. See also Mary Rebecca Sharpless, "Fertile Ground, Narrow Choices: Women on Cotton Farms of the Texas Blackland Prairie, 1900–1940" (Ph.D. diss., Emory University, 1993), 9.

58. U.S. Bureau of the Census, *Eighth Census of the United States, 1860: Agriculture* (Washington, D.C.: Government Printing Office, 1864), 216–17; idem, *Ninth Census of the United States, 1870: Agriculture* (Washington, D.C.: Government Printing Office, 1872), 3: 363; idem, *Tenth Census of the United States, 1880: Agriculture* (Washington, D.C.: Government Printing Office, 1883), 3: 133–36; idem, *Eleventh Census of the United States, 1890: Agriculture* (Washington, D.C.: Government Printing Office, 1895), 5: 229–31; and idem, *Twelfth Census of the United States, 1900: Agriculture*, part 2, *Crops and Irrigation* (Washington, D.C.: Government Printing Office, 1902), 5: 298–301.

59. Frank Putnam, "Texas in Transition," *Collier's*, January 22, 1910, 15; and William C. Pool, *A Historical Atlas of Texas* (Austin: Encino Press, 1975), 6–10.

60. Paul S. Taylor, "Mechanization in Agriculture and Its Effect on Farm Labor," typescript, n.d., box 6, C–B 893, Taylor Papers. A comparison of the cost of producing cotton in western Texas and the Piedmont of the Atlantic coastal states indicated that western Texas cotton was produced at one-third the cost per acre as was Piedmont cotton and that it required one-third of the man-hours per acre that were needed for Piedmont cotton. The report concluded that "the lower cost of production of cotton in the Western area will ultimately tend to wipe out the costly growing of cotton in the southeastern area." On the westward movement of cotton production between 1850 and 1900, see Gabbard and Rea, *Cotton Production in Texas*, 8–13; and Johnson, *Commercial and Industrial Development of Texas*, 65. A congressman from Alabama testified in 1928 that bollweevil infestation and the migration of blacks to the cities from 1919 to 1922 had transformed much of Alabama's cotton "black belt" to "hay lands" for livestock (statement of Hon. Miles C. Allgood, U.S. Congress, House Committee on Immigration and Naturalization, *Immigration from Countries of the Western Hemisphere*, 70th Cong., 1st sess., 1928, 742). On the role of irrigation in the development of the Panhandle, see Billy R. Brunson, *The Texas Land and Development Company: A Panhandle Promotion, 1912–1956* (Austin: University of Texas Press, 1970), 15–16, 61–62, 78–80.

61. Quoted in Charles W. Holman, "Landlord and Tenant: White Tenants versus Black Tenants," *Farm and Ranch*, November 4, 1911, 8.

62. *Final Report and Testimony* 9: 8954. See also *Report on Cotton Production*, 819. On the increase of white tenants in central Texas, see Neil Foley, "The New South in the Southwest: Anglos, Blacks, and Mexicans in Central Texas, 1880–1930" (Ph.D. diss., University of Michigan, 1990), 48–62; and Division of Public Welfare, Department of Extension, *Studies in Farm Tenancy in Texas*, with chapters by E. V. White and William F. Leonard, University of Texas Bulletin 21 (Austin: University of Texas, 1915), 16–18, 22–26, 103.

63. Clark, "Mexican Labor," 485; and Texas Applied Economics Club, *Survey of Southern Travis County*, 131. It is important to remember that although owners spoke of obtaining higher rents from Mexicans, these Mexican sharecroppers, like all sharecroppers, did not actually rent the land but raised cotton on it, for which they were paid at the end of the harvest, as wages, the proceeds from one-half of the cotton grown. Thus the statement that a Mexican sharecropper paid "higher rent" is equivalent to stating that the owner paid "lower wages." See also Ruth Allen, *The Labor of Women in the Production of Cotton*, University of Texas Bulletin 3134 (Austin: University of Texas, 1931), 13, 113.

64. T. J. Cauley, "Agricultural Land Tenure in Texas," *Southwestern Political and Social Science Quarterly* 11 (September 1930), 140; and Division of Public Welfare, *Farm Tenancy in Texas*, 27–30. On the growing reliance of farm operators, owners as well as tenants, on hired Mexican labor, see, for example, Texas Applied Economics Club, *Southern Travis County*, 130–32. On the presence of Mexican sharecroppers in Travis County, see Texas Applied Economics Club, *Southern Travis County*, 72–73; and in one area of Caldwell County between 1880 and 1910, where Mexican sharecroppers displaced Anglo and black tenants, see Robert H. Montgomery, "Keglar Hill," *Survey*, May 1, 1931, 171, 193–95.

65. Author interview with Andrés and Sabina Palomo Acosta.

66. U.S. Congress, House Committee on Immigration and Naturalization, *Temporary Admission of Illiterate Mexican Laborers*, 66th Cong., 2d sess., 1920, 19 (hereafter cited as *Temporary Admission*); and idem, *Seasonal Agricultural Laborers from Mexico*, 69th Cong., 1st sess., 1926, 213 (hereafter cited as *Seasonal Agricultural Laborers*).

67. Davis, *White Scourge*, 174. Davis used his research on illiteracy, tenancy, and other rural problems to produce this novel on poor white cotton farmers in Texas and on the menace of Mexican immigration into Texas.

68. Interview with Mr. Flynn, no. 184–773, folder "Nueces County," 74–187c, Taylor Papers; interview with W. C. Hatter, no. 156–745, Taylor Papers; Taylor, *American-Mexican Frontier*, 131–32; and Davis, "King Cotton," 1.

69. *Beeville Bee*, August 17, 1894, 7, cited in Arnoldo de León, *They Called Them Greasers: Anglo Attitudes toward Mexicans in Texas, 1821–1900* (Austin: University of Texas Press, 1983), 95.

70. *San Antonio Express*, December 28, 1897, 1, and April 28, 1898, 5, cited in de León, *Greasers*, 102.

71. James R. Green, *Grass-Roots Socialism: Radical Movements in the Southwest, 1895–1943* (Baton Rouge: Louisiana State University Press 1978), 111.

72. U.S. Congress, Senate, *Report of the Committee on Agriculture and Forestry on the Condition of Cotton Growers* . . . , 53d Cong., 3d sess., 1895, S. Rept. 986, 362; Walton Peteet, *Farming Credit in Texas*, Texas Agricultural Experiment Station, Extension Service Bulletin B–34 (College Station: Agricultural and Mechanical College of Texas, 1917), 54–55; and Charles W. Holman, "Preliminary Report on the Land Question in the United States," unpublished records of the U.S. Commission on Industrial Relations, Records of the Division of Research and Investigation, Department of Labor, reel 9, 28, 65–66, Record Group 174, National Archives and Records Administration, Washington, D.C. (hereafter cited as "Land Question" [final version]).

73. Division of Public Welfare, *Farm Tenancy in Texas*, 120; and Holman, "Land Question" [final version], 28, 65–66.

Chapter 2

1. Clark, "Mexican Labor," 485.

2. J. C. Brodie to John C. Box, March 4, 1928, Weeks Papers. For reference to the "second color menace" in the chapter subtitle, see President, Immigration Study Commission, to John C. Box, June 9, 1927, box 2, folder 6, LULAC Collection.

3. The debate can be traced through the numerous congressional hearings by the Immigration and Naturalization Committee during the 1920s. See, for example, U.S. Congress, House Committee on Immigration and Naturalization, *Immigration from Countries of the Western Hemisphere*, 70th Cong., 2d sess., 1930; idem, *Immigration from Countries of the Western Hemisphere*, 1928; idem, *Immigration from Mexico*, 71st Cong., 2d sess., 1930; idem, *Naturalization*, 71st Cong., 2d sess., 1930; idem, *Restriction of Immigration*, 68th Cong., 1st sess., 1924, Serial 1–A; *Seasonal Agricultural Laborers*, 1926; *Temporary Admission*; and idem, *Western Hemisphere Immigration*, 71st Cong., 2d sess., 1930. For a scholarly treatment and analysis of the immigration debate, see Mark Reisler, *By the Sweat of Their Brow: Mexican Immigrant Labor in the United States, 1900–1940* (Westport, Conn.: Greenwood Press, 1976).

4. Stoddard, *Rising Tide of Color*, v; President, Immigration Study Commission, to John C. Box, June 9, 1927, box 2, folder 6, LULAC Collection.

5. For a study of agricultural wages in Mexico around the turn of the century, see Walter E. Weyl, "Labor Conditions in Mexico," *Bulletin of the Department of Labor*, no. 38 (January 1902): 35–41. See also Paul S. Taylor, "Migratory Labor," typescript, n.d., box 3, 84/38c, Taylor Papers.

6. *Temporary Admission*; and idem, *Agricultural Laborers from Mexico*, 214, 337, 339, 341.

7. See interview with John Wuenche, no. 59–649, folder "Nueces County," 74–187c, Taylor Papers; interview with teacher at Mexican school, Luling, Texas, n.d., no. 199–370, folder "South Central Texas," 74–187c, Taylor Papers; and Davis, "King Cotton," 2. On disfranchisement and segregation in the Jim Crow South, see Woodward, *Jim Crow*; idem, *Origins of the New South*, 321–95; J. Morgan Kousser, *The Shaping of Southern Politics: Suffrage Restriction and the Establishment of the One-Party South, 1880–1910* (New Haven, Conn.: Yale University

Press, 1974); and LaWanda Cox, "From Emancipation to Segregation: National Policy and Southern Blacks," in *Interpreting Southern History: Historiographical Essays in Honor of Sanford W. Higginbotham*, ed. John B. Boles and Evelyn Thomas Nolen (Baton Rouge: Louisiana University Press, 1987), 199–253. On Jim Crow segregation in Texas, see Montejano, *Anglos and Mexicans*, esp. 220–54.

8. On eugenic notions of racial hygiene, see Thurman B. Rice, *Racial Hygiene: A Practical Discussion of Eugenics and Race Culture* (New York: Macmillan, 1929).

9. Interview with Mr. Flynn, no. 184–773, folder "Nueces County," 74–187c, Taylor Papers.

10. Davis, "King Cotton," 2.

11. Interview with Albert Gregg, San Antonio, Texas, n.d., no. 177–348, folder "South Central Texas," 74–187c, Taylor Papers.

12. Since making the distinction between white Mexicans and Indian or "Negro Mexicans" was almost always a function of skin color, in some Mexican families in Texas one child might be considered "white" while her dark-skinned brother or sister was not (interview with Miss Annie C. Watson, International Institute, San Antonio, Texas, n.d., no. 174–345, folder "South Central Texas," 74–187c, Taylor Papers). For an excellent discussion of hygiene as a metaphor for distinguishing between white and nonwhite Mexicans, see Montejano, *Anglos and Mexicans*, 225–34.

13. Interview with A. H. Dervinney, no. 65–655, folder "Nueces County," 74–187c, Taylor Papers.

14. On the difficulty of accurately estimating the Mexican population in the United States and the problem of undercounting by the census, see de León and Stewart, *Tejanos and the Numbers Game*; Corwin, "Early Mexican Labor Migration," 34–35; Martínez, "Chicano Population," 43–67; Davis, "King Cotton," 1–3; Clark, "Mexican Labor," 519; and Jordan, "Ethnic Change in Texas," 394. From an extant 1887 state census Jordan calculated that the Mexican population was actually around 83,000, or 4 percent of the population (Terry G. Jordan, "The 1887 Census of Texas' Hispanic Population," *Aztlán* 12 [Autumn 1981]: 271–78).

15. Texas had 68 percent in 1900, 56 percent in 1910, 52 percent in 1920, and 41 percent in 1930 (U.S. Bureau of the Census, *Sixteenth Census of the United States, 1940: Population* [Washington, D.C.: Government Printing Office, 1943], 2: 43, 781). See also Vernon Monroe McCombs, *From over the Border: A Study of the Mexicans in the United States* (1925; reprint, San Francisco: R & E Research Associates, 1970), 25–29.

16. Davis, "King Cotton," 1; Allen, *Labor of Women*, 236; Clark, "Mexican Labor," 475; and Max Sylvius Handman, "San Antonio: The Old Capital City of Mexican Life and Influence," *Survey*, May 1, 1931, 163–66.

17. Carrizo Springs *Javelin*, September 2, 1911, cited in Taylor, *American-Mexican Frontier*, 102. The *Javelin* article, Taylor notes, was apparently quoted from a San Antonio newspaper, so the city through which the migrants passed was San Antonio and not Carrizo Springs.

18. Paul S. Taylor, *Mexican Labor in the United States: Dimmit County, Winter Garden District of South Texas*, University of California Publications in Eco-

nomics, vol. 6, no. 5 (Berkeley: University of California Press, 1930), 358; García, *Desert Immigrants*, 37; and Clark, "Mexican Labor," 521. In many ways the primary force behind the northward expansion of Mexicans was not unlike that behind westward expansion—the family. See Elliott West, *Growing Up with the Country: Childhood on the Far Western Frontier* (Albuquerque: University of New Mexico Press, 1989); and Kathleen Neils Conzen, "A Saga of Families," in *The Oxford History of the American West*, ed. Clyde A. Milner II, Carol A. O'Connor, and Martha A. Sandweiss (New York: Oxford University Press, 1994), 315-57.

19. Clark, "Mexican Labor," 521.

20. In a study of women in the production of cotton in central Texas, Ruth Allen found that the proportion of unmarried Mexican women farmers—owners, tenants, laborers—(32 percent) was higher than that of either unmarried Anglo (21.1 percent) or African American (30 percent) farmers. See Allen, *Labor of Women*, 242; Texas Bureau of Labor Statistics, *Sixth Biennial Report, 1919–1920*, 18, 30; and Ruth A. Allen, "Mexican Peon Women in Texas," *Sociology and Social Research* 16 (November-December 1931): 131.

21. Quoted in the *Topeka Daily State Journal*, August 14, 1913, in file 52546/31–H, Subject Correspondence, U.S. Immigration and Naturalization Service, Record Group 85, National Archives, Washington, D.C. (hereafter cited as INS RG 85). On Mexicans employed by Texas railroads, see Samuel Bryan, "Mexican Immigrants in the United States," *Survey*, September 7, 1912, 727–28; Arthur F. Corwin and Lawrence A. Cardoso, "Vamos al Norte: Causes of Mass Mexican Migration to the United States," in *Immigrants—and Immigrants: Perspectives on Mexican Labor Migration to the United States*, ed. Arthur F. Corwin (Westport, Conn.: Greenwood Press, 1978), 49–50; García, *Desert Immigrants*, 14–16, 37–38; and statement of Charles McKemy, Commissioner of Labor of the state of Texas, House Committee on Immigration and Naturalization, *Immigration from Countries of the Western Hemisphere*, 1928, 733.

22. See Roediger, *Wages of Whiteness*, esp. 133–36; and Ignatiev, *How the Irish Became White*. On the Irish and Chinese in California, see Saxton, *Indispensable Enemy*. On whiteness, see Roediger, *Wages of Whiteness*; idem, *Towards the Abolition of Whiteness*, esp. 127–80; Saxton, *Rise and Fall of the White Republic*; Allen, *Racial Oppression and Social Control*; López, *White by Law*; and Harris, "Whiteness as Property," 1709–92.

23. O'Banion, "Caldwell County," 171; and Clark, "Mexican Labor," 470, 472, 476.

24. The Mexican newspaper *El Sol* referred to *coyotes* in 1924 as "Traficantes de Carne Humana" (traffickers in human flesh), quoted in García, *Desert Immigrants*, 249. See also Reisler, *By the Sweat of Their Brow*, 12, 24–25 (quotation); and Carey McWilliams, *North from Mexico: The Spanish-Speaking People of the United States* (1949; reprint, New York: Greenwood Press, 1968), 178–79.

25. Texas Bureau of Labor Statistics, *Sixth Biennial Report*, 19.

26. On the temporary admissions of Mexicans during World War I, see Reisler, *By the Sweat of Their Brow*, 24–42.

27. Labor Committee of Council of Defense, Victoria County, to Hon. W. B. Wilson, July 25, 1918, file 54261/202–C, INS RG 85; Roy Miller to J. F. Carl, September 6, 1918, telegram, box 2J370, folder "Nueces County Defense

Council," Texas War Records Collection, Center for American History, University of Texas at Austin (hereafter cited as Texas War Records, CAH); and Reisler, *By the Sweat of Their Brow*, 27–30.

28. Texas Bureau of Labor Statistics, *Ninth Biennial Report, 1925–1926*, 11; and Reisler, *By the Sweat of Their Brow*, 32–36.

29. *Final Report and Testimony* 10: 9201. On the ways in which labor contractors exploited the legal and economic spaces created by the contract labor law, see Gunther Peck, "Reinventing Free Labor: Immigrant Padrone and Contract Laborers in North America, 1880–1920" (Ph.D. diss., Yale University, 1994), 213–81.

30. J. W. Berkshire to Commissioner-General, January 30, 1913, file 52546/31–F, INS RG 85.

31. *Cleveland Press*, November 17, 1911, clipping in file 52456/31–D, INS RG 85.

32. In INS RG 85, Samuel Gompers to Charles Nagel, Secretary of Commerce and Labor, January 17, 1913, file 52546/31–F; Daniel J. Keefe to Samuel Gompers, January 16, 1912, file 52546/31–C; Wesley O. Staver to Supervisory Inspector, November 16, 1911; and Jonathan T. Parker to Secretary of Commerce and Labor, February 9, 1912, file 52546/31–E. Also interview with Consul Y. M. Vásquez, no. 7–12, folder "Mexican Officials," 74–187c, Taylor Papers.

33. McWilliams, *North from Mexico*, 178; and idem, *Ill Fares the Land: Migrants and Migratory Labor in the United States* (1942; reprint, New York: Arno Press, 1976), 250–51.

34. In INS RG 85, "Seraphic Report re Conditions on Mexican Border, 1906–1907," file 51423/1–A; "Report of Conditions Existing in Europe and Mexico Affecting Emigration and Immigration," n.d., file 51411/1; and Marcus Brown to Frank P. Sargent, Commissioner General of Immigration, February 12, 1907, file 52320/1. Texas laws regulating employment agencies were also ignored with impunity. See Texas Bureau of Labor Statistics, *Fifth Biennial Report, 1917–1918*, 13; and idem, *Sixth Biennial Report*, 11.

35. Virgil N. Lott to John C. Box, September 12, 1926, Weeks Papers.

36. M. F. Taryeye, Valley Fruit Growers Association, to Secretary of Labor, July 24, 1917, file 54261/202A, INS RG 85.

37. Texas Bureau of Labor Statistics, *Fourth Biennial Report, 1915–1916*, 12, 18; Daniel J. Keefe to Samuel Gompers, January 16, 1912, file 52546/31–C, INS RG 85; Wesley O. Staver to Supervisory Inspector, November 16, 1911, INS RG 85; and interview with Consul Y. M. Vásquez, no. 7–12, folder "Mexican Officials," 74–187c, Taylor Papers.

38. *Final Report and Testimony* 10: 9201–2. For other examples of abuses committed against Mexican laborers, see Texas Bureau of Labor Statistics, *First Biennial Report, 1909–1910*, 5; idem, *Third Biennial Report, 1913–1914*, 11; idem, *Sixth Biennial Report*, 16; idem, *Eleventh Biennial Report, 1929–1930*, 44–45; Handman, "Coming of the Mexican Immigrant," 608; and McWilliams, *North from Mexico*, 179. For other examples of violence against Mexicans in Texas, see Reisler, *By the Sweat of Their Brow*, 51–53.

39. Department of Labor, U.S. Employment Service, Bulletin 22, "Importation of Mexican Labor," May 25, 1918, memorandum, box 2J366, folder "Bell Co.," Texas War Records, CAH; and *Temporary Admission*, 302.

40. House Committee on Immigration and Naturalization, *Immigration*

from Countries of the Western Hemisphere, 1930, 625; and Crawford, "Menace of Mexican Immigration," 906.

41. Interview with Federal Farm Loan representative, no. 131–302, folder "Dimmit County," 74–187c, Taylor Papers. On "low-profile" forms of resistance among subordinate groups, see James C. Scott, *Domination and the Arts of Resistance: Hidden Transcripts* (New Haven, Conn.: Yale University Press, 1990). On the distinction between resistance and "oppositionality," see Ross Chambers, *Room for Maneuver: Reading (the) Oppositional (in) Narrative* (Chicago: University of Chicago Press, 1991), xi–xx.

42. T. C. Richardson, "The Little Brown Man in Gringo Land," *Farm and Ranch*, October 31, 1925, 2.

43. Texas Bureau of Labor Statistics, *Sixth Biennial Report*, 16; Taylor, "Migratory Labor," p. 9, box 3, 84/38c, Taylor Papers; and U.S. Congress, *Hearings before the Select Committee to Investigate the Interstate Migration of Destitute Citizens*, Pursuant to H. Res. 63 and H. Res. 491, 76th Cong., 3d sess., 1941, part 5, Oklahoma City Hearings, 1805–7 (hereafter cited as *Interstate Migration of Destitute Citizens*).

44. Texas Bureau of Labor Statistics, *Eighth Biennial Report, 1923–1924*, 10–11; and idem, *Ninth Biennial Report*, 16.

45. Works on the Bracero Program include Ernesto Galarza, *Merchants of Labor: The Mexican Bracero Story* (Charlotte, N.C.: McNally & Loftin, 1964); Richard B. Craig, *The Bracero Program: Interest Groups and Foreign Policy* (Austin: University of Texas Press, 1971); George O. Coalson, *The Development of the Migratory Farm Labor System in Texas, 1900–1954* (1955; reprint, San Francisco: R & E Research Associates, 1977); and Kitty Calavita, *Inside the State: The Bracero Program, Immigration, and the I.N.S.* (New York: Routledge, 1992). On the role of the federal government in displacing labor contractors elsewhere in the West, see Peck, "Reinventing Free Labor."

46. Handman, "Coming of the Mexican Immigrant," 606.

47. *Seasonal Agricultural Laborers*, 111. See also the letter of H. P. Davis of Canton, Texas, to John C. Box, 1921, 337. A journalist wrote in 1925 that scarcely twenty years earlier few Mexicans could be found residing north of San Antonio. "Now the Mexican farm tenant is common in counties where he was then unknown. Cotton pickers going to distant fields are finding opportunity for year-round work, and are settling in increasing numbers" (Richardson, "Little Brown Man," 3).

48. Caldwell County (Lockhart) Census Data Base. I am grateful to Myron Gutmann for providing me with the Lockhart data bases.

49. Montgomery, "Keglar Hill," 171, 193–95. Alabama Congressman Miles C. Allgood made the distinction between white people raising cotton in the "white belt" of the hilly area of the state and blacks on large plantations in the "black belt" of Alabama's cotton region. See statement of Hon. Miles C. Allgood, House Committee on Immigration and Naturalization, *Immigration from Countries of the Western Hemisphere*, 1928, 742–43.

50. From the field notes in Taylor, *American-Mexican Frontier*, 314.

51. Davis, *Illiteracy in Texas*, 10; and idem, *White Scourge*, 174.

52. Charles McKemy to John C. Box, February 6, 1928, box 2, folder 13, Weeks Papers.

53. The corn-and-pork diet of poor white and black cotton farmers, some-times called "hog and hominy," consisted of the "three M's": salt meat, meal, and molasses. See George B. Tindall, *The Emergence of the New South, 1913–1945* (Baton Rouge: Louisiana State University Press, 1967), 411; and Jack Temple Kirby, *Rural Worlds Lost: The American South, 1920–1960* (Baton Rouge: Louisiana State University Press, 1987), 188–90.

54. Ernest Galarza, "Without Benefit of Lobby," *Survey*, May 1, 1931, 181.

55. P. C. Gibson to Hon. Morris Sheppard, November 17, 1917, file 54261/202–A, INS RG 85; T. M. Campbell, "Report of Investigation on Negro Migration," General Correspondence, box 1, folder "Negroes, 1923," U.S. De-partment of Agriculture, Record Group 16, National Archives, Washington, D.C. (hereafter cited as USDA RG 16); García, *Desert Immigrants*, 47; and Coal-son, *Migratory Farm Labor System*, 27. An Austin journalist wrote that the "Negro as a class is migrating to the towns and cities, and those that remain in the country are, most of them, wage laborers, while there are few owners of land among them" ("Landlord and Tenant," *The Rebel*, October 28, 1911, 2).

56. H. W. Lewis to J. F. Carl, September 29, 1917, and December 24, 1917, Texas State Council of Defense, box 2J362, folder "Organization of Negroes," Texas War Records, CAH; and memorandum to the "Southern State Councils of Defense," February 23, 1918, Texas War Records, CAH. On the exodus of African Americans from rural areas of Texas from 1890 to 1910, see Haney, "In-dustrial Resources of Texas," 47–48.

57. *Temporary Admission*, 247.

58. Winegarten, *Black Texas Women*, 156; and House Committee on Immi-gration and Naturalization, *Immigration from Countries of the Western Hemi-sphere*, 1928, 21.

59. Nineteen men and eleven women served as extension agents for Texas's black farmers (T. M. Campbell to Dr. C. W. Warburton, June 21, 1924, General Correspondence, Negroes, box 2, USDA RG 16).

60. The standard study of nativism during the period in which Mexican im-migration was being debated is John Higham, *Strangers in the Land: Patterns of American Nativism, 1860–1925* (New Brunswick, N.J.: Rutgers University Press, 1955).

61. Quoted in ibid., 273. See also Gossett, *Race*, 402.

62. Charles Benedict Davenport, "The Effects of Race Intermingling," *Pro-ceedings of the American Philosophical Society* 56 (April 13, 1917), 367.

63. Chester H. Rowell, "Why Make Mexico an Exception?" *Survey*, May 1, 1931; and idem, "Chinese and Japanese Immigrants," *Annals of the American Academy* 34 (September 1909): 4.

64. According to one estimate, the Texas Chamber of Commerce had a membership of 10,000 during the 1920s in 355 affiliated towns and cities, 90 per-cent of which were opposed to immigration restriction. See, for example, in the Weeks Papers: H. D. Wade to John C. Box, January 31, 1928, box 2, folder 15; Chamber of Commerce and Farm Bureau, Beeville, Texas, to John C. Box, April 20, 1927, box 2, folder 5; and J. A. Glen, Gulf, Colorado and Santa Fe Railway Company, to John C. Box, January 11, 1927, box 2, folder 6.

65. Rowell, "Why Make Mexico an Exception?" 180.

66. Interview with F. E. Jackson, president of farm bureau, Ysleta, Texas, no. 85–90, folder "Along Rio Grande," 74–187c, Taylor Papers; Montejano, *Anglos and Mexicans*, 187.

67. *Seasonal Agricultural Laborers*, 46.

68. House Committee on Immigration and Naturalization, *Western Hemisphere Immigration*, 410.

69. Quoted in McWilliams, *North from Mexico*, 121.

70. John M. Lennon to John C. Box, January 14, 1926, box 2, folder 4, Weeks Papers. Excerpts from the letter are reproduced in *Seasonal Agricultural Laborers*, 340.

71. Dr. T. J. Williams to John C. Box, February 4, 1928, box 2, folder 15, Weeks Papers. Another white Texan who was worried about the potential of blacks to infect whites with their "germs" wrote to Box that a law should be passed "compelling every [fruit] packing house to stamp on the container if handled by white or black help" (Charles Cross to John C. Box, March 22, 1929, box 2, folder 19, Weeks Papers).

72. From *Bob Shuler's Magazine*, in House Committee on Immigration and Naturalization, *Immigration from Countries of the Western Hemisphere*, 1928, 28.

73. Montejano, *Anglos and Mexicans*, 181. Another complained that Mexicans were "in our social organization what a pound of putty would be in the stomach of a dyspeptic" (House Committee on Immigration and Naturalization, *Immigration from Countries of the Western Hemisphere*, 1928, 13). Madison Grant, nativist author and advocate of the "true greatness" of the Nordic race, wrote in 1934 that it would have been a disaster to annex all of northern Mexico after the U.S.–Mexico War of 1848 or to acquire Cuba after the Spanish-American War because Cuba would have brought into the union "an indigestible mass of Mediterraneans and blacks" (Madison Grant, *The Conquest of a Continent, Or Expansion of Races in America* [New York: Charles Scribner's Sons, 1934], 196–97).

74. W. D. Cannon to John C. Box, February 12, 1928, box 2, folder 8, Weeks Papers.

75. W. M. Branch, M.D., to John C. Box, December 14, 1927, box 2, folder 6, Weeks Papers.

76. Ibid.

77. J. E. Farnsworth to John C. Box, April 22, 1927, box 2, folder 8, Weeks Papers.

78. On the racial ambiguity of Italian immigrants in the West, see Gunther Peck, "Padrones and Protest: 'Old' Radicals and 'New' Immigrants in Bingham, Utah, 1905–1912," *Western Historical Quarterly* 24 (May 1993): 157–78. The loyalty and "Americanness" of German immigrants during World War I is discussed in Higham, *Strangers in the Land*, 196–200.

79. *Seasonal Agricultural Laborers*, 297.

80. *Temporary Admission*, 317; and House Committee on Immigration and Naturalization, *Immigration from Countries of the Western Hemisphere*, 1928, 14.

81. Quoted in *Congressional Record*, 70th Cong., 1st sess., p. 7, in box 1, ZR–4, Taylor Papers.

82. Don S. Biggers, Eastland, Tex., in a telegram to Congressman Hudspeth, January 29, 1920, in *Temporary Admission*, 209.

83. John T. Branhall to John C. Box, February 16, 1929, box 2, folder 18, Weeks Papers.

84. See Charles C. Cumberland, "Border Raids in the Lower Rio Grande Valley—1915," *Southwestern Historical Quarterly* 58 (January 1954): 301–24; William M. Hager, "The Plan of San Diego: Unrest on the Texas Border in 1915," *Arizona and the West* 5 (Winter 1963): 327–36; James A. Sandos, "The Plan of San Diego: War and Diplomacy on the Texas Border, 1915–1916," *Arizona and the West* 14 (Spring 1972): 5–24; idem, *Rebellion in the Borderlands: Anarchism and the Plan of San Diego, 1904–1923* (Norman: University of Oklahoma Press, 1992); Charles H. Harris and Louis R. Sadler, "The Plan of San Diego and the Mexican–United States Crisis of 1916: A Reexamination," *Hispanic American Historical Review* 58 (August 1978): 381–408; Rodolfo Acuña, *Occupied America: A History of Chicanos*, 3d ed. (New York: HarperCollins, 1988), 161–62; and Montejano, *Anglos and Mexicans*, 117–19.

85. *Temporary Admission*, 6.

86. Ibid., 88–89. The idea that Mexicans and other groups of farm workers could suddenly go "loco" was not merely a figurative statement. Carleton H. Parker, a labor economist who studied the causes of the Wheatland riot of 1913 in northern California, in which hundreds of hop workers rioted in response to squalid living conditions and low wages, claimed that farm workers suffered from a kind of "industrial psychosis" and "psychic ill-health" that resulted from their powerlessness and the "mentally insanitary" conditions of industrial agriculture. See Daniel, *Bitter Harvest*, 91–95.

87. J. C. Brodie to John C. Box, July 18, 1928, box 2, folder 16, Weeks Papers.

88. *Temporary Admission*, 33–34.

89. José E. Limón, "El Primer Congreso Mexicanista de 1911: A Precursor to Contemporary Chicanismo," *Aztlán* 5 (Spring-Fall 1974): 95. My translation.

90. On the Renters' Union and Mexican organizers, see Emilio Zamora, *The World of the Mexican Worker in Texas* (College Station: Texas A&M University Press, 1993), 133–61; and Foley, "New South," 295–358.

91. W. M. Bond to John C. Box, November 11, 1926, box 2, folder 2, Weeks Papers. I examine the role of Mexican radicals in the Texas Socialist Party and the PLM in chapter 4.

92. H. D. Wade to John C. Box, January 31, 1928, box 2, folder 15, Weeks Papers; and Gossett, *Race*, 406.

93. House Committee on Immigration and Naturalization, *Immigration from Countries of the Western Hemisphere*, 1928, 2.

94. *Temporary Admission*, 96, 161, 191; and House Committee on Immigration and Naturalization, *Immigration from Countries of the Western Hemisphere*, 1928, 2.

95. Statement of Harry H. Laughlin, Eugenics Record Office, ibid., 709, 712.

96. *Seasonal Agricultural Laborers*, 188. See also interview with superintendent of Gonzales County schools, no. 220–391, folder "South Central Texas," 74–187c, Taylor Papers.

97. *Seasonal Agricultural Laborers*, 112.

98. *Temporary Admission*, 113.

99. Taylor, *American-Mexican Frontier*, 315–16. For a fine study of the effect of Mexican immigration on the identity of Mexican Americans, see Gutiérrez, *Walls and Mirrors*.

100. *Final Report and Testimony* 10: 9200–9205.

101. Manuel de la O [withheld his family name], March 10, 1928, box 2, folder 23, Weeks Papers. Emphasis added.

102. Interview with Johnny Solís, Texas Mexican, San Antonio, Texas, no. 181–352, folder "South Central Texas," 74–187c, Taylor Papers. Solís also told Taylor that because most Mexican Americans "still feel and are treated like Mexicans," they are more comfortable taking their complaints to the Mexican consul than to Anglo officials.

103. Interview with Benito Rodríguez, no. 59–64, folder "Mexican Officials," 74–187c, Taylor Papers.

104. Douglas R. Cope, *The Limits of Racial Domination in Mexico: Plebeian Society in Colonial Mexico City, 1600–1720* (Madison: University of Wisconsin Press, 1994); and Patricia Seed, "Social Dimensions of Race: Mexico City, 1753," *Hispanic American Historical Review* 62 (1982): 559–606. See also Michael C. Meyer and William Sherman, *The Course of Mexican History*, 5th ed. (New York: Oxford University Press, 1995), 214–15; and Magnus Mörner, *Race Mixture in the History of Latin America* (Boston: Little, Brown, 1967), 9–19.

105. Mario T. García, "Mexican Americans and the Politics of Citizenship: The Case of El Paso, 1936," *New Mexico Historical Review* 59 (April 1984): 189. See also Martin S. Stabb, "Indigenism and Racism in Mexican Thought, 1857–1911," *Journal of Inter-American Studies* 1 (1959): 405–23.

106. Maud Burnette to John C. Box, April 12, 1927, box 2, folder 5, Weeks Papers.

107. Leonard Watkins, "Farm Labor," in Texas Applied Economics Club, *Southern Travis County*, 132.

108. Davis, *White Scourge*, ix.

109. Davis, "King Cotton," 1–3.

110. Davis, *White Scourge*, 174. See also interview with Charles McKenny, Labor Commissioner, Austin, Texas, no. 195–366, folder "South Central Texas," 74–187c, Taylor Papers.

111. Statement of Harry H. Laughlin, Eugenics Record Office, House Committee on Immigration and Naturalization, *Immigration from Countries of the Western Hemisphere*, 1928, 709, 711.

Chapter 3

1. Daniel, *Bitter Harvest*, 23.

2. "The Transition to the Industrial Farm in the United States," typescript, box 15, C–B893, Taylor Papers; Paul H. Johnstone, "Old Ideals versus New Ideas in Farm Life," in U.S. Department of Agriculture, *Yearbook of Agriculture, 1940* (Washington, D.C.: Government Printing Office, 1941), 139; and Stuart Jamieson, *Labor Unionism in American Agriculture* (1945; reprint, New York: Arno Press, 1976), 4–8.

3. Quoted in Billington and Ridge, *Westward Expansion*, 691. On the contested meaning of the closing of the frontier and the ethnocentric bias built into Frederick Jackson Turner's usage of "frontier," see Limerick, *Legacy of Conquest*, 23–27. For a history of the American West as the creation of a distinct region involving the interaction of many cultures rather than as an advancing frontier of

white settlers, see Richard White, *"It's Your Misfortune and None of My Own": A History of the American West* (Norman: University of Oklahoma Press, 1991).

4. See, for example, Karl E. Ashburn, "Economic and Social Aspects of Farm Tenancy in Texas," *Southwestern Social and Political Science Quarterly* 15 (March 1935): 301–2; and Cauley, "Agricultural Land Tenure in Texas," 139–40.

5. William Spillman, Address on Agricultural Education before the Montgomery County, Md., Pomona Grange, n.d., typescript, Reports, Speeches, and Articles Relating to Farm Management, 1902–20, Division of Farm Management, box 71, U.S. Department of Agriculture, Bureau of Agricultural Economics, Record Group 83, National Archives, Washington, D.C. (hereafter cited as USDA RG 83).

6. See, for example, E. A. Goldenweiser and Leon E. Truesdell, *Farm Tenancy in the United States: An Analysis of the Results of the 1920 Census Relative to Farms Classified by Tenure, Supplemented by Pertinent Data from Other Sources*, U.S. Bureau of the Census, Census Monograph 4 (Washington, D.C.: Government Printing Office, 1924), 83. Another analyst wrote, "Tenancy is not an institution to become alarmed about" (L. P. Gabbard, *An Agricultural Economic Survey of Rockwall County, Texas: A Typical Blackland Cotton Farming Area*, Texas Agricultural Experiment Station Bulletin 327 [College Station: Agricultural and Mechanical College of Texas, 1925], 142). See also A. M. Loomis, "The Trend in Tenancy and Ownership," *American Academy of Political and Social Science: The Annals* 117 (January 1925): 63. Another analyst called tenancy a "normal and healthful condition," in which young and inexperienced men acquired the skills and capital to purchase a farm (untitled document, July 22, 1919, General Correspondence, box 718, folder on tenancy, USDA RG 16).

7. See testimony of Judge Brooks in *Final Report and Testimony* 10: 9206; and "The Agricultural Revolution," *Manas*, August 25, 1948, in box 6, C–B 893, Taylor Papers. White tenancy in Texas accounted for numerous conflicts between landlords and tenants "unheard of in the Old South" (Charles S. Johnson, Edwin R. Embree, and W. W. Alexander, *The Collapse of Cotton Tenancy: Summary of Field Studies and Statistical Surveys, 1933–35* [Chapel Hill: University of North Carolina Press, 1935], 71–72).

8. Lee, "Theory of the Agricultural Ladder," 61; and W. J. Spillman, "The Agricultural Ladder," *American Economic Review*, Supplement: *Papers and Proceedings of the Thirty-First Annual Meeting of the American Economic Association* 9 (March 1919): 170–79.

9. Quoted in Division of Public Welfare, *Farm Tenancy in Texas*, 118–19.

10. George S. Wehrwein, "Size of Farms," in Texas Applied Economics Club, *Southern Travis County*, 89–90.

11. "Plutocratic Renters," *The Rebel*, October 28, 1911, 2.

12. *The Rebel*, August 12, 1911, 4.

13. From a collection of 247 interviews with owners, tenants, bankers, credit merchants, and farm laborers in twenty high-tenancy counties in central Texas (Peteet, *Farming Credit in Texas*, 54).

14. George S. Wehrwein, "Length of Tenure," in Texas Applied Economics Club, *Southern Travis County*, 77; and Charles L. Stewart, "Migration to and from Our Farms," *Annals: The Agricultural Situation in the United States, American Academy of Political and Social Science* 17 (January 1925): 53–60.

The chairman of the Commission on Industrial Relations asked J. Tom Padgitt, a landowner from Coleman County, whether landlords felt "any social responsibility for the housing of tenants." He wondered, for example, whether landowners provided screens to protect tenants from mosquitoes, which medical science had recently found to carry diseases. Padgitt replied: "Tenants never want screens, and the landlords don't furnish them, and if he did they wouldn't stay in 24 hours. . . . They [the tenants] wouldn't know how to take care of them" (*Final Report and Testimony* 10: 9106).

15. Holman, "Land Question" [draft], 63–64.

16. Ibid.; and E. C. Branson, "Farm Tenancy in the Cotton Belt: How Farm Tenants Live," *Journal of Social Forces* 1 (March 1923): 219.

17. Paul S. Taylor, "Again the Covered Wagon," *Survey Graphic*, July 1935, 349, in box 1, 84/38c, Taylor Papers.

18. Quoted in Jacqueline Jones, *Labor of Love, Labor of Sorrow: Black Women, Work, and the Family, from Slavery to the Present* (1985; reprint, New York: Vintage, 1995), 83. A North Carolina mail carrier offered a similar version of chicken behavior at moving time: "My daddy moved around so much that Mama used to tell him that every time the chickens heard a wagon they would set down in the yard and cross their legs to be tied" (Kirby, *Rural Worlds Lost*, 278).

19. *Farm and Ranch*, November 3, 1923, p. 8, quoted in Samuel Lee Evans, "Texas Agriculture, 1880–1930" (Ph.D. diss., University of Texas, 1960), 333.

20. Wehrwein, "Length of Tenure," 78–81.

21. Leonard Watkins, "Farm Labor," in Texas Applied Economics Club, *Southern Travis County*, 131–32.

22. More than 96 percent of loans to white owners were at rates of 8 percent or less, whereas only 49.7 percent of loans to black owners were at this rate. The same disparity existed between the percentage of loans to white tenants at rates 8 percent or less (65.4 percent) and to black (35.2 percent) and Mexican (38.4 percent) tenants (E. D. Penn, "Rural Credits," in Texas Applied Economics Club, *Southern Travis County*, 145–46; and George S. Wehrwein, "Productivity and the Value of the Land," in Texas Applied Economics Club, *Southern Travis County*, 20–21). For a more extended analysis of the racial basis of extending credit in central Texas, see Foley, "New South," 169–86.

23. U.S. Bureau of the Census, *Twelfth Census of the United States, 1900: Agriculture*, part 2, *Crops and Irrigation*, 418. The ten southern states are Alabama, Arkansas, Florida, Georgia, Louisiana, Mississippi, North Carolina, South Carolina, Tennessee, and Texas.

24. "Usurers Insult Renters," *The Rebel*, May 29, 1915, 4; and "The 'Shiftless' Tenant," *The Rebel*, December 26, 1914, 2.

25. "Short Talks to Renters," *The Rebel*, February 1, 1913, 3.

26. Penn, "Rural Credits," 145–46.

27. Haney, *Industrial Resources of Texas*, 49; and *Final Report and Testimony* 10: 9152.

28. Some tenants on blackland farms preferred renting to ownership (Division of Public Welfare, *Studies in Farm Tenancy in Texas*, 129).

29. Testimony of Judge Brooks, *Final Report and Testimony* 10: 9208–11. The Texas Socialist newspaper, *The Rebel*, described Judge Brooks as "one of the old-time R'ligion Bourbon democrats . . . who has bought and drank more whiskey

at the Iron Front saloon than any other man of his political standing" ("Story of the Federal Hearing," *The Rebel*, April 3, 1915, 2).

30. Raper, *Preface to Peasantry*, 174–175, quoted in Kirby, *Rural Worlds Lost*, 257.

31. "Story of the Federal Hearing," *The Rebel*, April 3, 1915, 2.

32. "A Commercial Secretary Editor," *The Rebel*, May 22, 1915, 2.

33. *Final Report and Testimony* 9: 9006–38.

34. Ibid. See also Rupert B. Vance, *Human Factors in Cotton Culture: A Study in the Social Geography of the American South* (Chapel Hill: University of North Carolina Press, 1929), 266–69.

35. Holman, "Land Question" [draft], 113. The conflict between business interests and social interests culminated in central Texas with the founding of the Renters' Union in 1911, which is the subject of the next chapter.

36. *Final Report and Testimony* 9: 9029.

37. Lewis H. Haney, "Farm Credit Conditions in a Cotton State," *American Economic Review* 4 (March 1914): 51.

38. Robin D. G. Kelley, *Hammer and Hoe: Alabama Communists during the Great Depression* (Chapel Hill: University of North Carolina Press, 1990), 36. See also chapter 8, in which I discuss the case of the black sharecropper's wife, Deacy Real, who insisted that her illiterate husband not surrender his parity checks to the landlord: Deacy understood the terms of the cotton contract and was prepared to take her case against the landlord to the Agricultural Adjustment Administration (H. L. Mitchell, *Mean Things Happening in This Land: The Life and Times of H. L. Mitchell, Co-Founder of the Southern Tenant Farmers Union* [Montclair, N.J.: Allanheld, Osmun, 1979], 22).

39. Charles W. Holman, "The Tenant Farmer: Country Brother of the Casual Worker," *Survey*, April 17, 1915, 62.

40. *Final Report and Testimony* 9: 9038–44; and Holman, "The Tenant Farmer," 62.

41. After the particularly depressing Dallas hearings, Harriman went to Brownsville to watch the "great show" across the Rio Grande, in which the troops of Villa and Carranza battled for control of Matamoros (Florence Jaffray Hurst Harriman, *From Pinafores to Politics* [New York: Henry Holt, 1923], 172, 176, 181). See also Graham Adams Jr., *Age of Industrial Violence, 1910–15: The Activities and Findings of the United States Commission on Industrial Relations* (New York: Columbia University Press, 1966), 200–202.

42. "Story of the Federal Hearing," *The Rebel*, April 3, 1915, 2.

43. Ibid., 1.

44. *Final Report and Testimony* 10: 9078. On the connection between birth control and eugenics, see Frank Hankins, "The Interdependence of Eugenics and Birth Control," *Birth Control Review* 15 (June 1931), 170–71.

45. Mrs. M. Alexander to editor of *Appeal to Reason*, n.d., in *Final Report and Testimony* 10: 9241–42.

46. Lewis Jones to T. A. Hickey, *The Rebel*, January 25, 1915, in *Final Report and Testimony* 10: 9266; and T. A. Squirer to T. A. Hickey, *The Rebel*, December 23, 1914, in *Final Report and Testimony* 10: 9269.

47. D. W. Sirkel to E. O. Meitzen and W. S. Noble, *The Rebel*, December 7, 1914, in *Final Report and Testimony* 10: 9270.

48. H. L. Cook to W. S. Noble, *The Rebel*, March 3, 1915, in *Final Report and Testimony* 10: 9248–49. The tenant J. H. Blackwell expressed the desperation of many tenants when he used the words of an "old negro" who once told him: "We will have to get on our own land in the public road and keep going, for if we stop they [owners and merchants] will pinch us for obstructing the public highway" (J. H. Blackwell to T. A. Hickey, *The Rebel*, December 21, 1914, in *Final Report and Testimony* 10: 9274).

49. Jones, *Labor of Love*, 86.

50. National Council concerning Mexicans and Spanish Americans in the United States, *Report of Commission on International and Interracial Factors in the Problem of Mexicans in the United States* (El Paso: Home Missions Council, 1926), 33.

51. *Final Report and Testimony* 10: 9282. Mr. Hernández was also an organizer for the Socialist Renters' Union and later the Land League. See chapter 4.

52. Peteet, *Farming Credit in Texas*, 5–6; and Division of Public Welfare, *Farm Tenancy in Texas*, 52.

53. Haney, "Farm Credit Conditions," 47–67; and *Final Report and Testimony* 10: 9153.

54. For a compelling analysis of the legal aspects of crop lien and chattel mortgage laws, see Woodman, *New South—New Law*, 28–66; and idem, "Southern Agriculture and the Law," 319–37. For a general discussion of the rise of sharecropping and the crop-lien system, see Fred A. Shannon, *The Farmer's Last Frontier: Agriculture, 1860–1897* (New York: Farrar and Rinehart, 1945), 83–95.

55. "A Typical Situation," *The Rebel*, December 26, 1914, 4.

56. Peteet, *Farming Credit in Texas*, 36.

57. Ibid., 35.

58. Ibid., 29.

59. From *Farm and Ranch*, October 14, 1911, quoted in Holman, "Land Question" [draft], 22, 25.

60. Charlie Black to M. A. Ferguson, August 12, 1934, folder 4, box 301–480, Miriam A. Ferguson Papers, Texas State Library, Archives Division, Austin (hereafter cited as Ferguson Papers); and W. F. Reden, L.L.B., to Hon. Henry Wallace, July 25, 1933, General Correspondence, Negroes, box 2, USDA RG 16.

61. Peteet, *Farming Credit in Texas*, 40. This was one of forty-six black owners in Rains County in 1910, who constituted 7.8 percent of all farmers in the county. Black tenants, of whom there were seventy-five, represented 12.8 percent of all farmers. Black owners constituted 38 percent of all black farmers in the county (U.S. Bureau of the Census, *Thirteenth Census of the United States, 1910: Agriculture* [Washington, D.C.: Government Printing Office, 1913], 7: 672). For examples of those who did lose their farms, see case numbers 94, 126, 132 in Peteet, *Farming Credit in Texas*, 51, 57–58.

62. M. M. Offutt, Observations and Conclusions upon East Texas, typescript, 1908–9, Reports, Speeches, and Articles Relating to Farm Management, 1902–20, Division of Farm Management, box 62, USDA RG 83.

63. *Interstate Migration of Destitute Citizens*, 1968.

64. William E. Leonard, "The Economic Aspects of the Tenant Problem in Ellis County," in Division of Public Welfare, *Farm Tenancy in Texas*, 108.

65. The practice of threatening to cut off a tenant's credit for growing a garden dates back to the nineteenth century. See M. B. Hammond, *The Cotton Industry: An Essay in American Economic History*, American Economic Association Publications, n.s., 1 (New York: Macmillan, for the American Economic Association, 1897), 151; and George K. Holmes, "The Peons of the South," *Annals of the American Academy of Political and Social Sciences* 4 (September 1893): 267. Some tenants were assessed a fee for any land they planted in a garden. One farmer recalled the case of a black tenant who planted "four rows in the edge of the yard where he lived, 30 or 40 feet long . . . and C. [the landowner] made him pay $4.00 for that little space. If they raise gardens they must plant them in their yards" (Division of Public Welfare, *Farm Tenancy in Texas*, 97).

66. Testimony of W. D. Lewis in *Final Report and Testimony* 10: 9234; and testimony of Patrick S. Nagle, *Final Report and Testimony* 10: 9075.

67. *The American Mercury*, February 1935, quoted in "A Statement concerning Farm Tenancy Submitted to the Governor's Commission on Farm Tenancy by the Executive Council, Southern Tenant Farmers' Union, in Records of the Division of Land Economics, Records relating to the President's Special Committee on Farm Tenancy, 1936–37, box 1, USDA RG 83.

68. William Faulkner, *Collected Stories* (New York: Random House, 1950), 153.

69. See Roediger, *Wages of Whiteness*.

70. The cropper "does not farm by lease, but by a *contract of hiring*. The possession of the crop and right of division remain with the landlord. The cropper has no property in his share of the crop until the division, which is made by the owner of the land" (W. C. Tichenor, *Farm Contracts between Landlord and Tenant* [Lebanon, Ohio: W. C. Tichenor, 1916], 13). On the origins of sharecropping in the South, see Oscar Zeichner, "The Transition from Slave to Free Agricultural Labor in the Southern States," *Agricultural History* 13 (January 1939): 22–32; and Ralph Shlomowitz, "The Origins of Southern Sharecropping," *Agricultural History* 53 (July 1979): 557–75.

71. Woodman, "Southern Agriculture and the Law," 333.

72. Rogers v. Frazier Bros. and Co., 108 S.W. 727, 728 (Tex. Civ. App. 1908), in Erling D. Solberg, *Legal Aspects of Farm Tenancy in Texas*, Texas Agricultural Experiment Station Bulletin 718 (College Station: Agricultural and Mechanical College of Texas, 1950), 107–8, 285–86; and Jesse Thomas Sanders, *Farm Ownership and Tenancy in the Black Prairie of Texas* U.S. Department of Agriculture Bulletin 1068 (Washington, D.C.: Government Printing Office), 16.

73. Steward testified before the commission that he rented "on the halves" on more than six farms in central Texas, and on all but one he did not own his own team or implements. However, his contract permitted him to take his share of the cotton to town, have it graded, and to sell it himself (*Final Report and Testimony* 9: 9026).

74. The landlord's crop lien, of course, protected his half of the crop for rent and any part of his tenant's half for advances. The landlord could still execute a chattel mortgage on any other property the tenant owned, a mortgage he could foreclose if the tenant could not repay advances from his half. See Woodman, "Southern Agriculture and the Law," 319–37.

75. Harold Hoffsommer, ed., *The Social and Economic Significance of Land*

Tenure in the Southwestern States: A Report of the Regional Land Tenure Research Project (Chapel Hill: University of North Carolina Press, 1950), 250; Tichenor, *Farm Contracts*, 20; and C. O. Brannen, "Problems of Croppers on Cotton Farms," *Journal of Farm Economics* 20 (February 1938): 153–58.

76. In *The Rebel*: "A Renter's Letter," October 7, 1911, 3; "How to Get After 'Em," December 21, 1912, 1; and "Attracting Nationwide Attention," February 7, 1919, 1.

77. "Texas Land Troubles," *The Rebel*, September 16, 1911, 1.

78. From a 1911 article by Carl Crow, "What the Tenant Farmer Is Doing in the South," quoted in Holman, "Land Question" [final version], 145.

79. Newspaper clipping, November 15, 1922, in folder "South Texas, General History," box 2, ZR–4, Taylor Papers. On the activities of the Ku Klux Klan in Texas cities, see Norman Brown, *Hood, Bonnet, and Little Brown Jug: Texas Politics, 1921–1928* (College Station: Texas A&M University Press, 1984), 49–87; Charles C. Alexander, *The Ku Klux Klan in the Southwest* (Lexington: University Press of Kentucky, 1965); and Max Bentley, "The Ku Klux Klan in Texas," *McClure's Magazine* 57 (May 1924): 11–21.

80. On the transition from tenancy to wage labor in Texas, see L. C. Gray, Charles L. Stewart, Howard A. Turner, J. T. Sanders, and W. J. Spillman, "Farm Ownership and Tenancy," in U. S. Department of Agriculture, *Yearbook, 1923* (Washington, D.C.: Government Printing Office, 1924), 532.

81. J. E. Davis to T. A. Hickey, *The Rebel*, December 17, 1914, in *Final Report and Testimony* 10: 9270–72.

82. Ibid. Tindel was permitted by another statute to seize the crop because it was "not lawful for the tenant, while rent or advances remain unpaid, to remove from the premises . . . any of the crops . . . without his [the landlord's] consent" (Holman, "Land Question" [draft], 32).

83. For an analysis of the legal distinctions between croppers and tenants in the postbellum South, see Woodman, *New South—New Law*, esp. 67–94.

84. William Bennett Bizzell, *Farm Tenancy in the United States: A Study of the Historical Development of Farm Tenancy and Its Economic and Social Consequences on Rural Welfare, with Special References to Conditions in the South and Southwest*, Texas Agricultural Experiment Station Bulletin 278 (College Station: Agricultural and Mechanical College of Texas, 1921), 188.

85. Oscar Schulz v. F. A. Hernández, in *Final Report and Testimony* 10: 9284.

86. Holman, "Land Question" [draft], 40–42.

87. Ibid.

88. Ibid., 46; and Division of Public Welfare, *Farm Tenancy in Texas*, 118.

89. Lewis H. Haney, ed., *Studies in the Land Problem in Texas*, University of Texas Bulletin 39 (Austin: University of Texas Press, 1915), 9.

90. Texas Applied Economics Club, *Southern Travis County*, 2. See also "The 'Shiftless' Tenant," *The Rebel*, December 26, 1914, 2.

91. *The Rebel*, October 10, 1914.

92. Peteet, *Farming Credit in Texas*, 55.

93. "Land League," *The Rebel*, February 13, 1915, 2.

94. Peteet, *Farming Credit in Texas*, 73.

95. See Adams, *Age of Industrial Violence*.

96. *Final Report and Testimony* 9: 8952.

97. "Socialism in Texas, 1890–1925," typescript, n.d., box 3E278, folder 4, Ruth Allen Papers, 1943–1973, Center for American History, University of Texas at Austin (hereafter cited as Ruth Allen Papers).

Chapter 4

1. On the Populist Party in Texas, see Roscoe Coleman Martin, *The People's Party in Texas: A Study in Third Party Politics*, University of Texas Bulletin 3308 (Austin: University of Texas Press, 1933); Lawrence Goodwyn, *Democratic Promise: The Populist Moment in America* (New York: Oxford University Press, 1976); Robert Lee Hunt, *A History of the Farmer Movements of the Southwest, 1837–1925* (College Station: Texas A&M University Press, 1935); and Donna A. Barnes, *Farmers in Rebellion: The Rise and Fall of the Southern Farmers Alliance and Peoples Party in Texas* (Austin: University of Texas Press, 1984).

2. In *The Rebel*: "Texas Land and Speculators," August 31, 1912, 2; "Arouse, Ye Renters," October 12, 1912, 1; "The Land—The Paramount Issue in Dixie," February 24, 1912, 1; and "The Rebel Goes to Austin," March 29, 1916, 1. The slogan, "Land for the Landless and Homes for the Homeless," appeared in *The Rebel*, November 1, 1913. See also "Thomas A. Hickey and Socialism in Texas," typescript, n.d., folder 2, Ruth Allen Papers.

3. See Lewis L. Gould, *Progressives and Prohibitionists: Texas Democrats in the Wilson Era* (Austin: University of Texas Press, 1973); and Sam Hanna Acheson, *Joe Bailey: The Last Democrat* (New York: Macmillan, 1932).

4. "Statutory v. Fundamental Law," *The Rebel*, April 17, 1915, 4; and "To a Texas Professor," *The Rebel*, July 3, 1915, 2.

5. *The Rebel*, November 28, 1914, 2; and "The Enemy Within: The Land Grabber," *The Rebel*, May 29, 1915, 2.

6. "The Fake of Ferguson," *The Rebel*, April 11, 1914, 1, and April 25, 1914, 1; and "A Little Leaven Leaveneth the Whole," *The Rebel*, July 11, 1914, 1.

7. On the Ferguson campaign, see Gould, *Progressives and Prohibitionists*, 120–49; and Green, *Grass-Roots Socialism*, 295–97.

8. "Story of the Federal Hearing," *The Rebel*, April 3, 1915, 1.

9. "Socialism in Texas," Ruth Allen Papers; and "Hickey and Socialism," folder 2, Ruth Allen Papers.

10. T. A. Hickey, "The Land Renters Union in Texas," *International Socialist Review* 13 (September 1912): 239–44; and "Land League," *The Rebel*, April 24, 1915, 4. On Texas Socialist Party activity and recruitment of tenants, see James R. Green, "Tenant Farmer Discontent and Socialist Protest in Texas, 1901–1917," *Southwestern Historical Quarterly* 81 (October 1977): 133–54. By 1910 tenant-operated farms in Texas constituted 52.6 percent of all farms, and in the Blackland Prairie of central Texas tenancy exceeded 60 percent. See U.S. Bureau of the Census, *Thirteenth Census of the United States, 1910: Agriculture*, vol. 5, part 1, 124–31.

11. "Renters' Union," *The Rebel*, September 2, 1911, 1. Examples abounded of landlords who had "rented out" Socialist tenants and replaced them with less politically active renters, but the conflict between the Socialist tenants of Coleman County and the superintendent of the Day Ranch received widespread cov-

erage. See, in *The Rebel*: "The Trouble at Leaday," November 2, 1919, 1; "Renters' Union," November 16, 1913, 2; "Blacklisting Socialists," November 23, 1912, 4; and "Renters Out!" January 24, 1914, 1.

12. "An Arlington Addle Pate," *The Rebel*, December 16, 1911, 3.

13. "Land League of America," *The Rebel*, December 5, 1914, 3.

14. Scholarship on biracial unionism was pioneered by Herbert G. Gutman, "The Negro and the United Mine Workers of America: The Career and Letters of Richard L. Davis and Something of Their Meaning: 1890–1900," in *The Negro and the American Labor Union*, ed. Julius Jacobson (Garden City, N.Y.: Anchor Books, 1968); Paul B. Worthman, "Black Workers and Labor Unions in Birmingham, Alabama, 1897–1904," *Labor History* 10 (Summer 1969): 375–407; James R. Green, "The Brotherhood of Timber Workers, 1910–1913: A Radical Response to Industrial Capitalism in the Southern U.S.A.," *Past and Present* 60 (August 1973): 161–200; idem, *Grass-Roots Socialism*; Paul B. Worthman and James Green, "Black Workers in the New South," in *Key Issues in the Afro-American Experience*, ed. Nathan Higgins, Martin Kilson, and Daniel Fox (New York: Harcourt, Brace, Jovanovitch, 1971), 2: 47–69; and Stephen Brier, "Interracial Organizing in the West Virginia Coal Industry: The Participation of Black Mine Workers in the Knights of Labor and the United Mine Workers, 1880–1894," in *Essays in Southern Labor History*, ed. Gary M. Fink and Merl E. Reed (Westport, Conn.: Greenwood Press, 1977), 18–41. Recent works that examine patterns of biracial unionism include Roediger, *Abolition of Whiteness*, chap. 10; Vicki L. Ruiz, *Cannery Women, Cannery Lives: Mexican Women, Unionization, and the California Food Processing Industry, 1930–1950* (Albuquerque: University of New Mexico Press, 1987); Eric Arnesen, *Waterfront Workers of New Orleans: Race, Class, and Politics, 1863–1923* (New York: Oxford University Press, 1991); Joe William Trotter Jr., *Coal, Class, and Color: Blacks in Southern West Virginia, 1915–1932* (Urbana: University of Illinois Press, 1990); Guerin-Gonzales, *Mexican Workers*; Henry M. McKiven Jr., *Iron and Steel: Class, Race, and Community in Birmingham, Alabama, 1875–1920* (Chapel Hill: University of North Carolina Press, 1995); and Daniel Letwin, "Interracial Unionism, Gender, and 'Social Equality' in the Alabama Coalfields, 1878–1908," *Journal of Southern History* 61 (August 1995): 519–54.

15. My analysis of interracial unionism in Texas is deeply indebted to David Roediger's fine essay, "Gaining a Hearing for Black-White Unity: Covington Hall and the Complexities of Race, Gender and Class," in his *Abolition of Whiteness*, 127–80, 143 (quotation). The best work on the Socialist Party in the Southwest is Green, *Grass-Roots Socialism*. Standard works on the Socialist Party in America are Ira Kipnis, *The American Socialist Movement, 1897–1912* (New York: Columbia University Press, 1952); David Shannon, *The Socialist Party of America: A History* (New York: Macmillan, 1955); and James Weinstein, *The Decline of Socialism in America, 1912–1925* (New York: Monthly Review Press, 1967). See also Nick Salvatore, *Eugene V. Debs: Citizen and Socialist* (Urbana: University of Illinois Press, 1982). On the Industrial Workers of the World, see Melvyn Dubofsky, *We Shall Be All: A History of the Industrial Workers of the World*, 2d ed. (Urbana: University of Illinois Press, 1988); and Joseph R. Conlin, *Big Bill Haywood and the Radical Union Movement* (Syracuse, N.Y.: Syracuse University Press, 1969).

16. "Race Equality and Free Love," *The Rebel*, October 5, 1912, 1. See also "Who [S]aid Race Equality?" *The Rebel*, December 7, 1912, 1.

17. "Social Equality," *The Rebel*, December 23, 1911, 1; and Green, *Grass-Roots Socialism*, 113.

18. "Social Equality," *The Rebel*, December 23, 1911, 1.

19. "Renters' Union," *The Rebel*, September 9, 1911, 1.

20. Works dealing with Mexicans in the Socialist Party in Texas include Green, "Tenant Farmer Discontent and Socialist Protest in Texas," 133–54; idem, *Grass-Roots Socialism*; Ruth Allen, Labor Movements in Texas Papers, Center for American History, Austin (hereafter cited as Labor Movements Papers); Zamora, *Mexican Worker in Texas*, 133–61; and Foley, "New South," 295–358.

21. In *The Rebel*: "Renters' Union of America," November 11, 1911, 2; "The Gathering of Land Tenants," November 4, 1911, 1; and "Renters' Convention," November 16, 1912, 2.

22. In *The Rebel*: "Renters' Convention," 2; "The Gathering of Land Tenants," 1; and "Renters' Union of America," 2. On the biracial BTW, see Roediger, "Gaining a Hearing," 127–80; idem, "Covington Hall: The Poetry and Politics of Labor Radicalism and Southern Nationalism," *History Workshop Journal* 19 (Spring 1985): 162–68; Green, "Brotherhood of Timber Workers"; idem, *Grass-Roots Socialism*, 204–13; and Jeff Ferrel and Kevin Ryan, "The Brotherhood of Timber Workers and the Southern Trust: Legal Repression and Worker Response," *Radical America* 19 (July-August 1985): 55–74.

23. *The Rebel*, May 17, 1913, 1.

24. Green, *Grass-Roots Socialism*, 111, 223; and "Land League of America," *The Rebel*, December 5, 1914, 3. Green notes the parallel between Hickey's exclusion of blacks in Texas and California Socialist Frank Roney's venomous hostility toward the Chinese. See Saxton, *Indispensable Enemy*.

25. On the Molly Maguires, see Wayne G. Broehl Jr., *The Molly Maguires* (Cambridge, Mass.: Harvard University Press, 1964); James Walter Coleman, *The Molly Maguire Riots: Industrial Conflict in the Pennsylvania Coal Region* (Richmond, Va.: Garrett & Massie, 1936); Kevin Kenny, *Making Sense of the Molly Maguires* (New York: Oxford University Press, 1997); and M. R. Beames, *Peasants and Power: The Whiteboy Movements and Their Control in Pre-Famine Ireland* (New York: St. Martin's Press, 1983), 75, 78, 79, 92, and 123. I am thankful to Kevin Kenny for bringing these works to my attention.

26. "Hickey and Socialism," folder 2, Ruth Allen Papers; Eric Foner, "Class, Ethnicity, and Radicalism in the Gilded Age: The Land League and Irish-America," *Marxist Perspectives* 1 (Summer 1978): 10; and S. T. Clark, *Social Origins of the Irish Land War* (Princeton, N.J.: Princeton University Press, 1979).

27. "Socialism in Texas," Ruth Allen Papers; and Green, *Grass-Roots Socialism*, 303.

28. "Socialism in Texas," Ruth Allen Papers. See also typescripts, n.d., folders 2 and 4, Ruth Allen Papers.

29. "Hickey and Socialism," folder 2, Ruth Allen Papers. For a discussion of the nineteenth-century experience of Irish immigrants who became white by embracing white supremacy, see Roediger, *Wages of Whiteness*, 133–63; and Ignatiev, *How the Irish Became White*.

30. Green, *Grass-Roots Socialism*, 146.

31. "Hickey and Socialism," folder 2, Ruth Allen Papers; and "Socialism in Texas," Ruth Allen Papers.

32. Martin, *People's Party in Texas*, 234. See also Dick Smith, "Texas and the Poll Tax," *Southwestern Social Science Quarterly* 45 (September 1964): 167–73; and Donald S. Strong, "The Poll Tax: The Case of Texas," *American Political Science Review* 38 (August 1944): 693–709. See also Darlene Clark Hine, *Black Victory: The Rise and Fall of the White Primary in Texas* (Millwood, N.Y.: KTO Press, 1979); and Woodward, *Career of Jim Crow*.

33. "Tom Watson and the McNamaras," *The Rebel*, December 16, 1911, 1. See also C. Vann Woodward, *Tom Watson: Agrarian Rebel* (1938; reprint, New York: Oxford University Press, 1963).

34. Quoted in Roediger, "Covington Hall," 162–64.

35. "A Miracle in Dixie," *The Rebel*, December 21, 1912, 2.

36. Quoted in Roediger, "Gaining a Hearing," 156.

37. Hubert Harrison, "Socialism and the Negro," *International Socialist Review* 13 (July 1912): 67.

38. *Mother Earth* 6 (October 1911), 198, quoted in Sally M. Miller, "The Socialist Party and the Negro, 1901–20," *Journal of Negro History* 56 (July 1971): 225.

39. Green, *Grass-Roots Socialism*, 108. I found no references in *The Rebel* or any other source describing the efforts of Hickey or the Land League to organize black sharecroppers.

40. "Correspondence," *The Rebel*, July 18, 1914, 3.

41. "A Word of Encouragement," *The Rebel*, July 1, 1916, 1.

42. "Hickey and Socialism," folder 2, Ruth Allen Papers; and Green, *Grass-Roots Socialism*, 166–67.

43. "Correspondence," *The Rebel*, July 18, 1914, 3.

44. "Hickey and Socialism," folder 2, Ruth Allen Papers.

45. "The Renters' Union," *The Rebel*, November 18, 1911, 1; and "An Arlington Addle Pate," *The Rebel*, December 16, 1911, 3.

46. "A Word of Encouragement," *The Rebel*, July 1, 1916, 1.

47. "Flashes from Our Correspondents," *The Rebel*, March 16, 1912, 3.

48. Roediger, "Gaining a Hearing," 135–36. Roediger alludes here to W. E. B. Du Bois's notion of the "double-consciousness" of black Americans: "One ever feels his two-ness,—an American, a Negro; two souls, two thoughts, two unreconciled strivings" (W. E. B. Du Bois, *The Souls of Black Folk* [1903; reprint, New York: Alfred A. Knopf, 1993], 9).

49. On the social isolation of poor whites, see George S. Wehrwein, "Social Life," in Texas Applied Economics Club, *Southern Travis County*, 53–63; and Julian B. Roebuck and Mark Hickson III, *The Southern Redneck: A Phenomenological Class Study* (New York: Praeger, 1982), 72–75, 83–87. See also J. Wayne Flynt, *Dixie's Forgotten People: The South's Poor Whites* (Bloomington: Indiana University Press, 1979).

50. In 1912 *The Rebel* reported that Padgitt owned 20,000 acres and rented a portion of it to fifty tenants. Three years later Padgitt testified before the Commission on Industrial Relations that he owned 12,000 acres, 2,000 of which were rented to twenty-two tenants. It is possible that in the intervening three years Padgitt sold 8,000 acres and reduced the number of tenants from fifty to

twenty-two. See *Final Report and Testimony* 10: 9102; and "Report of the Resolution Committee of the Land Renters' Union of North America, Held at Waco, November 8, 1912," *The Rebel*, November 16, 1912, 2.

51. *Final Report and Testimony* 10: 9102–12; and "The New Slavery in the New South," *The Rebel*, October 26, 1912, 1.

52. "The New Slavery in the New South," *The Rebel*, October 26, 1912, 1.

53. Ibid., 1–2.

54. *Final Report and Testimony* 10: 9102–12; and "The New Slavery in the New South," *The Rebel*, October 26, 1912, 1.

55. In *The Rebel*: "The Trouble at Leaday," November 2, 1912, 1; "Gal.-Dal. News and the Renter," February 1, 1913, 1; and "Renters' Union," August 12, 1911, 1. Hickey learned about the actions of prohibitionist landlords from testimony taken before a special committee of the 32d Texas Legislature.

56. "Renters' Union," *The Rebel*, November 16, 1912, 2.

57. *Final Report and Testimony* 20: 9107–11.

58. "The New Slavery in the New South," *The Rebel*, October 26, 1912, 2.

59. Noble, who had met with 112 delegates from twenty-eight counties at the second annual convention of the Renters' Union, reported that "the Leaday trouble is no uncommon affair, and the same thing is being done all over the state" ("Renters' Union," *The Rebel*, November 16, 1912, 2).

60. *Final Report and Testimony* 1: 86–88.

61. "The New Slavery in the New South," *The Rebel*, October 26, 1912, 2.

62. "Plutocratic Renters," *The Rebel*, October 28, 1911, 2.

63. "Some Awful Statistics," *The Rebel*, February 28, 1914, 1.

64. "Renters' Union," *The Rebel*, September 9, 1911, 1.

65. "Farm Renters and Laborers," *The Rebel*, April 19, 1913, 2.

66. "Negroes and Laborers Barred," *The Rebel*, April 24, 1915, 3.

67. Quoted in Roediger, "Gaining a Hearing," 127.

68. "The Race Question," *The Rebel*, April 22, 1916, 3.

69. Green, *Grass-Roots Socialism*, 113.

70. "Renters' Union," *The Rebel*, August 30, 1913, 3.

71. For a discussion of the influence of Mexican magonistas and members of the radical PLM in Texas, see Zamora, *Mexican Worker in Texas*, 133–61. The influence of the Mexican Revolution on northern Mexico and Texas are explored in John M. Hart, *Anarchism & the Mexican Working Class, 1860–1931* (Austin: University of Texas Press, 1978); Sandos, *Rebellion in the Borderlands*; W. Dirk Raat, *Revoltosos: Mexico's Rebels in the United States, 1903–1923* (College Station: Texas A&M University Press, 1981); Cumberland, "Border Raids"; Limón, "Primer Congreso Mexicanista"; and Juan Gómez-Quiñones, *Sembradores, Ricardo Flores Magón y el Partido Liberal Mexicano: A Eulogy and a Critique*, rev. ed. (Los Angeles: Chicano Studies Center Publications, University of California at Los Angeles, 1977).

72. On the early development of Texas Anglo attitudes toward Mexicans, see de León, *They Called Them Greasers*.

73. See Arnoldo de León, *In Re Ricardo Rodríguez: An Attempt at Chicano Disfranchisement in San Antonio, 1896–1897* (San Antonio, Tex.: Caravel Press, 1979), 8; Almaguer, *Racial Fault Lines*, 162–64; Fernando Padilla, "Early Chi-

cano Legal Recognition, 1846–1897," *Journal of Popular Culture* 13 (Spring 1980): 564–74; and Martha Menchaca, "Chicano Indianism: A Historical Account of Racial Repression in the United States," *American Ethnologist* 20 (August 1993): 583–601. For an analysis of the legal decisions that barred numerous groups from claiming white racial status, see Stanford M. Lyman, "The Race Question and Liberalism: Casuistries in American Constitutional Law," *International Journal of Politics, Culture, and Society* 5 (Winter 1991): 183–247. For a fascinating personal history involving the legal and cultural complexities of racial identity, see Ernest Evans Kilker, "Black and White in America: The Culture and Politics of Racial Classification," *International Journal of Politics, Culture, and Society* 7 (Winter 1993): 229–58.

74. "Land League," *The Rebel*, October 23, 1915, 4.

75. Zamora, *Mexican Worker*, 133–61; Hart, *Anarchism*; Raat, *Revoltosos*; Cumberland, "Border Raids"; and Limón, "Primer Congreso Mexicanista."

76. "Land League Organizer Arrested," *The Rebel*, October 23, 1915, 2; "Hernandez Goes Free," *The Rebel*, January 22, 1916, 1; and Nils H. Hanson, "Texas Justice! 99 Years!" *International Socialist Review* 16 (February 1916): 476–78.

77. "Land League," *The Rebel*, October 9, 1915, 3.

78. In *The Rebel*: "Hernández Case," November 6, 1915, 4; "Land League," September 23, 1915, 3; and "Land League Organizer Arrested," October 23, 1915, 1.

79. In *The Rebel*: "Land League," October 9, 1915, 3; "Land League Organizer Arrested," October 23, 1915, 1; "Hernández Case," November 6, 1915, 4; "Land League," September 23, 1915, 3; and "Land League Convention," December 4, 1915, 2. See also Foley, "New South," 332–50; and Zamora, *Mexican Worker*, 133–61.

80. "Mexican Land Given Up," *The Rebel*, February 12, 1916, 4.

81. "Real Rebels," January 29, 1916, 2. Hickey and *The Rebel* sought to unseat Senators James B. Wells and James L. Slayden, whom Hickey called corrupt "bosses" and "landhog-politicians" ("Hernandez Goes Free," *The Rebel*, January 22, 1916, 1).

82. "State News," *The Rebel*, January 30, 1915, 3.

83. In *The Rebel*, "Renters' Union," April 26, 1913, 4; "Renters' Union," May 3, 1913, 4; and "Renters' Union," May 10, 1913, 3.

84. "Renters' Union," *The Rebel*, May 10, 1913, 3; "Land League Convention," *The Rebel*, December 4, 1915, 2; and Zamora, *Mexican Worker*, 136–38.

85. "Renters' Union," *The Rebel*, September 27, 1913, 3. On working-class constructions of whiteness, see Roediger, *Wages of Whiteness*. On Germans in Texas after the Civil War, see Jordan, *German Seed*.

86. "The Renting Situation," *The Rebel*, September 12, 1914, 1; and *Final Report and Testimony* 10: 9284–85.

87. From *The Rebel*: "Renters' Union," May 3, 1913, 4; "Renters' Union," February 1, 1913, 4; "Renters' Union," April 5, 1913, 3; and "Land League Organizer Arrested," October 23, 1915, 1 (quotation).

88. W. S. Noble, secretary of the Land League, paid Hernández the highest compliment when he wrote that he had "organized more locals and accomplished more by his generalship than any one organizer in the League" ("Land League," *The Rebel*, May 29, 1915, 3; and "Land League," *The Rebel*, February 13, 1915, 2). Weekly reports between 1911 and 1917 indicated that Hernández and

other Mexican organizers established locals of the Renters' Union and Land League in fourteen counties in south and central Texas: Atacosa, Bexar, Caldwell, Comal, DeWitt, Goliad, Gonzales, Guadalupe, Karnes, Live Oak, McMullen, Medina, Milam, and Nueces.

89. "Land for the People," *The Rebel*, June 29, 1912, 3. Shortly after organizing several unions in Travis and adjoining counties, Antonio Valdés left to return to Mexico to liberate "the slaves in his native country" ("Renters' Union," *The Rebel*, April 5, 1913, 3).

90. "Mexican Immigration," *The Rebel*, April 4, 1914, 2; Emilio Zamora, "Mexican Labor Activity in South Texas, 1900–1920" (Ph.D. diss., University of Texas, 1983), 182; idem, *Mexican Worker*, 158–60; and Foley, "New South," 343–45. See also *Temporary Admission*, 4, 19, 65, 133, 174, 203–4; *Seasonal Agricultural Laborers*, 214, 337, 341; Clark, "Mexican Labor in the United States," 500, 512; Crawford, "Menace of Mexican Immigration," 906; Handman, "Coming of the Mexican Immigrant," 606, 609; idem, "Mexican Immigrant in Texas," 36; and Paul S. Taylor, "Mexicans North of the Rio Grande," *Survey*, May 1, 1931, 136, 201.

91. On Anglo "race-thinking" and Texas Mexicans, see Montejano, *Anglos and Mexicans*, 222–34. My use of the phrase "not-quite-white" is an adaptation of David Roediger's phrase "not-yet-white," which he uses to describe the process of "becoming white" for some European immigrant groups. See his *Abolition of Whiteness*, 181–98.

92. From *The Rebel*: "Renters' Union," May 3, 1913, 4; "Renters' Union," February 1, 1913, 4; "Renters' Union," April 5, 1913, 3; and "Land League Organizer Arrested," October 23, 1915, 1 (quotation).

93. Black timber workers in east Texas demonstrated their "white-hearted manliness" to whites when they walked off their jobs rather than "scabbing." Quoted in Roediger, *Abolition of Whiteness*, 152–53.

94. On political repression of the Socialist Party in the Southwest during World War I, see Green, *Grass-Roots Socialism*, 345–95.

95. H. Wirt Steele to District and County Administrators, May 16, 1918, box 2J366, Bell Co., Texas War Records, CAH; and Green, *Grass-Roots Socialism*, 374–75.

96. Hunt, *Farmer Movements in the Southwest*, 145–46, 156–60; and Green, *Grass-Roots Socialism*, 381–82.

97. National Nonpartisan League, Texas Branch, December 22, 1917, box 3k423, Thomas A. Hickey Papers, Center for American History, University of Texas at Austin (hereafter cited as Hickey Papers).

98. "Rebel Editor Kidnapped!" *The Rebel*, May 26, 1917, 1.

99. "Socialism in Texas," folder 4, Ruth Allen Papers.

100. Ibid.

101. Ibid. The edition of June 2, 1917, is the last extant copy of *The Rebel*. The Center for American History in Austin, Texas, and the New York Public Library are, as far as I know, the only depositories in the country that have copies of *The Rebel*, and neither set runs beyond this date.

102. Circular, "To the Friends of *The Rebel*," June 30, 1917; "Texas Landlord-Banker Plutocracy Strikes at Rebel," Hickey Papers; and Green, *Grass-Roots Socialism*, 356–57.

103. Quoted in Donald Johnson, "Wilson, Burleson, and Censorship in the First World War," *Journal of Southern History* 28 (February 1962): 51–52.

104. Oscar Ameringer, *If You Don't Weaken: The Autobiography of Oscar Ameringer* (New York: Henry Holt, 1940), 319–20; and "Texas Landlord-Banker Plutocracy Strikes at Rebel," Hickey Papers. Burleson also barred from the mail seven other Socialist publications, as well as *New York Call* and *The Nation* ("A. S. Burleson Takes Pride in Blows at Him," newspaper clipping, n.d., Albert S. Burleson Papers, Center for American History, University of Texas at Austin).

105. "Hickey and Socialism," folder 2, Ruth Allen Papers.

106. Tom Hickey, "Frontier Smashers," *Calliham Caller and Three Rivers Oil News* (Calliham), n.d., Hickey Papers.

107. *Tom Hickey's Magazine* 1 (April 1925): 10–11, 14, Hickey Papers. See also L. P. Gabbard and F. R. Jones, *Large-Scale Cotton Production in Texas*, Texas Agricultural Experiment Station Bulletin 362 (College Station: Agricultural and Mechanical College of Texas, 1927).

Chapter 5

1. Harold Woodman, who pioneered the study of business plantations, writes that "the key characteristic of these business plantations was centralized management and supervision of labor—not the periodic checking by absentee landlords . . . but the control by management of all decisions from plowing to sales" (Harold D. Woodman, "Postbellum Social Change and Its Effect on Marketing the South's Cotton Crop," *Agricultural History* 56 [January 1982]: 225, 228). To underscore the fact that tenants were no longer independent operators, the AAA referred to some share tenants, along with sharecroppers, as "nonmanaging tenants," or people who are "merely laborers and not tenants at all." See the discussion by T. Lynn Smith at the conclusion of C. O. Brannen, "Problems of Croppers on Cotton Farms," *Journal of Farm Economics* 20 (February 1938): 161–62.

2. On the development of corporate cotton ranches in California, see Paul S. Taylor, "Mechanization in Agriculture and Its Effect on Farm Labor," typescript, n.d., box 6, C–B 893, Taylor Papers; John Turner, *White Gold Comes to California* (Bakersfield: California Planting Cotton Seed Distributors, 1981), 29–52; Daniel, *Bitter Harvest*, 40–70; McWilliams, *Factories in the Field*, 48–65, 81–102, 185–99; Guerin-Gonzales, *Mexican Workers*, 11–24; and Weber, *Dark Sweat, White Gold*. See also the testimony of various agricultural specialists in U.S. Congress, Senate, Committee on Education and Labor, *Violations of Free Speech and Rights of Labor*, 76th Cong., 3d sess., 1940, Supplementary Hearings, parts 1–3, The American Farmer and the Rise of Agribusiness: Seeds of Struggle (New York: Arno Press, 1975) (hereafter cited as *Violations of Free Speech*).

3. On the development of cotton ranches in Texas in the context of the South, see *Final Report and Testimony* 9: 9044–56 and 10: 9214–28; L. P. Gabbard, "Effect of Large-Scale Production on Cotton Growing in Texas," *Journal of Farm Economics* 10 (April 1928): 211–24; Gabbard and Jones, *Large-Scale Cotton Production in Texas*, 5–24; Montejano, *Anglos and Mexicans*; Pete Daniel, *Breaking the Land: The Transformation of Cotton, Tobacco, and Rice Cultures since 1880*

(Urbana: University of Illinois Press, 1985); Vance, *Cotton Culture*; Gilbert C. Fite, *Cotton Fields No More: Southern Agriculture, 1865–1980* (Lexington: University of Kentucky Press, 1984); Kirby, *Rural Worlds Lost*; Woodman, "Postbellum Social Change"; idem, "The Reconstruction of the Cotton Plantation in the New South" in *Essays on the Postbellum Southern Economy*, ed. Thavolia Glymph and John J. Kushma (College Station: Texas A&M University Press, 1985), 95–119; A. Ray Stephens, *The Taft Ranch: A Texas Principality* (Austin: University of Texas Press, 1964); and Taylor, *American-Mexican Frontier*.

4. On plantation agriculture in the South in the twentieth century, see Daniel, *Breaking the Land*; Rupert B. Vance, "Cotton and Tenancy," in *Problems of the Cotton Economy: Proceedings of the Southern Social Science Research Conference, New Orleans, March 8 and 9, 1935* (Dallas: Arnold Foundation, for the Southern Regional Committee of the Social Science Research Council, 1936); idem, *Cotton Culture*; Jay R. Mandle, *The Roots of Black Poverty: The Southern Plantation Economy after the Civil War* (Durham, N.C.: Duke University Press, 1978); Fite, *Cotton Fields No More*; Charles S. Johnson, *Shadow of the Plantation* (Chicago: University of Chicago Press, 1934); Kirby, *Rural Worlds Lost*; idem, "The Transformation of Southern Plantations ca. 1920–1960," *Agricultural History* 57 (July 1983): 257–76; Woodman, "Postbellum Social Change"; and idem, "Reconstruction of the Cotton Plantation."

5. U.S. Bureau of the Census, *Thirteenth Census of the United States, 1910: Agriculture*, 5: 877–92. The special report based the findings of the 1910 census on plantations in U.S. Bureau of the Census, *Plantation Farming in the United States* (Washington D.C.: Government Printing Office, 1916 [hereafter cited as *Plantation Farming*]). The 325 selected counties were distributed throughout eleven southern states, as follows: 47 in Alabama, 23 in Arkansas, 1 in Florida, 70 in Georgia, 29 in Louisiana, 45 in Mississippi, 21 in North Carolina, 35 in South Carolina, 11 in Tennessee, 41 in Texas, and 2 in Virginia (*Plantation Farming*, 16).

6. O. C. Payne, "Corporation Farming in Texas," *Farm and Ranch*, May 30, 1914, 2–3.

7. "The Solution of the Land Problem," *The Rebel*, July 5, 1913, 1 (first quotation); testimony of Cullen F. Thomas, *Final Report and Testimony* 10: 9191 (second quotation); and "The Taft Farm," 1 (third quotation). See also Tom Lea, *The King Ranch*, 2 vols. (Boston: Little, Brown, 1957); and Stephens, *Taft Ranch*. A study of the ownership of tenant farms conducted by the U.S. Department of Agriculture (USDA) in 1920 and published in 1926 concluded that "large holdings of rented farms are few in the Northern States but fairly common in the Southern States; the largest holdings being in cotton-plantation counties." The study included data from 184 counties in twenty-four states, including the Texas cotton-producing counties of Bell, Ellis, Hill, and McLennan. These counties lie in the fertile Blackland Prairie of central Texas. See Howard A. Turner, *The Ownership of Tenant Farms in the United States*, U.S. Department of Agriculture Bulletin 1432 (Washington, D.C.: Government Printing Office, 1926), 3, 46 (quotation). These four cotton-producing Texas counties are among the counties included in the 1910 decennial census special study of plantation farming. See *Plantation Farming*. See also Rural Problem Areas Survey Report No. 62: The Western Cotton Growing Area, San Patricio County, Texas, Federal Emergency Relief Administration, January 11, 1935, Division of Farm Population and Rural

Life, Reports on Rural Problem Areas, box 1, County Reports, 1934–35 USDA RG 83 (hereafter cited as San Patricio County, USDA RG 83).

8. In *The Rebel*: "Land Question the Big Question," September 21, 1912, 3; "The Rebel Has Made Land the Question," October 19, 1912, 1; and "The Small Farmer," February 24, 1912, 2 (Hickey quotation).

9. Brannen, *Relation of Land Tenure to Plantation Organization*, U.S. Department of Agriculture Bulletin 1269 (Washington, D.C.: Government Printing Office, 1924), 31; Holman, "Land Question" [draft], 46; idem, "Land Question" [final version], 13; and Division of Public Welfare, *Farm Tenancy in Texas*, 118. Forty-two percent of all farmlands in San Patricio County was owned by nonresidents, including the Taft Ranch (San Patricio County, USDA RG 83).

10. Edward Sherwood Mead and Bernhard Ostrolenk, *Harvey Baum: A Study of the Agricultural Revolution* (Philadelphia: University of Pennsylvania Press, 1928), 85.

11. Ibid., 85; and Lynn W. Ellis, "How the Machine Is Making History on the Farm," *International Socialist Review* 12 (April 1912): 647.

12. Interview with Mr. Thompson, Chapman Ranch, no. 200–789, folder "Nueces County," 74–187c, Taylor Papers; and Davis, "Next Great American Industry," 580, 586.

13. Taylor, *American-Mexican Frontier*, 103.

14. Taylor, "Mechanization in Agriculture," Taylor Papers.

15. Taylor, *American-Mexican Frontier*, xi, 103. See also Gabbard, "Effect of Large-Scale Production"; and Gabbard and Jones, *Large-Scale Cotton Production in Texas*, 5–24.

16. Interview with Mr. Thompson, Chapman Ranch, no. 200–789, folder "Nueces County," 74–187c, Taylor Papers; and Davis, "Next Great American Industry," 580, 586.

17. *Final Report and Testimony* 1: 86–88.

18. For the history of the Taft Ranch, see Stephens, *Taft Ranch*. Stephens's work is largely an uncritical panegyric of Taft management that includes little information on the Mexican workers themselves. His main purpose is to tell "the story of a corporation . . . that led the Texas Coastal bend to unprecedented prosperity through progressive techniques, maintenance of soil fertility, and aggressive leadership" (p. ix). I was afforded a different view of Taft management from the unpublished reports of the special investigators Charles W. Holman and David J. Saposs for the Commission on Industrial Relations at the National Archives and from the Socialist newspaper *The Rebel*, sources that Stephens did not use in his book.

19. Coleman-Fulton Pasture Company, Charter No. 1206, May 1, 1880, Office of the Texas Secretary of State, quoted in Stephens, *Taft Ranch*, 41; see also pp. 43, 57, 79–80, 93.

20. Davis, "Next Great American Industry," 580, 586.

21. Testimony of Charles H. Alvord, superintendent of farms for Coleman-Fulton Pasture Company, in *Final Report and Testimony* 10: 9214; and Stephens, *Taft Ranch*, 137, 148–50.

22. "Meeting Held in Auditorium," newspaper clipping [July 1913] in scrapbook, folder 1, box 2N276, May Mathis Green Watson Papers, Center for Amer-

ican History, University of Texas at Austin (hereafter cited as Watson Papers); and *Seasonal Agricultural Laborers*, 213.

23. "Farming Experience on Taft Farm Told," newspaper clipping, 1913, folder 1, box 2N276, Watson Papers; and Stephens, *Taft Ranch*, 150–51, 165.

24. Stephens, *Taft Ranch*, 130; and George Frederic Stratton, "Mr. Taft's Tenants: How They Earn Farms on His Big Texas Ranch," *Country Gentleman*, March 1, 1919, 5, 37. See also Payne, "Corporation Farming in Texas," 2.

25. *Final Report and Testimony* 10: 9220; Stephens, *Taft Ranch*, 174 (quotation); and David J. Saposs interview with J. J. Runck, August, 19, 1914, p. 22, in typescript entitled "Taft Ranch," a series of interviews conducted by field investigator Saposs, in U.S. Commission on Industrial Relations, Records of the Division of Research and Investigation, Department of Labor, Record Group 174, National Archives and Records Administration, Washington, D.C. (hereafter cited as Saposs, "Taft Ranch").

26. Interviews with George Rhodes, Portland, Texas, August 20, 1914, and T. D. Williams, carpenter, Sinton, Texas, August 22, 1914, in ibid., 1–2 (Rhodes) and 16 (Williams). See also David J. Saposs, "Self-Government and Freedom of Action in Isolated Industrial Communities" [January 20, 1915], 1–17, reel P71–1690, CIR Records, SHSW (hereafter cited as Saposs, "Industrial Communities").

27. Saposs, "Taft Ranch," 1, 3. See also interviews with J. C. Albertson, grocer, and J. C. Russell, lawyer, insurance agent and former editor of the local newspaper, Sinton, Texas, August 21, 1914, pp. 12, 14. D. F. Jones, a farmer near Taft, Texas, told Russell and others that the company was offering only $12.00 per ton of cottonseed, whereas independent agents offered $24.00. For Joseph Green's testimony, see *Final Report and Testimony* 10: 9225–27.

28. *Final Report and Testimony* 10: 9225–26; and Saposs, "Taft Ranch," 4, 9.

29. Saposs, "Taft Ranch," 2, 4; and Stephens, *Taft Ranch*, 177.

30. Saposs, "Taft Ranch," 5.

31. Saposs, "Industrial Communities," 26–27. Saposs's field report on industrial communities (one of which was the Taft Ranch) indicated that the industrial managers like Green were "vested with absolute power in anything affecting the operating end of the plant, as well as the policy to be pursued towards the inhabitants of the community in which the corporation is located." On Green's efforts to drive independent store operators out of business, see interview with M. K. Hunt, Gregory, Texas, August 20, 1914, in Saposs, "Taft Ranch," 8–9. *The Rebel* reported in July 1914 that Joseph Green's "understrappers beat up a field agent of the Industrial Relations Commission" who went to the Taft Ranch to investigate its operations ("Story of the Federal Hearing," *The Rebel*, April 3, 1915, 2).

32. Interviews with George Rhodes and J. H. Woods, Portland, Texas, August 20, 1914, in Saposs, "Taft Ranch," 5–7. For a more cheerful description of Taft Ranch tenant farmers, see Stratton, "Mr. Taft's Tenants," 5.

33. Interview with N. S. Tunnell, cashier and manager of Farmers' Bank, Gregory, Texas, August 20, 1914, in Saposs, "Taft Ranch," 5–6; *Final Report and Testimony* 10: 9217; and Stephens, *Taft Ranch*, 171.

34. *Final Report and Testimony* 10: 9223–24 (third quotation) and 9228 (first two quotations). Green's knowledge of all phases of company operations as revealed in various articles and in his own interview with Saposs belies his testi-

mony before the commission that he was ignorant of company-store policy and procedures. Saposs revealed that Green either inaugurated or approved all policies affecting the operations of the farms, stores, hospital, banks, gins, and other holdings associated with the company. See Saposs, "Taft Ranch," 8–9. Although it was clear from the line of questioning at the commission's Dallas hearings that Frank P. Walsh and other commission members remained unconvinced that the coupon system worked to the benefit of Taft employees, Ray Stephens came to the rather fatuous conclusion that Chairman Walsh "undoubtedly . . . marvelled at this arrangement, which represented a somewhat advanced agrarian social outlook for 1915" (Stephens, *Taft Ranch*, 195).

35. Scrapbook, 1887–1934, folder 1, box 2N276, Watson Papers.

36. One correspondent, for example, noted in 1913 that well-stocked stores were maintained on the ranch and, without seeking evidence from Taft employees or from independent farmers and store operators, reported that "there is no effort made to compel patronage." A year later another correspondent spent "several days" on the ranch marveling at the "wise direction" of Joseph Green, whose "company stores are models any way you consider them" (Theodore H. Price, "A 100,000-Acre Business," *World's Work* 25 [January 1913]: 273). See also Payne, "Corporation Farming in Texas," 2.

37. "100,000 Acres of Business Farming . . . ," 1915, clipping, folder 1, box 2N276, Watson Papers; and Taft Hospital Department Minute Book, box 2K154, Coleman-Fulton Pasture Company Records, Center for American History, University of Texas at Austin (hereafter cited as Coleman-Fulton Records). Rodolfo Flores was hired by the Taft Hospital to board "sick Mexicans" until a separate wing for them had been added to the hospital.

38. See, for example, Davis, "The Next Great American Industry," 580, 586; and Stratton, "Mr. Taft's Tenants," 5. On Taylorism, see Frederick W. Taylor, *The Principles of Scientific Management* (New York: Harper & Brothers, 1911). For an interesting essay on the logic of Fordism and Taylorism with respect to leisure and the work week, see David R. Roediger, "The Limits of Corporate Reform: Fordism, Taylorism, and the Working Week in the United States, 1914–1929," in *Worktime and Industrialization: An International History*, ed. Gary Cross (Philadelphia: Temple University Press, 1988), 135–54.

39. Stratton, "Mr. Taft's Tenants," 5, 37 (first quotation); Payne, "Corporation Farming in Texas," 2 (second quotation); *Final Report and Testimony* 10: 9219, 9226; and Stephens, *Taft Ranch*, 173, 196.

40. "Farming Experience on Taft Farm Told," 1913, folder 1, box 2N276, Watson Papers.

41. "Land for the People," *The Rebel*, June 29, 1912, 3; Charles W. Holman, "Charles P. Taft Absolute King over Thousands on Big Estate," *New York Call*, January 15, 1915, 1. The percentage of Mexicans living in San Patricio County more than doubled between 1920 and 1930. The population in 1920 was 11,386, of which 77.5 percent were native whites, 20.9 percent were foreign-born whites (the overwhelming majority of whom were Mexicans), and 1.5 percent were blacks. Ten years later the population increased to 23,836, of which 52.1 percent were Mexicans, 45 percent were native whites, 0.8 percent were non-Mexican foreign-born whites, and 2.1 percent were blacks (U.S. Bureau of the Census,

Fifteenth Census of the United States, 1930: Population Bulletin, First Series, *Texas* [Washington, D. C.: Government Printing Office, 1931], 1061). See also San Patricio County, USDA RG 83.

42. Holman, "Taft Absolute King," 1. C. O. Brannen recognized the increased efficiency of production and lower costs for the owners of large "tenant plantations," but he also recognized that changes wrought by large-scale production meant for the laborer "less consistent employment and lower incomes. . . . The immediate outlook, for tenants who revert to croppers, for croppers who revert to wage hands, and for wage hands who become unemployed, is distinctly unfavorable" (Brannen, "Croppers on Cotton Farms," 158). Another study demonstrated that in one Blackland Prairie county in Texas a high correlation existed between farm size and net income (Gabbard, *Survey of Rockwall County*, 65, 103–16). Other studies also demonstrated the profitability of large-scale farming using cropper and wage labor in conjunction with improved machinery. See L. A. Moorhouse and M. R. Cooper, *The Cost of Producing Cotton*, U.S. Department of Agriculture Bulletin 896 (Washington, D.C.: Government Printing Office, 1920); and C. D. Kinsman, *An Appraisal of Power Used on Farms in the United States*, U.S. Department of Agriculture Bulletin 1348 (Washington, D.C.: Government Printing Office, 1925).

43. Stratton, "Mr. Taft's Tenants," 5, 37; Payne, "Corporation Farming in Texas," 2; and Journal no. 47, vol. 13, 1910, box 4ZE50, Coleman-Fulton Records.

44. San Patricio County, USDA RG 83.

45. *Final Report and Testimony* 10: 9218–19.

46. Taylor, *American-Mexican Frontier*, 312.

47. Allen, *Labor of Women*, 113.

48. Grant, *Passing of the Great Race*, 34–35, 75. In 1905 an American army surgeon published a wondrously strange ethnographic study entitled *The Effects of Tropical Light on White Men*. See Gossett, *Race*, 225.

49. *Final Report and Testimony* 10: 6218.

50. Ibid., 10: 9201–2. See also interview with Federal Farm Loan representative, no. 131–302, folder "Dimmit County," 74–187c, Taylor Papers. On low-profile forms of resistance among subordinate groups, see Scott, *Arts of Resistance*.

51. Price, "100,000-Acre Business," 272, 275.

52. Interviews with George Rhodes and J. H. Woods, Portland, Texas, August 20, 1914, in Saposs, "Taft Ranch," 6.

53. Interviews with J. C. Russell, Mr. Mynier, and G. F. Haskins, Sinton, Texas, August 21, 1914, in Saposs, "Taft Ranch," 13, 17; and Saposs, "Industrial Communities, 45.

54. Saposs, "Industrial Communities," 48 (first two quotations); and interview with Mr. Callender, n.d., no. 31–36, folder "South Central Texas" (third quotation), 74–187c, Taylor Papers. Priests sometimes became involved in or founded agricultural unions among Mexican workers in South Texas. In 1930 the missionary priest Charles Taylor organized a "society" of Mexican agricultural workers in Crystal City, Texas, called Unión Católica de Trabajadores (Catholic Workers' Union). A group of 450 Mexican farm workers, not including their women and children, presented a list of demands to the growers. See, in box 15, C–B893, Taylor Papers: Charles Taylor to Paul S. Taylor, February 3, 1931; "To the Growers, or Farmers of Crystal City," November 10, 1930; and "La Respuesta," November 30, 1930.

55. Stephens, *Taft Ranch*, 183–84; and Payne, "Corporation Farming in Texas," 2–3.

56. See Cumberland, "Border Raids," 301–24; Hager, "Plan of San Diego," 327–36; Sandos, "Plan of San Diego," 5–24; idem, *Rebellion in the Borderlands*; Harris and Sadler, "Plan of San Diego," 381–408; Acuña, *Occupied America*, 161–62; and Montejano, *Anglos and Mexicans*, 117–19.

57. Minutes of Departmental Meeting, July 19, 1916, quoted in Stephens, *Taft Ranch*, 198–99.

58. Scrapbook on Joseph Green, folder 1, box 2N276, Watson Papers.

59. Price, "100,000-Acre Business," 275 (first quotation; see also *Final Report and Testimony* 10: 9169); and Stratton, "Mr. Taft's Tenants," 37 (second quotation). On the shift from the moral view of agrarianism, in which the farmer was the repository of virtue, to a more secular, economic view, in which the farmer was "simply another business man," see Clifford B. Anderson, "The Metamorphosis of American Agrarian Idealism in the 1920's and 1930's," *Agricultural History* 35 (October 1961): 182–88.

60. U.S. Department of Agriculture, Bureau of Agricultural Economics, *Farm Power and Farm Machines* (Washington, D.C.: Government Printing Office, 1953), 2–3; Records Relating to Studies, Projects and Surveys, Projects A-1-22–6, box 38, USDA RG 83. Tractor power on 140 farms in West Texas increased from 24.5 percent in 1931 to 78.6 percent in 1937. See Thomas C. Blaisdell Jr. and Paul S. Taylor, "Displacement of Agricultural Labor by Tractors," typescript, June 30, 1938, box 2, 84/38c, Taylor Papers. On the transcendent role of mules in cotton agriculture, see Kirby, *Rural Worlds Lost*, 195–204.

61. Progress Report, Texas Agricultural Experiment Station, "Mechanization and Its Relation to the Cost of Producing Cotton in Texas," typescript, June 1940, box 6, C–B 893, Taylor Papers.

62. On the mechanization of cotton in Texas and elsewhere in the South, see Warren Whatley, "Institutional Change and Mechanization in the Cotton South: The Tractorization of Cotton Farming" (Ph.D. diss., Stanford University, 1982); Moses S. Musoke, "Mechanizing Cotton Production in the American South: The Tractor, 1915–1960," *Explorations in Economic History* 18 (October 1987), 347–75; James H. Street, *The New Revolution in the Cotton Economy: Mechanization and Its Consequences* (Chapel Hill: University of North Carolina Press, 1957); and Richard H. Day, "The Economics of Technological Change and the Demise of the Sharecropper," *American Economic Review* 57 (June 1967), 427–49. See also Sally H. Clarke, *Regulation and the Revolution in United States Farm Productivity* (Cambridge, England: Cambridge University Press, 1994), esp. 83–135.

63. Minutes of the Board of Directors, August 24, 1912, Box 3171, 187a-187b, Coleman-Fulton Records. The minutes recorded that the statement was made by the owner of the King Ranch but added that "the Superintendent of this Company [Joseph Green] agrees with him in this regard." Stephens's paraphrase of the same statement omits the word "Mexican" before "laborers." See Stephens, *Taft Ranch*, 191. The decision to rent the Campbell picker was also reported in Minutes of the Stockholders' Meeting, May 5, 1913, box 3L30, Coleman-Fulton Records. In 1911 the Price-Campbell cotton-picking machine was exhibited in Dallas, where a USDA agent, S. M. Tracey, examined the efficiency of the machine and found it lacking: It gathered so much trash along with the

cotton that the cotton's value was seriously depreciated. Because it weighed 6,000 pounds, it could not be used on soft ground or on plants taller than 4 or 5 feet, which was a typical height for cotton plants grown in Texas. Of all the picking devices he examined, Tracey nevertheless concluded that only the Price-Campbell machine held any promise of success, and "even that one gives only a promise" (S. M. Tracey to W. J. Spillman, November 29, 1911, folder on cotton-picking machines, box 85, Reports, Speeches and Articles Relating to Farm Management, Division of Farm Management, USDA RG 83).

64. *Corpus Christi Caller*, February 25, 1925, quoted in Taylor, *American-Mexican Frontier*, 109; see also pp. 112–13.

65. Allis-Chalmers Tractor Division advertisement, in box 6, C–B 893, Taylor Papers.

66. "Renters' Union," *The Rebel*, March 30, 1912, 3; and "Hick's Page," *The Rebel*, September 2, 1911, 4.

67. Transcript of interview with cotton weigher on Weil Brothers' ranch, 1929, Corpus Christi, no. 100–690, folder "Nueces County," 74–187c, Taylor Papers; and Taylor, *American-Mexican Frontier*, 113. At times mechanization referred mainly to the substitution of mechanical power for animal power. At other times it meant the replacement of "hand labor" by mechanical harvesters. Ultimately, mechanization came to mean "the complete elimination of hand labor from cotton production" (Grady B. Crowe, "The Economic Implications of Mechanization in Cotton Production," typescript, February 6, 1952, Records Relating to Studies, Projects and Surveys, Projects A–1–20–25, box 33, USDA RG 83).

68. Paul S. Taylor to H. B. Walker, June 25, 1940, box 6, CB 893, Taylor Papers.

69. Undated newspaper clipping, "100,000 Acres of Business Farming . . . ," scrapbook, folder 1, box 24276, Watson Papers. More than fifteen years later, in 1933, Charles Alvord became an assistant to Cully Cobb, chief of the Cotton Section of the Agricultural Adjustment Administration. See C. H. Alvord to Mrs. Otto W. Thiel, November 9, 1933, AAA, Subject Correspondence files, folder on cotton pickers, box 28, U.S. Department of Agriculture, Bureau of Agricultural Economics, Record Group 83, National Archives, Washington, D.C. (hereafter cited as USDA RG 154). On the ties between corporate farms, government, and agricultural institutions, see Deborah Fitzgerald, *The Business of Breeding: Hybrid Corn in Illinois, 1890–1940* (Ithaca, N.Y.: Cornell University Press, 1990).

70. *Temporary Admission*, 48–51, 65.

71. Transcript of interview with John Wuenche, no. 59–649, folder "Nueces County," 74–187c, Taylor Papers.

72. See Street, *New Revolution*; and Whatley, "Institutional Change."

73. Morrison I. Swift, "Strengthen the Immigration Law and Improve the American Race," March 1926, folder 3, box 2, Weeks Papers. See also John T. Branhall to John C. Box, February 16, 1929, folder 18, box 2, Weeks Papers.

74. *Temporary Admission*, 61.

75. Ibid., 36 (Miller), 48 (Roberts), 205–9 (Walton); Johnson, Embree, and Alexander, *Collapse of Cotton Tenancy*, 12; and San Patricio County, USDA RG 83.

76. *Interstate Migration of Destitute Citizens*, 1955; *Violations of Free Speech*, 191; and Sanders, *Farm Ownership and Tenancy*, 16.

77. *Temporary Admission*, 133–38.

78. Interview with G. A. Talmadge, Corpus Christi, September 1929, box 2, Z–R4, Taylor Papers; and Taylor, *American-Mexican Frontier*, 299.

79. Interview with Mr. Wilkinson, no. 24–29, folder "Dimmit County," 74–187c, 1929, Taylor Papers.

80. U.S. Congress, Senate Committee on Immigration, *Restriction of Western Hemisphere Immigration*, 70th Cong., 1st sess., February 1, 1928, 148.

81. "The Agricultural Revolution," *Manas*, August 25, 1948, in box 6, C–B 893, Taylor Papers; William T. Ham, "Farm Labor in an Era of Change," in U.S. Department of Agriculture, *Yearbook of Agriculture, 1940* (Washington, D.C.: Government Printing Office, 1941), 912.

82. See Saposs, "Industrial Communities," 26–27.

83. "Farm Tenantry," *The Rebel*, October 30, 1915, 2.

84. "Ford Tractor," *The Rebel*, December 11, 1915, 2. On the effect of "Fordism" on industry, see David A. Hounshell, *From the American System to Mass Production, 1800–1932: The Development of Manufacturing Technology in the United States* (Baltimore, Md.: Johns Hopkins University Press, 1984), esp. chaps. 6 and 7. See also Roediger, "Limits of Corporate Reform," 135–54.

85. Horace Hamilton, "The Status and Future of Farm Tenantry in the South," paper read before the Southern Economic Association, Duke University, Records of the Division of Land Economics, Records Relating to the President's Special Committee on Farm Tenancy, 1936–37, Box 4, USDA RG 83; and Mead and Ostrolenk, *Harvey Baum*, 88–89. The moral superiority of independent yeoman farmers is one of the principal themes of Jefferson's "Notes on Virginia," 1784 (Adrienne Koch and William Peden, eds., *The Life and Selected Writings of Thomas Jefferson* [New York: Modern Library, 1944]). See also Anderson, "Metamorphosis of American Agrarian Idealism," 182–88.

86. Davis, "Next Great American Industry," 586.

87. James C. Cobb and Michael V. Namorato, eds., *The New Deal and the South* (Jackson: University Press of Mississippi, 1984), 7.

Chapter 6

1. Allen, *Labor of Women*, 250.

2. Ibid., 71.

3. See Commission on Country Life, *Report of the Commission on Country Life* (New York: Sturgis and Walton, 1917); and William L. Bowers, *The Country Life Movement in America, 1900–1920* (Port Washington, N.Y.: Kennikat Press, 1974).

4. Thomas Jefferson, *Notes on the State of Virginia*, ed. William Peden (New York: W. W. Norton, 1954), 164–65; and U.S. Department of Agriculture, *Yearbook of Agriculture, 1940*, 117.

5. Scholarship on gender and farm women useful for this chapter includes Wava G. Haney and Jane B. Knowles, eds., *Women and Farming: Changing Roles, Changing Structures* (Boulder, Colo.: Westview Press, 1988); Nancy Grey Osterud, *Bonds of Community: The Lives of Farm Women in Nineteenth-Century New York* (Ithaca, N.Y.: Cornell University Press, 1991); idem, "Gender and the Transition to Capitalism in Rural America," *Agricultural History* 67 (Spring 1993): 14–29; Jones, *Labor of Love*; Mary Neth, *Preserving the Family Farm:*

Women, Community, and the Foundations of Agribusiness in the Midwest, 1900–1940 (Baltimore, Md.: Johns Hopkins University Press, 1995); Katherine Jellison, *Entitled to Power: Farm Women and Technology, 1919–1963* (Chapel Hill: University of North Carolina Press, 1993); Marilyn Irvin Holt, *Linoleum, Better Babies, and the Modern Farm Woman, 1890–1930* (Albuquerque: University of New Mexico Press, 1995); Joan M. Jensen, *Promise to the Land: Essays on Rural Women* (Albuquerque: University of New Mexico Press, 1991); idem, *With These Hands: Women Working on the Land* (Old Westbury, N.Y.: Feminist Press, 1981); idem, *Loosening the Bonds: Mid-Atlantic Farm Women, 1750–1850* (New Haven, Conn.: Yale University Press, 1986); Louise Tilly, "Paths of Proletarianization: Organization of Production, Sexual Division of Labor, and Women's Collective Action," *Signs* 6 (Winter 1981): 400–417; Deborah Fink, *Agrarian Women: Wives and Mothers in Rural Nebraska, 1880–1940* (Chapel Hill: University of North Carolina Press, 1992); Gail Bederman, *Manliness & Civilization: A Cultural History of Gender and Race in the United States, 1880–1917* (Chicago: University of Chicago Press, 1995); Deutsch, *No Separate Refuge*; Allen, *Labor of Women*; Sharpless, "Fertile Ground, Narrow Choices"; Higginbotham, "African-American Women's History"; Ruth Schwartz Cowan, *More Work for Mother: The Ironies of Household Technology from the Open Hearth to the Microwave* (New York: Basic Books, 1983); and Carolyn E. Sachs, *The Invisible Farmers: Women in Agricultural Production* (Totowa, N.J.: Rowman & Allanheld, 1983).

6. Miss Leffler Corbitt, "Address to the Girls of the Home Economic Clubs," in Texas Department of Agriculture, *Proceedings of the Fifth Meeting of the Texas State Farmers' Institute, 1915*, Texas Department of Agriculture Bulletin 48 (Austin, 1915), 172–74. Other examples of routines and duties of women on cotton and tobacco farms can be found in Kirby, *Rural Worlds Lost*, 155–61.

7. Fink, *Agrarian Women*, 156.

8. See Lorraine Garkovich and Janet Bokemeier, "Agricultural Mechanization and American Farm Women's Economic Roles," in *Women and Farming: Changing Roles, Changing Structures*, ed. Wava G. Haney and Jane B. Knowles (Boulder, Colo.: Westview Press, 1988), 211–28; Sarah Elbert, "Women and Farming: Changing Structures, Changing Roles," in *Women and Farming*, 245–64; Neth, *Preserving the Family Farm*, 214–43; and Jellison, *Entitled to Power*, 1–65. For a critique of the concept of "separate spheres," see Elbert, "Women and Farming," 256–63; and Osterud, *Bonds of Community*.

9. Charles E. Gibbons, *Child Labor among Cotton Growers of Texas: A Study of Children Living in Rural Communities in Six Counties in Texas* (New York: National Child Labor Committee, 1925), 31.

10. U.S. Department of Agriculture, *Yearbook, 1928* (Washington, D.C.: Government Printing Office, 1929), 620; and Allen, *Labor of Women*, 137.

11. Allen, *Labor of Women*, 137.

12. U.S. Department of Agriculture, *Yearbook, 1930* (Washington, D.C.: Government Printing Office, 1930): 241–43.

13. Neth, *Preserving the Family Farm*, 26. On rural women doing "men's work," see Jensen, *With These Hands*; Osterud, *Bonds of Community*; and Delores E. Janiewski, *Sisterhood Denied: Race, Gender, and Class in a New South Community* (Philadelphia: Temple University Press, 1985).

14. Harry R. O'Brien, "'Ill Fares the Land': When the Wrongs of the Tenant System Go Unchecked," *Country Gentleman*, December 14, 1918, 3. The classic study of white women on tenant farms during the depression years is Margaret Jarman Hagood, *Mothers of the South: Portraiture of the White Tenant Farm Woman* (Chapel Hill: University of North Carolina Press, 1939).

15. Division of Public Welfare, *Studies in Farm Tenancy in Texas*, 128; and Allen, *Labor of Women*, 139, 195, 234.

16. George S. Wehrwein, "Age, Mortality, and Size of Farm Family," in Texas Applied Economics Club, *Southern Travis County*, 35.

17. Interview with J. Bonner Rackley, October 27, 1976, Caldwell County Oral History Collection, Center for American History, University of Texas at Austin.

18. *Farm and Ranch*, October 19, 1898, 16, quoted in Evans, "Texas Agriculture," 320.

19. Gibbons, *Child Labor*, 5–7.

20. Ibid., 52.

21. Wehrwein, "Age, Mortality, and Size of Farm Family," 35.

22. Allen, *Labor of Women*, 71.

23. Texas Applied Economics Club, *Southern Travis County*, 36–38; and Allen, *Labor of Women*, 214.

24. Report on Survey Rural Problem Area: Western Cotton Growing, Williamson County, Texas, September 7, 1934, Division of Farm Population and Rural Life, Reports on Rural Problem Areas, box 11, State Reports, 1934–35, USDA RG 83.

25. Hagood, *Mothers of the South*, 123. See also Kirby, *Rural Worlds Lost*, 164; and Vance, *Cotton Culture*, 299–300.

26. Quoted in Allen, *Labor of Women*, 108; on the size of African American families compared with white families, see p. 194.

27. Hagood, *Mothers of the South*, 123; and Janiewski, *Sisterhood Denied*, 34–35.

28. Allen, *Labor of Women*, 72, 241.

29. Gibbons, *Child Labor*, 5–7, 50.

30. Allen, *Labor of Women*, 78, 188, 223, 246–48.

31. Gibbons, *Child Labor*, 52.

32. Allen, *Labor of Women*, 121.

33. Gibbons, *Child Labor*, 32. For other examples of tenant women laboring from "sun to sun" while their husbands napped in the shade, see Kirby, *Rural Worlds Lost*, 156–57. In a novel published in 1932 on sharecroppers, the father says of his six-year-old daughter, Perla: "She puts her feet under the table to eat three times a day, don't she? Well, then, she's got to do her share of the work. Hit the grit, Perly" (Dorothy Scarborough, *The Stretch-Berry Smile* [Indianapolis, Ind.: Bobbs, Merrill, 1932], 9).

34. Gibbons, *Child Labor*, 47, 49, 51–52.

35. See, for example, oral history of Elvira Sánchez, July 20, 1977, Caldwell County Oral History Collection, Center for American History, University of Texas at Austin.

36. F. A. Hernández to E. O. Meitzen, December 5, 1914, in *Final Report and Testimony* 10: 9288–89.

37. Interview with Mr. McPeet, no. 312–483, folder "Dimmit County," 74–187c, Taylor Papers.

38. Gibbons, *Child Labor*, 47, 49, 51–52.

39. Mexican and African American farm women in all class categories worked off-farm in greater percentages than did white farm women (Allen, *Labor of Women*, 271, 274–75).

40. Interview at the Municipal Employment Bureau, Houston, n.d., no. 31–36, folder "South Central Texas," 74–187c, Taylor Papers; and García, *Desert Immigrants*, 76.

41. Interview with Mr. Patterson, no. 141–312, folder "Dimmit County," 74–187c, Taylor Papers.

42. Address of Mrs. G. E. Adams, Woman's Educational and Industrial Association, in Texas Department of Agriculture, *Twelfth Texas Farmers' Conference, 1909*, Texas Department of Agriculture Bulletin 10 (Austin, 1909), 308–9.

43. U.S. Department of Agriculture, *Social and Labor Needs of Farm Women*, Report 103 (Washington, D.C.: Government Printing Office, 1915), 54–55.

44. U.S. Department of Agriculture, *Economic Needs of Farm Women*, Report 106 (Washington, D.C.: Government Printing Office, 1915), 16.

45. *Wallace's Farmer*, July 5, 1930, 11, reproduced and quoted in Jellison, *Entitled to Power*, 47–48; and Neth, *Preserving the Family Farm*, 230–31.

46. Mary E. Gearing, "The Conservation of the Woman on the Farm," in Texas Department of Agriculture, *Sixteenth Texas Farmers' Congress, 1913*, Texas Department of Agriculture Bulletin 33 (Austin, 1913), 70–75. See also Fink, *Agrarian Women*, 3.

47. Leffler Corbitt, "Address," 172–74.

48. Allen, *Labor of Women*, 269, 273.

49. E. M. Barrett, "Woman's Problem on the Farm," in Texas Department of Agriculture, *Proceedings of the Fifth Meeting of the Texas State Farmers' Institute, 1915*, 175–78.

50. Gearing, "Conservation of the Woman," 74; and Fink, *Agrarian Women*, 1–10. Historian George Lipsitz notes that in the 1953 film *Salt of the Earth*, based on the 1951 zinc miners' strike in Silver City, New Mexico, Ramón Quintero, a union militant, and other strikers reluctantly take over the laundry and other household chores while their wives walk the picket lines. While hanging laundry on a clothesline, Ramón tells his neighbor that the union ought to include plumbing as one of its demands, having forgotten that he scoffed at the idea when his wife first proposed it (George Lipsitz, *Rainbow at Midnight: Labor and Culture in the 1940s* [Urbana: University of Illinois Press, 1994], 293).

51. U.S. Department of Agriculture, *Domestic Needs of Farm Women*, Report 104 (Washington, D.C.: Government Printing Office, 1915), 8–15. On the importance of designing homes with women's convenience in mind, see Texas Department of Agriculture, *Eleventh Texas Farmers' Conference, 1908*, Texas Department of Agriculture Bulletin 5 (Austin, 1908), 39.

52. See, for example, Allen, *Labor of Women*, 73, 213, 216–17.

53. Ibid., 181.

54. She signed her letter, "Yours for reasonable hours and—no hens" (U.S. Department of Agriculture, *Social and Labor Needs of Farm Women*, 51).

55. Jellison, *Entitled to Power*, 4.

56. Texas Department of Agriculture, *Proceedings of the Fourth Meeting: Texas State Farmers' Institute, 1914*, Texas Department of Agriculture Bulletin 39 (Austin, 1914), 76.

57. U.S. Department of Agriculture, *Social and Labor Needs of Farm Women*, 35.

58. Ibid., 35, 40–41.

59. Data on fieldwork for the three groups can be found in Allen, *Labor of Women*, 78, 188, 223; for automobile ownership, see pp. 183, 218, 245. For a discussion of informal patterns of interaction and mutuality in rural communities during this period, see Neth, *Preserving the Family Farm*, 40–70.

60. Wehrwein, "Social Life," 53–58.

61. Ibid.; and Sharpless, "Fertile Ground," 336–41.

62. Quoted in Wehrwein, "Social Life," 60.

63. Author interview with Fidencio Durán Sr., August 2, 1994, Maxwell, Texas; and Wehrwein, "Social Life," 59. On the origins of conjunto music, see Manuel Peña, *The Texas-Mexican Conjunto: History of a Working-Class Music* (Austin: University of Texas Press, 1985).

64. Galveston *Tri-Weekly News*, June 20, 1865, quoted in *The Handbook of Texas: A Dictionary of Essential Information* (Austin: Texas State Historical Association, 1952), 1: 934. See also *Austin American-Statesman*, June 18, 1992, p. 1; and Wehrwein, "Social Life," 60.

65. Wehrwein, "Social Life," 59–60.

66. R. B. Woods, "Religious Activity," in Texas Applied Economics Club, *Southern Travis County*, 64.

67. Ibid., 68–69. On the importance of religion to rural black women, see Jones, *Labor of Love*, 102–3. See also Evelyn Brooks Higginbotham, *Righteous Discontent: The Women's Movement in the Black Baptist Church, 1880–1920* (Cambridge, Mass.: Harvard University Press, 1993).

68. U.S. Department of Agriculture, *Social and Labor Needs of Farm Women*, 51.

69. Ibid., 51–52; and Neth, *Preserving the Family Farm*, 40–70.

70. Neth, *Preserving the Family Farm*, 244–46. For a discussion of the impact of automobiles on the lives of women during the Progressive Era, see Virginia Scharff, *Taking the Wheel: Women and the Coming of the Motor Age* (New York: Free Press, 1991); and Michael L. Berger, *The Devil Wagon in God's Country: The Automobile and Social Change in Rural America, 1893–1929* (Hamden, Conn.: Archon Books, 1979).

71. Allen, *Labor of Women*, 183, 218, 245. Of the 269 Mexican families in the study, none owned its own farm. In another Texas study more than half of the farm tenants and laborers, most of whom were Mexicans, owned their own automobile (see Tom Vasey and Josiah C. Folsom, *Survey of Agricultural Labor Conditions in Karnes County, Texas*, Farm Security Administration [Washington, D.C.: U.S. Department of Agriculture, 1937], 10).

72. Allen, *Labor of Women*, 40.

73. Interview with Caldwell County superintendent of schools, n.d., no. 31–36, folder "South Central Texas," 74–187c, Taylor Papers.

74. Allen, *Labor of Women*, 219.

75. Quoted in Jellison, *Entitled to Power*, 17.

76. Allen, *Labor of Women*, 86.

77. Charles R. Schultz, "Keeping the Wolves from Their Doors and the Shirts on Their Backs: Rural Texas Women at Work, 1930–1960," paper presented at the Women and Texas History Conference, October 4, 1990, Center for American History, University of Texas at Austin.

78. Allen, *Labor of Women*, 86, 89, 246, 275; and idem, "Mexican Peon Women," 133. Distrust of white demonstration agents may also have made Mexican women reluctant to adopt canning techniques. See, for example, Joan M. Jensen, "Canning Comes to New Mexico: Women and the Agricultural Extension Service, 1914–1919," in *New Mexico Women: Intercultural Perspectives*, ed. Joan M. Jensen and Darlis A. Miller (Albuquerque: University of New Mexico Press, 1986), 201–26.

79. U.S. Department of Agriculture, *Economic Needs of Farm Women*, 30.

80. Ibid., 38.

81. U.S. Department of Agriculture, *Yearbook, 1927* (Washington, D.C.: Government Printing Office, 1928), 665–69; and C. W. Warburton to Helen W. Atwater, September 29, 1926, General Correspondence, box 1199, folder on farm women's camps, USDA RG 16.

82. U.S. Department of Agriculture, *Yearbook, 1927*, 665–69.

83. Ibid.

84. *Wallace's Farmer*, May 8, 1908, in Texas Department of Agriculture, *Yearbook, 1908*, Texas Department of Agriculture Bulletin (Austin, 1909), 85. Gender bias is, of course, inherent in such terms as *owner, craft worker, farm worker, democracy*, and *agrarianism*. For a fine overview of the intersection of gender and labor history, see Ava Baron, "Gender and Labor History: Learning from the Past, Looking to the Future," in *Work Engendered: Toward a New History of American Labor*, ed. Ava Baron (Ithaca, N.Y.: Cornell University Press, 1991), 1–46.

85. *Farm and Ranch*, November 23, 1907, in Texas Department of Agriculture, *Yearbook, 1908*, 77–80.

86. Ibid., 81.

87. Paper read before the Woman's Industrial and Educational Association at the fourth session of the Texas Farmers' Congress, in ibid., 90.

88. U.S. Department of Agriculture, *Domestic Needs of Farm Women*, 3.

89. U.S. Department of Agriculture, *Social and Labor Needs of Farm Women*, 37, 39; and Miss Amanda Stoltzfus, "Social Life in the Country," in Texas Department of Agriculture, *Proceedings of the Fifth Meeting of the Texas State Farmers' Institute, 1915*, 184.

90. Miss Amanda Stoltzfus, "Better Babies on Texas Farms," in Texas Department of Agriculture, *Seventeenth Texas Farmers' Congress, 1914*, Texas Department of Agriculture Bulletin 40 (Austin, 1914), 95.

91. Barrett, "Woman's Problem," 175–78. I have corrected the spelling of *garten* in this quotation.

92. Ibid.

93. U.S. Department of Agriculture, *Educational Needs of Farm Women*, 64; and Hagood, *Mothers of the South*, 103.

94. Gearing, "Conservation of the Woman," 71.

95. Elbert, "Women and Farming," 254.

96. Quoted in U.S. Department of Agriculture, *Yearbook of Agriculture, 1940*, 162. One farmwife observed that if a man felt "he was judged by . . . his wife's ap-

pearance rather than his driving horse, the farm woman would not today be over-worked" (U.S. Department of Agriculture, *Economic Needs of Farm Women*, 11).

97. U.S. Department of Agriculture, *Yearbook, 1914* (Washington, D.C.: Government Printing Office, 1915), 312.

98. Gearing, "Conservation of the Woman," 70–75.

99. U.S. Department of Agriculture, *Social and Labor Needs of Farm Women*, 36; and "The American Farm Woman as She Sees Herself," in U.S. Department of Agriculture, *Yearbook, 1914*, 317–18. According to one estimate, there were 200 women's clubs in Texas in 1909 (Texas Department of Agriculture, *Fifteenth Texas Farmers' Congress, 1912*, Texas Department of Agriculture Bulletin 29 [Austin, 1913], 235).

100. Address of Mrs. S. E. Buchanan to the Women's Educational and Industrial Association, *Twelfth Texas Farmers' Conference, 1909*, 310–11. Also see Theodora Martin, *The Sound of Our Own Voices: Women's Study Clubs, 1860–1910* (Boston: Beacon Press, 1987).

101. In General Correspondence, Women/Labor, box 567, USDA RG 16: E. Merritt, "Farm Work of Women in War Time," June 20, 1918, typescript, Address before the National Conference of State Leaders of Home Demonstration Work in Northern and Western States; and "Women on the Farms," *Evening Star*, May 9, 1918.

102. In General Correspondence, Women/Labor, box 567, USDA RG 16: L. J. Christie to Professor W. F. Ganong, November 15, 1918; *Washington Post*, April 11, 1918; Ethel Puffer Howes to Hon. David F. Houston, March 15, 1918; and *Women on the Land* (New York: Advisory Council of the Women's Land Army of America, 1918), copy. The Women's Land Army was approved by President Wilson and endorsed by the women's committee of the Council of National Defense, the United States Employment Service, and the Bureau of Farm Management of the Department of Agriculture.

103. Spencer Borden to Mr. Vrooman, General Correspondence, Women/Labor, box 567, USDA RG 16.

104. G. T. McElderry to Hon. R. H. Tolley, March 12, 1936, letter attached to G. T. McElderry to Hon. Cully A. Cobb, March 12, 1936, Agricultural Adjustment Administration (AAA), Subject Correspondence, box 159, USDA RG 145.

105. Allen, *Labor of Women*, 193.

106. Ibid., 107.

Chapter 7

1. Mitchell, *Mean Things Happening*, 186; and Tindall, *Emergence of the New South*, 421.

2. Frank Tannenbaum to Paul H. Appleby, December 29, 1934, General Correspondence, Cotton, box 1963, USDA RG 16. Studies of the depression include Anthony J. Badger, *The New Deal: The Depression Years, 1933–1940* (New York: Hill and Wang, 1989); Lester V. Chandler, *America's Greatest Depression, 1929–1941* (New York: Harper & Row, 1970); Broadus Mitchell, *Depression Decade: From New Era through New Deal, 1929–1941* (New York: Rinehart, 1947); David A. Shannon, *The Great Depression* (Englewood Cliffs, N.J.: Prentice Hall, 1960); Gerald D. Nash, *The American West in the Twentieth Century: A Short History of*

an Urban Oasis (Englewood Cliffs, N.J.: Prentice Hall, 1973); and David E. Hamilton, *From New Day to New Deal: American Farm Policy from Hoover to Roosevelt, 1928–1933* (Chapel Hill: University of North Carolina Press, 1991).

3. M. M. Clayton to Herbert Hoover, April 5, 1932, General Correspondence, farm relief, box 1690, USDA RG 16.

4. The best general study of the New Deal and the South is Tindall, *Emergence of the New South*. On the effects of New Deal programs on southern tenant farmers, see David E. Conrad, *The Forgotten Farmers: The Story of Sharecroppers in the New Deal* (Urbana: University of Illinois Press, 1965); Pete Daniel, "Transformation of the Rural South, 1930 to the Present," *Agricultural History* 55 (July 1981): 231–48; idem, *Breaking the Land*; Donald H. Grubbs, *Cry from the Cotton: The Southern Tenant Farmers' Union and the New Deal* (Chapel Hill: University of North Carolina Press, 1971); Paul E. Mertz, *New Deal Policy and Southern Rural Poverty* (Baton Rouge: Louisiana State University Press, 1978); and Mitchell, *Mean Things Happening*.

5. From "Making Cotton Cheaper," *Delta Experiment Station Bulletin* no. 298, quoted in Paul S. Taylor, "Power Farming and Labor Displacement, Part 2: Southwestern Oklahoma and Mississippi Delta," U.S. Department of Labor, Bureau of Labor Statistics, *Monthly Labor Review* 46 (January-June 1938): 861.

6. Testimony of J. H. Youngblood, *Interstate Migration of Destitute Citizens*, 1791–92.

7. Testimony of Mrs. Val M. Keating, *Interstate Migration of Destitute Citizens*, 1886.

8. O. D. Britton to Hon. Franklin D. Roosevelt, January 9, 1935, AAA, Subject Correspondence Files, Criticism of Administration, box 159, USDA RG 145.

9. Taylor, "Power Farming and Labor Displacement, Part 2," 856.

10. Fred Matthews, Memorandum to the President's Special Committee on Farm Tenancy, January 4, 1937, Records of the Division of Land Economics, Records Relating to the President's Special Committee on Farm Tenancy, 1936–37, box 1, USDA RG 83.

11. Paul S. Taylor, "What Shall We Do With Them," typescript, Address before the Commonwealth Club of California, San Francisco, April 15, 1938, General Correspondence, Tenancy/Title III, box 2902, USDA RG 16; and U. S. Senate, *Extracts from Hearings before a Special Committee to Investigate Unemployment and Relief*, 75th Cong., 3d sess., February 28 to April 8, 1938, in vol. 3, 84/38c, Taylor Papers. On the mechanization of cotton in Texas and elsewhere in the South, see Whatley, "Institutional Change"; Musoke, "Mechanizing Cotton Production," 347–75; and Street, *New Revolution*. See also Clarke, *Farm Productivity*, esp. 83–135, 175–94.

12. J. E. Marshall to W. D. McFarlane, August 29, 1936, General Correspondence, Tenancy, box 2439, USDA RG 16. See also J. W. Hamilton to President Franklin D. Roosevelt, April 22, 1933, General Correspondence, Farms, box 1827, USDA RG 16.

13. Grady B. Cowe, "Farm Mechanization Research in the South," *Agricultural Economics Research* 3 (January 1951), in Records Relating to Studies, Projects, and Surveys, box 33, USDA RG 83; and Fred Matthews, Memorandum to the President's Special Committee on Farm Tenancy, January 4, 1937, Records

of the Division of Land Economics, Records Relating to the President's Special Committee on Farm Tenancy, 1936–37, box 1, USDA RG 83.

14. Frank Tannenbaum to Paul H. Appleby, December 29, 1934, General Correspondence, Cotton, box 1963, USDA RG 16; Plan for Cooperation between the Rural Rehabilitation Division of the Federal Emergency Relief Administration and the Agricultural Adjustment Administration in Handling Cases of Eviction of Tenants and Sharecroppers on Account of Inability of Landlords to Finance Them, typescript, 1935, AAA, Subject Correspondence Files, Cotton / Landlord-Tenant, box 26, USDA RG 145.

15. Tindall, *Emergence of the New South*, 393; and Henry I. Richards, *Cotton and the AAA* (Washington, D.C.: Brookings Institution, 1936).

16. Conrad, *Forgotten Farmers*, 37–63; and Fite, *Cotton Fields No More*, 140–42.

17. Henry A. Wallace to H. C. Stedman, April 30, 1934, General Correspondence, Farm Relief / Cotton, box 1985, USDA RG 16; W. J. Green to D. M. Allen, July 18, 1934, Central Correspondence Files, 1933–35, AAA, box 17, USDA RG 145; and Form No. Cotton 1a, 1934 and 1935 Cotton Acreage Reduction Contract, AAA, Subject Correspondence Files, Cotton: Landlord-Tenant, box 26, USDA RG 145. The controversial paragraph 7 of the cotton contract can be found in Conrad, *Forgotten Farmers*, 58.

18. Interview with Gardner Jackson, July 28, 1959, quoted in Conrad, *Forgotten Farmers*, 81; on Jackson's dismissal and other protenant officials of the AAA, see pp. 136–53. See also Harold Hoffsommer, "The AAA and the Cropper," *Social Forces* 13 (October 1934–May 1935): 496–97. Instructions sent out by the Cotton Section of the AAA specified that "only landowners, cash tenants and managing share-tenants should be eligible for membership on the county committees" (D. P. Trent, Memorandum for the Secretary, May 18, 1934, General Correspondence, Farm Relief / Cotton, box 1985 USDA RG 16).

19. Henry A. Wallace to Ira G. Tate, July 6, 1934, General Correspondence, Farm Relief / Cotton, box 1986, USDA RG 16. Emphasis added.

20. C. C. Davis to District Agents, May 5, 1934, General Correspondence, Farm Relief / Cotton Hearings, box 1987, USDA RG 16; and Statement of the Results of Cotton Program and Its Effect upon Tenant Farmer Situation in South, typescript, May 27, 1935, AAA, Subject Correspondence Files, Cotton: Landlord-Tenant, box 26, USDA RG 145.

21. U.S. Bureau of the Census, *Thirteenth Census of the United States, 1910: Agriculture*, 877–92; and *Plantation Farming*, 1916, 16.

22. Mordecai Ezekiel to Secretary of Agriculture, Memorandum, March 5, 1934, General Correspondence, Farm Relief / Cotton, box 1985, USDA RG 16.

23. U.S. Department of Agriculture, *Participation under A.A.A. Programs, 1933–55* (Washington, D.C.: Government Printing Office, 1938), 33, in Records Relating to Studies, Projects, and Surveys, AAA Publications, box 7, USDA RG 83; George Bishop to C. A. Cobb and Henry A. Wallace, Memorandum, February 21, 1934, General Correspondence, Farm Relief / Cotton, box 1985, USDA RG 16; and R. G. Tugwell to Hon. Morris Sheppard, August 30, 1934, General Correspondence, Tenancy, box 2081, USDA RG 16.

24. Author interview with Andrés and Sabina Palomo Acosta; author interview with Fidencio Durán Sr.; and interviews with Juan Flores, March 8, 1977,

and Vicente Corpus, January 6, 1977, in Caldwell County Oral History Collection, Center for American History, University of Texas at Austin.

25. Lillie Harthcock to George Bishop, March 21, 1934, General Correspondence, Tenancy, box 2081, USDA RG 16.

26. In Central Correspondence Files, 1933–35, AAA, box 17, USDA RG 145: D. M. Allen to C. A. Cobb, July 4, 1934; C. A. Cobb to D. M. Allen, July 12, 1934; and W. J. Green to D. M. Allen, July 18, 1934.

27. Daniel, *Breaking the Land*, 99.

28. In Central Correspondence Files, AAA, box 943, USDA RG 145: Walter F. Sanders to United States Department of Agriculture, September 29, 1934; E. A. Miller to Walter F. Sanders, October 8, 1934; and G. C. Ellison to R. M. Hooker, July 10, 1935. See also W. M. McClure to Wright Patman, April 15, 1939, General Correspondence, box 3117, USDA RG 16.

29. Conrad, *Forgotten Farmers*, 133; Daniel, *Breaking the Land*, 102; and Spencer McCullough, *St. Louis Post Dispatch*, January 25, 1936, quoted in A Statement concerning Farm Tenancy Submitted to the Governor's Commission on Farm Tenancy by the Executive Council, Southern Tenant Farmers' Union, in Records of the Division of Land Economics, Records relating to the President's Special Committee on Farm Tenancy, 1936–37, box 1, USDA RG 83. See also Johnson, Embree, and Alexander, *Collapse of Cotton Tenancy*, 60–61.

30. In Central Correspondence Files, AAA, box 5, USDA RG 145: Alvin Rose to Henry A. Wallace, February 20, 1934; C. H. Alvord to George E. Adams, April 11, 1934; George E. Adams to C. H. Alvord, March 26, 1934; C. H. Alvord to Mrs. [*sic*] Alvin Rose, March 1, 1934; and George E. Adams to V. T. Kallus, March 26, 1934.

31. L. B. Archer to Henry Wallace, January 20, 1936, AAA, Subject Correspondence File, box 160, USDA RG 145.

32. George Bishop to C. A. Cobb and Henry A. Wallace, Memorandum, February 21, 1934, General Correspondence, Farm Relief / Cotton, box 1985, USDA RG 16.

33. Plan for Applying the Agricultural Adjustment Act to the 1933 Cotton Crop, June 19, 1933, General Correspondence, Farm Relief / Cotton, box 1985, USDA RG 16.

34. Anonymous to U.S. Department of Agriculture, August 10, 1935, Central Correspondence Files, AAA, box 5, USDA RG 145; and Anonimous [*sic*] to Jerome Frank, November 23, 1934, quoted in Conrad, *Forgotten Farmers*, 76.

35. Testimony of C. A. Walton, Farm Tenancy Conference, Dallas, Texas, January 4, 1937, Records of the Division of Land Economics, Records Relating to the President's Special Committee on Farm Tenancy, 1936–37, box 1, USDA RG 83.

36. M. L. Wilson to B. F. Allen, December 26, 1934, Central Correspondence Files, AAA, box 17, USDA RG 145; R. G. Tugwell to S. D. Dixon, April 25, 1934, General Correspondence, Farm Relief / Cotton, box 1985, USDA RG 16; and Conrad, *Forgotten Farmers*, 78–79.

37. See, for example, C. A. Cobb to O. H. Cross, Central Correspondence Files, AAA, box 256, USDA RG 145; and Form No. Cotton 1a, 1934 and 1935 Cotton Acreage Reduction Contract, AAA, Subject Correspondence Files, Cotton: Landlord-Tenant, box 26, USDA RG 145.

38. C. C. Davis to District Agents, May 5, 1934, General Correspondence, Farm Relief / Cotton Hearings, box 1987, USDA RG 16; D. P. Trent, Memorandum for the Secretary, May 18, 1934, and George Bishop to C. A. Cobb and Henry A. Wallace, Memorandum, February 21, 1934, General Correspondence, Farm Relief / Cotton, box 1985, USDA RG 16; and untitled, undated typescript, AAA, Subject Correspondence Files, Cotton: Landlord-Tenant, box 26, USDA RG 145.

39. L. S. Sanders to President Roosevelt, September 30, 1935, Central Correspondence Files, AAA, box 943, USDA RG 145; and E. A. Miller to Ross Montgomery, November 7, 1935, Central Correspondence Files, AAA, box 28, folder "cotton pickers," USDA RG 145.

40. B. F. Miller to Gov. James Allred, December 10, 1935, box 4–14/283, Correspondence, James Allred Papers, Texas State Library, Austin.

41. San Patricio County, USDA RG 83.

42. Rafael de la Colina to Miriam A. Ferguson, March 5, 1934, Mexican Affairs, box 301–495, Ferguson Papers.

43. Interview with Scott Randall, no. 18–611, folder "Dimmit County," 74–187c, Taylor Papers.

44. Author interview with Fidencio Durán Sr.; and author interview with Andrés and Sabina Palomo Acosta.

45. Author interview with Fidencio Durán Sr. See also Dennis Nodín Valdés, *Al Norte: Agricultural Workers in the Great Lakes Region, 1917–1970* (Austin: University of Texas Press, 1991), 51–88; and Zaragosa Vargas, *Proletarians of the North: A History of Mexican Industrial Workers in Detroit and the Midwest, 1917–1933* (Berkeley: University of California Press, 1993).

46. The Mexican government preferred the term *repatriation* to *deportation*. See McKay, "Texas Mexican Repatriation," 200–206, 232–44, 270; George C. Kiser and David Silverman, "Mexican Repatriation during the Great Depression," *Journal of Mexican American History* 3 (1973): 139–64; and Hoffman, *Unwanted Mexican Americans*.

47. D. A. Blandon, Manager, West Texas Chamber of Commerce (a report of a special meeting of the West Texas Chamber of Commerce to discuss the farm-tenancy problem in west Texas, n.d.), Records of the Division of Land Economics, Records Relating to the President's Special Committee on Farm Tenancy, 1936–37, box 1, USDA RG 83.

48. In General Correspondence, Farm Relief / Cotton, box 1986, USDA RG 16: C. B. Baldwin to W. J. Greenwood, July 7, 1934; and C. B. Baldwin to W. J. Greenwood, August 6, 1934. See also D. P. Trent, Memorandum for the Secretary, May 18, 1934, General Correspondence, Farm Relief / Cotton, box 1985, USDA RG 16; and Conrad, *Forgotten Farmers*, 115–16.

49. C. C. Davis to District Agents, May 5, 1934, General Correspondence, Farm Relief / Cotton Hearings, box 1987, USDA RG 16.

50. Ibid.; and Survey of Results of 1934–35 Cotton Adjustment Program with Particular Reference to Status of Tenants, typescript, May 5, 1934, General Correspondence, Tenancy, box 2081, USDA RG 16.

51. Ibid.

52. Daniel, *Breaking the Land*, 107.

53. Mitchell, *Mean Things Happening*, 102.

54. "The real problem," according to economist Gavin Wright (*Old South, New South: Revolutions in the Southern Economy since the Civil War* [New York: Basic Books, 1986], 230), "was not 'eviction' but simply not adding new tenancies."

55. Fuller Jones to Victor Christgau, September 1934, AAA, Central Correspondence Files, box 547, USDA RG 145.

56. See Gregory, *American Exodus*; Street, *New Revolution*, 57–58; and Joe Motheral, *Recent Trends in Land Tenure in Texas*, Texas Agricultural Experiment Station, Bulletin 641 (College Station: Agricultural and Mechanical College of Texas, 1944), 5. Payson Irwin of the Resettlement Administration wrote in 1937 that California was witnessing a record influx of sharecroppers and tenant farmers from Arkansas, Oklahoma, and Texas, where they had lost their farms. Irwin noted that native whites made up about 50 percent of the migratory workers in California, followed by Mexicans (33 percent), Filipinos (11 percent), Chinese (3 percent), and Japanese (3 percent). Payson Irwin, Memorandum on California Migratory Agricultural Labor Camps, February 6, 1937, General Correspondence, Resettlement, box 2630, USDA RG 16.

57. See chapter 5; *Interstate Migration of Destitute Citizens*, 1955; *Violations of Free Speech*, part 1, 191; and Sanders, *Farm Ownership and Tenancy*, 16.

58. Paul S. Taylor, "Plantation Agriculture in the United States: Seventeenth to Twentieth Centuries," vol. 9, 84/38c, Taylor Papers.

59. *Violations of Free Speech*, part 1, 489.

60. Testimony of J. R. Butler, Farm Tenancy Conference, Dallas, Texas, January 4, 1937, Records of the Division of Land Economics, Records Relating to the President's Special Committee on Farm Tenancy, 1936–37, box 1, USDA RG 83; and Motheral, *Land Tenure in Texas*, 5.

61. J. B. Seago to Franklin D. Roosevelt, January 10, 1936, AAA, Subject Correspondence Files, box 160, USDA RG 145; W. T. Rogers to Henry A. Wallace, June 22, 1935, Subject Correspondence Files, AAA, box 922, USDA RG 145; and Mertz, *New Deal Policy*, 45–46.

62. Tindall, *Emergence of the New South*, 548; and Irene Ledesma, "New Deal Public Works Programs and Mexican-Americans in McAllen, Texas, 1933–36" (M.A. thesis, University of Texas at Edinburg, 1977).

63. Gabbard's assumptions about Mexicans and African Americans were not supported by at least one relief survey conducted in 1934 in San Patricio County, where Mexicans, both native-born and foreign-born, constituted 52 percent of the total population of the county while constituting only 27.3 percent of the relief cases, compared with 72.7 percent for whites on relief. (Only ten black families in the county were on relief and therefore were not included in the survey; blacks constituted 2.1 percent of the county's total population.) See L. P. Gabbard to Dr. A. B. Cox, October 20, 1934, AAA, Central Correspondence Files, box 1073, USDA RG 145; San Patricio County, USDA RG 83; and Statement of the Results of Cotton Program and Its Effect upon Tenant Farmer Situation in South, typescript, May 27, 1935, AAA, Subject Correspondence Files, Cotton: Landlord-Tenant, box 26, USDA RG 145.

64. Gabbard, *Survey of Rockwall County*, 142.

65. Quoted in Ledesma, "New Deal Public Works Programs," 54.

66. San Patricio County, USDA RG 83; D. P. Trent, Memorandum for the Secretary, May 18, 1934, General Correspondence, Farm Relief / Cotton, box 1985, USDA RG 16; Sam L. Crow to James A. Farley, January 28, 1936, General Correspondence, Cotton-Criticism, box 2336, USDA RG 16; "Farm labor and the WPA," typescript, n.d., Division of Land Economics, Records of the Land Tenure Section, Texas Tenancy Study, box 23, USDA RG 83; and Ledesma, "New Deal Public Works Programs," 52–53.

67. Dan Dove, representative of tenant farmers, Limestone County, Texas, statement to the committee on tenancy, January 4, 1937, Records of the Division of Land Economics, Records Relating to the President's Special Committee on Farm Tenancy, 1936–37, box 1, USDA RG 83.

68. Tenant Purchase Program, typescript, November 1939, Division of Land Economics, Records of the Land Tenure Section, FSA Reports and Information, box 6, USDA RG 83.

69. L. C. Gray to Henry A. Wallace, Memorandum, January 14, 1935, General Correspondence, Cotton, box 1963, USDA RG 16; and Horace Hamilton, "The Status and Future of Farm Tenantry in the South," paper read before the Southern Economic Association, Duke University, Records of the Division of Land Economics, Records Relating to the President's Special Committee on Farm Tenancy, 1936–37, box 4, USDA RG 83.

70. David E. Coffman to Dr. L. C. Gray, January 5, 1937, Records of the Division of Land Economics, Records Relating to the President's Special Committee on Farm Tenancy, 1936–37, box 7, USDA RG 83.

71. Davis, *White Scourge*, ix.

72. Tenant Purchase Program, typescript, November 1939, Division of Land Economics, Records of the Land Tenure Section, FSA Reports and Information, box 6, USDA RG 83; and Report No. 11, Tenant Purchase Division, General Correspondence, box 3117, USDA RG 16.

73. In Records of the Division of Land Economics, Records Relating to the President's Special Committee on Farm Tenancy, 1936–37, box 6, USDA RG 83: William E. Turner to Henry Wallace, January 5, 1937; and John Morris to President Roosevelt, January 9, 1937. In General Correspondence, Tenancy, box 2662, USDA RG 16: Chester Shoemaker to R. E. Thomason, August 11, 1937; James Monroe Smith to Morris Sheppard, August 11, 1937; and C. E. Flinn to George Mahon, August 10, 1937.

74. Farmers' Educational and Co-operative Union of American, Statement on Farm Tenancy, n.d., Records of the Division of Land Economics, Records Relating to the President's Special Committee on Farm Tenancy, 1936–37, box 1, USDA RG 83; and Mertz, *New Deal Policy*, 140–41. The history of the Farmers' Educational and Co-operative Union is recounted in Theodore Saloutos, *Farmer Movements in the South, 1865–1933*, University of California Publications in History 64 (Berkeley: University of California Press, 1960), 184–212 (quotation on p. 212); and Hunt, *Farmer Movements in the Southwest*, 41–143.

75. Paul S. Taylor and Clark Kerr, "Uprisings on the Farms," *Survey Graphic*, January, 1935, 19–22, 44; Paul S. Taylor, "Labor in Agriculture," typescript, n.d., p. 12, box 3, 84/38c, Taylor papers.

Chapter 8

1. Resolutions Adopted by Tenancy Committee of the Texas Agricultural Workers Association, Austin, Texas, February 15, 1940, Division of Land Economics, Records of the Land Tenure Section, Correspondence, box 23, USDA RG 83.

2. Jamieson, *Labor Unionism*, 298–99, 306–7.

3. Ibid., 30, 36.

4. Brannen, *Relation of Land Tenure to Plantation Organization*, 9.

5. On the development of plantation agriculture in Arkansas, see Jeannie Whayne, "Creation of a Plantation System in the Arkansas Delta in the Twentieth Century," *Agricultural History* 66 (Winter 1992): 63–84; on nonplantation white tenants in Texas, see Foley, "New South," 144–225.

6. On radical rural and urban unionizing among Communist blacks and whites in Alabama, see Kelley's fine study, *Hammer and Hoe*, 34–56. See also Rosengarten, *All God's Dangers*, 97–343, passim; and Jamieson, *Labor Unionism*, 289–302.

7. Jamieson, *Labor Unionism*, 7.

8. After the highly publicized roadside demonstration by Missouri sharecroppers in 1939, Secretary of Agriculture Henry Wallace and the AAA finally acknowledged that its cotton-reduction program had contributed to the shift from sharecropper to wage labor but hoped to "correct any tendency" in the program to "unduly accelerate the change from sharecropper to day laborer" (Henry A. Wallace to Thad Snow, March 18, 1939, General Correspondence, Cotton, box 3044, USDA RG 16). See also *St. Louis Post Dispatch*, March 5, 1939, in General Correspondence, Cotton, box 3044, USDA RG 16; Louis Cantor, *A Prologue to the Protest Movement: The Missouri Sharecropper Roadside Demonstration of 1939* (Durham, N.C.: Duke University Press, 1969); and Grubbs, *Cry from the Cotton*, 180–83.

9. Valdés, *Al Norte*, 51–88; and Vargas, *Proletarians of the North*.

10. H. L. Mitchell, Report to the Third Annual Convention, Membership Report, January 1937, reel 4, Southern Tenant Farmers' Union, Mircrofilm Collection of the STFU Papers at the Southern Historical Collection, University of North Carolina (hereafter cited as STFU Papers); and Jamieson, *Labor Unionism*, 264, 302–3, 314.

11. Texas Agricultural Experiment Station, *Cotton Production Practices in the High Plains Area, 1947*, Miscellaneous Publication 37, Records Relating to Studies, Projects and Surveys, Projects A–1–20–25, box 32, USDA RG 83. In 1934 Dawson County, in the lower Panhandle, had 91.4 percent of its total acreage in farmlands, whereas in 1910 the county was primarily a vast cattle range with only a few scattered farms. Cotton acreage increased from zero percent of the total acreage in 1900 to 67.7 percent in 1930, whereas cattle ranches decreased to 18.4 percent in 1930 (Report on Rural Problem Area, Western Cotton Growing, Dawson County, Texas, September 8, 1934, Division of Farm Population and Rural Life, Reports on Rural Problem Areas, box 1, County Reports, 1934–35, USDA RG 83).

12. In STFU Papers: Fred Matthews, Memorandum to the President's Special Committee on Farm Tenancy, Dallas, Texas, January 4, 1936, reel 4; Fred Matthews to Gertrude Orendorff, January 7, 1936, reel 1; and Matthews to Orendorff, February 17, 1936, reel 1.

13. In STFU Papers: J. R. Butler to H. L. Mitchell, October 30, 1935, reel 1; and Fred Matthews to H. L. Mitchell, February 4, 1937, reel 4. When Taft Ranch management refused to meet Mexican workers' demands for higher wages, a number of Mexicans walked off to seek work elsewhere. See testimony of Charles Alvord, *Final Report and Testimony* 10: 9218.

14. See chapter 4. The segregated locals of the STFU in Texas represented an improvement over the refusal of the Renters' Union and Land League to organize black tenants. The BTW was the only truly biracial union to emerge in Texas, forged mainly through the progressive racial ideology of the IWW, with whom the BTW affiliated. See Green, "Brotherhood of Timber Workers," 161–200. See also David Roediger's excellent analysis of the discourse of biracial unionism, "Gaining a Hearing," 127–80.

15. In STFU Papers: Fred Matthews, Circular Letter, July 12, 1936, reel 2; and Fred Matthews to H. L. Mitchell, September 27, 1936, reel 3. Thirty-one Anglos joined the white local, and twelve blacks formed their own local under Charles Deo.

16. In STFU Papers: Fred Matthews, Circular Letter, July 12, 1936, reel 2; Fred Matthews to Mr. Butler, July 27, 1936, reel 2; H. L. Mitchell to Charles Deo, December 31, 1936, reel 3; H. L. Mitchell to Donald Henderson, October 6, 1937, reel 5; and Aaron Levenstein to *New York Post*, January 17, 1937, reel 4 (I would like to thank Stuart Rockoff for bringing this citation to my attention). See also Mitchell, *Mean Things Happening*, 134.

17. F. R. Belton and H. L. Mitchell, "Land and Liberty for Mexican Farmers: Report of the STFU Delegation to Laguna Conference, Torreón, Coahuila, Mexico," typescript, July 1939, Benson Latin American Collection, University of Texas at Austin.

18. In STFU Papers: Fred Matthews to Donald Henderson, June 13, 1937, reel 4; and Fred Matthews, Circular Letter, July 12, 1936, reel 2.

19. Ibid.

20. G. P. Terry to STFU, February 22, 1938, reel 7, STFU Papers. On the pecan shellers' strike, see Zaragosa Vargas, "Tejana Radical: Emma Tenayuca and the San Antonio Labor Movement," *Pacific Historical Review* (forthcoming); Jamieson, *Labor Unionism*, 278–81; and Julia Kirk Blackwelder, *Women of the Depression: Caste and Culture in San Antonio, 1929–1939* (College Station: Texas A&M University Press, 1984), 140–51.

21. In STFU Papers: J. E. Clayton to H. L. Mitchell, March 9, 1938, reel 7; J. E. Clayton to H. L. Mitchell, April 15, 1938, reel 8; G. P. Terry to Southern Tenant Farmers' Union, December 24, 1937, reel 5; and Barney Egan to H. L. Mitchell, December 17, 1937, reel 5.

22. In STFU Papers: J. E. Clayton to H. L. Mitchell, December 28, 1937, reel 5; H. L. Mitchell to J. E. Clayton, March 25, 1938, reel 7; and H. L. Mitchell to J. E. Clayton, April 5, 1938, reel 8.

23. Mitchell to Egan, June 9, 1938, reel 8, STFU Papers.

24. Interview with J. R. Butler in Leah Wise and Sue Thrasher, "The Southern Tenant Farmers' Union," in *Working Lives: The "Southern Exposure" History of Labor in the South*, ed. Marc S. Miller (New York: Pantheon Books, 1980), 128.

25. Fred Matthews to H. L. Mitchell, November 9, 1937, reel 5, STFU Papers.

26. Mitchell, *Mean Things Happening*, 107. Mitchell also said that union lo-

cals could admit small landowners "who are in the same shape as croppers." The only owner who would be in the same shape as a sharecropper—that is, working for wages—would be a former owner.

27. On the role of UCAPAWA in farm-labor unionism in the late 1930s and its conflict with the STFU, see Jamieson, *Labor Unionism*, 164–68, 174–79, 320–26; Mitchell, *Mean Things Happening*, 155–56; Kelley, *Hammer and Hoe*, 170–71; and Grubbs, *Cry from the Cotton*. See also Ruiz, *Cannery Women*; and Walter J. Stein, *California and the Dust Bowl Migration* (Westport, Conn.: Greenwood Press, 1973). Mitchell is quoted in Green, *Grass-Roots Socialism*, 426.

28. Mitchell, *Mean Things Happening*, 155–56; and in STFU Papers: J. R. Butler to H. L. Mitchell, October 30, 1935, reel 1; Fred Matthews to H. L. Mitchell, February 4, 1937, reel 4; Fred Matthews to Donald Henderson, June 13, 1937, reel 4; and Fred Matthews, Circular Letter, July 12, 1936, reel 2. UCAPAWA, which organized cannery, packing, and agricultural workers, was considerably more successful in Texas than was the STFU, particularly in south Texas, where agricultural workers, mostly Mexicans, vastly outnumbered tenant farmers. See Victor B. Nelson-Cisneros, "UCAPAWA Organizing Activities in Texas, 1935–1970," *Aztlán* 9 (Spring-Summer-Fall 1978), 71–84.

29. Green, *Grass-Roots Socialism*, 426–30. On the DiGiorgio Strike, see Ernesto Galarza, *Farm Workers and Agri-business in California, 1947–1960* (Notre Dame, Ind.: University of Notre Dame Press, 1977), 98–117. On César Chávez, see Mark Day, *Forty Acres: César Chávez and the Farm Workers* (New York: Praeger, 1971); Peter Matthiessen, *Sal Si Puedes: César Chávez and the New American Revolution* (New York: Random House, 1973); Ronald Taylor, *Chávez and the Farm Workers* (Boston: Beacon Press, 1975); and Richard Griswold del Castillo and Richard A. García, *César Chávez: A Triumph of Spirit* (Norman: University of Oklahoma Press, 1995).

30. Works on the Bracero Program include Galarza, *Merchants of Labor*; Craig, *Bracero Program*; Coalson, *Migratory Farm Labor System*; Robert J. Thomas, *Citizenship, Gender, and Work: Social Organization of Industrial Agriculture* (Berkeley: University of California Press, 1985), 62–73; and Calavita, *Inside the State*.

31. "Farm Tenantry," *The Rebel*, October 30, 1915, 2; Mitchell, *Mean Things Happening*, 49, 202, 212, 290; Kirby, *Rural Worlds Lost*; Jamieson, *Labor Unionism*, 323–24; and U.S. Department of Agriculture, *Yearbook of Agriculture, 1940*, 144–46. The slogan, "Land for the Landless and Homes for the Homeless," appeared in *The Rebel*, November 1, 1913. See chapter 4 on the failure of biracial unionism and the Socialist Party in Texas.

32. Interview with George Stith, in Wise and Thrasher, "Southern Tenant Farmers' Union," 132; and Mitchell, *Mean Things Happening*, 113–14.

33. Interview with George Stith, in Wise and Thrasher, "Southern Tenant Farmers' Union," 132.

34. Ibid. Mitchell (*Mean Things Happening*, 119) recalled a slightly different version, in which the waiter at first refused to serve her: The restaurant owner approached her table and apologized to McGee, explaining that the waiter could not have known that she was "a visitor from a foreign land." In Washington, D.C., it was often possible for blacks to pass—or be passed—as "foreigners with dark skins" from one of the city's many embassies and therefore were not subject to the rigid segregation that otherwise prevailed in the capital city.

35. Quoted in ibid., 120–21; examples of white tenant farmer women's sometimes contentious relations with their husbands can be found in Hagood, *Mothers of the South*, 164–65.

36. On California cotton strikes in the 1930s, see Weber, *Dark Sweat, White Gold*; McWilliams, *Factories in the Field*, 48–65, 81–102, 185–99; Guerin-Gonzales, *Mexican Workers*, 11–24; and Daniel, *Bitter Harvest*, 40–70. See also testimony of various agricultural specialists in *Violations of Free Speech*, parts 1–3.

37. Quoted in John Steinbeck, *The Harvest Gypsies: On the Road to the Grapes of Wrath* (1936; reprint, Berkeley, Calif.: Heyday Books, 1988), xi–xii. For a fine study of Okie culture in California, see Gregory, *American Exodus*.

38. Weber, *Dark Sweat, White Gold*, 190; and Stein, *Dust Bowl Migration*, 258.

39. Stein, *Dust Bowl Migration*, 256; and Weber, *Dark Sweat, White Gold*, 193. UCAPAWA's failure in California must also be attributed to the union-busting tactics of California growers' associations, which John Steinbeck and Carey McWilliams called "farm fascism." On the failure to organize the Okies, see Stein, *Dust Bowl Migration*, 243–78.

40. *Violations of Free Speech*, 171–77.

41. Paul S. Taylor, "Migratory Farm Labor in the United States," *Monthly Labor Review*, Serial No. R. 530 (March 1937), 4, in box 1, 84/38c, Taylor Papers.

42. "The Struggle of Civil Liberty on the Land: The Story of the Recent Struggles of Land-owning Farmers, of Share-Croppers, Tenants and Farm Laborers for the Right to Organize, Strike, and Picket," American Civil Liberties Union, n.d., box 6, C–B893, Taylor Papers; Kelley, *Hammer and Hoe*, 34–56; Rosengarten, *All God's Dangers*, 97–343, passim; and Jamieson, *Labor Unionism*, 289–302. Carl E. Bailey, governor of Arkansas, claimed that despite the "lurid stories" surrounding the violations of sharecroppers' civil rights in his state, these "sordid" incidents were "of more infrequent occurrence than total eclipses of the sun" (*Congressional Record*, 75th Cong., 1st sess., "Farm Tenancy in the United States," in Records of the Division of Statistical and Historical Research, General Correspondence, box 53, USDA RG 83).

43. More than 450 Mexican agricultural workers in Crystal City, Texas, formed the Catholic Workers' Union in 1930 and conducted a successful strike to raise wages, end child labor, and hire only local laborers. In 1933 a diverse group of Mexican laborers that included carpenters and miners as well as agricultural workers formed the Asociación de Jornaleros and in 1935 led a strike of more than 1,200 onion workers. See Jamieson, *Labor Unionism*, 272–75; and Coalson, *Migratory Farm Labor System*, 61–63. For a comprehensive study of Mexican workers in south Texas from 1900 to 1930, see Zamora, *Mexican Worker in Texas*.

44. Victor B. Nelson-Cisneros, "La clase trabajadora en Tejas, 1920–1940," *Aztlán* 6 (Summer 1975): 239–65; and idem, "UCAPAWA Organizing Activities," 71–85.

45. Zamora, *Mexican Worker in Texas*, 205. Taft management mounted a machine gun on a wagon and organized vigilante clubs on the ranch to guard against Mexican uprisings and strikes. See Stephens, *Taft Ranch*, 198–99.

46. Hunt, *Farmer Movements in the Southwest*; and Jamieson, *Labor Unionism*, 270–81.

47. Taylor and Kerr, "Uprisings on the Farms," 19–22, 44; and Taylor, "Labor in Agriculture," typescript, n.d., p. 12, box 3, 84/38c, Taylor Papers.

48. On the politics of the KKK in Texas, see Brown, *Hood, Bonnet, and Little Brown Jug*, 49–87; Alexander, *Ku Klux Klan in the Southwest*; and Bentley, "Ku Klux Klan in Texas," 11–21.

49. See Caldwell, *Tobacco Road*; and idem, *God's Little Acre* (1933; reprint, Savannah, Ga.: Beehive Press, 1977).

Conclusion

1. *Austin American-Statesman*, June 11, 1996, 1, 6.

2. Holman, "Land Question" [draft], 20 (first quotation), 15 (second quotation).

3. Coalson, *Migratory Farm Labor System*, 124.

4. See Craig, *Bracero Program*; Coalson, *Migratory Farm Labor System*; and Calavita, *Inside the State*.

5. Quoted in Coalson, *Migratory Farm Labor System*, 128.

6. "Caucasian Race—Equal Privileges," H.C.R. No. 105, April 15, 1943, in *General and Special Laws of the State of Texas, Passed by the Regular Session of the Forty-Eighth Legislature, Austin, Convened January 12, 1943, and Adjourned May 11, 1943* (Austin: State of Texas, 1943).

7. Coalson, *Migratory Farm Labor System*, 176; Craig, *Bracero Program*, 50–51; O. M. Scruggs, "Texas and the Bracero Program, 1942–1947," *Pacific Historical Review* 32 (August 1962): 251–64; idem, "The United States, Mexico, and the Wetbacks," *Pacific Historical Review* 30 (May 1961): 149–64; "Texas, Good Neighbor?" *Southwestern Social Science Quarterly* 43 (September 1962): 118–25; and Johnny M. McCain, "Texas and the Mexican Labor Question, 1942–1947," *Southwestern Historical Quarterly* 85 (July 1981): 45–64.

8. Daniel, "Transformation of the Rural South," 245.

9. Craig, *Bracero Program*, 11; and Mario Barrera, *Race and Class in the Southwest: A Theory of Racial Inequality* (Notre Dame, Ind.: University of Notre Dame Press, 1979), 118.

10. See, for example, the testimony of Texas Congressman Joseph J. Mansfield in *Seasonal Agricultural Laborers*, 214.

11. Taylor, *American-Mexican Frontier*, 191.

12. Interview with Anna Moore Schwein, no. 106–696, folder "Nueces County," 74–187c, Taylor Papers.

13. Interview with H. H. Schultz, U.S. Department of Agriculture, Austin, Texas, no. 192–363, folder "American Government Officials," 74–187c, Taylor Papers. When whites married Mexicans, especially of the "peon" class (dark-skinned), they were said to have descended "to the level of the Mexicans" (interview with Mr. Martin, county agent, El Paso County, Texas, no. 85–90, folder "Along Rio Grande," 74–187c, Taylor Papers). For a fine study of miscegenation law and racial ideology, see Pascoe, "Miscegenation Law," 44–69.

14. Interview with Judge Wildenthal, no. 54–644, folder "Dimmit County," 74–187c, Taylor Papers.

15. Interview with John Asker, no. 42–634, folder "Dimmit County," 74–187c, Taylor Papers; and interview with Bob Lemmons, no. 246–417, folder "Dimmit County," 74–187c, Taylor Papers. Asker told Taylor that he liked Mexicans but added, "You can't make a rose out of an onion."

16. Studies of the Mexican American generation include Mario T. García, *Mexican Americans: Leadership, Ideology, & Identity, 1930–1960* (New Haven, Conn.: Yale University Press, 1989); George J. Sánchez, *Becoming Mexican American: Ethnicity, Culture and Identity in Chicano Los Angeles, 1900–1945* (New York: Oxford University Press, 1993); Gutiérrez, *Walls and Mirrors*; and Guadalupe San Miguel Jr., *"Let All of Them Take Heed": Mexican Americans and the Campaign for Educational Equality in Texas, 1910–1981* (Austin: University of Texas Press, 1987). On LULAC and the politics of Mexican American identity, see Benjamin Márquez, *LULAC: The Evolution of a Mexican American Political Organization* (Austin: University of Texas Press, 1993). See also Cynthia E. Orozco, "The Origins of the League of Latin American Citizens (LULAC) and the Mexican American Civil Rights Movement in Texas with an Analysis of Women's Political Participation in a Gendered Context, 1910–1929" (Ph.D. diss., University of California, Los Angeles, 1993).

17. Cornel West, "The New Cultural Politics of Difference," in *Out There: Marginalization and Contemporary Cultures*, ed. Russell Ferguson and others (Cambridge, Mass.: MIT Press, 1990), 29.

18. Quoted in Taylor, *American-Mexican Frontier*, 268.

19. García, "Mexican Americans and the Politics of Citizenship," 188–89; Márquez, *LULAC*, 32–33; and Gary A. Greenfield and Don B. Kates Jr., "Mexican Americans, Racial Discrimination, and the Civil Rights Act of 1866," *California Law Review* 63 (January 1975): 700.

20. Cleofas Calleros, quoted in García, "Politics of Citizenship," 191–92.

21. Quoted in Márquez, *LULAC*, 32–33.

22. Teresa Córdova et al., eds. *Chicana Voices: Intersections of Class, Race, and Gender* (1986; reprint, Albuquerque: University of New Mexico Press, 1993), 38. See also Vargas, "Tejana Radical"; and Blackwelder, *Women of the Depression*, 144–49.

23. Córdova et al., *Chicana Voices*, 38.

24. Lipsitz, "Possessive Investment in Whiteness," 369–87.

25. Limerick, *Legacy of Conquest*, 27.

26. The controversy surrounding the 1991 exhibit on western art, "The West as America," illustrates the fervor of that resistance. See William H. Truettner, ed., *The West as America: Reinterpreting Images of the Frontier, 1820–1920* (Washington, D.C.: Smithsonian Institution Press, 1991). On the mythology of the West, see the classic study by Henry Nash Smith, *Virgin Land: The American West and Symbol and Myth* (1950; reprint, Cambridge, Mass.: Harvard University Press, 1978).

27. House Committee on Immigration and Naturalization, *Immigration from Countries of the Western Hemisphere*, 1930, 619.

28. Roediger, *Abolition of Whiteness*, 13.

Bibliography

Primary Sources

ARCHIVAL AND MANUSCRIPT COLLECTIONS

Ruth Allen Papers, Texas Labor Archives, University of Texas at Arlington.

Ruth Allen Papers, 1943–1973, Center for American History, University of Texas at Austin.

Ruth Allen, Labor Movements in Texas Papers, Center for American History, University of Texas at Austin.

James Allred Papers, Texas State Library, Archives Division, Austin.

Bureau of Refugees, Freedmen, and Abandoned Land, Record Group 105, National Archives, Washington, D.C.

Albert S. Burleson Papers, Center for American History, University of Texas at Austin.

Coleman-Fulton Pasture Company Records (Taft Ranch), Center for American History, University of Texas at Austin.

George Clifton Edwards Papers, Texas Labor Archives, University of Texas at Arlington.

James Ferguson Papers, Texas State Library, Archives Division, Austin.

Miriam A. Ferguson Papers, Texas State Library, Archives Division, Austin.

Food, Tobacco, Agricultural, and Allied Workers Union of America–Congress of Industrial Organizations: Texas Locals, Texas Labor Archives, University of Texas at Arlington.

Thomas A. Hickey Papers, Center for American History, University of Texas at Austin.

Mance Libscomb Papers, Center for American History, University of Texas at Austin.

LULAC Collection, Benson Latin American Collection, University of Texas at Austin.

Frank J. and Dorothy Redus Robinson Papers, Center for American History, University of Texas at Austin.

Jacob I. Rodríguez Papers, LULAC Collection, Benson Latin American Collection, University of Texas at Austin.

George I. Sánchez Papers, Benson Latin American Collection, University of Texas at Austin.

Southern Tenant Farmers' Union, Mircrofilm Collection of the STFU Papers at the Southern Historical Collection, University of North Carolina; duplicates at the University of Texas at Austin.

Santiago Tafolla Papers, Benson Latin American Collection, University of Texas at Austin.

Paul S. Taylor Collection, Bancroft Library, Berkeley, California.

Texas War Records Collection, Center for American History, University of Texas at Austin.

Travis County Court Records, Civil Cases, Travis County Court House, Austin, Texas.

U.S. Commission on Industrial Relations, Records of the Division of Research and Investigation, Department of Labor, Record Group 174, National Archives, Washington, D.C.

U.S. Commission on Industrial Relations, Records of the Division of Research and Investigation, State Historical Society of Wisconsin, Madison.

U.S. Department of Agriculture, Agricultural Stabilization and Conservation Service, Record Group 145, National Archives, Washington, D.C.

U.S. Department of Agriculture, Bureau of Agricultural Economics, Record Group 83, National Archives, Washington, D.C.

U.S. Department of Agriculture, Record Group 16, National Archives, Washington, D.C.

U.S. Immigration and Naturalization Records, Record Group 85, National Archives, Washington, D.C.

May Mathis Green Watson Papers, Center for American History, University of Texas at Austin.

Oliver Douglas Weeks Papers, LULAC Collection, Benson Latin American Collection, University of Texas at Austin.

GOVERNMENT DOCUMENTS, REPORTS, BULLETINS, AND OTHER PRIMARY SOURCES

Allen, Ruth. *The Labor of Women in the Production of Cotton.* University of Texas Bulletin 3134. Austin: University of Texas, 1931.

Angelasto, A. M., C. B. Doyle, G. S. Meloy, and O. C. Stine. "The Cotton Situation." In U.S. Department of Agriculture, *Yearbook, 1921.* Washington, D.C.: Government Printing Office, 1922.

Austin, Charles Burgess, and George S. Wehrwein. *Co-operation in Agriculture, Marketing, and Rural Credit.* Division of Public Welfare, Extension Series 60. University of Texas Bulletin 355. Austin: University of Texas, 1914.

Azadian, Dee. *The Earth Has No Sorrow.* Oral History. Caldwell County, Tex.: Voluntary Action Center of Caldwell County, 1977.

Belton, F. R., and H. L. Mitchell. "Land and Liberty for Mexican Farmers: Report of the STFU Delegation to Laguna Conference, Torreón, Coahuila, Mexico." Typescript, July 1939. Benson Latin American Collection, University of Texas at Austin.

Biggers, Don H. *From Cattle Range to Cotton Patch*. Reprint, Abilene, Tex.: Abilene Printing, circa 1908. Micropublished in *Western Americana: Frontier History of the Trans-Mississippi West, 1550–1900*. New Haven, Conn.: Research Publications, 1975. Microfilm 512, reel 54.

Bonnen, C. A., B. H. Thibodeaux, and J. J. Criswell. *An Economic Study of Farm Organization in the Piney Woods Farming Area of Texas*. Texas Agricultural Experiment Station Bulletin 453. College Station: Agricultural and Mechanical College of Texas, 1932.

Brannen, C. O. *Relation of Land Tenure to Plantation Organization*. U.S. Department of Agriculture Bulletin 1269. Washington, D.C.: Government Printing Office, 1924.

"Caucasian Race—Equal Privileges." H.C.R. No. 115, April 15, 1943. In *General and Special Laws of the State of Texas, Passed by the Regular Session of the Forty-Eighth Legislature, Austin, Convened January 12, 1943, and Adjourned May 11, 1943*. Austin: State of Texas, 1943.

Clark, Victor S. "Mexican Labor in the United States." *Bulletin of the Bureau of Labor*, no. 78 (September 1908): 466–522.

Commissioner's Court Minutes, 1860, Refugio County. Reel 1012469, Local Records Division, Texas State Library, Austin.

Cox, James. *Historical and Biographical Record of the Cattle Industry and the Cattlemen of Texas and Adjacent Territory*. 1895; reprint, New York: Antiquarian Press, 1959.

Davis, Edward Everett. *A Report on Illiteracy in Texas*. University of Texas Bulletin 2328. Austin: University of Texas, 1923.

———. *A Study of Rural Schools in Karnes County*. University of Texas Bulletin 2246. Austin: University of Texas, 1922.

———. *A Study of Rural Schools in Travis County, Texas*. University of Texas Bulletin 67. Austin: University of Texas, 1916.

———. *A Study of Rural Schools in Williamson County*. University of Texas Bulletin 2238. Austin: University of Texas, 1922.

Division of Public Welfare, Department of Extension. *Studies in Farm Tenancy in Texas*. With chapters by E. V. White and William E. Leonard. University of Texas Bulletin 21. Austin: University of Texas, 1915.

Farm Ownership and Tenancy in the Black Prairie of Texas. U.S. Department of Agriculture Bulletin 1068. Washington, D.C.: Government Printing Office, 1922.

Gabbard, L. P. *An Agricultural Economic Survey of Rockwall County, Texas: A Typical Blackland Cotton Farming Area*. Texas Agricultural Experiment Station Bulletin 327. College Station: Agricultural and Mechanical College of Texas, 1925.

Gabbard, L. P., and F. R. Jones. *Large-Scale Cotton Production in Texas*. Texas Agricultural Experiment Station Bulletin 362. College Station: Agricultural and Mechanical College of Texas, 1927.

Gabbard, L. P., and H. E. Rea. *Cotton Production in Texas*. Texas Agricultural Experiment Station Circular 39. College Station: Agricultural and Mechanical College of Texas, 1926.

Gabbard, L. P., J. B. Hutson, and T. L. Gaston Jr. *Systems of Farming for the Black Waxy Prairie Belt of Texas*. Texas Agricultural Experiment Station Bulletin 395. College Station: Agricultural and Mechanical College of Texas, 1929.

Goldenweiser, E. A., and Leon E. Truesdell. *Farm Tenancy in the United States: An Analysis of the Results of the 1920 Census Relative to Farms Classified by Tenure, Supplemented by Pertinent Data from Other Sources*. U.S. Bureau of the Census, Census Monograph 4. Washington, D.C.: Government Printing Office, 1924.

Gray, L. C., Charles L. Stewart, Howard A. Turner, J. T. Sanders, and W. J. Spillman. "Farm Ownership and Tenancy." In U.S. Department of Agriculture, *Yearbook, 1923*. Washington, D.C.: Government Printing Office, 1924.

Hammond, M. B. *The Cotton Industry: An Essay in American Economic History*. American Economic Association Publications, n.s., 1. New York: Macmillan, for the American Economic Association, 1897.

Hawthorne, H. W. *The Family Living from the Farm*. U.S. Department of Agriculture Bulletin 1338. Washington, D.C.: Government Printing Office, 1925.

King, Edward. *Texas, 1874: An Eyewitness Account of Conditions in Post-Reconstruction Texas*. 1875; reprint, Houston: Cordovan Press, 1974.

Kinsman, C. D. *An Appraisal of Power Used on Farms in the United States*. U.S. Department of Agriculture Bulletin 1348. Washington, D.C.: Government Printing Office, 1925.

Lee, V. P. *Short Term Farm Credit in Texas*. Texas Agricultural Experiment Station Bulletin 351. College Station: Agricultural and Mechanical College of Texas, 1927.

Menefee, Sheldon C. "Mexican Migratory Workers of South Texas." In *Migratory Workers of the Southwest*. U.S. Work Projects Administration, Division of Research. 1941; reprint, Westport, Conn.: Greenwood Press, 1978.

Miller, Susan G. *Sixty Years in the Nueces Valley, 1870–1930*. San Antonio: Naylor, 1930.

Moorhouse, L. A., and M. R. Cooper. *The Cost of Producing Cotton*. U.S. Department of Agriculture Bulletin 896. Washington, D.C.: Government Printing Office, 1920.

National Council concerning Mexicans and Spanish-Americans in the United States. *Report of Commission on International and Interracial Factors in the Problem of Mexicans in the United States*. El Paso: Home Missions Council, 1926.

——. *A Study of Social and Economic Factors Relating to Spanish-Speaking People in the United States*. Report by the Commission on Social and Economic Factors. El Paso: Home Missions Council, 1926.

Origins and Problems of Texas Migratory Farm Labor. A brief prepared by the Farm Placement Service Division of the Texas State Employment Service. Austin, 1940.

Parisot, Pierre F. *The Reminiscences of a Texas Missionary*. San Antonio, 1899.

Peteet, Walton. *Farming Credit in Texas*. Texas Agricultural Experiment Station, Extension Service Bulletin B–34. College Station: Agricultural and Mechanical College of Texas, 1917.

Sanders, Jesse Thomas. *Farm Ownership and Tenancy in the Black Prairie of Texas*. U.S. Department of Agriculture Bulletin 1068. Washington, D.C.: Government Printing Office, 1922.

Sanderson, Ezra Dwight. *A Statistical Study of the Decrease in the Texas Cotton Crop Due to the Mexican Cotton Boll Weevil, and the Cotton Acreage of Texas, 1899 to 1904 Inclusive*. Austin: Department of Agriculture, Insurance, Statistics and History, 1905.

Texas Almanac and State Industrial Guide for 1904. N.p.: Galveston-Dallas News, 1904.

Texas Applied Economics Club. *Social and Economic Survey of Southern Travis County, Texas*. Edited by Lewis H. Haney and George S. Wehrwein. University of Texas Bulletin 65. Austin: University of Texas, 1916.

Texas Bureau of Labor Statistics. *Biennial Reports*, 1909–1930.

Texas Department of Agriculture. *Eleventh Texas Farmers' Congress, 1908*. Texas Department of Agriculture Bulletin 5. Austin, 1908.

———. *Fifteenth Texas Farmers' Congress, 1912*. Texas Department of Agriculture Bulletin 29. Austin, 1913.

———. *Proceedings of the Fifth Meeting of the Texas State Farmers' Institute, 1915*. Texas Department of Agriculture Bulletin 48. Austin, 1915.

———. *Proceedings of the Fourth Meeting of the Texas State Farmers' Institute, 1914*. Texas Department of Agriculture Bulletin 39. Austin, 1914.

———. *Proceedings of the Ninth Annual Meeting of the Texas State Farmers' Institute, 1919*. Texas Department of Agriculture Bulletin 67. Austin, 1919.

———. *Seventeenth Texas Farmers' Congress, 1914*. Texas Department of Agriculture Bulletin 40. Austin, 1914.

———. *Seventh Annual Report of the Commissioner of Agriculture, 1914*. Austin, 1914.

———. *Sixteenth Texas Farmers' Congress, 1913*. Texas Department of Agriculture Bulletin 33. Austin, 1913.

———. *Tenth Annual Report of the Commissioner of Agriculture, 1917*. Austin, 1917.

———. *Twelfth Texas Farmers' Congress, 1909*. Texas Department of Agriculture Bulletin 10. Austin, 1909.

———. *Yearbook: 1908*. Texas Department of Agriculture Bulletin. Austin, 1909.

Texas State Board of Education. *Report of the Results of the Texas Statewide School Adequacy Survey*. Austin: Texas State Board of Education, 1937.

Truesdell, Leon E. *Farm Population of the United States*. U.S. Bureau of the Census, Census Monograph 6. Washington, D.C.: Government Printing Office, 1927.

Turner, Howard A. *The Ownership of Tenant Farms in the United States*. U.S. Department of Agriculture Bulletin 1432. Washington, D.C.: Government Printing Office, 1926.

U.S. Bureau of the Census. *Census of Agriculture, 1954*. Washington, D.C.: Government Printing Office, 1956.

———. *A Compendium of the Eleventh Census, 1890. Population*. Washington, D.C.: Government Printing Office, 1892.

———. *A Compendium of the Ninth Census, 1870*. Washington, D.C.: Government Printing Office, 1872.

———. *Eighth Census of the United States, 1860. Agriculture*. Washington, D.C.: Government Printing Office, 1864.

——. *Eighth Census of the United States, 1860. Population.* Washington, D.C.: Government Printing Office, 1864.

——. *Eleventh Census of the United States, 1890. Agriculture.* Washington, D.C.: Government Printing Office, 1895.

——. *Fifteenth Census of the United States, 1930. Agriculture.* Washington, D.C.: Government Printing Office, 1932.

——. *Fifteenth Census of the United States, 1930. Population.* Population Bulletin, First Series. *Texas.* Washington, D.C.: Government Printing Office, 1931.

——. *Fifteenth Census of the United States, 1930. Population.* Vol. 1. Washington, D.C.: Government Printing Office, 1931.

——. *Fifteenth Census of the United States, 1930. Population.* Vol. 3, part 2. Washington, D.C.: Government Printing Office, 1932.

——. *Fourteenth Census of the United States, 1920. Agriculture.* Vol. 6, part 2. Washington, D.C.: Government Printing Office, 1922.

——. *Negro Population, 1790–1915.* Washington, D.C.: Government Printing Office, 1918.

——. *Ninth Census of the United States, 1870. Agriculture.* Washington, D.C.: Government Printing Office, 1872.

——. *Ninth Census of the United States, 1870. Population.* Washington, D.C.: Government Printing Office, 1872.

——. *Plantation Farming in the United States.* Washington, D.C.: Government Printing Office, 1916.

——. *Report on Cotton Production in the United States; Also Embracing Agricultural and Physico-Geographical Descriptions of the Several Cotton States and of California.* Part 1, *Mississippi Valley and Southwestern States.* Vol. 5, *Cotton Production of the State of Texas.* Washington, D.C.: Government Printing Office, 1884.

——. *Report on the Productions of Agriculture as Returned at the Tenth Census, 1880.* Washington, D.C.: Government Printing Office, 1883.

——. *Report on the Statistics of Agriculture in the United States at the Eleventh Census, 1890.* Vol. 5. Washington, D.C.: Government Printing Office, 1895.

——. *Sixteenth Census of the United States, 1940. Population.* Washington, D.C.: Government Printing Office, 1943.

——. *Tenth Census of the United States, 1880. Agriculture.* Washington, D.C.: Government Printing Office, 1883.

——. *Tenth Census of the United States, 1880. Population.* Washington, D.C.: Government Printing Office, 1882.

——. *Thirteenth Census of the United States, 1910. Agriculture.* Washington, D.C.: Government Printing Office, 1913.

——. *Thirteenth Census of the United States, 1910. Population.* Washington, D.C.: Government Printing Office, 1911.

——. *Twelfth Census of the United States, 1900. Agriculture.* Part 1, *Farm Live Stock, and Animal Products.* Washington, D.C.: Government Printing Office, 1902.

——. *Twelfth Census of the United States, 1900. Agriculture.* Part 2, *Crops and Irrigation.* Washington, D.C.: Government Printing Office, 1902.

——. *Twelfth Census of the United States, 1900. Population.* Washington, D.C.: Government Printing Office, 1901.

———. *United States Census of Agriculture, 1925. Texas*. Washington, D.C.: Government Printing Office, 1927.

U.S. Congress. *Hearings before the Select Committee to Investigate the Interstate Migration of Destitute Citizens*. Pursuant to H. Res. 63 and H. Res. 491, 76th Cong., 3d sess., 1941, part 5: Oklahoma City Hearings.

U.S. Congress. Committee on Education and Labor. *Violations of Free Speech and Rights of Labor*. 76th Cong., 3d sess., 1940. Hearings, parts 1–3. The American Farmer and the Rise of Agribusiness: Seeds of Struggle. New York: Arno Press, 1975.

U.S. Congress. House. Committee on Immigration and Naturalization. *Immigration from Countries of the Western Hemisphere*. 70th Cong., 1st sess., 1928.

———. *Immigration from Countries of the Western Hemisphere*. 70th Cong., 2d sess., 1930.

———. *Immigration from Mexico*. 71st Cong., 2d sess., 1930.

———. *Naturalization*. 71st Cong., 2d sess., 1930.

———. *Restriction of Immigration*. 68th Cong., 1st sess., 1924. Serial 1–A.

———. *Restriction of Immigration*. 68th Cong., 2d sess., 1924. Serial 2–A.

———. *Restriction of Western Hemisphere Immigration*. 70th Cong., 1st sess., 1928.

———. *Seasonal Agricultural Laborers from Mexico*. 69th Cong., 1st sess., 1926.

———. *Temporary Admission of Illiterate Mexican Laborers*. 66th Cong., 2d sess., 1920.

———. *Western Hemisphere Immigration*. 71st Cong., 2d sess., 1930.

———. *Letter from the Secretary of the Treasury in Regard to the Range and Cattle Traffic in the Western States and Territories*. Report prepared by Joseph Nimmo Jr. 48th Cong., 2d sess., 1885. Ex. Doc. 267. Serial 2304.

U.S. Congress. Senate. *Report of the Committee on Agriculture and Forestry on the Condition of Cotton Growers*. . . . 53d Cong., 3d sess., 1895. S. Rept. 986.

———. Senate Commission on Industrial Relations. *Final Report and Testimony*. 64th Cong., 1st sess., 1916. S. Doc. 415, vols. 1, 9–10.

U.S. Department of Agriculture. *Domestic Needs of Farm Women*. Report 104. Washington, D.C.: Government Printing Office, 1915.

———. *Economic Needs of Farm Women*. Report 106. Washington, D.C.: Government Printing Office, 1915.

———. *Social and Labor Needs of Farm Women*. Report 103. Washington, D.C.: Government Printing Office, 1915.

———. *Yearbook, 1914*. Washington, D.C.: Government Printing Office, 1915.

———. *Yearbook, 1923*. Washington, D.C.: Government Printing Office, 1924.

———. *Yearbook, 1927*. Washington, D.C.: Government Printing Office, 1928.

———. *Yearbook, 1928*. Washington, D.C.: Government Printing Office, 1929.

———. *Yearbook, 1930*. Washington, D.C.: Government Printing Office, 1930.

———. *Yearbook of Agriculture, 1940*. Washington, D.C.: Government Printing Office, 1941.

———. Bureau of Agricultural Economics. *Farm Power and Farm Machines*. Washington, D.C.: Government Printing Office, 1953.

———. Farm Security Administration. *Survey of Agricultural Labor Conditions in Karnes County, Texas*. Washington, D.C.: Government Printing Office, 1937.

Vasey, Tom, and Josiah C. Folsom. *Survey of Agricultural Labor Conditions in Karnes County, Texas*. Washington, D.C.: U.S. Department of Agriculture, 1937.

———. *U.S. Farm Security Administration Survey of Agricultural Labor Conditions*. Washington, D.C.: Government Printing Office, 1937.

The Welfare of Children in Cotton-Growing Areas of Texas. U.S. Children's Bureau Publication 134. Washington, D.C.: Government Printing Office, 1924.

Wilcox, E. V. *Lease Contracts Used in Renting Farms on Shares*. U.S. Department of Agriculture Bulletin 650. Washington, D.C.: Government Printing Office, 1918.

Williard, Rex E. *A Farm Management Study of Cotton Farms of Ellis County, Texas*. U.S. Department of Agriculture Bulletin 659. Washington, D.C.: Government Printing Office, 1918.

Winkler, Ernest W., ed. *Platforms of Political Parties in Texas*. University of Texas Bulletin 53. Austin: University of Texas, 1916.

Works, George A. *Texas Educational Survey Report*. Austin, 1925.

Yantis, Robert Enoch. *Farm Acreage, Values, Ownership, and Tenancy; Production of Principal Crops by Counties*. Texas Department of Agriculture Bulletin 89 (revision of Bulletin 70). Austin: Texas Department of Agriculture, 1927.

NEWSPAPERS

Austin American-Statesman
Beeville Bee
Beeville Weekly Picayune
Corpus Christi Caller
La Crónica (Laredo)
Dallas Morning News
El Demócrata Fronterizo (Laredo)
The Laborer (Dallas)
New York Times
La Prensa (San Antonio)
The Rebel (Halletsville)
San Antonio Light
San Antonio Weekly Express
Topeka Daily State Journal
Vanguardia (Austin)

INTERVIEWS

Andrés Acosta and Sabina Palomo Acosta, March 16, 1993, McGregor, Texas.

Vicente Corpus, January 6, 1977, Caldwell County Oral History Collection, Center for American History, University of Texas at Austin.

Rev. S. L. Davis, February 17, 1977, Caldwell County Oral History Collection, Center for American History, University of Texas at Austin.

Fidencio Durán Sr., August 2, 1994, Maxwell, Texas.

Juan Flores, March 8, 1977, Caldwell County Oral History Collection, Center for American History, University of Texas at Austin.

Florentina Granado and Dolores Mojica, July 5, 1977, Caldwell County Oral History Collection, Center for American History, University of Texas at Austin.

J. Bonner Rackley, October 27, 1976, Caldwell County Oral History Collection, Center for American History, University of Texas at Austin.

Elvira Sánchez, July 20, 1977, Caldwell County Oral History Collection, Center for American History, University of Texas at Austin.

SECONDARY SOURCES

Abramowitz, Jack. "The Negro in the Populist Movement." *Journal of Negro History* 38 (July 1953): 257–71.

Acheson, Sam Hanna. *Joe Bailey: The Last Democrat*. New York: Macmillan, 1932.

Acuña, Rodolfo. *Occupied America: A History of Chicanos*. 3d ed. New York: HarperCollins, 1988.

Adams, Graham, Jr. *Age of Industrial Violence, 1910–1915: The Activities and Findings of the United States Commission on Industrial Relations*. New York: Columbia University Press, 1966.

Adams, Larry Earl. "Economic Development in Texas during Reconstruction." Ph.D. diss., North Texas State University, 1980.

Agee, James, and Walker Evans. *Let Us Now Praise Famous Men*. Boston: Houghton Mifflin, 1941.

Alba, Richard D. *Ethnic Identity: The Transformation of White America*. New Haven, Conn.: Yale University Press, 1990.

Alexander, Charles C. *The Ku Klux Klan in the Southwest*. Lexington: University Press of Kentucky, 1965.

Allen, Ruth A. *Chapters in the History of Organized Labor in Texas*. University of Texas Publication 4143. Austin: University of Texas, Bureau of Research in the Social Sciences, 1941.

——. "Mexican Peon Women in Texas." *Sociology and Social Research* 16 (November-December 1931): 131–42.

Allen, Theodore W. *The Invention of the White Race*. Vol. 1, *Racial Oppression and Social Control*. London and New York: Verso, 1994.

Almaguer, Tomás. *Racial Fault Lines: The Historical Origins of White Supremacy in California*. Berkeley: University of California Press, 1994.

Ameringer, Oscar. *If You Don't Weaken: The Autobiography of Oscar Ameringer*. New York: Henry Holt, 1940.

Anders, Evan. *Boss Rule in South Texas: The Progressive Era*. Austin: University of Texas Press, 1982.

Anderson, Benedict. *Imagined Communities: Reflections on the Origin and Spread of Nationalism*. Rev. ed. London and New York: Verso, 1991.

Anderson, Clifford B. "The Metamorphosis of American Agrarian Idealism in the 1920's and 1930's." *Agricultural History* 35 (October 1961): 182–88.

Anderson, Rodney. *Outcasts in Their Own Land: Mexican Industrial Workers, 1906–1911*. DeKalb: Northern Illinois University Press, 1976.

Anzaldúa, Gloria. *Borderlands / La Frontera: The New Mestiza*. San Francisco: Spinster / Aunt Lute, 1987.

App, Frank. "The Industrialization of Agriculture." *American Academy of Political and Social Science, Annals: Farm Relief* 142 (March 1929): 228–34.

Arnesen, Eric. *Waterfront Workers of New Orleans: Race, Class, and Politics, 1863–1923*. New York: Oxford University Press, 1991.

Ashburn, Karl E. "The Development of Cotton Production in Texas." Ph.D. diss., Duke University, 1932.

———. "Economic and Social Aspects of Farm Tenancy in Texas." *Southwestern Social and Political Science Quarterly* 15 (March 1935): 298–306.

Atherton, Lewis E. *The Cattle Kings*. Bloomington: Indiana University Press, 1961.

Ayers, Edward L. *The Promise of the New South: Life after Reconstruction*. New York: Oxford University Press, 1992.

———. "The South, the West, and the Rest." *Western Historical Quarterly* 25 (Winter 1994): 473–76.

———. "What We Talk about When We Talk about the South." In *All over the Map: Rethinking American Regions*, edited by Edward L. Ayers, Patricia Nelson Limerick, Stephen Nissenbaum, and Peter S. Onuf. Baltimore, Md.: Johns Hopkins University Press, 1996.

Badger, Anthony J. *The New Deal: The Depression Years, 1933–1940*. New York: Hill and Wang, 1989.

Baker, Andrew. "Recent Trends in the Nordic Doctrine." *Journal of Psychology* 2 (1936): 151–59.

Balderama, Francisco E., and Raymond Rodríguez. *Decade of Betrayal: Mexican Repatriation in the 1930s*. Albuquerque: University of New Mexico Press, 1995.

Barkan, Elazar. *The Retreat of Scientific Racism: Changing Concepts of Race in Britain and the United States Between the World Wars*. Cambridge, England: Cambridge University Press, 1992.

Barker, Eugene C. *The Life of Stephen F. Austin: Founder of Texas, 1793–1836*. 1926; reprint, Austin: University of Texas Press, 1985.

Barnes, Donna A. *Farmers in Rebellion: The Rise and Fall of the Southern Farmers Alliance and People's Party in Texas*. Austin: University of Texas Press, 1984.

Baron, Ava. "Gender and Labor History: Learning from the Past, Looking to the Future." In *Work Engendered: Toward a New History of American Labor*, edited by Ava Baron. Ithaca, N.Y.: Cornell University Press, 1991.

Barr, Alwyn. *Black Texans: A History of Negroes in Texas, 1528–1971*. Austin: Jenkins, 1973.

———. "Occupational and Geographical Mobility in San Antonio, 1870–1900." *Social Science Quarterly* 51 (September 1970): 396–403.

———. *Reconstruction to Reform: Texas Politics, 1876–1906*. Austin: University of Texas Press, 1976.

Barrera, Mario. *Race and Class in the Southwest: A Theory of Racial Inequality*. Notre Dame, Ind.: University of Notre Dame Press, 1979.

Beames, M. R. *Peasants and Power: The Whiteboy Movements and Their Control in Pre-Famine Ireland*. New York: St. Martin's Press, 1983.

Bederman, Gail. *Manliness and Civilization: A Cultural History of Gender and Race in the United States, 1880–1917*. Chicago: University of Chicago Press, 1995.

Bell, Mattie. "The Growth and Distribution of the Texas Population." Ph.D. diss., Baylor University, 1955.

Bentley, Max. "The Ku Klux Klan in Texas." *McClure's Magazine* 57 (May 1924): 11–21.

Berger, Michael L. *The Devil Wagon in God's Country: The Automobile and Social Change in Rural America, 1893–1929*. Hamden, Conn.: Archon Books, 1979.

Billington, Ray Allen, and Martin Ridge. *Westward Expansion: A History of the American Frontier*. 5th ed. New York: Macmillan, 1982.

Binkley, William C. *The Expansionist Movement in Texas, 1836–1850*. Berkeley: University of California Press, 1925.

Bizzell, William B. *Farm Tenancy in the United States: A Study of the Historical Development of Farm Tenancy and Its Economic and Social Consequences on Rural Welfare, with Special References to Conditions in the South and Southwest.* Texas Agricultural Experiment Station Bulletin 278. College Station: Agricultural and Mechanical College of Texas, 1921.

——. "Rural Housing and the Tenant Farmer." *Survey*, April 3, 1920, 26–28.

——. *Rural Texas*. New York: Macmillan, 1924.

Blackwelder, Julia Kirk. *Women of the Depression: Caste and Culture in San Antonio, 1929–1939*. College Station: Texas A&M University Press, 1984.

Boas, Franz. "This Nordic Nonsense." *Forum* 74 (October 1925): 502–11.

Bodnar, John. *The Transplanted: A History of Immigrants in Urban America*. Bloomington: Indiana University Press, 1985.

Bogardus, Emory. *The Mexican in the United States*. Los Angeles: University of Southern California Press, 1934.

Boles, John B., and Evelyn Thomas Nolen, eds. *Interpreting Southern History: Historiographical Essays in Honor of Sanford W. Higginbotham*. Baton Rouge: Louisiana University Press, 1987.

Bonacich, Edna. "A Theory of Ethnic Antagonism: The Split Labor Market." *American Sociological Review* 37 (October 1972): 547–59.

Bowers, William L. *The Country Life Movement in America, 1900–1920*. Port Washington, N.Y.: Kennikat Press, 1974.

Brack, Gene M. *Mexico Views Manifest Destiny: An Essay on the Origins of the Mexican War*. Albuquerque: University of New Mexico Press, 1975.

Brannen, C. O. "Problems of Croppers on Cotton Farms." *Journal of Farm Economics* 20 (February 1938): 153–58.

Branson, E. C. "Farm Tenancy in the Cotton Belt: How Farm Tenants Live." *Journal of Social Forces* 1 (March 1923): 213–21.

Brewer, Thomas B. "State Anti-Labor Legislation: Texas—A Case Study." *Labor History* 11 (Winter 1970): 58–76.

Brier, Stephen. "Interracial Organizing in the West Virginia Coal Industry: The Participation of Black Mine Workers in the Knights of Labor and the United Mine Workers, 1880–1894." In *Essays in Southern Labor History*, edited by Gary M. Fink and Merl E. Reed. Westport, Conn.: Greenwood Press, 1977.

Brody, David. "The Old Labor History and the New: In Search of an American Working Class." *Labor History* 20 (1979): 111–26.

Broehl, Wayne G., Jr. *The Molly Maguires*. Cambridge, Mass.: Harvard University Press, 1964.

Brookings, Robert S. *Economic Democracy: America's Answer to Socialism and Communism*. New York: Macmillan, 1929.

Brown, Elsa Barkley. "Uncle Ned's Children: Negotiating Community and Freedom in Postemancipation Richmond, Virginia." Ph.D. diss., Kent State University, 1994.

———. "Womanist Consciousness: Maggie Lena Walker and the Independent Order of Saint Luke." *Signs* 14 (Spring 1989): 610–33.

Brown, Norman. *Hood, Bonnet, and Little Brown Jug: Texas Politics, 1921–1928.* College Station: Texas A&M University Press, 1984.

Brunson, Billy R. *The Texas Land and Development Company: A Panhandle Promotion, 1912–1956.* Austin: University of Texas Press, 1970.

Bruton, Paul W. "Cotton Acreage Reduction and the Tenant Farmer." *Law and Contemporary Problems* 1 (June 1934): 274–91.

Bryan, Samuel. "Mexican Immigrants in the United States." *Survey,* September 7, 1912, 726–30.

Buenger, Walter L. *Secession and the Union in Texas.* Austin: University of Texas Press, 1984.

Buenger, Walter L., and Robert A. Calvert, eds. *Texas through Time: Evolving Interpretations.* College Station: Texas A&M University Press, 1991.

Bugbee, Lester G. "Slavery in Early Texas." *Political Science Quarterly* 13 (September–December 1898): 389–412; 648–68.

Calavita, Kitty. *Inside the State: The Bracero Program, Immigration, and the I.N.S.* New York: Routledge, 1992.

Caldwell, Erskine. *God's Little Acre.* 1933; reprint, Savannah, Ga.: Beehive Press, 1977.

———. *Tobacco Road.* 1934; reprint, New York: Signet, 1962.

Caldwell, Erskine, and Margaret Bourke-White. *You Have Seen Their Faces.* New York: Viking Press, 1937.

Callcott, Frank. "The Mexican Peon in Texas." *Survey,* June 26, 1920, 437–38.

Camarillo, Albert. *Chicanos in a Changing Society: From Mexican Pueblos to American Barrios in Santa Barbara and Southern California, 1848–1930.* Cambridge, Mass.: Harvard University Press, 1979.

Campbell, Randolph B. *An Empire for Slavery: The Peculiar Institution in Texas, 1821–1865.* Baton Rouge: Louisiana State University Press, 1989.

Cantor, Louis. *A Prologue to the Protest Movement: The Missouri Sharecropper Roadside Demonstration of 1939.* Durham, N.C.: Duke University Press, 1969.

Cantrell, Gregg. "John B. Raynor: A Study in Black Populist Leadership." *Southern Studies: An Interdisciplinary Journal of the South* 24 (Winter 1985): 432–43.

Cardoso, Lawrence A. *Mexican Immigration to the United States, 1897–1931.* Tucson: University of Arizona Press, 1980.

Carnes, Mark C., and Clyde Griffen, eds. *Meanings for Manhood: Constructions of Masculinity in Victorian America.* Chicago: University of Chicago Press, 1990.

Castañeda, Antonia I. "Women of Color and the Rewriting of Western History: The Discourse, Politics, and Decolonization of History." *Pacific Historical Review* 61 (November 1992): 501–33.

Cauley, T. J. "Agricultural Land Tenure in Texas." *Southwestern Political and Social Science Quarterly* 11 (September 1930): 135–47.

Chafe, William H. *The Paradox of Change: American Women in the 20th Century.* New York: Oxford University Press, 1991.

——. "Women's History and Political History: Some Thoughts on Progressivism and the New Deal." In *Visible Women: New Essays on American Activism*, edited by Nancy A. Hewitt and Suzanne Lebsock. Urbana: University of Illinois Press, 1993.

Chambers, Ross. *Room for Maneuver: Reading (the) Oppositional (in) Narrative*. Chicago: University of Chicago Press, 1991.

Chan, Sucheng. *This Bittersweet Soil: The Chinese in California Agriculture, 1860–1910*. Berkeley: University of California Press, 1986.

Chandler, Lester V. *America's Greatest Depression, 1929–1941*. New York: Harper & Row, 1970.

Chávez, John R. *The Lost Land: The Chicano Image of the Southwest*. Albuquerque: University of New Mexico Press, 1984.

Clark, S. T. *Social Origins of the Irish Land War*. Princeton, N.J.: Princeton University Press, 1979.

Clarke, Sally H. *Regulation and the Revolution in United States Farm Productivity*. Cambridge, England: Cambridge University Press, 1994.

Coalson, George O. *The Development of the Migratory Farm Labor System in Texas, 1900–1954*. 1955; reprint, San Francisco: R and E Research Associates, 1977.

Cobb, James C. "Beyond Planters and Industrialization: A New Perspective on the New South." *Journal of Southern History* 54 (February 1988): 45–68.

——. *The Most Southern Place on Earth: The Mississippi Delta and the Roots of Regional Identity*. New York: Oxford University Press, 1992.

——. *The Selling of the South: The Southern Crusade for Industrial Development, 1936–1990*. 2d ed. Urbana: University of Illinois Press, 1993.

Cobb, James C., and Michael V. Namorato, eds. *The New Deal and the South*. Jackson: University Press of Mississippi, 1984.

Cohen, Lizabeth. *Making a New Deal: Industrial Workers in Chicago, 1919–1939*. Cambridge, England: Cambridge University Press, 1990.

Cohen, William. "Negro Involuntary Servitude in the South, 1865–1940: A Preliminary Analysis." *Journal of Southern History* 42 (February 1976): 31–61.

Coleman, James Walter. *The Molly Maguire Riots: Industrial Conflict in the Pennsylvania Coal Region*. Richmond, Va.: Garrett & Massie, 1936.

Commission on Country Life. *Report of the Commission on Country Life*. New York: Sturgis and Walton, 1917.

Conlin, Joseph R. *Big Bill Haywood and the Radical Union Movement*. Syracuse, N.Y.: Syracuse University Press, 1969.

Conrad, David E. *The Forgotten Farmers: The Story of Sharecroppers in the New Deal*. Urbana: University of Illinois Press, 1965.

Conzen, Kathleen Neils. "A Saga of Families." In *The Oxford History of the American West*, edited by Clyde A. Milner II, Carol A. O'Connor, and Martha A. Sandweiss. New York: Oxford University Press, 1994.

Cook, Sylvia Jenkins. *From Tobacco Road to Route 66: The Southern Poor White in Fiction*. Chapel Hill: University of North Carolina Press, 1976.

Cope, Douglas R. *The Limits of Racial Domination in Mexico: Plebeian Society in Colonial Mexico City, 1600–1720*. Madison: University of Wisconsin Press, 1994.

Córdova, Teresa, Norma Cantú, Gilberto Cárdenas, Juan García, and Christine M. Sierra, eds. *Chicana Voices: Intersections of Class, Race, and Gender*. 1986; reprint, Albuquerque: University of New Mexico Press, 1993.

Corwin, Arthur F. "Early Mexican Labor Migration: A Frontier Sketch, 1848–1900." In *Immigrants—and Immigrants: Perspectives on Mexican Labor Migration to the United States*, edited by Arthur F. Corwin. Westport, Conn.: Greenwood Press, 1978.

———, ed. *Immigrants—and Immigrants: Perspectives on Mexican Labor Migration to the United States*. Westport, Conn.: Greenwood Press, 1978.

Corwin, Arthur F., and Lawrence A. Cardoso. "Vamos al Norte: Causes of Mass Mexican Migration to the United States." In *Immigrants—and Immigrants: Perspectives on Mexican Labor Migration to the United States*, edited by Arthur F. Corwin. Westport, Conn.: Greenwood Press, 1978.

Cott, Nancy F. *The Bonds of Womanhood: "Woman's Sphere" in New England, 1780–1835*. New Haven, Conn.: Yale University Press, 1977.

———. "On Men's History and Women's History." In *Meanings for Manhood: Constructions of Masculinity in Victorian America*, edited by Mark C. Carnes and Clyde Griffen. Chicago: University of Chicago Press, 1990.

Cotton, Walter F. *History of Negroes of Limestone County from 1860 to 1939*. Mexia, Tex.: J. A. Chatman and S. M. Merriwether, 1939.

Cowan, Ruth Schwartz. *More Work for Mother: The Ironies of Household Technology from the Open Hearth to the Microwave*. New York: Basic Books, 1983.

Cox, LaWanda Fenlason. "From Emancipation to Segregation: National Policy and Southern Blacks." In *Interpreting Southern History: Historiographical Essays in Honor of Sanford W. Higginbotham*, edited by John B. Boles and Evelyn Thomas Nolen. Baton Rouge: Louisiana University Press, 1987.

———. "Tenancy in the United States, 1865–1900: A Consideration of the Validity of the Agricultural Ladder Hypothesis." *Agricultural History* 18 (July 1944): 97–105.

Craig, Richard B. *The Bracero Program: Interest Groups and Foreign Policy*. Austin: University of Texas Press, 1971.

Crawford, Remsen. "The Menace of Mexican Immigration." *Current History* 31 (February 1930): 903–7.

Creel, George. "Feudal Towns of Texas." *Harper's Weekly*, January 23, 1915, 76–78.

Cronon, William. "The West: A Moving Target." *Western Historical Quarterly* 25 (Winter 1994): 476–81.

Cronon, William, George Miles, and Jay Gitlin, eds. *Under an Open Sky: Rethinking America's Western Past*. New York: W. W. Norton, 1992.

Cross, Gary, ed. *Worktime and Industrialization: An International History*. Philadelphia: Temple University Press, 1988.

Cuellar, Robert A. *A Social and Political History of the Mexican-American Population of Texas, 1929–1963*. San Francisco: R and E Research Associates, 1974.

Cumberland, Charles C. "Border Raids in the Lower Rio Grande Valley—1915." *Southwestern Historical Quarterly* 58 (January 1954): 301–24.

Currie, Barton W. "100,000 Acres of Business Farming: The Taft Ranch Has Revolutionized the Cattle Industry." *Country Gentleman*, June 12, 1915, 1010–11.

Dale, Edward Everett. *The Range Cattle Industry: Ranching on the Great Plains from 1865 to 1925*. 1930; reprint, Norman: University of Oklahoma, 1960.

Daniel, Cletus. *Bitter Harvest: A History of California Farmworkers, 1870–1941.* Ithaca, N.Y.: Cornell University Press, 1981.

Daniel, Pete. *Breaking the Land: The Transformation of Cotton, Tobacco, and Rice Cultures since 1880.* Urbana: University of Illinois Press, 1985.

———. *The Shadow of Slavery: Peonage in the South, 1901–1969.* Urbana: University of Illinois Press, 1972.

———. "Transformation of the Rural South, 1930 to the Present." *Agricultural History* 55 (July 1981): 231–48.

Davenport, Charles Benedict. "The Effects of Race Intermingling." *Proceedings of the American Philosophical Society* 56 (April 13, 1917): 364–68.

Davis, Allen F. "The Campaign for the Industrial Relations Commission, 1911–13." *Mid-America* 45 (October 1963): 211–27.

Davis, Edward Everett. "King Cotton Leads Mexicans into Texas." *Texas Outlook* 9 (April 1925): 1–3.

———. *The White Scourge.* San Antonio: Naylor, 1940.

Davis, John H. "From Agriculture to Agribusiness." *Harvard Business Review* 34 (January-February 1956): 107–15.

Davis, K. C. "The Next Great American Industry." *Outlook,* August 8, 1928, 580, 586.

Day, Mark. *Forty Acres: César Chávez and the Farm Workers.* New York: Praeger, 1971.

Day, Richard H. "The Economics of Technological Change and the Demise of the Sharecropper." *American Economic Review* 57 (June 1967): 427–49.

De Lara, Gutiérrez, and Edgcumb Pinchon. *The Mexican People: Their Struggle for Freedom.* New York: Doubleday, Page, 1914.

De León, Arnoldo. *In Re Ricardo Rodríquez: An Attempt at Chicano Disfranchisement in San Antonio, 1896–1897.* San Antonio: Caravel Press, 1979.

———. *The Tejano Community, 1836–1900.* Albuquerque: University of New Mexico Press, 1982.

———. *They Called Them Greasers: Anglo Attitudes toward Mexicans in Texas, 1821–1900.* Austin: University of Texas Press, 1983.

De León, Arnoldo, and Kenneth L. Stewart. *Tejanos and the Numbers Game: A Socio-Historical Interpretation from the Federal Censuses, 1850–1900.* Albuquerque: University of New Mexico Press, 1989.

Del Castillo, Richard Griswold. *The Treaty of Guadalupe Hidalgo: A Legacy of Conflict.* Norman: University of Oklahoma Press, 1990.

Del Castillo, Richard Griswold, and Richard A. García. *César Chávez: A Triumph of Spirit.* Norman: University of Oklahoma Press, 1995.

Deutsch, Sarah. *No Separate Refuge: Culture, Class, and Gender on an Anglo-Hispanic Frontier in the American Southwest, 1880–1940.* New York: Oxford University Press, 1987.

DeVoto, Bernard. *The Year of Decision, 1846.* Boston: Little, Brown, 1943.

Dixon, Frederick K. "A History of Gonzales County in the Nineteenth Century." M.A. thesis, University of Texas, 1964.

Dobie, J. Frank. "Ranch Mexicans." *Survey,* May 1, 1931, 168–70.

Dorsett, Jesse. "Blacks in Reconstruction Texas, 1865–1877." Ph.D. diss., Texas Christian University, 1981.

Dowd, Douglas F. "A Comparative Analysis of Economic Development in the American West and South." *Journal of Economic History* 16 (December 1956): 558–74.

Dubofsky, Melvyn. *We Shall Be All: A History of the Industrial Workers of the World*. 2d ed. Urbana: University of Illinois Press, 1988.

Du Bois, W. E. B. *Black Reconstruction: An Essay toward a History of the Part Which Black Folk Played in the Attempt to Reconstruct Democracy in America, 1860–1880*. New York: Harcourt, Brace, 1935.

———. *The Souls of Black Folk*. 1903; reprint, New York: Alfred A. Knopf, 1993.

Dyer, Thomas G. *Theodore Roosevelt and the Idea of Race*. Baton Rouge: Louisiana State University Press, 1980.

Elbert, Sarah. "Women and Farming: Changing Structures, Changing Roles." In *Women and Farming: Changing Roles, Changing Structures*, edited by Wava G. Haney and Jane B. Knowles. Boulder, Colo.: Westview Press, 1988.

Elliott, Edwin A. "Classification and Economic Status of the Tenantry of a Texas Cotton Plantation." *Southwestern Political and Social Science Quarterly* 11 (March 1931): 408–35.

———. "An Economic Survey of a Texas Cotton Plantation as to Tenantry, Tenancy, and Management." Ph.D. diss., University of Texas, 1930.

Ellis, Lynn W. "How the Machine Is Making History on the Farm." *International Socialist Review* 12 (April 1912): 641–49.

Emmons, David M. "Constructed Province: History and the Making of the Last American West." *Western Historical Quarterly* 25 (Winter 1944): 437–59.

Evans, Samuel Lee. "Texas Agriculture, 1880–1930." Ph.D. diss., University of Texas, 1960.

Faue, Elizabeth. *Community of Suffering & Struggle: Women, Men, and the Labor Movement in Minneapolis, 1915–1945*. Chapel Hill: University of North Carolina Press, 1991.

Faulkner, William. *Collected Stories*. New York: Random House, 1950.

———. *Snopes: The Hamlet, The Mansion, and The Town*. New York: Random House, Modern Library Edition, 1994.

Ferguson, Russell, ed. *Out There: Marginalization and Contemporary Cultures*. Cambridge, Mass.: MIT Press, 1990.

Ferrel, Jeff, and Kevin Ryan. "The Brotherhood of Timber Workers and the Southern Trust: Legal Repression and Worker Response." *Radical America* 19 (July-August 1985): 55–74.

Fields, Barbara J. "Ideology and Race in America." In *Region, Race, and Reconstruction: Essays in Honor of C. Vann Woodward*, edited by J. Morgan Kousser and James M. McPherson. New York: Oxford University Press, 1982.

———. "Slavery, Race, and Ideology in the United States of America." *New Left Review* 181 (May-June 1990): 95–118.

Fine, Michelle, Lois Weis, Linda C. Powell, and L. Mun Wong, eds. *Off White: Readings on Race, Power, and Society*. New York and London: Routledge, 1997.

Fink, Deborah. *Agrarian Women: Wives and Mothers in Rural Nebraska, 1880–1940*. Chapel Hill: University of North Carolina Press, 1992.

Fink, Gary M., and Merl E. Reed, eds. *Essays in Southern Labor History*. Westport, Conn.: Greenwood Press, 1977.

Fishkin, Shelley Fisher. "Interrogating 'Whiteness,' Complicating 'Blackness': Re-mapping American Culture." *American Quarterly* 47 (September 1995): 428–66.

Fite, Gilbert C. *Cotton Fields No More: Southern Agriculture, 1865–1980.* Lexington: University Press of Kentucky, 1984.

——. *Farmers' Frontier, 1865–1900.* New York: Holt, Rinehart and Winston, 1966.

Fitzgerald, Deborah. *The Business of Breeding: Hybrid Corn in Illinois, 1890–1940.* Ithaca, N.Y.: Cornell University Press, 1990.

Fitzgerald, F. Scott. *The Great Gatsby.* New York: Charles Scribner's Sons, 1925.

Flynt, J. Wayne. *Dixie's Forgotten People: The South's Poor Whites.* Bloomington: Indiana University Press, 1979.

Foerster, Robert F. *The Racial Problems Involved in Immigration from Latin America and the West Indies.* Washington, D.C.: Government Printing Office, 1925.

Foley, Douglas E. *From Peones to Politicos: Class and Ethnicity in a South Texas Town, 1900–1987.* Rev. ed. Austin: University of Texas Press, 1988.

Foley, Neil. "Mexicans, Mechanization, and the Growth of Corporate Cotton Culture in South Texas: The Taft Ranch, 1900–1930." *Journal of Southern History* 62 (May 1996): 275–302.

——. "The New South in the Southwest: Anglos, Blacks, and Mexicans in Central Texas, 1880–1930." Ph.D. diss., University of Michigan, 1990.

Foner, Eric. "Class, Ethnicity, and Radicalism in the Gilded Age: The Land League and Irish-America." *Marxist Perspectives* 1 (Summer 1978): 6–55.

——. "The Meaning of Freedom in the Age of Emancipation." *Journal of American History* 81 (September 1994): 435–60.

Foucault, Michel. *Discipline and Punish: The Birth of the Prison.* New York: Vintage Books, 1979.

Frank, Dana. *Purchasing Power: Consumer Organizing, Gender, and the Seattle Labor Movement, 1919–1929.* New York: Cambridge University Press, 1994.

Frankenberg, Ruth. *White Women, Race Matters: The Social Construction of Whiteness.* Minneapolis: University of Minnesota Press, 1993.

Fredrickson, George M. *The Black Image in the White Mind: The Debate on Afro-American Character and Destiny, 1817–1914.* New York: Harper and Row, 1971.

Freeman, James W., ed. *Prose and Poetry of the Livestock Industry of the United States.* Kansas City, Mo.: National Livestock Historical Association, 1905.

Gabbard, L. P. "Effect of Large-Scale Production on Cotton Growing in Texas." *Journal of Farm Economics* 10 (April 1928): 211–24.

Galarza, Ernesto. *Barrio Boy.* Notre Dame, Ind.: University of Notre Dame Press, 1971.

——. *Farm Workers and Agri-Business in California, 1947–1960.* Notre Dame, Ind.: University of Notre Dame Press, 1977.

——. *Merchants of Labor: The Mexican Bracero Story.* Charlotte, N.C.: McNally & Loftin, 1964.

——. *Spiders in the House and Workers in the Field.* Notre Dame, Ind.: University of Notre Dame Press, 1970.

——. "Without Benefit of Lobby." *Survey,* May 1, 1931, 181.

Gamio, Manuel. *Mexican Immigration to the United States: A Study of Human Migration and Adjustment.* Chicago: University of Chicago Press, 1930.

——. "Migration and Planning." *Survey,* May 1, 1939, 174–75.

———, comp. *The Mexican Immigrant: His Life-Story*. Chicago: University of Chicago Press, 1931.

García, Mario T. "Americanization and the Mexican Immigrant, 1880–1930." *Journal of Ethnic Studies* 6 (Summer 1978): 19–34.

———. *Desert Immigrants: The Mexicans of El Paso, 1880–1920*. New Haven, Conn.: Yale University Press, 1981.

———. *Mexican Americans: Leadership, Ideology, & Identity, 1930–1960*. New Haven, Conn.: Yale University Press, 1989.

———. "Mexican Americans and the Politics of Citizenship: The Case of El Paso, 1936." *New Mexico Historical Review* 59 (April 1984): 187–204.

———. "Racial Dualism in the El Paso Labor Market, 1880–1920." *Aztlán* 6 (Summer 1975): 197–217.

García, Richard A. *Rise of the Mexican American Middle Class: San Antonio, 1929–1941*. College Station: Texas A&M University Press, 1991.

Gard, Wayne. "The Fence Cutters." *Southwestern Historical Quarterly* 51 (July 1947): 1–15.

Garkovich, Lorraine, and Janet Bokemeier. "Agricultural Mechanization and American Farm Women's Economic Roles." In *Women and Farming: Changing Roles, Changing Structures*, edited by Wava G. Haney and Jane B. Knowles. Boulder, Colo.: Westview Press, 1988.

Gibbons, Charles E. *Child Labor among Cotton Growers of Texas: A Study of Children Living in Rural Communities in Six Counties in Texas*. New York: National Child Labor Committee, 1925.

Gibbons, Edward J. "Frank Walsh and the United States Commission on Industrial Relations." M.A. thesis, University of Notre Dame, 1958.

Gilmore, Glenda Elizabeth. *Gender and Jim Crow: Women and the Politics of White Supremacy in North Carolina, 1896–1920*. Chapel Hill: University of North Carolina Press, 1996.

Glasrud, Bruce Alden. "Black Texans, 1900–1930: A History." Ph.D. diss., Texas Technological College, 1969.

Glymph, Thavolia, and John J. Kushma, eds. *Essays on the Postbellum Southern Economy*. College Station: Texas A&M University Press, 1985.

Goddard, H. H. *The Kallikak Family: A Study in the Heredity of Feeble-mindedness*. New York: Macmillan, 1912.

Gómez-Quiñones, Juan. "The First Steps: Chicano Labor Conflict and Organizing, 1900–1920." *Aztlán* 3 (Spring 1972): 13–49.

———. *Sembradores, Ricardo Flores Magón y el Partido Liberal Mexicano: A Eulogy and a Critique*. Rev. ed. Los Angeles: Chicano Studies Center Publications, University of California at Los Angeles, 1977.

González, Gilbert G. *Labor and Community: Mexican Citrus Worker Villages in a Southern California County, 1900–1950*. Urbana: University of Illinois Press, 1994.

González, Jovita. "America Invades the Border Towns." *Southwest Review* 15 (Summer 1930): 469–77.

Goodwyn, Lawrence C. *Democratic Promise: The Populist Moment in America*. New York: Oxford University Press, 1976.

———. "Populist Dreams and Negro Rights: East Texas as a Case Study." *American Historical Review* 76 (December 1971): 1435–56.

Gordon, John Ramsey. "The Negro in McLennan County, Texas." M.A. thesis, Baylor University, 1932.

Gossett, Thomas F. *Race: The History of an Idea in America*. Dallas: Southern Methodist University Press, 1963.

Gould, Lewis L. *Progressives and Prohibitionists: Texas Democrats in the Wilson Era*. Austin: University of Texas Press, 1973.

Gould, Steven Jay. *The Mismeasure of Man*. 1981; reprint, New York: W. W. Norton, 1993.

Gracy, David B., II. *Littlefield Lands: Colonization on the Texas Plains, 1912–1920*. Austin: University of Texas Press, 1968.

Grant, Madison. *The Conquest of a Continent, Or Expansion of Races in America*. New York: Charles Scribner's Sons, 1934.

——. *The Passing of the Great Race, Or the Racial Basis of European History*. New York: Charles Scribner's Sons, 1916.

Gray, L. C. "Trend in Farm Ownership." *American Academy of Political and Social Science, Annals: Farm Relief* 142 (March 1929): 20–26.

Green, James R. "The Brotherhood of Timber Workers, 1910–1913: A Radical Response to Industrial Capitalism in the Southern U.S.A." *Past and Present* 60 (August 1973): 161–200.

——. *Grass-Roots Socialism: Radical Movements in the Southwest, 1895–1943*. Baton Rouge: Louisiana State University Press, 1978.

——. "Tenant Farmer Discontent and Socialist Protest in Texas, 1901–1917." *Southwestern Historical Quarterly* 81 (October 1977): 133–54.

Greenfield, Gary A., and Don B. Kates Jr. "Mexican Americans, Racial Discrimination, and the Civil Rights Act of 1866." *California Law Review* 63 (January 1975): 662–731.

Gregory, James N. *American Exodus: The Dust Bowl Migration and Okie Culture in California*. New York: Oxford University Press, 1989.

Grubbs, Donald H. *Cry from the Cotton: The Southern Tenant Farmers' Union and the New Deal*. Chapel Hill: University of North Carolina Press, 1971.

Guerin-Gonzales, Camille. *Mexican Workers and American Dreams: Immigration, Repatriation, and California Farm Labor, 1900–1939*. New Brunswick, N.J.: Rutgers University Press, 1994.

Gutiérrez, David G. *Walls and Mirrors: Mexican Americans, Mexican Immigrants, and the Politics of Identity*. Berkeley: University of California Press, 1995.

——. "Significant to Whom?: Mexican Americans and the History of the West." *Western Historical Quarterly* 24 (November 1993): 519–39.

Gutiérrez, Ramón A. "The Erotic Zone: Sexual Transgression on the U.S.–Mexican Border." In *Mapping Multi-Culturalism*, edited by Avery F. Gordon and Christopher Newfield. Minneapolis: University of Minnesota Press, 1996.

——. "Unraveling America's Hispanic Past: Internal Stratification and Class Boundaries." *Aztlán* 17 (Spring 1986): 79–101.

——. *When Jesus Came, the Corn Mothers Went Away: Marriage, Sexuality, and Power in New Mexico, 1500–1846*. Stanford, Calif.: Stanford University Press, 1991.

Gutman, Herbert C. "The Negro and the United Mine Workers of America: The Career and Letters of Richard L. Davis and Something of Their Meaning: 1890–1900." In *The Negro and the American Labor Union*, edited by Julius Jacobson. Garden City, N.Y.: Anchor Books, 1968.

———. *Work, Culture, and Society in Industrializing America: Essays in American Working-Class and Social History*. New York: Random House, 1977.

Hager, William M. "The Plan of San Diego: Unrest on the Texas Border in 1915." *Arizona and the West* 5 (Winter 1963): 327–36.

Hagood, Margaret Jarman. *Mothers of the South: Portraiture of the White Tenant Farm Woman*. Chapel Hill: University of North Carolina Press, 1939.

Hahn, Steven. *The Roots of Southern Populism: Yeoman Farmers and the Transformation of the Georgia Upcountry, 1850–1890*. New York: Oxford University Press, 1983.

Hahn, Steven, and Jonathan Prude, eds. *The Countryside in the Age of Capitalist Transformation: Essays in the Social History of Rural America*. Chapel Hill: University of North Carolina Press, 1985.

Hall, Jacquelyn Dowd. "Disorderly Women: Gender and Labor Militancy in the Appalachian South." *Journal of American History* 73 (September 1986): 354–82.

———. *Revolt against Chivalry: Jessie Daniel Ames and the Women's Campaign against Lynching*. New York: Columbia University Press, 1993.

Hamilton, C. Horace. *The Social Effects of Recent Trends in Mechanization of Agriculture*. Progress Report 579. College Station: Agricultural and Mechanical College of Texas, 1938.

Hamilton, David E. *From New Day to New Deal: American Farm Policy from Hoover to Roosevelt, 1928–1933*. Chapel Hill: University of North Carolina Press, 1991.

The Handbook of Texas: A Dictionary of Essential Information. Vol. 1. Austin: Texas State Historical Association, 1952.

Handman, Max Sylvius. "Economic Reasons for the Coming of the Mexican Immigrant." *American Journal of Sociology* 35 (January 1930): 601–11.

———. "The Mexican Immigrant in Texas." *Southwestern Political and Social Science Quarterly* 7 (June 1926): 33–41.

———. "San Antonio: The Old Capital City of Mexican Life and Influence." *Survey*, May 1, 1931, 163–66.

Haney, Lewis H. "Farm Credit Conditions in a Cotton State." *American Economic Review* 4 (March 1914): 47–67.

———, ed. *Studies in the Industrial Resources of Texas*. University of Texas Bulletin 3. Austin: University of Texas, 1915.

———. *Studies in the Land Problem in Texas*. University of Texas Bulletin 39. Austin: University of Texas, 1915.

Haney, Wava G., and Jane B. Knowles, eds. *Women and Farming: Changing Roles, Changing Structures*. Boulder, Colo.: Westview Press, 1988.

Haney-López, Ian F. *White by Law: The Legal Construction of Race*. New York: New York University Press, 1996.

Hankins, Frank. "The Interdependence of Eugenics and Birth Control." *Birth Control Review* 15 (June 1931): 170–71.

Hanson, Nils H. "Texas Justice! 99 Years!" *International Socialist Review* 16 (February 1916): 476–78.

Harper, Cecil, Jr. "Farming Someone Else's Land: Farm Tenancy in the Texas Brazos River Valley, 1850–1880." Ph.D. diss., University of North Texas, 1988.

Harriman, Florence Jaffray Hurst. *From Pinafores to Politics*. New York: Henry Holt, 1923.

Harris, Charles H., and Louis R. Sadler. "The Plan of San Diego and the Mexican–United States Crisis of 1916: A Reexamination." *Hispanic American Historical Review* 58 (August 1978): 381–408.

Harris, Cheryl I. "Whiteness as Property." *Harvard Law Review* 106 (June 1993): 1709–91.

Harrison, Hubert. "Socialism and the Negro." *International Socialist Review* 13 (July 1912): 65–68.

Hart, John M. *Anarchism & the Mexican Working Class, 1860–1931*. Austin: University of Texas Press, 1978.

Hartigan, John, Jr. "Name Calling: Objectifying 'Poor Whites' and 'White Trash' in Detroit." In *White Trash: Race and Class in America*, edited by Matt Wray and Annalee Newitz. New York and London: Routledge, 1997.

Hewitt, Nancy A. "Politicizing Domesticity: Anglo, Black, and Latin Women in Tampa's Progressive Movements." In *Gender, Class, Race, and Reform in the Progressive Era*, edited by Noralee Frankel and Nancy S. Dye. Lexington: University Press of Kentucky, 1991.

———. *Women's Activism and Social Change: Rochester, New York, 1822–1872*. Ithaca, N.Y.: Cornell University Press, 1984.

Hibbard, Benjamin H. "Tenancy in the Southern States." *Quarterly Journal of Economics* 27 (May 1913): 482–96.

Hickey, T. A. "The Land Renters Union in Texas." *International Socialist Review* 13 (September 1912): 239–44.

Hietala, Thomas R. *Manifest Design: Anxious Aggrandizement in Late Jacksonian America*. Ithaca, N.Y.: Cornell University Press, 1985.

Higginbotham, Evelyn Brooks. "African-American Women's History and the Metalanguage of Race." *Signs* 17 (Winter 1992): 251–74.

———. *Righteous Discontent: The Women's Movement in the Black Baptist Church, 1880–1920*. Cambridge, Mass.: Harvard University Press, 1993.

Higgins, Nathan, Martin Kilson, and Daniel Fox, eds. *Key Issues in the Afro-American Experience*. Vol. 2. New York: Harcourt, Brace, Jovanovitch, 1971.

Higham, John. *Strangers in the Land: Patterns of American Nativism, 1860–1925*. New Brunswick, N.J.: Rutgers University Press, 1955.

Hine, Darlene Clark. *Black Victory: The Rise and Fall of the White Primary in Texas*. Millwood, N.Y.: KTO Press, 1979.

Hoffman, Abraham. *Unwanted Mexican Americans in the Great Depression: Repatriation Pressures, 1929–1939*. Tucson: University of Arizona Press, 1974.

Hoffsommer, Harold. "The AAA and the Cropper." *Social Forces* 13 (October 1934–May 1935): 494–502.

———, ed. *The Social and Economic Significance of Land Tenure in the Southwestern States: A Report of the Regional Land Tenure Research Project*. Chapel Hill: University of North Carolina Press, 1950.

Holman, Charles W. "Charles P. Taft Absolute King over Thousands on Big Estate." *New York Call*, January 15, 1915, 1.

———. "A First Hand View of the Renter Class." *Farm and Ranch*, November 25, 1911, 1.

———. "Governor Jim of Texas." *Harper's Weekly* 61 (1915): 279–80.

———. "Landlord and Tenant: White Tenants versus Black Tenants." *Farm and Ranch*, November 4, 1911, 7–8.

———. "The Tenant Farmer: Country Brother of the Casual Worker." *Survey*, April 17, 1915, 62–64.

Holmes, George K. "The Peons of the South." *Annals of the American Academy of Political and Social Sciences* 4 (September 1893): 265–74.

Holt, Marilyn Irvin. *Linoleum, Better Babies, and the Modern Farm Woman, 1890–1930*. Albuquerque: University of New Mexico Press, 1995.

Holt, R. D. "The Introduction of Barbed Wire into Texas and the Fence Cutting War." *West Texas Historical Year Book* 6 (June 1930): 65–79.

Holt, Thomas C. "Marking: Race, Race-Making, and the Writing of History." *American Historical Review* 100 (February 1995): 1–20.

Honey, Michael K. *Southern Labor and Black Civil Rights: Organizing Memphis Workers*. Urbana: University of Illinois Press, 1993.

Horsman, Reginald. *Race and Manifest Destiny: The Origins of American Racial Anglo-Saxonism*. Cambridge, Mass.: Harvard University Press, 1981.

Hounshell, David A. *From the American System to Mass Production, 1800–1932: The Development of Manufacturing Technology in the United States*. Baltimore, Md.: Johns Hopkins University Press, 1984.

Hufford, Charles H. *The Social and Economic Effects of the Mexican Migration into Texas*. 1929; reprint, San Francisco: R and E Research Associates, 1971.

Huginnie, A. Yvette. "Historical Construction, Multiple Casualties, and the American West." *Western Historical Quarterly* 25 (Winter 1994): 463–66.

Hunt, Robert Lee. *A History of the Farmer Movements of the Southwest, 1837–1925*. College Station: Texas A&M University Press, 1935.

Hunter, Tera W. "Domination and Resistance: The Politics of Wage Household Labor in New South Atlanta." *Labor History* 34 (Spring-Summer 1993): 205–20.

Hurtado, Albert L. "The Proffered Paradigm: Finding the West in Time and Space." *Western Historical Quarterly* 25 (Winter 1994): 467–69.

Ignatiev, Noel. *How the Irish Became White*. New York and London: Routledge, 1995.

I'll Take My Stand: The South and the Agrarian Tradition, by Twelve Southerners. 1930; reprint, Baton Rouge: Louisiana State University Press, 1977.

Jacobson, Julius, ed. *The Negro and the American Labor Union*. Garden City, N.Y.: Anchor Books, 1968.

Jamieson, Stuart. *Labor Unionism in American Agriculture*. 1945; reprint, New York: Arno Press, 1976.

Janiewski, Dolores E. *Sisterhood Denied: Race, Gender, and Class in a New South Community*. Philadelphia: Temple University Press, 1985.

Jefferson, Thomas. *Notes on the State of Virginia*. Edited by William Peden. New York: W. W. Norton, 1954.

Jellison, Katherine. *Entitled to Power: Farm Women and Technology, 1913–1963*. Chapel Hill: University of North Carolina Press, 1993.

Jensen, Joan M. "Canning Comes to New Mexico: Women and the Agricultural Extension Service, 1914–1919." In *New Mexico Women: Intercultural Perspectives*, edited by Joan M. Jensen and Darlis A. Miller. Albuquerque: University of New Mexico Press, 1986.

——. *Loosening the Bonds: Mid-Atlantic Farm Women, 1750–1850*. New Haven, Conn.: Yale University Press, 1986.

——. "Old vs. New History: Reconfiguration and Regionalism in the American West." *Western Historical Quarterly* 25 (Winter 1994): 461–63.

——. *Promise to the Land: Essays on Rural Women*. Albuquerque: University of New Mexico Press, 1991.

——. *With These Hands: Women Working on the Land*. Old Westbury, N.Y.: Feminist Press, 1981.

Jensen, Joan M., and Darlis A. Miller, eds. *New Mexico Women: Intercultural Perspectives*. Albuquerque: University of New Mexico Press, 1986.

Johannsen, Robert W. *To the Halls of the Montezumas: The Mexican War in the American Imagination*. New York: Oxford University Press, 1985.

Johnson, Charles S. *Shadow of the Plantation*. Chicago: University of Chicago Press, 1934.

Johnson, Charles S., Edwin R. Embree, and W. W. Alexander. *The Collapse of Cotton Tenancy: Summary of Field Studies and Statistical Surveys, 1933–35*. Chapel Hill: University of North Carolina Press, 1935.

Johnson, Donald. "Wilson, Burleson, and Censorship in the First World War." *Journal of Southern History* 28 (February 1962): 46–58.

Johnson, Elmer Harrison. *The Basis of the Commercial and Industrial Development of Texas*. University of Texas Bulletin 3309. Austin: University of Texas, 1933.

——. *The Natural Regions of Texas*. Bureau of Business Research, University of Texas Bulletin 3113. Austin: University of Texas, 1931.

Johnstone, Paul H. "Old Ideals versus New Ideas in Farm Life." In U.S. Department of Agriculture, *Yearbook of Agriculture, 1940*. Washington, D.C.: Government Printing Office, 1941.

Jones, Jacqueline. *The Dispossessed: America's Underclasses from the Civil War to the Present*. New York: Basic Books, 1992.

——. *Labor of Love, Labor of Sorrow: Black Women, Work, and the Family, from Slavery to the Present*. 1985; reprint, New York: Vintage, 1995.

Jordan, Terry G. "A Century and a Half of Ethnic Change in Texas, 1836–1986." *Southwestern Historical Quarterly* 89 (April 1986): 385–422.

——. "The 1887 Census of Texas' Hispanic Population." *Aztlán* 12 (Autumn 1981): 271–78.

——. *German Seed in Texas Soil: Immigrant Farmers in Nineteenth-Century Texas*. Austin: University of Texas Press, 1966.

——. *Trails to Texas: Southern Roots of Western Cattle Ranching*. Lincoln: University of Nebraska Press, 1981.

Jordan, Terry G., John L. Bean Jr., and William M. Holmes. *Texas: A Geography*. Geographies of the United States Series. Boulder, Colo.: Westview Press, 1984.

Katz, Friedrich. "Labor Conditions on Haciendas in Porfirian Mexico: Some Trends and Tendencies." *Hispanic American Historical Review* 54 (February 1974): 1–47.

Keefe, Susan E., and Amado Padilla. *Chicano Ethnicity*. Albuquerque: University of New Mexico Press, 1987.

Kelley, Robin D. G. *Hammer and Hoe: Alabama Communists during the Great Depression*. Chapel Hill: University of North Carolina Press, 1990.

———. "Notes on Deconstructing 'The Folk.'" *American Historical Review* 97 (December 1992): 1400–1408.

———. *Race Rebels: Culture, Politics, and the Black Working Class.* New York: Free Press, 1994.

———. "'We Are Not What We Seem': Rethinking Black Working-Class Opposition in the Jim Crow South." *Journal of American History* 80 (June 1993): 75–112.

Kenny, Kevin. *Making Sense of the Molly Maguires.* New York: Oxford University Press, 1997.

Kerr, Homer L. "Migration into Texas, 1860–1880." *Southwestern Historical Quarterly* 70 (October 1966): 184–216.

Kester, Howard. *Revolt among the Sharecrops.* New York: Covici Friede, 1936.

Kevles, Daniel J. *In the Name of Eugenics: Genetics and the Uses of Human Heredity.* New York: Knopf, 1985.

Kilker, Ernest Evans. "Black and White in America: The Culture and Politics of Racial Classification." *International Journal of Politics, Culture, and Society* 7 (Winter 1993): 229–58.

Kinsey, Winston Lee. "Negro Labor in Texas, 1865–1876." M.A. thesis, Baylor University, 1965.

Kipnis, Ira. *The American Socialist Movement, 1897–1912.* New York: Columbia University Press, 1952.

Kirby, Jack Temple. *Rural Worlds Lost: The American South, 1920–1960.* Baton Rouge: Louisiana State University Press, 1987.

———. "The Transformation of Southern Plantations ca. 1920–1960." *Agricultural History* 57 (July 1983): 257–76.

Kiser, George C., and David Silverman. "Mexican Repatriation during the Great Depression." *Journal of Mexican American History* 3 (1973): 139–64.

Koch, Adrienne, and William Peden, eds. *The Life and Selected Writings of Thomas Jefferson.* New York: Modern Library, 1944.

Korges, William Henry. "Bastrop County, Texas: Historical and Educational Development." M.A. thesis, University of Texas, 1933.

Kousser, J. Morgan. *The Shaping of Southern Politics: Suffrage Restriction and the Establishment of the One-Party South, 1880–1910.* New Haven, Conn.: Yale University Press, 1974.

Kousser, J. Morgan, and James M. McPherson, eds. *Region, Race, and Reconstruction: Essays in Honor of C. Vann Woodward.* New York: Oxford University Press, 1982.

Kraut, Alan M. *Silent Travelers: Germs, Genes, and the "Immigrant Menace."* New York: Basic Books, 1994.

Lack, Paul D. "Slavery and Vigilantism in Austin, Texas, 1840–1860." *Southwestern Historical Quarterly* 85 (July 1981): 1–20.

———. *The Texas Revolutionary Experience: A Political and Social History, 1835–1836.* College Station: Texas A&M University Press, 1992.

Laird, Judith Fincher. "Argentine, Kansas: The Evolution of a Mexican-American Community." Ph.D. diss., University of Kansas, 1975.

Lamar, Howard. *Texas Crossings: The Lone Star State and the American Far West, 1836–1986.* Austin: University of Texas Press, 1991.

Lange, Dorothea, and Paul S. Taylor. *American Exodus: A Record of Human Erosion*. New York: Reynal & Hitchcock, 1939.

Larson, Edward J. *Sex, Race, and Science: Eugenics in the Deep South*. Baltimore, Md.: Johns Hopkins University Press, 1995.

Lea, Tom. *The King Ranch*. 2 vols. Boston: Little, Brown, 1957.

Ledesma, Irene. "New Deal Public Works Programs and Mexican-Americans in McAllen, Texas, 1933–36." M.A. thesis, University of Texas at Edinburg, 1977.

Lee, Shu-Chung. "The Theory of the Agricultural Ladder." *Agricultural History* 21 (January 1947): 53–61.

Leonard, Karen Isaksen. *Making Ethnic Choices: California's Punjabi Mexican Americans*. Philadelphia: Temple University Press, 1992.

Leonard, William E. "Migratory Tenants of the Southwest." *Survey*, January 29, 1916, 511–12.

Lerner, Gerda. "Reconceptualizing Differences among Women." *Journal of Women's History* 1 (Winter 1990): 106–22.

Letwin, Daniel. "Interracial Unionism, Gender, and 'Social Equality' in the Alabama Coalfields, 1878–1908." *Journal of Southern History* 61 (August 1995): 519–54.

Levine, Lawrence. *Black Culture and Black Consciousness: Afro-American Folk Thought from Slavery to Freedom*. New York: Oxford University Press, 1977.

Lewis, David Levering. *W. E. B. Du Bois: Biography of a Race, 1868–1919*. New York: Henry Holt, 1993.

Lewis, Earl. *In Their Own Interests: Race, Class, and Power in Twentieth-Century Norfolk, Virginia*. Berkeley: University of California Press, 1991.

———. "To Turn as on a Pivot: Writing African Americans into a History of Overlapping Diasporas." *American Historical Review* 100 (June 1995): 765–87.

Lewis, Oscar. *On the Edge of the Black Waxy: A Cultural Survey of Bell County, Texas*. Saint Louis, Mo.: Washington University Studies, New Series, 1948.

Limerick, Patricia Nelson. *Legacy of Conquest: The Unbroken Past of the American West*. New York: W. W. Norton, 1987.

———. "Region and Reason." In *All over the Map: Rethinking American Regions*, edited by Edward L. Ayers, Patricia Nelson Limerick, Stephen Nissenbaum, and Peter S. Onuf. Baltimore, Md.: Johns Hopkins University Press, 1996.

Limón, José E. "El Primer Congreso Mexicanista de 1911: A Precursor to Contemporary Chicanismo." *Aztlán* 5 (Spring-Fall 1974): 85–118.

Lipsitz, George. "The Possessive Investment in Whiteness: Racialized Social Democracy and the 'White' Problem in American Studies." *American Quarterly* 47 (September 1995): 369–87.

———. *Rainbow at Midnight: Labor and Culture in the 1940s*. Urbana: University of Illinois Press, 1994.

———. *Time Passages: Collective Memory and American Popular Culture*. Minneapolis: University of Minnesota Press, 1990.

Lott, Eric. *Love and Theft: Blackface Minstrelsy and the American Working Class*. New York: Oxford University Press, 1993.

Luebke, Frederick C., ed. *Ethnicity on the Great Plains*. Lincoln: University of Nebraska Press, for the Center for Great Plains Studies, 1980.

Lyman, Stanford M. "The Race Question and Liberalism: Casuistries in American Constitutional Law." *International Journal of Politics, Culture, and Society* 5 (Winter 1991): 183–247.

McBride, George. *The Land Systems of Mexico*. New York: American Geographical Society, 1923.

McCain, Johnny M. "Texas and the Mexican Labor Question, 1942–1947." *Southwestern Historical Quarterly* 85 (July 1981): 45–64.

McCallum, Henry D., and Frances T. McCallum. *The Wire That Fenced the West*. Norman: University of Oklahoma Press, 1965.

McCombs, Vernon Monroe. *From over the Border: A Study of the Mexicans in the United States*. 1925; reprint, San Francisco: R & E Research Associates, 1970.

McConnell, Grant. *The Decline of Agrarian Democracy*. New York: Atheneum, 1969.

McDonald, Archie P. *The Mexican War: Crisis for American Democracy*. Lexington, Mass.: D. C. Heath, 1969.

McIlwaine, Shields. *The Southern Poor-White, from Lubberland to Tobacco Road*. New York: Cooper Square Publishers, 1970.

McKay, Reynolds R. "Texas Mexican Repatriation during the Great Depression." Ph.D. diss., University of Oklahoma, 1982.

McKitrick, Reuben. *The Public Land System of Texas, 1823–1910*. University of Wisconsin Bulletin 905. Madison: University of Wisconsin, 1918.

McKiven, Henry M., Jr. *Iron and Steel: Class, Race, and Community in Birmingham, Alabama, 1875–1920*. Chapel Hill: University of North Carolina Press, 1995.

McLean, Robert N. "Goodbye, Vicente!" *Survey*, May 1, 1931, 182–83, 195–97.

McLemore, S. Dale. "The Origins of Mexican-American Subordination in Texas." *Social Science Quarterly* 53 (March 1973): 656–70.

McWilliams, Carey. *Factories in the Field: The Story of Migratory Farm Labor in California*. Boston: Little, Brown, 1939.

———. *Ill Fares the Land: Migrants and Migratory Labor in the United States*. 1942; reprint, New York: Arno Press, 1976.

———. *North from Mexico: The Spanish-Speaking People of the United States*. 1949; reprint, New York: Greenwood Press, 1968.

Mandle, Jay R. *The Roots of Black Poverty: The Southern Plantation Economy after the Civil War*. Durham, N.C.: Duke University Press, 1978.

Márquez, Benjamin. *LULAC: The Evolution of a Mexican American Political Organization*. Austin: University of Texas Press, 1993.

Marr, John Columbus. "The History of Matagorda County, Texas." M.A. thesis, University of Texas, 1928.

Marshall, F. Ray. *Rural Workers in Rural Labor Markets*. Salt Lake City, Utah: Olympus Publishing, 1974.

———. "Some Reflections on Labor History." *Southwestern Historical Quarterly* 75 (October 1971): 139–57.

Martin, James C. *Maps of Texas and the Southwest, 1513–1900*. Albuquerque: University of New Mexico Press, 1984.

Martin, Roscoe Coleman. *The People's Party in Texas: A Study in Third Party Politics*. University of Texas Bulletin 3308. Austin: University of Texas, 1933.

Martin, Theodora. *The Sound of Our Own Voices: Women's Study Clubs, 1860–1910*. Boston: Beacon Press, 1987.

Martínez, John R. "Mexican Emigration to the United States, 1910–1930." Ph.D. diss., University of California, 1957.

Martínez, Oscar J. "On the Size of the Chicano Population: New Estimates, 1850–1890." *Aztlán* 6 (Spring 1975): 43–67.

Matthiessen, Peter. *Sal Si Puedes: César Chávez and the New American Revolution*. New York: Random House, 1973.

Mead, Edward Sherwood, and Bernhard Ostrolenk. *Harvey Baum: A Study of the Agricultural Revolution*. Philadelphia: University of Pennsylvania Press, 1928.

Meinig, Donald W. *Imperial Texas: An Interpretive Essay in Cultural Geography*. Austin: University of Texas Press, 1969.

———. *The Shaping of America: A Geographical Perspective on 500 Years of History*. Vol. 2, *Continental America, 1800–1867*. New Haven, Conn.: Yale University Press, 1993.

———. *Southwest: Three Peoples in Geographical Change, 1600–1970*. New York: Oxford University Press, 1971.

Menchaca, Martha. "Chicano Indianism: A Historical Account of Racial Repression in the United States." *American Ethnologist* 20 (August 1993): 583–601.

Meredith, H. L. "Agrarian Socialism and the Negro in Oklahoma, 1900–1918." *Labor History* 11 (Summer 1970): 277–84.

Merk, Frederick. *Manifest Destiny and Mission in American History: A Reinterpretation*. 1963; reprint, New York: Vintage Books, 1966.

———. *Slavery and the Annexation of Texas*. New York: Knopf, 1972.

Mertz, Paul E. *New Deal Policy and Southern Rural Poverty*. Baton Rouge: Louisiana State University Press, 1978.

Meyer, Michael C., and William Sherman, *The Course of Mexican History*. 5th ed. New York: Oxford University Press, 1995.

Miller, Marc S., ed. *Working Lives: The "Southern Exposure" History of Labor in the South*. New York: Pantheon Books, 1980.

Miller, Sally M. "The Socialist Party and the Negro, 1901–20." *Journal of Negro History* 56 (July 1971): 220–29.

Miller, Thomas L. *The Public Lands of Texas, 1519–1970*. Norman: University of Oklahoma Press, 1972.

Mintz, Sidney W. "A Note on the Definition of Peasantries." *Journal of Peasant Studies* 1 (October 1973): 91–106.

———. "The Rural Proletariat and the Problem of Rural Proletarian Consciousness." *Journal of Peasant Studies* 1 (April 1974): 308–11.

Mitchell, Broadus. *Depression Decade: From New Era through New Deal, 1929–1941*. New York: Rinehart, 1947.

Mitchell, H. L. *Mean Things Happening in This Land: The Life and Times of H. L. Mitchell, Co-Founder of the Southern Tenant Farmers Union*. Montclair, N.J.: Allanheld, Osmun, 1979.

Monroy, Douglas. *Thrown among Strangers: The Making of Mexican Culture in Frontier California*. Berkeley: University of California Press, 1990.

Montejano, David. *Anglos and Mexicans in the Making of Texas, 1836–1986*. Austin: University of Texas Press, 1987.

Montgomery, David. *The Fall of the House of Labor: The Workplace, the State, and American Labor Activism, 1865–1925*. Cambridge, England: Cambridge University Press, 1987.

Montgomery, Robert H. "Keglar Hill." *Survey*, May 1, 1931, 171, 193–95.

Moraga, Cherrie, and Gloria Anzaldúa, eds. *This Bridge Called My Back: Writings by Radical Women of Color*. Watertown, Mass.: Persephone Press, 1981.

Mörner, Magnus. *Race Mixture in the History of Latin America*. Boston: Little, Brown, 1967.

Motheral, Joe. *Recent Trends in Land Tenure in Texas*. Texas Agricultural Experiment Station Bulletin 641. College Station: Agricultural and Mechanical College of Texas, 1944.

Musoke, Moses S. "Mechanizing Cotton Production in the American South: The Tractor, 1915–1960." *Explorations in Economic History* 18 (October 1987): 347–75.

Myrdal, Gunnar. *An American Dilemma: The Negro Problem and Modern Democracy*. New York: Harper & Brothers, 1944.

Myres, S. D., Jr., ed. *The Cotton Crisis: Proceedings of Second Conference Institute of Public Affairs*. Dallas: Southern Methodist University, 1935.

Nash, Gerald D. *The American West in the Twentieth Century: A Short History of an Urban Oasis*. Englewood Cliffs, N.J.: Prentice Hall, 1973.

Nelson-Cisneros, Victor B. "La clase trabajadora en Tejas, 1920–1940." *Aztlán* 6 (Summer 1975): 239–65.

———. "UCAPAWA Organizing Activities in Texas, 1935–1970." *Aztlán* 9 (Spring-Summer-Fall 1978): 71–84.

Neth, Mary. *Preserving the Family Farm: Women, Community, and the Foundations of Agribusiness in the Midwest, 1900–1940*. Baltimore, Md.: Johns Hopkins University Press, 1995.

Nimmo, Joseph, Jr. *Report in Regard to the Range and Cattle Business of the United States*. 1885; reprint, New York: Arno Press, 1972.

Nourse, Edwin Griswold. "The Place of Agriculture in Modern Industrial Society." *Journal of Political Economy* 27 (June-July 1919): 466–97, 561–82.

O'Banion, Maurine M. "The History of Caldwell County." M.A. thesis, University of Texas, 1931.

O'Brien, Harry R. " 'Ill Fares the Land': When the Wrongs of the Tenant System Go Unchecked." *Country Gentleman*, December 14, 1918, 3–4, 28, 30–31.

Olmsted, Frederick Law. *A Journey through Texas: Or, a Saddle Trip on the Southwestern Frontier*. 1857; reprint, Austin: University of Texas Press, 1978.

Omi, Michael, and Howard Winant. *Racial Formation in the United States: From the 1960s to the 1980s*. New York: Routledge, 1986.

Orozco, Cynthia E. "The Origins of the League of Latin American Citizens (LULAC) and the Mexican American Civil Rights Movement in Texas with an Analysis of Women's Political Participation in a Gendered Context, 1910–1929." Ph.D. diss., University of California, Los Angeles, 1993.

Osgood, Ernest S. *The Day of the Cattlemen*. Minneapolis: University of Minnesota Press, 1929.

Osterud, Nancy Grey. *Bonds of Community: The Lives of Farm Women in Nine-teenth-Century New York*. Ithaca, N.Y.: Cornell University Press, 1991.

———. "Gender and the Transition to Capitalism in Rural America." *Agricultural History* 67 (Spring 1993): 14–29.

Owens, William. *This Stubborn Soil: A Frontier Boyhood*. New York: Charles Scribner's Sons, 1966.

Padilla, Fernando. "Early Chicano Legal Recognition, 1846–1897." *Journal of Popular Culture* 13 (Spring 1980): 564–74.

Painter, Nell Irvin. *Exodusters: Black Migration to Kansas after Reconstruction*. New York: Alfred A. Knopf, 1976.

———. " 'Social Equality,' Miscegenation, and the Maintenance of Power." In *The Evolution of Southern Culture*, edited by Numan B. Bartley. Athens: University of Georgia Press, 1988.

Pannell, W. W. "Mexican Workers in the Southwest." *International Socialist Review* 16 (September 1915): 168–69.

———. "Tenant Farming in the United States." *International Socialist Review* 16 (January 1916): 421–23.

Paredes, Américo. *A Texas-Mexican Cancionero: Folksongs of the Lower Border*. Urbana: University of Illinois Press, 1976.

———. *"With His Pistol in His Hand": A Border Ballad and Its Hero*. Austin: University of Texas Press, 1958.

Pascoe, Peggy. "Miscegenation Law, Court Cases, and Ideologies of 'Race' in Twentieth-Century America." *Journal of American History* 83 (June 1996): 44–69.

Payne, O. C. "Corporation Farming in Texas." *Farm and Ranch*, May 30, 1914, 2–3.

Peck, Gunther. "Padrones and Protest: 'Old' Radicals and 'New' Immigrants in Bingham, Utah, 1905–1912." *Western Historical Quarterly* 24 (May 1993): 157–78.

———. "Reinventing Free Labor: Immigrant Padrone and Contract Laborers in North America, 1880–1920." Ph.D. diss., Yale University, 1994.

Pelzer, Louis. *The Cattlemen's Frontier*. Glendale, Calif.: Arthur H. Clark, 1936.

Peña, Manuel. *The Texas-Mexican Conjunto: History of a Working-Class Music*. Austin: University of Texas Press, 1985.

Perales, Alonso S. *Are We Good Neighbors?* San Antonio: Artes Gráficas, 1948.

Percy, William Alexander. *Lanterns on the Levee: Recollections of a Planter's Son*. New York: Alfred A. Knopf, 1941.

Perry, Douglas Geraldyne. "Black Populism: The Negro in the People's Party in Texas." M.A. thesis, Prairie View A&M College, 1945.

Pickens, Donald K. *Eugenics and the Progressives*. Nashville, Tenn.: Vanderbilt University Press, 1968.

Pletcher, David M. *The Diplomacy of Annexation: Texas, Oregon, and the Mexican War*. Columbia: University of Missouri Press, 1973.

Pool, William C. *A Historical Atlas of Texas*. Austin: Encino Press, 1975.

Portes, Alejandro, and Robert L. Bach. *Latin Journey: Cuban and Mexican Immigrants in the United States*. Berkeley: University of California Press, 1985.

Potts, Charles S. *Railroad Transportation in Texas*. University of Texas Bulletin 119. Austin: University of Texas, 1909.

Price, Theodore H. "A 100,000-Acre Business." *World's Work* 25 (January 1913): 271–75.

Putnam, Frank. "Texas in Transition." *Collier's*, January 22, 1910, 15.

Raat, W. Dirk. *Revoltosos: Mexico's Rebels in the United States, 1903–1923*. College Station: Texas A&M University Press, 1981.

Rabinowitz, Howard N. *The First New South, 1865–1920*. Arlington Heights, Ill.: Harlan Davidson, 1992.

Rafter, Nicole Hahn. *White Trash: The Eugenic Family Studies, 1877–1919*. Boston: Northeastern University Press, 1988.

Raper, Arthur F. *Preface to Peasantry: A Tale of Two Black Belt Counties*. Chapel Hill: University of North Carolina Press, 1936.

Reed, S. G. *A History of the Texas Railroads and of Transportation Conditions under Spain and Mexico and the Republic and the State*. Houston: St. Clair, 1941.

Reisler, Mark. *By the Sweat of Their Brow: Mexican Immigrant Labor in the United States, 1900–1940*. Westport, Conn.: Greenwood Press, 1976.

"Results of Admission of Mexican Laborers, under Departmental Orders for Employment in Agricultural Pursuits." Publication of the Bureau of Statistics, Department of Labor 11. *Monthly Labor Review* (November 1920): 221–23.

Rice, Lawrence D. *The Negro in Texas, 1874–1900*. Baton Rouge: Louisiana State University Press, 1971.

Rice, Thurman B. *Racial Hygiene: A Practical Discussion of Eugenics and Race Culture*. New York: Macmillan, 1929.

Richards, Henry I. *Cotton and the AAA*. Washington, D.C.: Brookings Institution, 1936.

Richardson, T. C. "The Little Brown Man in Gringo Land." *Farm and Ranch*, October 31, 1925, 1–3.

Roebuck, Julian B., and Mark Hickson III. *The Southern Redneck: A Phenomenological Class Study*. New York: Praeger, 1982.

Roediger, David R. "Covington Hall: The Poetry and Politics of Labor Radicalism and Southern Nationalism." *History Workshop Journal* 19 (Spring 1985): 162–68.

———. "The Limits of Corporate Reform: Fordism, Taylorism, and the Working Week in the United States, 1914–1929." In *Worktime and Industrialization: An International History*, edited by Gary Cross. Philadelphia: Temple University Press, 1988.

———. *Towards the Abolition of Whiteness: Essays on Race, Politics, and Working-Class History*. London and New York: Verso, 1994.

———. *The Wages of Whiteness: Race and the Making of the American Working Class*. London and New York: Verso, 1991.

Rogers, William J. "A Study of the Work of the Fort Worth Branch of the Farm Labor Division of the United States Employment Service." M.A. thesis, Texas Christian University, 1930.

Romo, Ricardo. *East Los Angeles: History of a Barrio*. Austin: University of Texas Press, 1983.

———. "Responses to Mexican Immigration, 1910–1930." *Aztlán* 5 (Summer 1975): 173–94.

——. "The Urbanization of Southwestern Chicanos in the Early Twentieth Century." *New Scholar* 6 (Fall 1977): 183–207.

Rosaldo, Renato. *Culture and Truth: The Remaking of Social Analysis*. Boston: Beacon Press, 1993.

Rosengarten, Theodore. *All God's Dangers: The Life of Nate Shaw*. New York: Alfred A. Knopf, 1975.

Rotundo, E. Anthony. *American Manhood: Transformations in Masculinity from the Revolution to the Modern Era*. New York: Basic Books, 1993.

Rousse, Thomas Andrew. *Government Control of Cotton Production*. University of Texas Bulletin 3538. Austin: University of Texas, 1935.

Rowell, Chester H. "Chinese and Japanese Immigrants." *Annals of the American Academy* 34 (September 1909): 4.

——. "Why Make Mexico an Exception?" *Survey*, May 1, 1931, 180.

Rubinow, S. G. "Putting the Factory on the Farm." *Current History* 30 (September 1929): 1069–74.

Ruiz, Ramón Eduardo, ed. *The Mexican War: Was It Manifest Destiny?* New York: Holt, Rinehart and Winston, 1963.

Ruiz, Vicki L. *Cannery Women, Cannery Lives: Mexican Women, Unionization, and the California Food Processing Industry, 1930–1950*. Albuquerque: University of New Mexico Press, 1987.

Ryan, Mary P. *The Cradle of the Middle Class: The Family in Oneida County, New York, 1790–1865*. New York: Cambridge University Press, 1981.

——. *Women in Public: Between Banners and Ballots, 1825–1880*. Baltimore, Md.: Johns Hopkins University Press, 1990.

Sachs, Carolyn E. *The Invisible Farmers: Women in Agricultural Production*. Totowa, N.J.: Rowman & Allanheld, 1983.

Saloutos, Theodore. *The American Farmer and the New Deal*. Ames: Iowa State University Press, 1982.

——. *Farmer Movements in the South, 1865–1933*. University of California Publications in History, 64. Berkeley: University of California Press, 1960.

Salvatore, Nick. *Eugene V. Debs: Citizen and Socialist*. Urbana: University of Illinois Press, 1982.

Sánchez, George J. *Becoming Mexican American: Ethnicity, Culture and Identity in Chicano Los Angeles, 1900–1945*. New York: Oxford University Press, 1993.

Sandos, James A. "The Plan of San Diego: War and Diplomacy on the Texas Border, 1915–1916." *Arizona and the West* 14 (Spring 1972): 5–24.

——. *Rebellion in the Borderlands: Anarchism and the Plan of San Diego, 1904–1923*. Norman: University of Oklahoma Press, 1992.

San Miguel, Guadalupe, Jr. *"Let All of Them Take Heed": Mexican Americans and the Campaign for Educational Equality in Texas, 1910–1981*. Austin: University of Texas Press, 1987.

Saposs, David J. *Left Wing Unionism: A Study in Radical Policies and Tactics*. New York: International Publishers, 1926.

Saunders, Lyle. *The Spanish-Speaking Population of Texas*. Inter-American Education Occasional Papers, 5. Austin: University of Texas Press, 1949.

Saville, Julie. *The Work of Reconstruction: From Slave to Wage Laborer in South Carolina, 1860–1870*. New York: Cambridge University Press, 1994.

Saxton, Alexander. *The Indispensable Enemy: Labor and the Anti-Chinese Movement in California*. Berkeley: University of California Press, 1971.

———. *The Rise and Fall of the White Republic: Class Politics and Mass Culture in Nineteenth-Century America*. London and New York: Verso, 1990.

Scarborough, Dorothy. *The Stretch-Berry Smile*. Indianapolis, Ind.: Bobbs, Merrill, 1932.

Scharff, Virginia. *Taking the Wheel: Women and the Coming of the Motor Age*. New York: Free Press, 1991.

Schlissel, Lillian, Vicki L. Ruiz, and Janice Monk, eds. *Western Women: Their Land, Their Lives*. Albuquerque: University of New Mexico Press, 1993.

Schmidt, Louis Bernard. "Some Significant Aspects of the Agrarian Revolution in the United States." *Iowa Journal of History and Politics* 18 (July 1920): 371–95.

Schoen, Harold. "The Free Negro in the Republic of Texas." *Southwestern Historical Quarterly* 41 (January-April 1937): 83–108.

Schreiner, George A. "The Taft Ranch." *Texas Magazine*, December 1909, 35–38.

Schultz, Charles R. "Keeping the Wolves from Their Doors and the Shirts on Their Backs: Rural Texas Women at Work, 1930–1960." Paper presented at the Women and Texas History Conference, October 4, 1990, Center for American History, University of Texas at Austin.

Schwartz, Rosalie. *Across the Rio to Freedom: U.S. Negroes in Mexico*. El Paso: Texas Western Press, University of Texas at El Paso, 1975.

Scott, Anne Firor. "After Suffrage: Southern Women in the 1920s." In *Making the Invisible Woman Visible*, edited by Anne Firor Scott. Urbana: University of Illinois Press, 1984.

———. *The Southern Lady: From Pedestal to Politics, 1830–1930*. Chicago: University of Chicago Press, 1970.

Scott, James C. *Domination and the Arts of Resistance: Hidden Transcripts*. New Haven, Conn.: Yale University Press, 1990.

———. *Weapons of the Weak: Everyday Forms of Peasant Resistance*. New Haven, Conn.: Yale University Press, 1985.

Scott, Joan Wallach. *Gender and the Politics of History*. New York: Columbia University Press, 1988.

Scott, Rebecca J. "Defining the Boundaries of Freedom in the World of Cane: Cuba, Brazil, and Louisiana after Emancipation." *American Historical Review* 99 (February 1994): 70–102.

———. *Slave Emancipation in Cuba: The Transition to Free Labor, 1860–1899*. Princeton, N.J.: Princeton University Press, 1985.

Scruggs, O. M. "Texas and the Bracero Program, 1942–1947." *Pacific Historical Review* 32 (August 1962): 251–64.

———. "The United States, Mexico, and the Wetbacks." *Pacific Historical Review* 30 (May 1961): 149–64.

Seed, Patricia. "Social Dimensions of Race: Mexico City, 1753." *Hispanic American Historical Review* 62 (1982): 559–606.

Shankman, Arnold. "The Image of Mexico and the Mexican-American in the Black Press, 1890–1935." *Journal of Ethnic Studies* 3 (Summer 1975): 43–56.

Shannon, David A. *The Great Depression*. Englewood Cliffs, N.J.: Prentice Hall, 1960.

———. *The Socialist Party of America: A History*. New York: Macmillan, 1955.

Shannon, Fred A. *The Farmer's Last Frontier: Agriculture, 1860–1897*. New York: Farrar and Rinehart, 1945.

Shapiro, Harold. "The Labor Movement in San Antonio." *Southwestern Social Science Quarterly* 36 (June 1955): 160–75.

Sharpless, Mary Rebecca. "Fertile Ground, Narrow Choices: Women on Cotton Farms of the Texas Blackland Prairie, 1900–1940." Ph.D. diss., Emory University, 1993.

Shlomowitz, Ralph. "The Origins of Southern Sharecropping." *Agricultural History* 53 (July 1979): 557–75.

Silverthorne, Elizabeth. *Plantation Life in Texas*. College Station: Texas A&M University Press, 1986.

Sims, N. L., ed. *The Rural Community, Ancient and Modern*. New York: Charles Scribner's Sons, 1920.

Sitkoff, Harvard. *A New Deal for Blacks: The Emergence of Civil Rights as a National Issue*. New York: Oxford University Press, 1978.

Sitton, Thad, and Dan K. Utley. *From Can See to Can't: Texas Cotton Farmers on the Southern Prairies*. Austin: University of Texas Press, forthcoming.

Slayden, James L. "Some Observations on Mexican Immigration." *Annals of the American Academy of Political and Social Science* 93 (January 1921): 121–26.

Slotkin, Richard. *The Fatal Environment: The Myth of the Frontier in the Age of Industrialization, 1800–1890*. 1985; reprint, New York: HarperCollins, 1994.

———. *Gunfighter Nation: The Myth of the Frontier in Twentieth-Century America*. New York: Harper Perennial, 1993.

Smallwood, James M. *Time of Hope, Time of Despair: Black Texans during Reconstruction*. Port Washington, N.Y.: Kennikat Press, 1981.

———. "When the Klan Rode: White Terror in Reconstruction Texas." *Journal of the West* 25 (October 1986): 4–13.

Smith, Dick. "Texas and the Poll Tax." *Southwestern Social Science Quarterly* 45 (September 1964): 167–73.

Smith, H. P., and D. L. Jones. *Mechanized Production of Cotton in Texas*. Texas Agricultural Experiment Station Bulletin 704. College Station, Tex.: Agricultural and Mechanical College, 1948.

Smith, H. P., D. T. Killough, M. H. Byrom, D. Scoates, and D. L. Jones. *The Mechanical Harvesting of Cotton*. Texas Agricultural Experiment Station Bulletin 452. College Station: Agricultural and Mechanical College of Texas, 1932.

Smith, Henry Nash. *Virgin Land: The American West and Symbol and Myth*. 1950; reprint, Cambridge, Mass.: Harvard University Press, 1978.

Smith, J. David. *The Eugenic Assault on America: Scenes in Red, White, and Black*. Fairfax, Va.: George Mason University Press, 1993.

Smith, Lillian. *Killers of the Dream*. New York: W. W. Norton, 1961.

Smith, Ralph. "The Farmers' Alliance in Texas, 1875–1900." *Southwestern Historical Quarterly* 48 (January 1945): 346–69.

Smith, T. Lynn. "Discussion by T. Lynn Smith." *Journal of Farm Economics* 20 (February 1938): 161–62.

Solberg, Erling D. *Legal Aspects of Farm Tenancy in Texas*. Texas Agricultural Experiment Station Bulletin 718. College Station: Agricultural and Mechanical College of Texas, 1950.

Sollors, Werner. *Beyond Ethnicity: Consent and Descent in American Culture*. New York: Oxford University Press, 1986.

——, ed. *The Invention of Ethnicity*. New York: Oxford University Press, 1989.

Speek, Peter A. "The Psychology of Floating Workers." *Annals of the American Academy of Political and Social Science* 69 (January 1917): 72–78.

Spillman, W. J. "The Agricultural Ladder." *American Economic Review*, Supplement: *Papers and Proceedings of the Thirty-First Annual Meeting of the American Economic Association* 9 (March 1919): 170–79.

Spratt, John S. *The Road to Spindletop: Economic Change in Texas, 1875–1901*. Dallas: Southern Methodist University, 1955.

Stabb, Martin S. "Indigenism and Racism in Mexican Thought, 1857–1911." *Journal of Inter-American Studies* 1 (1959): 405–23.

Stein, Walter J. *California and the Dust Bowl Migration*. Westport, Conn.: Greenwood Press, 1973.

Steinbeck, John. *The Grapes of Wrath*. New York: Viking Press, 1939.

——. *The Harvest Gypsies: On the Road to the Grapes of Wrath*. 1936; reprint, Berkeley, Calif.: Heyday Books, 1988.

Stephanson, Anders. *Manifest Destiny: American Expansionism and the Empire of Right*. New York: Hill and Wang, 1995.

Stephens, A. Ray. *The Taft Ranch: A Texas Principality*. Austin: University of Texas Press, 1964.

Stephens, P. H. "Mechanization of Cotton Farms." *Journal of Farm Economics* 13 (January 1931): 27–36.

Stewart, Charles L. "Migration to and from Our Farms." *Annals: The Agricultural Situation in the United States, American Academy of Political and Social Science* 17 (January 1925): 53–60.

Stock, Catherine McNicol. *Main Street in Crisis: The Great Depression and the Old Middle Class on the Northern Plains*. Chapel Hill: University of North Carolina Press, 1992.

Stoddard, Lothrop. *The Rising Tide of Color against White World-Supremacy*. New York: Charles Scribner's Sons, 1920.

Stratton, George Frederic. "Mr. Taft's Tenants: How They Earn Farms on His Big Texas Ranch." *Country Gentleman*, March 1, 1919, 5, 37, 40.

Street, James H. *The New Revolution in the Cotton Economy: Mechanization and Its Consequences*. Chapel Hill: University of North Carolina Press, 1957.

Strong, Donald S. "The Poll Tax: The Case of Texas." *American Political Science Review* 38 (August 1944): 693–709.

Sullivan, Patricia. *Days of Hope: Race and Democracy in the New Deal Era*. Chapel Hill: University of North Carolina Press, 1996.

Takaki, Ronald T. *A Different Mirror: A History of Multicultural America*. Boston: Little, Brown, 1993.

——. *Iron Cages: Race and Culture in 19th-Century America*. Seattle: University of Washington Press, 1979.

——, ed. *From Different Shores: Perspectives on Race and Ethnicity in America*. New York: Oxford University Press, 1987.

Taylor, Frederick W. *The Principles of Scientific Management*. New York: Harper & Brothers, 1911.

Taylor, Henry C. *Agricultural Economics*. New York: Macmillan, 1919.

Taylor, Paul S. *An American-Mexican Frontier: Nueces County, Texas*. 1934; reprint, New York: Russell and Russell, 1971.

———. *Mexican Labor in the United States: Dimmit County, Winter Garden District, South Texas*. University of California Publications in Economics, vol. 6, no. 5. Berkeley: University of California Press, 1930.

———. "Mexicans North of the Rio Grande." *Survey*, May 1, 1931, 135–40, 197, 200–202, 205.

———. "Opportunities for Research in the Far West." *Publication of the American Sociological Society* 29 (August 1935): 103–4.

———. "Power Farming and Labor Displacement in the Cotton Belt, 1937, Part 1: Northwest Texas." U.S. Department of Labor, Bureau of Labor Statistics. *Monthly Labor Review* 46 (March-April 1938): 595–607.

———. "Power Farming and Labor Displacement, Part 2: Southwestern Oklahoma and Mississippi Delta." U.S. Department of Labor, Bureau of Labor Statistics. *Monthly Labor Review* 46 (January-June 1938): 852–67.

Taylor, Paul S., and Clark Kerr. "Uprisings on the Farms." *Survey Graphic*, January 1935, 19–22, 44.

Taylor, Quintard. "Blacks and Asians in a White City: Japanese Americans and African Americans in Seattle, 1890–1940." *Western Historical Quarterly* 22 (November 1991): 401–30.

Taylor, Ronald. *Chávez and the Farm Workers*. Boston: Beacon Press, 1975.

Tenayuca, Emma, and Homer Brooks. "The Mexican Question in the Southwest." *Political Affairs* (March 1939): 257–68.

"Texas, Good Neighbor?" *Southwestern Social Science Quarterly* 43 (September 1962): 118–25.

Thomas, Robert J. *Citizenship, Gender, and Work: Social Organization of Industrial Agriculture*. Berkeley: University of California Press, 1985.

Tichenor, W. C. *Farm Contracts between Landlord and Tenant*. Lebanon, Ohio: W. C. Tichenor, 1916.

Tijerina, Andrés A. *History of Mexican Americans in Lubbock, Texas*. Lubbock:: Texas Tech University Press, 1979.

Tilly, Louise. "Paths of Proletarization: Organization of Production, Sexual Division of Labor, and Women's Collective Action." *Signs* 6 (Winter 1981): 400–417.

Tindall, George B. *The Emergence of the New South, 1913–1945*. Baton Rouge: Louisiana State University Press, 1967.

Tinsley, James Aubrey. "The Progressive Movement in Texas." Ph.D. diss., University of Wisconsin, 1953.

"Trash Talk." *Lingua Franca* 5 (April 1995): 8–10.

Trotter, Joe William, Jr. *Coal, Class, and Color: Blacks in Southern West Virginia, 1915–1932*. Urbana: University of Illinois Press, 1990.

Truesdell, Leon E. "Farm Tenancy Moves West." *Journal of Farm Economics* 8 (1926): 443–50.

Truettner, William H., ed. *The West as America: Reinterpreting Images of the Frontier, 1820–1920*. Washington, D.C.: Smithsonian Institution Press, 1991.

Turner, John. *White Gold Comes to California*. Bakersfield: California Planting Cotton Seed Distributors, 1981.

Tyler, Ron, ed. *The New Handbook of Texas*. Vols. 1–6. Austin: Texas State Historical Association, 1996.

Tyler, Ronnie C. "The Callahan Expedition of 1855: Indians or Negroes?" *Southwestern Historical Quarterly* 70 (April 1967): 574–85.

———. "Fugitive Slaves in Mexico." *Journal of Negro History* 57 (January 1972): 1–12.

Valdés, Dennis Nodín. *Al Norte: Agricultural Workers in the Great Lakes Region, 1917–1970*. Austin: University of Texas Press, 1991.

Vance, Rupert B. "Cotton and Tenancy." In *Problems of the Cotton Economy: Proceedings of the Southern Social Science Research Conference, New Orleans, March 8 and 9, 1935*. Dallas: Arnold Foundation, for the Southern Regional Committee of the Social Science Research Council, 1936.

———. *Human Factors in Cotton Culture: A Study in the Social Geography of the American South*. Chapel Hill: University of North Carolina Press, 1929.

Vandiver, Frank. *The Southwest: South or West*. College Station: Texas A&M University Press, 1975.

Vargas, Zaragosa. "Tejana Radical: Emma Tenayuca and the San Antonio Labor Movement." *Pacific Historical Review*, forthcoming.

———. *Proletarians of the North: A History of Mexican Industrial Workers in Detroit and the Midwest, 1917–1933*. Berkeley: University of California Press, 1993.

Vogel, Joe Bill. "History of Caldwell County Newspapers." M.A. thesis, University of Texas, 1948.

Von Tunglen, G. L. "Some Observations of the So-Called Agricultural Ladder." *Journal of Farm Economics* 9 (January 1927): 94–106.

Vrooman, Carl. "The Agricultural Revolution: The Place of Agriculture in Modern Industrial Society." *Century* 93 (November 1916): 111–23.

Walden, Donald W. "No Way for White People to Live: Travellers' Visions of Poor Whites in the Nineteenth Century." M.A. thesis, University of Texas, 1992.

Ware, Vron. *Beyond the Pale: White Women, Racism, and History*. London and New York: Verso, 1992.

Waters, Mary C. *Ethnic Options: Choosing Identities in America*. Berkeley: University of California Press, 1990.

Weber, David J., ed. *Foreigners in Their Native Land: Historical Roots of the Mexican Americans*. Albuquerque: University of New Mexico Press, 1973.

Weber, Devra. *Dark Sweat, White Gold: California Farm Workers, Cotton, and the New Deal*. Berkeley: University of California Press, 1994.

Weeks, O. Douglas. "The League of United Latin-American Citizens: A Texas-Mexican Civic Organization." *Southwestern Political and Social Science Quarterly* 10 (December 1929): 257–78.

Weinberg, Albert K. *Manifest Destiny: A Study of Nationalist Expansion in American History*. 1935; reprint, Chicago: Quadrangle Books, 1963.

Weinstein, James. *The Decline of Socialism in America, 1912–1925*. New York: Monthly Review Press, 1967.

Wellman, David T. *Portraits of White Racism*. 2d ed. Cambridge, England: Cambridge University Press, 1993.

West, Cornel. "The New Cultural Politics of Difference." In *Out There: Marginalization and Contemporary Cultures*, edited by Russell Ferguson, Martha Gever, Trinh T. Minh-ha, and Cornel West. Cambridge, Mass.: MIT Press, 1990.

West, Elliott. *Growing Up with the Country: Childhood on the Far Western Frontier*. Albuquerque: University of New Mexico Press, 1989.

Weyl, Walter E. "Labor Conditions in Mexico." *Bulletin of the Department of Labor*, no. 38 (January 1902): 1–94.

Whatley, Warren. "Institutional Change and Mechanization in the Cotton South: The Tractorization of Cotton Farming." Ph.D. diss., Stanford University, 1982.

Whayne, Jeannie. "Creation of a Plantation System in the Arkansas Delta in the Twentieth Century." *Agricultural History* 66 (Winter 1992): 63–84.

White, E. V., and E. E. Davis. *A Study of Rural Schools in Texas*. University of Texas Bulletin 364. Austin: University of Texas, 1914.

White, Richard. *"It's Your Misfortune and None of My Own": A History of the American West*. Norman: University of Oklahoma Press, 1991.

White, William W. "The Texas Slave Insurrection of 1860." *Southwestern Historical Quarterly* 52 (January 1949): 259–85.

Wilkison, Kyle. "The End of Independence: Social and Political Consequences of Economic Growth in Texas, 1870–1914." Ph.D. diss., Vanderbilt University, 1995.

Wilson, Charles Reagan. "In Search of the True West: Looking for Answers in the South." *Western Historical Quarterly* 25 (Winter 1994): 470–73.

Winant, Howard. *Racial Conditions: Politics, Theory, Comparisons*. Minneapolis: University of Minnesota Press, 1994.

Winegarten, Ruthe. *Black Texas Women: 150 Years of Trial and Triumph*. Austin: University of Texas Press, 1995.

Winters, Jet Corine. *A Report on the Health and Nutrition of Mexicans Living in Texas*. University of Texas Bulletin 3127. Austin: University of Texas, 1931.

Wise, Leah, and Sue Thrasher. "The Southern Tenant Farmers' Union." In *Working Lives: The "Southern Exposure" History of Labor in the South*, edited by Marc S. Miller. New York: Pantheon Books, 1980.

"Without Quota." *Survey*, May 15, 1924, 219–20.

Woodman, Harold D. *King Cotton and His Retainers: Financing and Marketing the Cotton Crop of the South, 1800–1925*. Lexington: University Press of Kentucky, 1968.

———. *New South—New Law: The Legal Foundations of Credit and Labor Relations in the Postbellum Agricultural South*. Baton Rouge: Louisiana State University Press, 1995.

———. "Postbellum Social Change and Its Effect on Marketing the South's Cotton Crop." *Agricultural History* 56 (January 1982): 215–30.

———. "Post–Civil War Southern Agriculture and the Law." *Agricultural History* 53 (January 1979): 319–37.

———. "The Reconstruction of the Cotton Plantation in the New South." In *Essays on the Postbellum Southern Economy*, edited by Thavolia Glymph and John J. Kushma. College Station: Texas A&M University Press, 1985.

———. "Sequel to Slavery: The New History Views the Postbellum South." *Journal of Southern History* 43 (November 1977): 523–54.

Woodson, Carter Godwin. *The Rural Negro*. 1930; reprint, New York: Russell and Russell, 1969.

Woodward, C. Vann. *Origins of the New South, 1877–1913*. Rev. ed. Baton Rouge: Louisiana State University Press, 1971.

———. *The Strange Career of Jim Crow*. 3d rev. ed. New York: Oxford University Press, 1974.

———. *Tom Watson: Agrarian Rebel*. 1938; reprint, New York: Oxford University Press, 1963.

Woofter, Thomas Jackson, Jr. "The Negro and the Farm Crisis." *Social Forces* 6 (June 1928): 615–20.

———. *Negro Migration: Changes in Rural Organization and Population of the Cotton Belt*. 1920; reprint, New York: Negro Universities Press, 1969.

Wooten, Mattie Lloyd. "Racial, National, and Nativity Trends in Texas, 1870–1930." *Southwestern Social Science Quarterly* 14 (June 1933): 62–69.

Work Projects Administration. *WPA Guide to Texas*. 1940; reprint, Texas Monthly Press, 1986.

Worthman, Paul B. "Black Workers and Labor Unions in Birmingham, Alabama, 1897–1904." *Labor History* 10 (Summer 1969): 375–407.

Worthman, Paul B., and James Green. "Black Workers in the New South." In *Key Issues in the Afro-American Experience*, edited by Nathan Higgins, Martin Kilson, and Daniel Fox. Vol. 2. New York: Harcourt, Brace, Jovanovitch, 1971.

Wray, Matt, and Annalee Newitz, eds. *White Trash: Race and Class in America*. New York and London: Routledge, 1997.

Wright, Gavin. *Old South, New South: Revolutions in the Southern Economy since the Civil War*. New York: Basic Books, 1986.

Young, Elliott Gordon. "Twilight on the Texas-Mexico Border: Catarino Garza and Identity at the Cross-Roads, 1880–1915." Ph.D. diss., University of Texas at Austin, 1997.

Young, Robert J. C. *Colonial Desire: Hybridity in Theory, Culture and Race*. London and New York: Routledge, 1995.

Zamora, Emilio. "Chicano Socialist Labor Activity in Texas, 1900–1920." *Aztlán* 6 (Summer 1975): 221–36.

———. "Mexican Labor Activity in South Texas, 1900–1920." Ph.D. diss., University of Texas, 1983.

———. *The World of the Mexican Worker in Texas*. College Station: Texas A&M University Press, 1993.

Zeichner, Oscar. "The Legal Status of the Agricultural Laborer in the South." *Political Science Quarterly* 55 (September 1940): 424–28.

———. "The Transition from Slave to Free Agricultural Labor in the Southern States." *Agricultural History* 13 (January 1939): 22–33.

Index

Acosta, Andrés, 35–36

Acreage reduction programs. *See* Depression era tenant displacement

Adams, John Quincy, 21

AFL. *See* American Federation of Labor

African Americans. *See* Blacks

Agee, James, 201

Agrarian ideology, 10, 139, 259n85; and agrarian labor militancy, 183–84, 185, 187, 194–95, 200; and depression era tenant displacement, 183; and farm women, 142, 156; and Socialist Party, 69. *See also* Agricultural ladder ideal

Agrarian labor militancy, 11, 183–86, 197–201; and agrarian ideology, 183–84, 185, 187, 194–95, 200; blacks, 188, 189, 190–91, 195–96, 198–99, 240n38, 273n14, 273n15; and Bracero Program, 207; California strikes, 197–98; and corporate cotton ranches, 185, 186, 187, 199, 275n45; Missouri, 186, 272n8; Texas failure of, 184, 197, 199–200. *See also* Agrarian labor militancy repression; Mexican agrarian labor militancy; Renters' Union/Land League; Socialist Party; Southern Tenant Farmers' Union

Agrarian labor militancy repression: blacks, 195–96; California, 198, 275n39; corporate cotton ranches, 199, 275n45; Day Ranch conflict, 101–4, 118, 244–45n11, 247–48n50, 248n59; Mexicans, 109–10, 111, 112, 113, 199, 275n45;

and World War I, 114–15, 200, 250n101, 251n104

Agricultural Adjustment Act (AAA), 140, 164, 166. *See also* Depression era tenant displacement

Agricultural extension services, 142–43, 155–56, 161, 264n78

Agricultural ladder ideal, 9–11, 64; depression collapse of, 163–64, 200; turn-of-century problems with, 11, 35, 65, 74, 140; and white tenants' loss of status, 69, 75–76, 238n6. *See also* Agrarian ideology

Alabama, 184–85, 198–99

Alamo, Battle of, 18–19

Alderete, Narciso, 35

Alien Contract Labor Law (1885), 46–47, 48

Allen, D. M., 170

Allen, Ruth, 43, 98, 131, 142, 143, 145, 154, 231n20

Alvord, Charles, 127, 130, 131, 132, 258n69

American Farm Bureau Federation, 206

American Federation of Labor (AFL), 47, 193, 194, 199

Ameringer, Oscar, 94, 115

Anarchism, 108

"Anglo" label, 7–8

Archer, L. B., 171

Arkansas, 184–85, 186, 191, 275n42

Arrendondo, Joaquín de, 17

Asociación de Jornaleros, 199, 275n43

Austin, Charles B., 79

Austin, Moses, 17

317

Compositor:	Impressions Book and Journal Services, Inc.
Text:	10/13 Galliard
Display:	Galliard
Printer:	Edwards Brothers
Binder:	Edwards Brothers